Trapeze

Swallow Press Books by Anaïs Nin

FICTION

Children of the Albatross
Cities of the Interior
Collages
The Four-Chambered Heart
House of Incest
Ladders to Fire
Seduction of the Minotaur
A Spy in the House of Love
Under a Glass Bell
Waste of Timelessness and Other Early Stories
Winter of Artifice

NONFICTION

D. H. Lawrence: An Unprofessional Study

Mirages: The Unexpurgated Diary of Anaïs Nin, 1939–1947, edited by Paul Herron

The Novel of the Future

A Woman Speaks: The Lectures, Seminars, and Interviews of Anaïs Nin, edited by Evelyn J. Hinz

Swallow Press Books about Anaïs Nin

Arrows of Longing: The Correspondence between Anaïs Nin and Felix Pollak, 1952–1976, edited by Gregory H. Mason

Writing an Icon: Celebrity Culture and the Invention of Anaïs Nin, by Anita Jarczok

Recollections of Anaïs Nin by Her Contemporaries, edited by Benjamin Franklin V

TRAPEZE

The Unexpurgated Diary of Anaïs Nin

1947-1955

Preface by Paul Herron
Introduction by Benjamin Franklin V
Edited by Paul Herron

SWALLOW PRESS / OHIO UNIVERSITY PRESS
Athens, Ohio

PUBLISHED IN ASSOCIATION WITH SKY BLUE PRESS

Swallow Press
An imprint of Ohio University Press, Athens, Ohio 45701
www.ohioswallow.com

Digital trade edition published by Sky Blue Press, San Antonio, Texas, USA. Inquiries about worldwide electronic sales from all digital trade vendors should be directed to Sky Blue Press (skybluepress.com).

Print edition and institutional digital edition published by Swallow Press/Ohio University Press, Athens, Ohio (www.ohioswallow.com). To obtain permission to quote, reprint, or otherwise reproduce or distribute material from Swallow Press / Ohio University Press publications, please contact our rights and permissions department at (740) 593-1154 or (740) 593-4536 (fax).This book may not be circulated in any other binding or cover.

1st Edition. Unexpurgated.

Edited by: Paul Herron

Published by:
Sky Blue Press
San Antonio, Texas, USA

Copublished by:
Ohio University Press/Swallow Press
Athens, Ohio, USA

Typesetting and design: Sara A. Herron, Sky Blue Press
Cover photo: Courtesy of The Anaïs Nin Trust
Cover design: Ohio University Press/Swallow Press

Printed in the United States of America.
Swallow Press/Ohio University Press books are printed on acid-free paper ♾ ™.

23 22 21 20 19 18 17 5 4 3 2 1

Sky Blue Press Electronic ISBN: 978-0-9987246-0-7

Library of Congress Cataloging-in-Publication Data
Names: Nin, Anaïs, 1903–1977, author. | Franklin, Benjamin, 1939– writer of introduction. | Herron, Paul (Paul S.), editor.
Title: Trapeze : the unexpurgated diary of Anaïs Nin, 1947–1955 / preface by Paul Herron ; introduction by Benjamin Franklin V ; edited by Paul Herron.
Description: Athens, Ohio : Swallow Press, 2017. | Includes bibliographical references and index.
Identifiers: LCCN 2016051835| ISBN 9780804011815 (hardback) | ISBN 9780804040778 (pdf)
Subjects: LCSH: Nin, Anaïs, 1903–1977—Diaries. | Authors, American—20th century—Diaries.
Classification: LCC PS3527.I865 Z46 2017 | DDC 818/.5209 [B] —dc23
LC record available at https://lccn.loc.gov/2016051835

Dedicated to the memory of Rupert Pole

Acknowledgments

The editor gratefully acknowledges Sara Herron, Benjamin Franklin V, John Ferrone, Denise Brown, and Kim Krizan for their guidance and dedication to this book.

Correspondence from James Leo Herlihy used by permission of the James Leo Herlihy Literary Estate.

Anaïs Nin, 1950s

TABLE OF CONTENTS

PREFACE

Trapeze was transcribed from the handwritten diary of Anaïs Nin, which was no longer kept in bound journals, but mostly on loose paper. When Nin left New York with Rupert Pole in 1947, she reported that she had put her diary "into the vault." During her long trip to California, she kept no diary, no notes...the account of the voyage found in *The Diary of Anaïs Nin, Vol. 4, 1944-1947* is based on recollection long after the fact. *Trapeze* contains only original material.

Because the paper was loose, oftentimes it became out of sequence. Once the entire collection was transcribed, a significant amount of detective work had to be done to put it back in order—and one extremely valuable aid in this endeavor was a massive calendar Nin kept that was found in her Silver Lake house recently. It not only assisted in sequencing, it also filled in some of the long and mysterious gaps in the diary. Nin's diary-keeping had become erratic and intermittent due to her "bi-coastal" life, the constant swinging between a husband in New York and a lover in California. A habit she developed was the use of her eight-hour flights to record the events of the previous month or two, and these passages were often very long and detailed. But sometimes she went for months without writing anything at all, and that's where the calendar became critical...in *Trapeze*, entries from the calendar are used to identify where Nin was or what she was doing during those gaps. Even so, there are events found neither in the diary nor in the calendar, such as Nin's visit to Gore Vidal in Antigua, Nicaragua, in 1947, and they therefore do not appear in this volume.

Once everything was in sequence, then the true editing could begin, the elimination of repetitions, irrelevant correspondence, etc., but Nin's prose remains intact except in cases of misspellings or serious grammatical errors; sometimes translations of obscure phrases or terms in foreign languages are provided. The transcription of some 4,500 handwritten pages of the original diary yielded nearly 1,400 typewritten pages, from which this volume has been edited.

What *Trapeze* boils down to is the previously unknown account of one of the most fascinating periods of Nin's life—the incredible feat of secretly maintaining two men, two houses, and two lives, not to mention the enormous strain this put on her both physically and psychologically. Here, we find out exactly how Anaïs Nin was able to perform this seemingly impossible juggling act.

PAUL HERRON, EDITOR

San Antonio, Texas
May 2016

INTRODUCTION

Despite publishing six novels and numerous short stories from the 1930s into the 1960s, Anaïs Nin (1903-1977) failed to gain acceptance as a fiction writer. Yet she became famous in the mid-1960s with the publication of *The Diary of Anaïs Nin, 1931-1934* and *The Diary of Anaïs Nin, 1934-1939* (volumes 1 and 2). These books appealed to a wide audience and still please not only because of their attractive authorial persona but also because they record Nin's involvement in Paris with such memorable, fully drawn individuals as Henry Miller, June Miller, Otto Rank, and a man known only as Gonzalo. With friends less significant and less detailed, with themes less developed, and with an increasing reliance on letters to and from Nin to chronicle her life, the next five volumes of the diary are not so impressive as the initial two.[1] All seven diaries leave questions unanswered. In *The Diary of Anaïs Nin, 1947-1955* (volume 5), for instance, a reader might reasonably wonder why the cosmopolitan Nin, a resident of New York City, also dwelled in Sierra Madre, on the edge of a woods outside Los Angeles. Did she live alone on the two coasts? And then, how could this author whose books did not sell well and who held no job afford to maintain two homes, fly frequently between them, and take occasional trips to Mexico? Covering the same years as *The Diary of Anaïs Nin, 1947-1955*, *Trapeze* answers these questions while providing a compelling narrative of Nin's life during this period.

Trapeze is the sixth volume to offer versions of Nin's life substantially different from those Nin presented in the initial sequence of diaries.[2] Described as unexpurgated, these alternative treatments of events resulted from her withholding information from the diaries as originally published, information that would have embarrassed and probably harmed her and certain of her associates. Her death and the deaths of her friends eliminated such concerns. The first revised volume, *Henry and June*, divulges, among many other things, that Nin had a husband, the banker Hugh Guiler. The name of this man she wed in 1923 and to whom she remained married is absent from all diaries published during her lifetime.[3]

The year after their marriage Guiler was transferred from New York City to Paris, where the couple lived until 1939 and where he provided funds for his wife to live as an independent woman. As such in the 1930s, Nin devoted herself to literary pursuits and had sexual affairs with some men, including, first and most notably, Henry Miller. *Trapeze* reveals that Guiler continued supporting her even when, after repatriation, she established a residence in California in the 1940s. There she cohabited with Rupert Pole, a printer and failed actor as well as, later, a forest ranger, which accounts for her presence in Sierra Madre. He was the son of the actor Reginald Pole and stepson of the architect Lloyd Wright (son of Frank Lloyd Wright), his mother's second husband. These relationships explain why Reginald Pole and the Wrights appear in *The Diary of Anaïs Nin, 1947-1955*, which does not mention Rupert Pole.

Trapeze primarily documents Nin's lives with and attitudes toward Guiler and Pole. The one mainly provided security; the other, passion. Her feelings for these men were complex. Ambivalent toward them, Nin sometimes even pitied them. Guiler was too stolid and willful for her; he lacked charisma. His personal habits disgusted her. She disapproved of his profession, even though his banking success, which she belittled, enabled her to live as she wished to a large degree. Some of his business decisions upset her, including one to retire before being made a vice president. More than once she stated that she did not love him, yet guilt over being indebted to him and the need of his munificence kept her from divorcing him, despite vowing to end their marriage. When he adopted the name Ian Hugo and entered the art world as engraver and filmmaker, though, she supported him, including by using some of his engravings as illustrations in her books and by appearing in his films. Ultimately, his kindness, generosity, and seemingly limitless love permitted her to have a rewarding physical life with Pole, about which he was then unaware.[4]

With her ardor for longtime lover Gonzalo Moré dead, with her most recent paramour Bill Pinckard stationed in Korea, with the impossibility of an affair with the desirable but gay Gore Vidal, and with Guiler abroad in Cuba, Nin wanted a lover in early 1947. She found one at a party in New York City. She was smitten with this man, Rupert Pole, to the extent that she soon agreed to motor with him to California in his Ford Model A.[5] Thus began a romance that lasted the remainder of her life and that brought her both joy and frustration. The joy was sex; the frustration was almost everything else. Not only was his family insufferable at times, but his fault finding, temper, frugality, pettiness, and bourgeois values irritated her; his wandering eye distressed her. As an amateur guitarist and violist he was somewhat artistic, but was otherwise shallow. His job requirements dictated that he live among forest rangers, people she considered mediocre. She anesthetized herself against unpleasantness with Martinis and occasional visits to Acapulco. In other words, her lives with Guiler and

Pole were less than ideal, even maddening, but because they both provided something she needed, she endured their shortcomings. This acceptingness is perhaps most obvious in her agreeing to marry Pole. Becoming his wife made her a bigamist. With each man she lived half a life.

Nin had numerous friends who assisted her to one degree or another during the years covered in *Trapeze*. They include author and editor Gore Vidal; Jim Herlihy, writer and her spiritual child; critic Maxwell Geismar and his wife, Anne; Louis and Bebe Barron, early composers of electronic music; and bookstore owner Lawrence Maxwell. She relied on doctors, especially the analysts Clement Staff and Inge Bogner, with whom she discussed issues relating to her double life, but also Max Jacobson, whose medications energized her. He was later known as Dr. Feelgood for giving his patients amphetamines. In writing about some of these people she reveals a trait she describes as a character flaw: intolerance of others' deficiencies. For example, Herlihy was one of her greatest supporters, serving as a refuge from her travails with Guiler and Pole and living with Guiler when he, her husband, needed help while she was in California. Appreciative of his numerous services, Nin nonetheless thought him childish, believed he should have done more for Guiler, and disapproved of his writing, which she considered banal.

While living alternately with Guiler and Pole, Nin continued writing. Though she had some literary success, by the mid-1950s she was dispirited. Until the mid-1940s her books had been published only by small firms, including her own Gemor Press. Things changed when Gore Vidal, an editor at E. P. Dutton, arranged for his company to publish three of her books in consecutive years, beginning in 1946. They were the novels *Ladders to Fire* and *Children of the Albatross*, plus *Under a Glass Bell*, a collection of stories enlarged from earlier editions. She was disappointed when Dutton rejected *The Four-Chambered Heart*, a novel Duell, Sloan and Pearce published in 1950. The next novel, *A Spy in the House of Love*, caused problems that led to her considering herself a literary failure. Written in Sierra Madre and completed in June 1950, it did not attract a publisher, mainly, according to Nin, because the character known as the lie detector was too amorphous and the story was too much a fantasy. After the manuscript was rejected many times, she rewrote it, retaining the lie detector but reducing or eliminating the fantastical elements in order to make it more understandable. Additional rejections followed. Finally, British Book Centre agreed to publish it if Nin paid the company's costs, which Guiler did, though the firm's financial difficulties and distribution issues delayed publication. When the novel appeared in 1954, it sold poorly, generating less than $200 in royalties. Despite feeling defeated in the literary marketplace, Nin retained a belief in her artistry, going so far as to consider herself the equal of Djuna Barnes, Anna Kavan, and Virginia Woolf as a force in what she considered new writing.

The revelations in *Trapeze* make understandable the fragmentary, relatively undeveloped nature of *The Diary of Anaïs Nin, 1947-1955*. When preparing the earlier book for publication, Nin could not include the most important events in her life, which revolved around Guiler and Pole, because she was not at liberty to identify these men.[6] In that volume she presents herself as free, as a woman confronting life on her own without romantic attachment or financial support. In detailing her lives with Guiler and Pole and the emotional toll these relationships took on her, *Trapeze* sets the record straight.

BENJAMIN FRANKLIN V

University of South Carolina
August 2015

Notes

1 The first series of diaries consists of *The Diary of Anaïs Nin, 1931-1934* (1966); *The Diary of Anaïs Nin, 1934-1939* (1967); *The Diary of Anaïs Nin,1939-1944* (1969); *The Diary of Anaïs Nin, 1944-1947* (1971); *The Diary of Anaïs Nin, 1947-1955* (1974); *The Diary of Anaïs Nin, 1955-1966* (1976); and *The Diary of Anaïs Nin, 1966-1974* (1980). Gunther Stuhlmann, Nin's agent, edited and introduced all of them. Paperbacks of these titles number them sequentially, from volume 1 to volume 7.

2 This later series of diaries consists of *Henry and June* (1986), *Incest* (1992), *Fire* (1995), *Nearer the Moon* (1996), and *Mirages* (2013). Rupert Pole, executor of the Anaïs Nin Trust, wrote prefatory material for the first four of these books. John Ferrone, Nin's editor at Harcourt Brace Jovanovich, edited the initial volume; under Pole's supervision, Gunther Stuhlmann edited the next three diaries. Paul Herron edited and Kim Krizan introduced *Mirages*.

3 Guiler is also not mentioned in two volumes published posthumously, *Linotte: The Early Diary of Anaïs Nin, 1914-1920* (1978), which concludes before Nin met him, and *The Diary of Anaïs Nin, 1966-1974*. First as beau and then as husband, he figures prominently in books that recount her life from 1920 to 1931 and that, with *Linotte*, constitute another grouping of her diaries: *The Early Diary of Anaïs Nin, Volume Two, 1920-1923* (1982); *The Early Diary of Anaïs Nin, Volume Three, 1923-1927* (1983); and *The Early Diary of Anaïs Nin, Volume Four, 1927-1931* (1985). Joaquín Nin-Culmell, Nin's brother, introduced all four of the early diaries. John Ferrone edited *Linotte*; Rupert Pole edited the other volumes.

4 Guiler knew of his wife's bond with Pole by the mid-1960s. In a letter to Pole dated 23 February 1977, he states that for more than a decade he has known of Pole's "special relationship with Anaïs" ("Rupert Pole and Hugh Guiler: An Unlikely Partnership," *A Café in Space: The Anaïs Nin Literary Journal* 8 [2011]: 18).

5 The original published version of Nin's decision to make the trip reads: "I found a friend who was driving to Las Vegas to get a divorce, and we agreed to share expenses," with the name and sex of the companion unspecified (*The Diary of Anaïs Nin, 1944-1947* [New York: Harcourt Brace Jovanovich, 1971], 197).

6 Though Nin mentions the art of Ian Hugo (Hugh Guiler) in the initial series of diaries, including *The Diary of Anaïs Nin, 1947-1955*, she implies that her relationship with him is strictly professional.

CHRONOLOGY

1903 Anaïs Nin is born in Neuilly, France to the Spanish/Cuban pianist and composer Joaquín Nin y Castellanos and French/Danish/Cuban Rosa Culmell, a singer from a wealthy family

1905 Brother Thorvald is born in Havana

1908 Second brother Joaquín is born in Berlin

1912 Nearly dies from burst appendix in Brussels

1913 Nin's father abandons his family for a young lover; Nin's mother Rosa and the children stay with Joaquín Sr.'s parents in Barcelona

1914 Nin, her mother and two brothers come to New York; Nin begins her diary, in French

1919 Nin leaves school at the end of her junior year; becomes increasingly skeptical of Catholicism

1920 Begins to write her diary in English

1922 Becomes an artists' model to help with the family income

1923 Marries Hugh P. Guiler, a banker, in Cuba

1924 Nin and Guiler move to Paris where he takes a position with the Paris branch of his New York bank; Nin continues her diary and dabbles in fiction

1927 Begins Spanish dance lessons with Paco Miralles

1929 Has an unconsummated affair with American author and scholar John Erskine, which haunts her for years

1930 Moves from a lavish Paris apartment to a more economical house in Louveciennes, a suburb of Paris

1931 Meets controversial American novelist Henry Miller in Louveciennes

1932 Becomes Miller's lover and is infatuated with his wife June; Edward Titus publishes Nin's first book, *D. H. Lawrence: An Unprofessional Study*; Nin begins psychotherapy with René Allendy

1933 Reunites with her father and begins an incestuous relationship with him in the south of France, which would last for several months; begins psychoanalysis with Otto Rank

1934 Becomes Rank's lover; has a horrific late-term abortion; comes to New York to help Rank psychoanalyze patients; Miller secretly comes with her

1935 Moves from Louveciennes to Paris with Guiler

1936 Self-publishes *The House of Incest* (Siana Editions); meets Peruvian communist Gonzalo Moré and begins a sexual relationship with him; rents a houseboat on the Seine for their trysts

1937 Meets Lawrence Durrell; she, Miller and Durrell begin planning a series of books

1939 Obelisk Press prints Nin's *The Winter of Artifice*; Nin and Guiler fly to New York to avoid oncoming war

1940 Nin reunites with her two lovers, Miller and Moré, in New York; begins an affair with the young artist John Dudley

1941 Meets the Viennese singer Edward Graeffe (Chinchilito) in Provincetown and begins a long-lasting affair with him

1942 Self-publishes the expurgated version of *Winter of Artifice* (Gemor Press); breaks with Miller; begins psychoanalysis with Martha Jaeger

1943 Meets Haitian sculptor Albert Mangones and has a brief affair with him

1944 Self-publishes *Under a Glass Bell* (Gemor Press)

1945 Meets seventeen-year-old William Pinckard and begins an affair with him; self-publishes *This Hunger* (Gemor Press); meets Gore Vidal; begins psychoanalysis with Clement Staff; begins a brief affair with critic Edmund Wilson

1946 Falls in love with Vidal; with his help, E. P. Dutton publishes Nin's *Ladders to Fire*; briefly resumes affair with Mangones

1947 Dutton publishes *Children of the Albatross*; meets Rupert Pole; breaks with Moré

PART TWO OF MY LIFE

1947

New York, March 1947

I was recovering from all the deep wounds of Bill Pinckard's absence, of Gore Vidal's unattainableness, of the disintegration of my love for Gonzalo. Hugo was away in Cuba, and I was going out with Bernard Pfriem, a vital, charming man who desired me but whom I did not desire. Hazel McKinley is a burlesque queen in private life who literally strips herself bare at her parties, and then the next day she informs all her friends of the previous night's doings over the telephone. Hazel is blonde, very fat, weighing at least 200 pounds, a painter of childish watercolors proclaiming her age to be all of thirteen, an insatiable nymphomaniac who is always starved for men because they rarely stay more than one night. She telephoned me: "Oh Anaïs, bring me some men. I'm having a little party, and I haven't any men I could be interested in! Please, Anaïs."

I, thinking that she would attack Bernard and keep him there, agreed to come.

When I arrived at the hotel, I was ushered into an elevator with a tremendously tall young man. As I saw his handsome face, I said to myself: Caution. Danger. He is probably homosexual.

His name was Rupert Pole.

In Hazel's room, he and I stood talking for a moment. Rupert spoke first, having heard I was Spanish. Ordinary remarks. We discussed Schoenberg whom he had met in Hollywood. He intimated his belief in pacifism and mystical studies.

Later we found ourselves on the couch with his friend from California. I was on my guard with Rupert. But somehow or other we talked about printing (he excused himself for the condition of his hands) and that created a bond. I told him I had printed my books; he told me he was printing Christmas cards to earn a living. I told him I was a writer; he told me he was an actor out of work.

He was born in Hollywood.

He is twenty-eight.

His mother is re-married, this time to the son of Frank Lloyd Wright.

His father is a writer.

I remember that as we talked, we plunged deep, deep eyes into each other.

Then people intervened.

The homosexual is passive, so I was surprised when Rupert came up to me when I was ready to leave (early because Bernard was frightened by Hazel's advances and wanted to make love to me) and said, "I would like to see you again."

Hazel told me afterward, "He asked about you. He was interested in you."

That night while Bernard made love to me, it was Rupert's face that hung before my eyes.

Later Rupert called me. Hugo was away in Cuba. I invited him for dinner. I lit all the candles I had placed on the Spanish feast table. He took charge of the dinner. I sat far from him on the couch. We did not talk very long. His eyes were wet and glistening, and he was hungry for caresses. The radio was playing the love scene of *Tristan and Isolde*. We stood up. My mood was, above all, amazement—to see this beautiful, incredible face over mine, and to find in this slender, dreamy, remote young man a burst of electric passion.

The second surprise was that I, who never responded the first time in any love affair, responded to Rupert. He was so vehement, lyrical, passionate, and electric. His arms were strong. He pressed his body against mine as if he wanted to penetrate it from head to foot. He churned, thrashing sensually as if he would make love once and forever, with his whole force. The candles burned away. Tristan and Isolde sang sadly. But Rupert and I twice were shaken by such tremors of desire and pleasure that I thought we would die, like people who touched a third rail in the subway tunnel.

He stayed on. We talked. We made sandwiches. We fell asleep on my small bed. In the morning he was amazed by the painted window, like a pagan church of festive colors. I wore a white kimono. It was snowing. I made breakfast. I was expected at Thurema Sokol's, and he was driving to the country for the weekend at a friend's house. When I went downstairs with him, I was introduced to Cleo, his Ford Model A. Rupert dropped me off at Thurema's, said something lyrical, poetic, and drove off, leaving the light of his sea eyes to illumine the day. I went to see Thurema in a high state of exaltation. This was more than Bill. It was Bill handsomer, warmer, older, full of passion and love.

Would it only last one night? I asked myself, no longer able to believe in happiness.

He disappeared for several days. He had an infected finger. He was entangled with an ex-wife and a mistress he did not love.

Hugo returned.

Hugo was out for the evening when Rupert came with his guitar and sang. At midnight I had to send him away. I went to see him at his printing press. Rupert, so unique in appearance, so poetic, so aristocratic, seemed incongruous printing trite Christmas cards designed by his friend Eyvind Earle. That day I intended to stay an hour. I had an important dinner engagement arranged by Tana de Gamez at some celebrity's house with Hugo there. But when I called Tana and said, "*Te veo más tarde*," Rupert said no, I was having dinner with him. So I invented some absurd story for Tana, freed myself and went off with Rupert in Cleo. This time he took me to his shabby and unkempt little apartment. He kicked his soiled clothes into the closet, blushed for the disorder, but all I minded was the bare, glaring electric bulbs. The lovemaking was less intense. It may have been my mood. He gave me his kimono to wear and a bad metaphysical book he admired.

Our next encounter was at the Bibbiena Spanish restaurant on 14th Street. Rupert said in the middle of dinner, "I am driving back to Los Angeles soon. You once said you wanted to go to Mexico. Why don't you drive with me to Los Angeles and then go on with your trip from there?"

"Yes, why not?" I said.

Later, Rupert came with his arms full of maps and wearing a white scarf. The white scarf (the first was worn by Bill Pinckard) was for me a continuation of the broken experience with Bill. I watched Rupert's short, boyish hands pointing to the map. He was planning our trip. It was for my sake that Rupert would not take the shortest way—through the Middle West—because it is a dull way. He chose a southwest route and began to plan what he would show me.

Aside from our marvelous nights, what most attracted me was our harmony of rhythm. We got dressed at equal speed; we packed quickly. We leaped into the car; all our responses and reflexes were swift. There was a great elation in this for me, after living with Hugo's slow, laborious rhythm.

His voice over the telephone is clear like a perfect bell. Some deep part of his being is unknown to him, protected by this manly heartiness.

I am happy.

"Does it make you happy to know you have brought me back to life?" I asked.

"You seemed very alive to me."

"But sad."

"Yes, sad. But I shall make you happier still. I have our trip all planned."

To Dr. Clement Staff: "I fear my inadequate physical endurance. But now I know all these are fears of leaving."

Staff: "When you are happy you are relaxed and you do not get ill; these are anxieties."

The causes of anxiety are removed: I have not set myself to possess Rupert, win him, keep him! I have not strained after an illusion. I have been simple and truthful. My anxieties, fear of loss, are less than before; they do not strangle me as they did before.

Oh to win, to win freedom, enjoyment.

Looking back on my relationships, I feel I live in a ghostly world of shadows, of feebleness.

In Rupert there is enough physical resemblance to Bill Pinckard that I feel I am continuing my love for Bill, that I do not feel I am deserting Bill. A more hot-blooded Bill he is, a Bill ten years older.

Or will Bill always be passive and fearful?

Rupert is capable. He takes over the cooking, expertly. He repairs his own car. He does not ask as Gonzalo does: "Where is the knife? Where is the salt?"

I bought, for Rupert, my first pair of slacks.

Gonzalo comes every day. We kiss on the cheeks. He looks like a tired old lion. He works at the Press, at home. I get him printing jobs. I gave him a story, and *House of Incest* to do. Very little money.

March 30, 1947

When I went to Hazel's last night and met Guy Blake, a handsome young actor I had seen there before, I felt immune, unresponsive. To escape a loud movie director's monologue, Hazel and I went into her bedroom to talk, closing the door. Blake entered. Slim, dark-haired, blue-eyed, with a lovely voice. Hazel had said, "He does not like women," so I was not on my guard. He asked her to leave us. She closed the door. He began to kiss me and I to resist. I resisted because I knew that he knew Rupert, that Hazel would know and Rupert might hear of it. I wanted so much to be faithful, and above all not to endanger my relationship with Rupert. So I resisted. And it was difficult, because he was beautiful, ardent and violent.

As I tried to move away from his kiss, he pushed me onto the bed and lay over me. He was so violent. He took my hair into his hands and pulled it to keep my mouth welded to his.

"No, no, no, no—I want to be faithful to someone," I said. "No, no, no, no."

And got up.

"Let me walk you home!"

"But I have a husband. He is home, waiting."

"It's Rupert, isn't it?"

"I can't say."

"I know it's Rupert."

"I can't say."

He was disconcerted by my resistance. He went back to the party. I repainted my lips.

Then he walked me home.

"Let's stop for a drink."

"No, it's late."

But he was willful.

We sat at the back of a bar. He said, "Will you come to my room one night?"

"No."

"Why?"

"I told you why."

"Oh, women! I want you to come."

"I'll spend an evening with you."

"Oh, no, a whole night, or nothing at all. A night and a day. I want to know you. I never cared about Hazel; it would only be physical. With you…"

He was like a hypnotist, using all his assertiveness. His hand under my dress. Or pulling my hair again. At times I could not keep answering his kiss. The ardor, the fervor affected me. If only he had not known Rupert. With his fingers he knew I was not unresponsive. I liked his violence. He bit me.

"Come with me tonight. I want you."

"No, no, no."

We walked home.

Any other time I would have yielded. But I would not risk the loss of Rupert. (Who said Rupert expected faithfulness? I want to give it to him.) Blake had said, "Rupert is a nice fellow, but a dreamer."

A dreamer…

At the door he kissed me again and then held me wildly, violently. I fought to move away, but the more I fought the harder he clutched me, and this clutching aroused me; now and then I would rub against him as he rubbed against me, then tear myself away. Then he held me in such frenzy that he came, and I was still; I was unable to pull away in the middle of this frenzy.

To free myself I promised another night. Yes, I would come. He affected me sensually.

He was the first seductive man I ever resisted. I took pleasure in resisting; I was angry at his sensual power, at the way his violence aroused me. At one moment the way he pulled my hair to be able to kiss me reminded me of how I once twisted the reins on my horse when he started to run away, the bit pulled sideways to hurt him.

But what most affected me was that since the sensual barriers were removed in me how obvious it is that I could always have had this marvelous violence instead of seeking it from sickly boys, from Gore Vidal or Bill Burford or Lanny Baldwin, Marshall Barer...

My instinct now draws or seeks the violent lovers. What a mysterious pattern. If I had not known Rupert and felt tied to him, Blake would have delighted me. But Rupert is the dreamer—Rupert. Rupert.

Gore still has the power to melt me. It is no longer erotic, but this power to dissolve me with compassion melts my whole body so that still, if he chose to take me,

I would be happy. He gives me his softness, his sickness. At the sight of his face my heart is won each time. He puts on his glasses and acts like a senator, watching my love-life as my brother Joaquín did, with a sad resignation, asking me to marry him, to bear his child by "artificial insemination." He says when no one else wants me he will still love me.

But now I can keep them separate—even if Gore melts me, I can leave him and dream of Rupert. Violence and life with Rupert. Tenderness with Gore.

Last night Bill Burford took me out. We made our peace, exchanged confessions. At the door I kissed him tenderly, disregarding the deforming mirror of his neurosis, listening to and trusting only my own impulses.

It is the confusion of relationships that causes the misery, seeking to make them what they are not.

Everything is clear now.

I could be completely happy now if I had money to send Gonzalo to France, to travel, to dress, to make myself more beautiful.

Hugo is still completely in love with me.

All I ask is passion with Rupert—romance—a dream.

April 3, 1947

A dream, I said. I prayed for a dream.

Rupert returned from the weekend and called me Monday night (I had shut off the phone during a dinner for Richard Wright and Albert Mangones). He called me Tuesday; I was out (as I hadn't heard from him during the day, I tried not to think of him). Then last night he said, "I have been reading the stories from *Under a Glass Bell.* Oh, my darling, what beautiful writing. I felt I was living everything. I could smell the houseboat. And the language—I have never read writing like this. I used to read with my intellect. Those words about the crystal chandelier like blue icicles, I read them slowly."

I felt such happiness.

I had been so careful not to overwhelm him, not to reveal the stature of my work, to let him discover me slowly, by himself.

Midnight

We cook dinner together. He assumes leadership. He is planning our trip. He speaks humanly, and not callously (as Bill Pinckard did), of our "relationship." It may be the only trip we will have together. It must be wonderful. He likes the heat and the South, so we're going to New Orleans, which he has never seen. Slowly the trip becomes more wonderful.

Afterwards, during a stormy, nervous, wiry, electric lovemaking—so harmonious, virile, violent, without sadism (he does not need to bite or to hurt to feel lusty and strong), he said, "If it's like this in this cold city, my God, what will it be in the heat, in the sun, on the beach? What will happen to us?"

"Our bodies understand each other."

He talks of how his father will like me.

It all harmonizes—our primitive life—orchestrates into pleasure.

My only fear is my endurance! (Bad food, strain, all the hardships of casual traveling.)

But I must remember—Anaïs, remember—this relationship is not forever. Do not seek it forever. His choice of vocation, forestry, will take him to Colorado: "I want to do something simple, work with my hands, take root." Or will his love of acting take him to Hollywood? (He has already had a screen test.)

But I am happy. I do not have anxiety or the need for reassurance. I live in the present at last.

I feel great tenderness for Hugo, a grateful tenderness.

I feel altogether grateful; Rupert complains that on screen he looked too young, that his appeal was too boyish, not manly. He is a strange mixture. It is true that he looks younger than twenty-eight (alas!), yet in many ways he behaves more maturely than most men I have known.

It is his extreme slenderness and lankiness that give him the appearance of a boy at times. He is so tall, as tall as Hugo or Gonzalo, but weighs half, certainly. Then his neck is so slender, long.

It is in his hands that lies the great difference.

All the hands I have loved (except Gonzalo's) were aesthetic hands, especially Pinckard's, slender, white, fragile, soft-skinned.

Rupert's hands are sensitive but ruddy, roughened by activity—firm, not childish.

After lovemaking he said, "We are like two electrically charged magnets; when we touch it sets off a terrific light and fire; when we separate we die."

I *will not* say, "Come with me to Mexico." But that is what I want. He has just enough money for the trip to Hollywood, where his mother is, where he will look for a job.

I feel impelled not to clutch, not to seek words of permanence, as I did before. Perhaps if I could have behaved like this with Bill Pinckard my relationship with him might have been better.

At the first sign of jealousy I think: Anaïs, have faith. Have faith in the way he takes you.

It is wonderful, the erotic excitement into which he pours the elements of his nature: swiftness, lightning, mercury, a string instrumentalist's fingers.

More electricity than with Albert.

He does *not* like slacks! I had bought my first slacks as a concession to his Americanism, thinking them inevitable on a trip. But he likes femininity.

When we kiss with our eyes closed I like to open mine and see his long-lashed ones closed in the utter druggedness of desire.

When I lie on the couch, and he swoops down on me, then his eyes are open.

A penis has all the characteristics of its owner. There are lazy penises, like Gonzalo's; there are leaping, frigid ones; there are piercing and stabbing ones. When inside the womb they act so differently!

Rupert's is slender, active, leaping, wiry. He teases me into a frenzy before, by kisses, by caresses, by his hands, by friction, by undulations of the body.

I feel that Rupert and I connect electrically on a subterranean level; he is not aware of it as I am.

He was born February 18, 1919 at three in the morning in Los Angeles, and I feel superstitious about this. He has the love of the sea.

He comes to activate me.

Two trends conflict in him: he wants security, roots, wife, children, but he wants adventure and freedom. His desire for children is very strong.

Home is important. "I want music, and you can't have music without stability."

Oh, *mon journal*, Anaïs, the love-starved child, is fulfilled in a plenitude of love.

I open my eyes to reach for a letter from Bill Pinckard, a love-letter, dreaming of photographing me naked, of our going to Paris alone together: "You are so wonderful in every way."

Then I weep desperately once more over the death of my love for Gonzalo, and though we both know the passion is dead, he can't weep; he can only deceive himself as he has always done.

"It will all heal up...it will heal."

"No, no, we are separated," I shout. "It is over, I am going away. I don't want to see the death, the utter death of the love! I won't ever return to the hell you made with your violence and doubts."

He feels old, worn; he has no desire at all for anyone. He embraces me fraternally; it is unbearably sad. He seeks to destroy me with criticism. I am weakened by the past and have pity for Gonzalo left in Helba's prison.

And the other night Gore repeated: "Marry me, marry me, marry me. I will lock you up in Guatemala and allow you only clay pigeons" (casual lovers). He looked at me adoringly, and when he is there I feel only his presence. I want to enfold him inside my womb, warm him, nourish him.

Today at four, Carter Harman came to work on making *House of Incest* into an opera. For the first time I see him alone. We work so well, understanding each other and creating together, recreating *House of Incest*. It fills him with music.

Towards the end, in the twilight, I start to tell him about my marriage because I know he will hear about my life sooner or later. "I want you to know the truth because you are fond of Hugo. I am not betraying Hugo. I am not in love with him; I tried to preserve the marriage, but it's not a marriage. I don't seek justification; perhaps I would have had other loves anyway. I don't know."

I did not want to lie about my trip. I told him the truth. As I did this I thought I was *preventing* or dissolving the emotion we have, which I have always sensed in him. I thought I was destroying the feeling that should not be allowed since his marriage is good.

But then I saw he was disturbed and saddened. I said, "You seem sad. Are you worried about Hugo?"

"Oh, no, Anaïs."

We faced each other. He was leaving. We moved closer: "I'm so fond of you," he said. "I don't want you unhappy." We looked at each other: "I'm so...attracted to you."

"I, too...I feel so close."

Faces drawing nearer.

"Kiss me once, Carter."

He kissed me with passion.

Once.

At the door he paused.

Incoherent words: "Two years ago we could have been so happy together, Anaïs."

"But now you're happily married to Nancy."

"Yes."

"I love to work with you, Carter."

"I love to work with *you*. Let's be close friends."

"Yes, yes."

He was gentle.

It was I who asked him to kiss me.

He is gentle...gentle.

He is not as good for me as Rupert, but he affects me emotionally, deeply.

Oh, Anaïs...

That was Monday.

Then Tuesday he came again.

It is hard to work—the air is charged with desire. We sit on the couch. I write down what we agree on. He lies near. When he is too near, I tremble inwardly. I want violence. I feel his turmoil.

Again we talked. He told me: "Before my marriage I was in the army; I was so lonely. What I most wanted when I returned was to be married. Now, after two years, this is the first time I have been tempted. You are dangerous for me. I am afraid that someday I will have to live as you do. But now I couldn't."

"I know. That is why I'm leaving New York."

At the door he says, "Aren't you going to kiss me?"

Then we kiss longer. He is not violent, but sensual in a melting way. It is not electricity, but a flowing together that is piercingly sweet.

When he leaves, I feel lost.

This is not at all the way I feel with Rupert. With Carter I feel this sickness, this hauntingness. I'm afraid because Carter has the intense blue eyes of Bill (Rupert has eyes like mine, chameleon, now gold, now green, now blue, now grey), the fair skin. My desire for him is like my desire for Bill. I feel dissolved. It is painful.

That evening Carter, Nancy, Hugo and I went out together to see Lincoln Kirstein of the Ballet Society.

I felt depressed. I longed for Rupert to come and rescue me. The next day he came and kissed me but did not take me. Instead he drove me out to the East River to contemplate a red birch tree. It had a beautiful bark the color and texture of a chestnut. I tried to invest this one tree with all possible symbolizations: the tree of life, manly, not a tree of genealogy, but the mystical tree in Hindu mythology occupied by gods and dancers. This was the tree Rupert wanted to protect from devastation, fire, lumberjacks, the tree he wanted to help reproduce, nourish, house, shade.

He says, "Cleo is our houseboat."

He returns home with me. I dress for a formal dinner and he drives me to Peter Wreden's house on Park Avenue. He says, "You look pure and Grecian, all in white." *Mariposa blanca, Princesita.*

But he was annoyed by my preface to *Tropic of Cancer* and horrified by the book itself.

He is volatile.

I fought the anxiety I felt at his not making love. Anaïs, Anaïs. *Confiance.* On the East River he kissed me. He noticed I had no gloves. He wanted me to wear his. He asked: "Are you cold? Do you like my driving?" He took one of my photographs of me: "In this one your eyes are like jewels, and your mouth I love."

I love…

"To live like this," I said, "to dare to live without knowledge of tomorrow."

But Anaïs has *angoisse, angoisse.* I still add up the kisses, I still register the words; I fear it is all unreal. I do not believe.

At the Wredens', homeliness, comfort, bourgeois solidity. I am bored. Gore is there. He takes me home, and in the taxi we hold hands, or rather I take his hands and nestle them. I rest my head on his shoulder. He kisses me as warmly as one can kiss without sex.

I am lost in three loves (Rupert, Carter, Gore) that are orchestrations of my love and desire for Bill Pinckard.

Sad today.

But I am shopping and delighting in new cotton dresses.

Carter is twenty-eight. He is not tall; he is my height. He has light brown hair. He is very slender. Blond-skinned. His face has great beauty, emotion. He has large, very blue, very brilliant eyes, a bird's profile, a rich, full mouth. He has an irresistible grin. When he is not smiling fully he looks sad. Above all, he looks sensitive and frail. Yet he went to India during the war, flew a helicopter.

I don't know if it is my obsession with Bill or reality, but Carter has, as I imagine, physical traits like Bill's.

But why, why do I have with him this drugged state, fever, illness of love?

Rupert awakens wildness.

Carter comes humbly, almost, with his score in a valise, the metronome.

He and Nancy have music in common. She plays the piano and can copy music for him. Now I wish I had studied with my father. Why did I have this obstinate refusal to study music with my father?

The subtle, the sad, the terrible thing that happens in my life with Hugo. I cannot describe it clearly, only in terms of climate. As soon as he returned from Cuba I felt it. I feel I lose the sun. I feel the climate change to heaviness, greyness, death. I hear his voice. So many times he is like a zombie. He is *absent*; he is almost invariably depressed.

His analyst speaks of an old childhood sulkiness, resentment. He is full of negative reactions: forgetfulness, absent-mindedness, automatism in talking.

He behaves like an old man. After dinner he falls asleep. Saturdays he wants to sleep. Sundays too. I feel my life clogged, slowed down. I feel oppressed by his face, the solemnity of it. His conversation all factual, his constant budgeting, his total absence of playfulness.

At fifty, he moves slowly, deliberately, without buoyancy. Never has a quick reflex. Our rhythm is discordant. He goes to sleep early, and then at dawn he awakens and reads.

I feel caged, trapped, weighed down. All his good qualities cannot balance this climate in which I cannot *live*.

Even when I give him my individual attention and we spend an evening together—we went to Chinatown last night—he has pleasure in terms of taking me down in a taxi, but nothing comes out of him to illuminate the evening.

Poor Hugo.

I miss Rupert. I want him to possess me this minute, to keep me. It is only the fears I have that keep me unstable, escaping towards Carter because I feel that Rupert is not for me.

I feel the attraction between Rupert and me is unconscious. He is not fully aware of it as I am now.

April 15, 1947

Staff fights the anxiety. Anxiety is dispersing, splitting the loves. Anxiety because Rupert is the adventure I want, and I fear the instability of it, the unknown.

Staff points out the fears: my own duality between security and freedom—Hugo and Rupert.

When Hugo is absent I feel I could live without him. When he returns the dependency begins again.

After talking with Staff about my fear of giving to Rupert because there is no permanency, I flow again. And when Rupert came I was exuberant and joyous. He always responds to this. I tease him. I say I am going to spend our trip investigating whether he is taking up the study of trees because he loves them or because people have hurt him.

We sit on the couch, and again he becomes the burning lover, his tongue possessing my ear, his mouth on my mouth…

Oh, my diary, I am out of hell, I have known happiness.

Our lovemaking is all I want. He has my temperament. He teases me with caresses so much that I have to beg him: "Oh take me, *take* me!" His slender, slender body pushes against mine; he touches every nook, every curve. We fit so close—lean and pliable. Something is so exciting and tantalizing in him that I get into a frenzy. His quickness, alertness, volatile quality, his constant moving, his flying about in his car all enter into his lovemaking.

The complete frenzy. And then he stayed inside me. He lay over me, and after a moment he began again.

Then he fell asleep, laying his full length over me. And when he awakened he said, "I thought I was far from you, and now I find myself in your arms; it's so beautiful."

After violent sensuality, tenderness, more kisses, full and sensual.

Then we go out to shop, and he cooks the dinner as I do, in ten minutes, and enjoys it. And after dinner he lies over me again, at rest, tender, relaxed. A full, complete cycle.

And I am relaxed, natural. I feel the plentitude, the sweetness, the warmth of love. I am happy. We can talk together. We can enjoy together.

Now he is impatient to leave.

Such a being: so well balanced, a poet, mystic, musician, sensualist. He can win me, keep me, hold me if he wants to. He could stop all these flights and divisions. He is more dynamic than Carter.

I love his activity, his kindness.

Whenever he comes, because I think about his fiery intensity, I am surprised to see him slender, delicate; one expects a very big man.

I am happy, happy.

April 20, 1947

Then, after this merging, Rupert vanishes for a few days. Goes here and there, sees his ex-wife, his young girl, does not call, does not say when we will meet again, volatizes, and I feel anxiety. About the girl, Martha, he had said, "I cannot consider her seriously. She is too young, confused, under her mother's domination, a Christian Scientist, rich and spoiled. You say I'm in love with her? I don't know. There is no physical attraction. I think of her as a friend. I would have liked her to bear my children."

(That is how I used to write about Hugo!)

His need of stability—I am his passion. He probably does not feel sure of me.

Anxiety.

And the next day Carter came.

Now Carter I *trust*. Carter, I feel, loves me deeply. He telephones, he is *there*. With him, even though he belongs to Nancy, I feel that we are bound, that he will remain close, that he needs and wants continuity. No leaps, no vanishings, no elusiveness.

As does Gore, he settles within me, he nestles, he flows.

I said, "When Hugo and I first came to your house I felt an affinity, a closeness. We talked so easily."

The desire grows. We work together, awaiting the kiss at the end. The moment our bodies touch I feel his desire aroused. Intoxication. Drunkenness.

We separate.

It hurts.

He fears a split of his being, expansion, and I know all the pain this causes.

Then that same evening I received five yards of luxuriant, fire-red brocade from Bill in Korea wrapped around a secret box, which must have been sent before he received *Children of the Albatross*, in which I mention such a secret Chinese box as an image of his character. This came to me as an omen: he will like my writing. It will not separate us (I have been anxious). And the next morning I received his letter:

"Cherie, reading the book and comprehending what lay beneath it made me understand you and love you even more. With my heart I say those words. My heart was deeply moved throughout the book."

Happiness...happiness...happiness... Fullness...fullness...fullness...richness...

I knew what Carter felt, but I knew it more by his keenness to see me when Nancy, fearing me, began to withdraw from him. Vibration...vibration... So sad. I know I bring sadness, conflict to Carter, and yet I know too that I can unleash great music in him, that I am necessary to his growth, that his childish marriage is not enough, that I arouse, shake, stir him to greater things. I know the music in me and my words fire him. I know I am for him what Henry and June Miller were for me, who took me out of a small world into a vaster, more terrible and more magnificent realm.

Oh, Carter, the human treacheries for the sake of greater evolutions. Touching me is another Carter who could not be born out of Nancy—a deeper and wilder Carter—born today.

Last night I had a small farewell party for me. I invited Nancy and Carter. Carter came alone. The cell of the dream makes everything wonderful, transfigured.

I want to dance with him because it means holding him and melting together. This melting together, melting.

Oh Rupert, why don't you stay close? He has these airy spaces he leaps into. In his little car, he is far away. Cold Springs. Mount Kisko. His ex-wife Janie Lloyd Jones and Martha and friends I don't know.

Because Carter is faithful to Nancy I trust him, because I know he is caught not by a whim, a casual fantasy, but a deep feeling.

Once I wove a vast fire out of Henry and Gonzalo. Now, again, I feel a vast love encompassing very similar men, stemming from the source of Bill Pinckard.

Oh, Rupert, take all of me, hold me, hold me, hold me. I said to you wildly in the middle of possession: "I belong to you," and you tightened your grip exultantly, proudly. You too are afraid now?

You said, "We create our own sea!"

PART TWO OF MY LIFE
I feel loved
I feel united with the world
I feel free

Last night at the party I felt beloved.

Pablo said, "Oh, Anaïs, I'm jealous—I feel terribly jealous that someone is taking you away."

Woody Parrish-Martin, Stanley Haggart...

"I will miss you."

Friends, warm, devoted.

It took me years to conquer hell, to gain faith and peace.

My body is blooming.

I do not feel responsibility for others. I have not made Hugo's gloom or Gonzalo's prison. In fact, I fought too long to lighten Hugo and to free Gonzalo.

Friday night both Hugo and I were drained, exhausted. Hugo made dinner solemnly, and sat stagnant. I, equally tired, become more acutely humorous, bubbling, for visitors. I told Hugo I am traveling with Thurema.

NEW YORK, APRIL 23, 1947

Last entry before the trip. Now the diary goes into the vault. On Monday I leave with Rupert. Staff said my anxiety that this trip should not happen is a projection of my own guilt at deserting Hugo, Gore, Gonzalo, Carter, all my friends. The guilt is a myth, he warned. The only traces left of the old illness are anxiety, fear of catastrophe, of pain, of tragedy.

I became tense, tense again.

Suddenly there is no time for all my relationships. No time to see Albert, no time for Edward Graeffe (Chinchilito), no time for Guy Blake pleading over the telephone. One visit from Richard Wright and he falls in love with me and calls me today and says, "Come to France with me."

Henry Miller writes that he awaits my visit impatiently.

Carter: I keep time for him. We work together. But oh, the sweet torment, the sweet torment. The way he lies on the couch. I realize he is not good for me; he is not violent enough. He is gentle, yielding. He is not daring. He wants the kiss, but I have to lead. It is not good.

It is I who must act.

He responds. I am afraid to lose my control. I want him so much. His mouth, his eyes, his beautiful expression.

He is too quiet for me. But I could be at peace with him. It would be gentle.

My fiery one is absent. Dashed to the country. Darts here and there.

Staff said, "When the anxiety catches you, lie down and think of the analysis. Know you create the myth, the fiction. It is not reality. *You* are constantly deserting Rupert in your mind because you are afraid to give yourself."

Rupert Pole in "Cleo," his Model A Ford, 1947

July 2, 1947	New York. Beach with Carter and wife
July 3, 1947	Staff
July 5, 1947	Staff
July 6, 1947	Chinchilito
July 7, 1947	Jacobson
July 8, 1947	Staff
July 10, 1947	Chinchilito
July 11, 1947	Staff
July 12, 1947	Jacobson
July 13, 1947	Staff
July 18-27, 1947	Los Angeles. Rupert Pole
July 28, 1947	Leave Los Angeles
July 29, 1947	Mexico City, alone
July 30-September 10, 1947	Acapulco

September 11, 1947	Left for San Francisco
September 13-18, 1947	Trip to Utah with Rupert
October 26, 1947	Lecture at Black Mountain College; met Jim Herlihy
October 28, 1947	New York. Gotham Book Mart party for *Children of the Albatross*
November 1, 1947	Albert Mangones
November 5-6, 1947	Bennington lecture
November 12, 1947	Lecture Chicago with Wallace Fowlie
November 25, 1947	Gonzalo Moré
November 29, 1947	Radio broadcast, New York City
December 3, 1947	Lecture at Berkeley
December 6, 1947	Los Angeles to Mexico
December 8, 1947	Bought house in Acapulco
December 19, 1947	Rupert arrives in Acapulco

LA JOIE

1948

January 1948

Acapulco

New York, Spring 1948

Rupert's gift to me was a special, selected view of America. The nature was beautiful, full of variety and surprises. Canyons, marshes, fields, rivers, swamps, desert lakes.

During that trip none of his dogmatic traits were revealed to me. True, he talked about a home, wife and nine children, but I did not believe him altogether. We played at my being the other woman, the foreign woman who would lure him away from his home now and then!

I talked about my travels, the panorama of Europe paralleling America, sometimes created out of contrast, sometimes by association. Two warnings my heart did not heed: one, that his life was not interesting, just ordinary; the other, that he did not know or understand his relationships with other women, his lover of four or five years, or his ex-wife. I probed in vain. He gave me a blurred, confused image, with many gaps and black-outs.

Once he was jealous of my abundant mail and threw it on the floor.

I had my difficulties on that trip. My eyes were wind-burnt and caused me much suffering and humiliation. In South Carolina I wanted to quit; I felt homely and inadequate. Rupert was kind. But I realize now that true kindness would have been to put the top up, and that he never did. I had to learn the hard way, to find glasses with sides against the wind, to wear a base of makeup over my eyelids and face as protection.

I also felt utterly tired; we kept a daredevil pace, and this intensity, without pause, made the trip an ordeal.

On that trip I accepted his leadership totally. I did not know the road, the restaurants, the motels, or anything about cars. He was an experienced traveler. So Rupert may have had the illusion that I was easily dominated! I enjoyed his leadership then.

We stopped to see Henry Miller in Big Sur. The road to his home was steep and dangerous, mountain driving, and Rupert's car wasn't quite equal to it. But as we climbed, the view of the sea below, the rocks, the pines, was beautiful. The car drove into a courtyard, and there was Henry sitting out of doors, typing. He seemed healthier than in New York. He was proud to own the modest cottage we entered. It was simple and uncluttered, reminiscent of the old Henry's tidiness. His wife Lepska appeared. There was tension between them. He criticized her. He thought my trip west and to Mexico was a flight from my life in New York, and that he should help me in some way. I made it clear I needed no help.

I should not have visited Miller. As soon as one ceases to know a person intimately, the knowledge of them is from the outside, as if you stood at a window looking in. Intimacy takes trust and faith. That was over.

"See! See!" said Rupert, "See the Lord's candle cactus flower." When I saw them I thought: we are nearing his home. It is time for me to return the ring he gave me so that during the trip I would be known as Mrs. Pole. In so many registers all through the United States, Mr. and Mrs. Pole. But when I tried to return the ring Rupert turned his face away: "No, keep it. As a remembrance of the trip." It was the wedding ring from his marriage to Janie. On the last day of our trip together, entering Los Angeles, he expressed sorrow at the termination of our dream.

"It's hell," he said upon awakening to the reality of our parting. But he did not act to hold me, to affix me. He surrendered me. I wept as I sat at the airport, watching him drive away.

There was a honeymoon couple being celebrated, rice was thrown, a champagne bottle was opened, and the cork fell at my feet. I was weeping and looking at the couple. They did not love each other as Rupert and I had loved each other during our eighteen-day trip, yet they were married, secure for years, and that would never happen to us. We were separating, perhaps forever.

"Deep feelings have continuity," I said to Rupert before leaving, to sustain my faith, but in reality there was nothing to reassure me. He was entering a new profession: two years of university courses to attain a degree as forester, and a forestry job in the summer.

I asked, "What would you have done if I had run away, gone to Europe?"

"I would have dropped my work and pursued you, brought you back. In New York I wasn't sure you'd come with me."

"Suppose I hadn't at the last moment?"

"I would have abducted you."

As we parted, I was returning a comb, a newspaper, and I said, "Do I have anything else of yours?"

"My heart."

I returned to New York, to all my nightmares, to find Gonzalo still preying upon me, taking, asking, destroying the last shreds of respect, of illusion. Life with Hugo, insincere, a role. Then came a government injunction that I must leave the United States until a re-entry permit was in order. I left for Acapulco alone. In sensual, drugging Acapulco I wanted Rupert desperately. He haunted me. I haunted him equally. He wrote me that he saw me peeping behind every tree. He wrote of wanting me. He wrote of needing to be with me, but he didn't write: "I'm coming."

But just before last Christmas he did come to Acapulco. I had a little home and rented a car. All that I had imagined when I had been there alone took place and was fulfilled. We swam. We made love wildly in the tropical nights, after siestas. We took a trip. He got ill. I nursed him. We lived in rhythm. No clashes. We spent two days in Taxco. The only anguish he caused me was by turning to look at every pretty woman, and once when a Mexican girl stared at him he turned completely to stare back at her as if I were not there.

I am aware of the reality of our relationship. Rupert is kind, responsible and loyal, but he is susceptible to women's charms. He has an adolescent curiosity and multiple enthusiasms. I am not to expect faithfulness.

Three days at Ensenada. When we got into the car, as for our first voyage, Rupert became free. He changed, expanded, grew wild. He became Pan. We were sitting on the bed talking. He has a brusque, impetuous way of throwing himself on me. We had three days and nights of wild and frenzied passion. Sometimes it begins gently and ends in fire, or sometimes it begins with fire and ends in gentleness, but it is always complete, all the movements are there, slow and sad, quick and gay, a rhythm below the surface. The sea, the sand, the wind, the trees are marshaled for our desire, our décor, and our language. Our moods are their moods. High, low, cold, warm, peaceful, tempestuous. Very few words. It is alchemy. Is there a mysterious rhythm between people, mysterious flows? Is it that he turns off the music I don't like at the precise moment it grates on me, or that I am silent when his nerves are tired from driving? Is it that I sit passively in the shadow of his driving, basking in his leadership, his swift decisions? "We sleep here. We stay here." His lightning quickness, his easy entrances and exits, his restlessness at restaurant tables. Oh, darling, how our bodies fit into one another and how our two vehemences knead caresses into each other to the point of pain. The fever mounts. In sleep it coils between our hips. Our faces veiled and dissolved by sleep, eyes closed, his desire is there, taut against my hips. In sleep he turns towards me, in sleep, in sleep...

The road swallowed us. The night. The mountain. A heavy snow cloud lying over the mountain, over every crevice, falling like a hand over us; it aroused the feeling of a caress, a union, as that of certain trees paired together, the aspen and the pine.

Dawn, day, and night were welded. Food a delight, drink a delight, and words too simple to contain this well of music made by our collisions, our desires, our caresses. Bathed in music, in the quick drumming of his fingers on my body, drumming out of my body every cord, and in the core, the vortex, the volcanic center where the two points of fire meet, a possession takes place of such high alchemy that no element is missing and each one has fused, not one drop lost or strayed or foreign or contrary.

Return to New York.

Los Angeles, May 8, 1948

The book entitled *La Joie* by Georges Bernanos always entranced me not for its contents as much as for the power of the words: *La Joie*, the mystery, the quality of an Unknown Land.

It was the unattainable state. When Rupert, a year ago, asked me to leave New York with him, I did not know it was to be a voyage not only across the United States, pausing at New Orleans, the canyons, but that ultimately we were to reach this new land together, this unfamiliar country of *La Joie*.

We are in my Hollywood hotel room, anonymous and banal, but white. His pipe lies forgotten on my desk. His bathing suit hangs in my bathroom. He, the volatile, the uncapturable Chief Heat Lightning as I call him, has left, but he is not lost. He has to sleep at home because his stepfather Lloyd Wright is severe, because he has to be up at seven to be at the College of Forestry at eight, because his mother is conventional and worried about his reputation, but he will telephone me at midnight, or earlier, every night, of his own free will. And when he can, he will rush over. His clear, light, breathless voice of a boy. This habit only began a month ago when I left for a lecture in Houston, one of the intermittent trips he imposed on me by his fear of permanence. When I left, he said over the telephone: "You have all my love."

It took years of sorrow to learn these airy birds' spirals around the lover so that the love should never crystallize into prison bars. Flights. Swoops. Circles. For a year I circled around him so lightly, so lightly. And so it was away to Houston for two weeks, and a return to California with Hugo who then returned to New York to complete his psychoanalysis. Rupert, then anxious, said over the telephone: "I missed you. I need to be with you again." And he came over one night in Cleo and drove up the hills and we lay under a pepper tree, so avid, so hungry. Then he began to call, as we can only see each other on weekends.

La Joie. The present. When he comes he wears the sandals he bought in Acapulco. He lost the peaked green Tyrolean hat he wore on his trip, which gave him such a pixie air, for his face is small, pointed, and is eclipsed by his eyes. His eyes. His entire being is concentrated in his eyes. So large. So deep. So remote and yet so brilliant. Tropical sea eyes, sometimes veiled as if he had wept, passionate. I leap at his arrival. The current is so strong, a current of fire and of water, of nerves, and of mists, of mysteries.

Two lean bodies embracing always with vehemence, except when he is tired, so very tired, and then he rests his head on my stomach. If we drank the potion the first time we made love in New York to the tune of *Tristan and Isolde*, neither one of us ac-

Anaïs Nin signing her books in Houston, 1948

knowledged it until a year later, acknowledged the impossibility of separation. For after two weeks in Acapulco, he was able to leave without any plans for the future. He feared my presence in Los Angeles because he had too little time and imagined a demanding relationship. But when he saw how I behaved, how I disappeared, did not even call or expect him, weighed so little on him, he learned to enjoy the short moments with me. It was not until recently that he uttered the words I needed to hear: "You are the closest; no one has ever been closer to me." Or: "You understand me so well." Or: "We always want the same thing. I approve of you as I didn't of Janie. But Anaïs, you are not being given all that you deserve."

"Lord and Lady Windchime," I say in our moments of aristocracy, for he has that to a high degree. Lord and Lady Windchime go out in Hugo's gift to me, a Chrysler Deluxe convertible that Rupert baptized Perseus. Perseus is exchanged for Cleo for long trips. Perseus has speed. Cleo has a dogged, spirited character. Perseus is polished and new. Cleo has gusto.

When we first met we were both poor, badly dressed, worn out, unhappy and defeated by life. Today he is no richer but he has a good home, refined, artistic, comfortable; he goes to UCLA every day. When he comes, we pack our bathing suits and drive to the beach along the richly flowered roads lined with dignified palm trees. We swim, we lie in the sun, we sleep. Or we run along the edge of the sea. Another time it is dark when he arrives. I wear my black and turquoise cotton dress from Acapulco. We rush to a movie, where we hold hands and where he laughs so exuberantly that he squeezes me to suffocation, and his gayety is expressed by his encircling me with his two wiry arms. And always this firm, strong, feverish lovemaking.

This love is full of sparks, and it is blinding. There is a potion that was drunk on our first trip, a mingling with the desert, the canyons, the mountains, a part that is mythical and dreamed. He who never planned, never crystallized, never foresaw, never promised, never longed, now says, "Next winter when I am in Berkeley you could take a little house in Monterey."

I am awakened by the singing of birds. I cannot introduce them. I ask their names and then forget like a careless hostess. But they sing well and gaily. The sun shines through the venetian blinds. I have a choice of beautiful dresses to wear. (Hugo has resigned from the bank, has made money on the outside, and travels again as he used to and wanted to.) The pleasure I have indulged in for the first time in my whole life, of dressing according to my taste, of taking care of my body and face. I walk down the hill to breakfast at Musso. The banality and vulgarity of Hollywood does not disturb me. I see another Hollywood, young artists of all kinds. I help Rupert to increase his knowledge of art, to develop taste.

At night, alone, sometimes I suffer again from the mysterious malady of anxiety and marvel by what alchemy this is transmuted and given to others as a life source, wondering if it is not the alchemy itself that is killing me, as if I kept the poisons in my being, sadness, loneliness, and gave out only the gold. Everywhere I go life and creation burst open, yet I remain lonely, I remain without the twin I seek.

The oneness with Rupert is being destroyed by its intermittences, leaving me in between in deserts of mistrust.

This morning I got into my car that I learned to drive painstakingly and now enjoy. Alone, still amazed naïvely at the miracle of driving a beautiful, suave, powerful car in the sun. I go to Elizabeth Arden where the two women who attend to me have read my books, pamper me and come to my readings, and are proud of me. A quest for beauty, to efface some of the harm done by my years in the hell of New York. At times it seems like a convalescence. The sun shines on the nickel of the car, on my new dress, on my new dash, on my new confidence. This image of the quest for beauty is a fulfillment of a childhood dream, for when I was a girl I had to wait once for Tia Antolina at the Elizabeth Arden salon and I saw her appear so groomed, so radiant, so beautiful. I longed to be able to enter as she did and reappear, smooth as porcelain, a glitter of the eyes enhanced by eye-drops! Oh, Anaïs, such frivolity. No longer ashamed, for the deep life runs securely like a river, and the rest is adornment. And I no longer fear to be cursed by my father's shallowness for daring to fulfill a natural elegance that is suitable to my body and face. I reappear then, as my beautiful Tia Antolina, powdered and ironed, patted out and refreshed, and get into my Nile-green car. When I return there is a letter from Hugo, finishing his analysis and planning for our future and "remarriage;" there is a letter from Bill Pinckard scolding me because my letters are impersonal (after two years it is he who is looking for a personal word as I used to look in his letters for a sign of love). He is on his way back from Korea. There is a letter filled with newspaper clippings on *Under a Glass Bell*, just published by Dutton. There are telephone messages from Rupert's father, from Paul Mathieson, Kenneth Anger, Curtis Harrington, Claiborne Adams, other friends. There are flowers from an admirer. I can do as I please, but I can't write. The present being beautiful, I can extract from the past its essence without pain. But still, I like this moment. I am absorbed by my love for Rupert. I meditate on his strong, hardy, rough eyebrows, his woman's eyelashes so long and thick, his passionate eyes. His long deer neck, his lean and wiry body. His strange, unpredictable nature, chaotic, full of intuitions and seeking in nature a reality. I see him playing the viola in quartets at home, planting the lawn, helping his mother, cleaning the windows, taxiing the family, doing his homework, rushing to school. When we drive into the desert, Rupert knows the names of the trees and flowers; he is familiar with the roads. In Acapulco once he got very ill with a high fever. I was frightened. I remember the fragility of his face burning in my hands, a fragility like mine, though ultimately strong with will and spiritedness and a desperate courage. His lungs are not strong, but instinctively he seeks to harden himself, to lead a healthy life.

Chiquito, I call him.

How gaily he came Sunday, pretending to be drunk and sliding down the stairs, three steps at a time, dragging me by the hand, running to the car.

The birds here sing at night.

As in Acapulco, there is a constant air of Fiesta.

He loves what my sorrows have made me, my efforts, my courage, my aspirations. He loves what I have created, lost, loved, surrendered. With all his beauty, he looks upon the beautiful girls in his college (he could have them all) but he says, "They do not have this...this...this..." (he cannot find the words) "...this warmth you have, this growth." *C'est moi qu'il aime*, my flavors, my elixirs, and I feel worthy because it was my labor, my effort, my struggle to become what I am, every word, color, every form I had to make, to create.

Last night: he was asleep on my breast, and I was caressing his infinitely delicate temples, the sleep veil over his face. It was three o'clock. He should have been home. We lay there in a trance of human sweetness. We had laughed at the movies. His talk and his words are but a small fraction of what he knows, and by this secret other sense we commune, we mingle.

Beethoven Quartet: on Saturday afternoons Rupert plays the viola in a string quartet. He asked me to go to his home yesterday to hear them. His face, leaning over his viola, was so beautiful and grave. So pure and emotional. The gravity of his wholeness. He plays with his whole being. This slender body contains passion and music. His bare arms are wiry and strong. His small, square hands so lusty and yet so sensitive. He is sad that his hands are not beautiful, but it is their character that saves him from too much delicacy, that gives a balance to his delicate face. His strong, square hands and feet save him from being too exquisite, too aesthetic. He plays with the same vehemence with which he makes love. Listening to him, I knew this was his language.

He wants me to study piano so I can accompany him.

Once again the diary becomes the extension of moments I want to retain forever. You cannot enclose fire or tenderness, but their echoes, their vibrations, their imprints. Love is the drug at first, and one is asleep during its fecundations.

"It's strange, Anaïs, that I cannot take you for granted. Other people, you feel, will love you forever. With you I feel I must begin anew each time. Or is it that you mean so much to me that I fear losing you and I make greater efforts?" Jealousy is our only enemy. His and mine. In Acapulco, when the son of the man who rented me the house came to the door to deliver a message (an invitation for New Year's Eve) or stopped his motorboat to hail us while we fished, to invite us to his father's house, Rupert was anxious.

There are times when he makes love to me so profoundly, so magnetically, that I want to cry out, and the moan that seeps through is a faint echo of the wild turmoil of the body in this lightning storm, this charged current, vibrations with such violence through the nerves, the moment when he enfolds me, encircles me. Once he locked me in his arms so vigorously, so hard it left me breathless, and he murmured: "I'm just an inhibited man, but all I can say I say with my arms around you."

After the quartet it happened we were both high-keyed, elated. I said, "Let's run away" (from his home, mother and stepfather). We climbed into Perseus and drove to the sea and to an amusement park. And then I found my fear again, all the fears I thought I had conquered, fear and terror of speed, heights, the scenic railway, of violence and darkness, of labyrinths, of enclosures, of chutes, of darkness, traps. Why? Why? Rupert holding my hand, Rupert unafraid, Rupert elated by danger.

I am not made for happiness. Will I hear the birds sing again? Will I feel pleasure tomorrow when I see the jacaranda tree in bloom? Am I condemned to tragedy? Rupert and I had talked of jealousy. That was it.

And I had a dream. Rupert was telling me about a woman he had seen at a restaurant, and was fascinated with. He had made a drawing. He was asking me how to conquer her. I said, “Must you torment me by discussing her?” I sought him, and went to the restaurant. I examined the drawing of the woman. She wore an oriental veil, a Spanish mantilla that half covered her face. It was me.

Last night, returning to my room, he wanted to stay all night, so we had passion and fell asleep locked together until dawn. He is my music, my dance, my wine, my sea, my mountain, my fever.

And he has an important role to play, for it was he who took me by the hand and led me into nature, who took me out of artifice and into my own innocence again.

His airiness—how I love his airiness. Today he had only a moment with me. He leaped upon me and enveloped me so that I found myself caught between his legs, between his arms, and lying down.

With equal agility he climbs into Cleo and vanishes, and I feel a slight constriction of anxiety. Then, ironically, it is I who enter the hairdresser's to have my hair washed and the girl says to me: “You always look as if you were about to fly away.” The first day she had said, “Are you a ballerina?”

Rupert in his car and I in mine. At San Diego he was given a car to deliver to his mother. And as he drove it back I had to follow in Perseus. It took all my wits, dexterity, and nimbleness to keep his pace! And how I laughed when even while driving in another car he kept pointing to things I must see, as he did all during our first trip. Thus I choose always the one who will take me out into the open, and my interior journeys become the journey outside. Rupert is always outside, always watchful, alert, responsive. Only after playing his viola does he sink into a mood, distance, absorption. The music sucks him under, into silent depths. He said once he had sent me away because he thought he was not good enough for me, and was not free to give me enough. When he saw that I was not unhappy in Los Angeles when he could not come, then he did not even send me away during his final examinations.

Yesterday I saw him for a few minutes in his own house. He was alone. He prepared a drink with mint that he planted himself. How difficult it is to be together for only a little while. Such desire I have for him. He has a way of dropping his head suddenly on my breast, with such abandon. So happy I am today dreaming of our next trip together. He sent me far from here yesterday to buy a cookbook from the famous French cook Henri Charpentier, for our life in San Francisco where he will study forestry at Berkeley. He said, “When we amalgamate our libraries we shall have a system. I don't think certain books should be mixed together.” At times he calls me twice a day. He calls me at midnight sometimes, when I am asleep.

I fear his adolescent Don Juanism, his need to charm and conquer, his pleasure in being liked. He teases me. And I feel him react to every pretty woman as he reacts to flowers, trees, music, skies—with enthusiasm. Yet I feel so fortunate to be deeply loved by him, that I want to have faith and courage. Great lovers never trust each other. I imagine him as impetuous as he was with me. He imagines me, no doubt, as impetuously responsive to others as I was with him. Strange life, strange boy, too. Few understand his whims and fancies as I do. Few, perhaps none, understand that his compassion for others means he needs compassion himself. He is vulnerable and requires care and warmth.

Every trip is an adventure, because we explore new realms of love. This one came after his final examination at UCLA when we knew we would not see each other for a week or ten days, and I suggested traveling with him to his summer job in Colorado. At the last minute I teased him: "Perhaps I won't come." And then he became anxious and fully aware of how much he wanted me to come. So again Cleo is waiting at the door and we are off.

The first night in Las Vegas, in the little motel room, our caresses became electrical and feverish, wild. He fell asleep murmuring: "The desert is good for us."

Our lovemaking was like the desert heat, the hair-fine desert flowers, the sharp smells and the hot and warmed-toned sand.

Second night: again the hunger and fever.

Third day: we stopped by a river and took our clothes off. In the water he took me, floating and swaying, cool, lying on the shallow edge, and then he planted a tiny poplar tree by the place. So small and fragile, on the river's edge, and I was afraid it would be carried away. Our bodies, our moods, our fevers, seem to fight for permanency. His acts moved me, like tender rituals. A poplar tree planted where we loved each other. I laughed and said, "I have met Pan." I always wanted to meet Pan. He was wonderful. He came out of the river and took me. "You're a water sprite," he said.

Again a river. A very wide and wild one, the Colorado. Ice cold. But as we came out the sun was warm and Rupert bent me down on the sand and took me. But this time the cruel green flies stung us while we made love.

At dawn his soft, full mouth on my cheek. Before he opens his eyes he turns to embrace me.

Depression the last day. Cleo broke down. The wild and beautiful voyage was over. He put me on a bus, and although he had said, "This time you're not unhappy, this time you know it will be a short separation," I felt pain, pain at leaving him. When I arrived in Hollywood, in my room, I had the feeling of something torn from my body, this painful emptiness, his vivid face, his eagerness, his swiftness, his voice, his telephone calls at night. His warm, lithe body so kneaded with mine. The sensation of his slender body like a vine, all tangled with mine. Often during the trip he told me what kind of place he wanted me to take in San Francisco. How he would paint it, fix it up.

Los Angeles, June 26, 1948

Dream: Bill is there. But there is an older woman, severe looking, who is always watching him like a nurse or a governess. She is without pity, never leaves us alone. I try to soften her by telling her Bill and I have been separated for two years and want to talk to each other, but she says she has been told to watch over us. Finally Bill and I manage to come close, physically, but he uses a red gel and we are not happy.

I think of Gonzalo as dead—the Gonzalo I loved is dead. The one I knew at the end, without illusion, I did not love. People create an illusion together and then it is disintegrated by reality.

So I am now writing a book about Gonzalo as he was and I began simply and humanly. It is my last act of love. It is the monument that he will not be able to destroy as he destroyed our life together.

Of the fragments I did, only a few survive. Nothing of what I wrote in Acapulco. Out of hundred pages only twenty are good. I am only beginning now to work seriously. I am lonely; I am hungry for Chiquito. It is a difficult moment. I have acquired a mood of economy, having spent lavishly and now atoning. I eat plainly and frugally. A discipline. An enforced asceticism. Bill is coming to visit soon. I do not want to yield to him physically. I want to be true to Rupert.

The feminine desire to espouse the faith of those I love, as I espoused my father's and then my mother's, then Hugo's. I only swerved from each as my love changed. I swerved from admiration of my father's values to those of my mother's, from my mother to Hugo, Hugo to Henry, Henry to Gonzalo (with ramifications of each in minor terms). The curious fact is that I have returned to Hugo by way of Bill and Rupert, who are Hugo's sons, physically, in build and race (Irish, Welsh, English), mentally and emotionally, men of responsibility and of certain repressions and rigidities in conflict with their emotional and wild natures, men of aristocracy and of certain conventionalism of principle, of kindness, of nobility and honesty. Quite far from Henry and Gonzalo, who were completely neurotic, false primitives, twisted men of nature.

Rupert is more like Hugo than any of them, except that in temperament he has less control over his natural impulses, but equal guilt and control intermittently, which causes a rhythm of expansion and contraction alternately.

At fifty, Rupert will be more like Hugo than like Henry or Gonzalo, except for the Don Juanism, which he has in common with Henry. But Rupert is a man of love, and Henry was not. With his great beauty he could have been narcissistic, pampered, beloved by all women and given everything, protection, wealth. But instead he remained sincere.

There was masochism in my relationship with Henry and Gonzalo, and their brutality and violence may have seemed like necessary elements of primitive life, but in my life today there is an aliveness of emotion, a keenness of sensation that does not need to seek danger, pain or violence to feel its aliveness.

Los Angeles, June 27, 1948

In spite of all my machinations I cannot avoid these abysms in which I find myself as in Acapulco, without Rupert and without Hugo, and lonely. Alone with my writing. Alone at night. And never resigned, never able to live like this. I feel depressed, invaded by the past because my work forces me to remember, because it is the source of my stories, my life. If only I could always create out of the present, but the present is sacred to me, to be lived, to be passionately absorbed, but not transfigured into fiction.

The alchemy of fiction is for me an act of embalming. Bill, having been subjected to this process because of his two years in Korea, has lost a good deal of his human reality. What will I feel when I see him? What a hopeless relationship, due to his subjection to his parents, his childishness, his fears and submissions, guilts. What will he make of his life? Such a selfish love! He has never once written me when I asked him to, answered my cables when I wanted to visit him, never answering a need, complete passivity. And when he was staying with Frances Brown, if I called him up to ask him to come, he would rebel. All the rebellions he did not dare at home he dared with me.

Chiquito. When I came in February for our birthdays he said, "Friends have asked me: 'How old is Anaïs?' I had to say I don't know. I don't know and I don't care."

"Guess."

"From all you have told me, not from your appearance, I would say thirty-two or thirty-three. If you said less I would believe it. But if you say more I won't believe it."

He seemed anxious as he looked at me. I laughed. At first I said nothing, but I assented to his guess and added a year or two—thirty-five. And we celebrated his twenty-nine years and my thirty-five gaily. I laughed at my fear, my tragic fear of discovery.

What makes me feel the right to love him is that he was hurt by his first love and by his second. The first was physically good but emotionally and intellectually bad for him ("She was stupid and boring—just a beautiful girl, that's all") and the second, hard and selfish. I knew I could love him better. He is so vulnerable, so easily hurt, so susceptible, so easily harmed by criticism. He needs reassurance, warmth, understanding. He is often inarticulate, stubborn. He is naïve and candid. He needs subtlety. He is emotional and soft.

Bill did not write me for five months. Did not answer my request for news. And then a letter of desire, not of love. "About love, I don't know," he wrote. "But I want you."

As Rupert won me with a deeper love, warmth, humanity, he detached me from Bill. Bill observed the coolness of my letters, acknowledged that he deserved to lose my love. I did not have the courage to write him: "You have lost my love," but I felt it. And I would choose Rupert who gives me so much.

I can't be harsh with Bill because he is twenty, lost and confused. But I bless Rupert for freeing me.

Now Bill cables that he arrives July 15.

Los Angeles, June 30, 1948

While Hugo is finishing his analysis and preparing to come July 16, Bill is on his way from Korea.

I work at the story of Gonzalo with mixed feelings of love and pity for the dream of Gonzalo, and a full knowledge of its death. I know how Gonzalo killed it, and I pity him. I have forgotten my torment. There is an enduring love for the dream, with a knowledge of its death. Henry must have thusly buried June again and again with misgiving because the corpse is illumined, as it were, alive by the light of our first illusion, and one is uneasy about burying it, doubting its death. I have remembered Gonzalo with feeling and also the torment of the last years.

Los Angeles, July 2, 1948

I am exhausted with writing and with the conflict of making a river bed for the flow of the diary so that it may not seem a diary, but a monologue by Djuna in *The Four-Chambered Heart*. Not yet solved. The diary cannot ever be published. How can it seep into the work, not as a diary, but as a Joyceian flow of inner consciousness? Last night I wanted to give up writing. It seemed wrong to make a story of Gonzalo. I felt the inhumanity of art. I thought of my story of Bill in *Children of the Albatross*. But it touched his heart. It destroyed nothing. The story of Gonzalo will be perhaps an inspiration of love, a gift to the world, the only thing born of our caresses. It may be its monument, its only enduring image.

Last night, hurt and moved by memories, I was a woman acknowledging the continuity of love. This morning I was an artist, but I had come to terms with the woman and said, "It must be sincere, it must be truthful." And I worked gravely, sincerely.

I talked with Chiquito by telephone. I want to be with him. He loses nothing by remembrance. He is to me equally magnificent as a lover, warm, tender and interesting, though he had repressed his wildness and he is younger and less free, less asserted than was Gonzalo. In his eyes there are worlds and memories, depths he does not know. He is not harmful to me as Gonzalo was. He is undiscovered, unexplored, and not free, but it is all there, and he manifests it in music and in his love of nature, in his love for me.

Early awakenings, songs of birds, and a gentle sun, downhill to Musso, a hearty, masculine restaurant. Then writing. Rereading volumes 49 to 54.

I never told the truth in *Children of the Albatross*, an idealized story without the destructive part. Shall I go to the end this time?

One handles the truth like dynamite. Literature is one vast hypocrisy, a slant, deception, treachery. All the writers have concealed more than they have revealed.

Yet, I too do not have the courage to tell all, because of its effect on Hugo and Rupert.

It is not imagination; it is memory, memory that stirs in the blood obscurely at certain spectacles, a city, a mountain, a face. Some are like dormant animals, and atrophied memories, but others feel this extension of themselves into the past, and easily slip into other periods.

The idea of memory is very persistent. I think of it all day. I believe the blood carries cells down through the ages, transmitting physical traits and characteristics. They lie dormant until aroused by a face, a city, a situation. The simple explanation of "we have lived before," of recognition and familiarity. Racial and collective memory also continues, forming the subconscious.

Los Angeles, July 6, 1948

Awaiting Hugo and Bill, but without feeling for Bill, only friendship. No feeling for him at all. He has harmed me so much, has given so little of himself. I am nearest to Rupert. I feel him in me, inside me. I can feel the pain, his efforts, his courage up there in the mountains.

Hugo I admire terribly, his courage and effort in analysis, his immense struggle to be happy and free.

Hollywood for me is palms, flowers, flaming eucalyptus, jacaranda, the sun on gleaming cars, slacks and gold sandals, beautiful men and women, but standard, nondescript. Natural beauty of hills, sea, fogs and mists.

A relief to be far from New York, from Gonzalo, enclosure and ill health. I have gained health here. I feel like Rimbaud, that I walked out of my madness, and away from my demon. I am happy, but lazy and uninspired.

Bill telephoned: "Hello! I am on my way to San Francisco. I will be going to the University of California for some courses."

He had not tried to see me. He was not going to New York. He did not know I was planning to live in San Francisco. I said very casually: "I'll be there this winter. We may run into each other."

July 15, 1948	Bill Pinckard returns from Korea
July 24, 1948	Los Angeles
August 1948	Move to San Francisco with Rupert
October 1948	Return to New York
November 1, 1948	Albert Mangones
December 1948	Acapulco with Rupert

A TYPICAL AMERICAN WIFE

1949

San Francisco, February 1949

I moved to San Francisco after one more return to New York and attempting to live with Hugo on his houseboat, which he took on Long Island Sound. Was he trying to relive my life? To find me? Or to lure me by offering me what he thought I wanted? At the time I felt completely estranged from him. He was trying for closeness and I could not feel it. My life with him seemed unreal, a role.

He came to San Francisco, before Rupert did. I persuaded him to let me have an apartment there. Our relationship was at its worst then. We could not communicate. Did he think this was the end of it? I did not say so. I merely admitted to needing to be by myself at periods. He let me choose the apartment. He was angry, but we did not break. He left. I fixed it up with furniture from Goodwill and with shelves and glass bricks.

But I had not thought at first of Rupert living in the apartment. I had found a tea house in the back of a big house, in the center of a garden. I could see it from the road, near Ruth Witt Diamond's house. I thought it would be beautiful for when Rupert came to stay with me on weekends; he was living at International House and going to forestry school at Berkeley. I still thought of the apartment as for me and Hugo. I fixed up the tea house. It was an enormous task. An unkempt old man had lived there, never cleaned it. I had to fill twenty boxes with garbage; for days I carried old newspapers and detritus up the hill for the garbage man. I had a shower built in the cellar. It was poetic. A true Japanese tea house.

Rupert loved it. I painted it, fixed it up, but it was damp. The garden was cold and damp. San Francisco was damp. The sun did not reach it.

By contrast the apartment was spacious, sunny, and with a beautiful open view of the Bay. But I felt Rupert would believe that I could afford the tea house, while he would not believe I could afford the apartment. I began to wish I could tell him about the apartment. So I concocted the following story and here it is:

"Darling Chiquito: I'm writing you instead of waiting to talk with you because sometimes I get intimidated by the big eyes of your conscience, and lose sight of my explanations. When my Americanization process began I was stumped by the following illogical law: I can't get Americanized unless I'm self-supporting, and I can't take a job with my present papers because I am here as a visitor, that is, not allowed to work for a living. To fix this I would have to leave the country for an indefinite period of time while they studied my case and perhaps risk never entering again because I would have to apply for entry as one intending to work and be self-supporting! Such are the laws. I was gravely concerned about this, as when I asked you if I could accept Hugo's support for a year you felt definitely I shouldn't, and I felt so too, yet I could see no solution. Finally, talking with a lawyer while Hugo was here, we reached this compromise. If Hugo paid my rent for a year, and could show the contract, it would suffice as proof of support and I would need not show any other proof. That was fine, except that I didn't want Hugo to see the tea house as he would deem me romantic, living in an unhealthy, inadequately warmed place. And I certainly did not want him to pay for our tea house. So I tried to postpone all until he had gone, but as he had to sign the lease, I couldn't, and so I had to accept the apartment or be sent to Mexico and not be with you for an unknown time and with fear of a refusal of a re-entry permit. Once I am Americanized then I can begin to work, or earn without having to leave the United States and return. Then I was disturbed as to how you would feel. I considered renting the apartment to a friend. Then I thought of many things: my belongings from France arriving and having no room for them in the tea house, our not having room for your music and a place for me to take up dancing again. I thought of waiting and letting you decide. I wanted to surprise you and have it fixed up. Many other problems came up. There are people I can't imagine visiting the tea house, people I would not like to see there, like my brother, or some professors I know. I could see the tea house invaded by the wrong people and no place for our little house of love. I thought of how many moods you and I have, how we love Cleo and yet find Perseus useful on long trips, how we like casas and casitas, how you love a good kitchen and that we don't have one in the tea house. Then we have no garage for Perseus, and sometimes during the rainy season our tea house will be very damp for your chest. And I decided to let you decide, to think it over. I feel we can always have the tea house as a retreat for our togetherness, but that you need space sometimes. And so darling, that is the story. You decide."

Rupert, who had been slightly taken aback by the smallness of the tea house, took one look at the new apartment and decided very simply and without romanticism that it was a far better place to live in and for him to come to on weekends. That was the end of the tea house.

We live quietly. Ruth comes to tell me I owe it to the community to go to gatherings, parties, etc., but I feel when going out that I enter a colder world in which I am not at home. I only want to be with Rupert. On weekends we drive to the beach, which is cold, to the mountains, which are foggy.

Then came the ordeal of the poison ivy. Rupert was gathering leaves and flowers for his botanical studies, right in the hills surrounding us. That evening we went to a movie. The virulent poison ivy broke out on his face and hands. It was as frightening as leprosy. In one night the beautiful face was the face of Frankenstein's monster. He could not sleep. I had to cover him with balm, clean the suppurations. He was inflamed beyond recognition. He was humiliated, cowered. We saw the doctor. He did not want to be seen. His eyes would be closed by crusts in the morning and had to be carefully washed. It was a nightmare for him. He suffered physically and in his pride. Once while he was taking a bath I saw his desire and bathed with him, a proof of love, a proof that it was not only his beauty I loved.

Recovery. I could not believe his face would return to normal—the delicacy of the skin, the delicacy of the ears. It slowly emerged unspoilt—a miracle.

We went sailing with Jean Varda, but it was bitterly cold and I dressed like an Eskimo. And we were becalmed and stayed in one spot almost all the time.

Varda is living in a loft. He gave a party. We arrived early and Varda was showering under a contraption used in the army, a pail of water pulled by a string, pouring water over him. Rupert played his guitar and sang. I was filled with anxiety. I felt Rupert was like the Crown Jewels and that would be stolen from me, that he could not continue to be mine.

On his trip west, Hugo had met the young filmmaker Kenneth Anger. Hugo bought a bargain movie camera and began to film. Kenneth encouraged him to film and not to study with anyone, to become self-taught. In Mexico he began to film whatever he liked, without plan. With time, adding a little with each trip, he finally edited and finished *Ai-Ye* (mankind), his first real film.

He impulsively resigned from the bank. He was free. He was living on his capital. It was a period of freedom and recklessness, economically and emotionally.

He left the 13th Street studio and moved to 9th Street, a furnished apartment that had to be transformed.

San Francisco, April 15, 1949

Rupert left the International House, where he was staying, and began to live in the apartment, going to Berkeley from there.

At six-thirty the alarm clock buzzes and makes me jump. In the long, wide bed, I turn to the right where I can see through a slit in the venetian blinds the little garden stretching uphill, flowers, the reflection of a ceiling of fog, and to the left where I look at Rupert asleep. His face causes me a surprise each time. How could a face be assigned with such finesse, so close to the bones, the bones so delicate that it might represent the essence of a face rather than a face of flesh? His tousled black hair: boy and man. His features have a generous, bold proportion. They were designed for a rich, full nature, on a face so delicate that they portray instantly the duality of his nature: a generous, expansive, full nature blooming on a vulnerable, fragile structure, in danger of injury, the full flower of sensuality and imagination on an oscillating stem of adolescence. He turns towards me, still half asleep, and kisses me on the cheek. Only later will the kiss of hunger turn into the possessiveness of desire, not on the cold mornings of duty tearing us both out of the warmth, cutting the sleep and the embrace short, sending me first out of bed so that I can wash my face and comb my hair and button on my slacks and sweater. I start the coffee and light the oven for the rolls. I push the button that gives heat. I open the venetian blinds. The fog has lifted and the sun dapples the breakfast table, the San Francisco Chronicle sign, the other houses, other windows, children starting off for school, other garage doors opening, men going to work, women waiting for the bus.

While I set the table Rupert goes to the bathroom. On school days he does not sing. On early mornings he is like a newborn kitten and not yet awake or aware. His blue eyes are without recognition of human beings. He has been wrenched out of the depths of sleep and he is still swimming in it. On other days, Saturday and Sunday, when he can sleep, he comes out with clear, open eyes and embraces me, rocking me, whispering, or inserting his tongue in my ear like a direct message from his desire, and I know that this signal comes from his manhood, by the kiss that is not tender, not adolescent, but hungry and aggressive.

When he is dressed I have to remind him of all he forgets: "Do you have your keys? Change? Handkerchief?"

"Will you make me a sandwich?"

If he is late, or if the gas has leaked out of old and tired Cleo who waits outside in the rain while Perseus stands sheltered in the garage, I drive him down the hill to the bus, like a typical American wife. We never talk very much. When I return I finish my coffee. I wash the dishes. Out of the window of the kitchen I look down upon a wing of San Francisco, white houses on hillsides, upon a span of the Bridge, on a stretch of the Bay, and beyond, where there is fog, Berkeley where Rupert is going to study forestry. In his room I have to empty the scrap basket of the dried flowers he did not paste in his botany scrapbook, pick up his clothes and hang them.

At eleven o'clock or eleven-thirty the mailman comes. It is a lone letter from Hugo, a very long one, describing his trip to Brazil. Our relationship is, for me, a playing for time, an edifice of lies, a postponement. I won the last game. He returned to New York on April 1st and I expected to have to go to see him but managed by infinite intricacies to postpone homecoming until June because he is going to France in May. In June

Rupert will have a summer job where I can't be with him. I can't desert Hugo altogether and I can't leave Rupert.

I await news from Dutton. I sent them *The Four-Chambered Heart* a few days ago, the story of Gonzalo without its sordid, degrading end, for Gonzalo, like June, had the power to descend to the greatest vulgarities, and I cannot even transcribe the slime into which our love dissolved.

I telephoned the antique dealer: will you come and see some antiques I have for sale? A Spanish-Moorish bedstead, an Indian lamp, an Arabian mirror, an Arabian coffee set, a Kali goddess. They have served their purpose. They furnished and decorated my days with Henry, my days with Gonzalo on the houseboat, and they were catalogued in my diary, glorified in the *Under a Glass Bell* stories. After that they died the death of objects no longer illumined by a living essence. My attachment to them died, and objects lose their glow as soon as we do not inhabit them, caress them. When they arrived from France after years in storage, I saw they were dead. Antiques. Wreckage from great emotional journeys. I had moved away. They looked incongruous in this apartment, this place. With Rupert I looked at the bed of my past loves, the lamps of my nights of caresses, and my memory swathed them in the robes of mortuary winters. They were objects I no longer loved, as I no longer loved the people I had shared them with, and I was eager to destroy them.

Letter from Anaïs Nin to Hugh Guiler:

San Francisco, April 1949

Darling: Our uncertain plans suspended our correspondence and I was happy to have talked with you by telephone—it is so much more real. I hope you are taking care of yourself, resting. I am always worried about you straining.

Your long letter about your adventures in Brazil was fascinating, really like a novel. And you write it all so *vividly*, so I felt I had been there with you. The funny thing is that what you felt about the man whose will forced you to take the trip under dangerous conditions is what I feel about you. I might say that if I tried to sum up the main characters of the life I lead alone it might be described as "effortless"—seeking to live according to my nature and energy. Of course I realize it is only possible due to the results of your work, but I hope you will strain less later. I do miss you and want to be with you, but in postponing the big move till June, I have an unconscious resistance to "strain." I always hope that if I wait for you to be farther along in your analysis I won't return to an experience that characterizes strain. On the one side is the love, the desire to be with you, but on the other is the sense of compulsion, the strain in your life that destroys me. We are now at this moment looking at each other but not at the same goal, or perhaps the same goal but in space. The result of my finding my true self is that I discovered a Cuban who does not like to *force nature. Dios gana* [God wins]. I admire your courage on your Brazil adventure, but as a woman I would dislike returning from this trip you wanted me to take with you depleted and exhausted. That is why here, though it isn't the best climate in the world, I become absolutely healthy—by a *petite vie, douce et humaine*—where I never force myself. I work, but I stop when I have to.

In June I am hoping you will have finished your tense, quick trips and be ready for seven weeks of enjoyment. I do look forward to that. I also know I should be helping you now to entertain, so that gets me in a conflict of guilt. The resolution there seems to be one that I can't take because of our love: to live on a small income but to live without effort, or forcing, that is the only "other" life I achieve alone. Anyway, I believe you are on your way to achieving a marvelous life and you are now all that I wished you were before: flowing and vital. Once the strain is taken out I believe we will want the same things.

Perhaps I am wrong to hope that the farther you push into analysis the happier you will be. I believe now that the short stays in New York were not good—too intense—and you felt resentful of my leaving so soon. When I come in June it will be different. Your feeling that I am returning for good may make a difference.

Anyway, I told you now about the course in composition I took all this year. It was interesting and strange.

I haven't heard from Dutton yet. I speak before the Writers Conference April 8th at Berkeley.

You gave me money (cash and credit at bank) for five weeks. If you want me to come now, can I draw the cost of the trip from the bank and if I don't leave on the 8th or 10th shall I take the allowance from the bank account? I await your plans.

People come to see the "antiques" but don't buy.

Anaïs

San Francisco, May 1, 1949

No alarm clock, a week of holiday. But Rupert is recuperating from an acute bronchitis. He needs his sleep. I always awaken earlier. A shaft of light awakens me, or the neighbor's loud talk on the floor above.

The front room is flooded with sun. This morning it highlighted the newly stained table, in a pale violet blue, the last of our work on the furniture. Rupert has put a great deal of his own substance into the house. He worked on sandpapering the shelves and stained them. He is a perfectionist in craft. He built the coffee table.

But there is an organic weakness in him: the devastating bronchitis, the cough that racks his body. Lying in bed, defenseless, tender, he called me as I passed: "Come here." His mouth trembled. "I am lucky to have you." I took care of him with utter devotion. The love I feel is deep. His gestures move me. The fixity of his eyes, rigid with anxiety. The shape of his hands and feet.

Today I made breakfast and had coffee alone. I answered Gore's letter, Hugo's letter. On June 1st Rupert takes his summer job and I go to New York. I owe Hugo that.

Then Rupert awakened and began tinting the furniture. He is sad because the job is almost over and then he will have to face his dull, dry, monotonous schoolwork. So he dreams of Bali. But he does not dare to live on what I have because of his conscience and because he wants to be useful.

I wash dishes. I clean the apartment. I wash his socks (the first time I washed his socks was in New Orleans—he had work to do on the car, and I offered to wash his socks because he was suffering from poison oak and needed fresh ones). I go marketing. I buy what he likes. I have become fearfully domestic because the peace, the monotony of housework is broken by our wild lovemaking, our lyrical, stormy, lightning caresses.

Every day I question the mystery of my physical life with Hugo. What happened? What destroyed it? Was it inexperience on his part, and on mine? Was it inadequacy on his part? He has always reached the climax too soon. Was it dissatisfaction, sensual unfulfillment that estranged me from him? Now that I have this fulfillment with Rupert I have become faithful, domestic. I can sew, mend, repair, clean, wash, because there will be a climax, a lyrical moment, a sensation, a certitude of high living. The high living moment must have been absent from my marriage because I always had the feeling I was trapped by such experience, waiting, living *en marge* with Hugo, that this high moment lay outside, in the night, in the absent lover. Poor Hugo. What could I do? Sometimes I tried, delicately, to impart what I had learned, but his manhood rebelled then. Our lovemaking was tragic, ineffectual. He inhibited me.

A night of fog. Music on the radio. Leave the past alone.

I look at the dressing table I made from four shelves, a mirror, and six glass bricks. Brilliant, multicolored Japanese dolls on the shelves, princesses of a lavish glitter of gestures and clothes, like a Christmas tree of light, tinsel, satin, jewels. Elaborate, iridescent. I bought two of them. Hugo bought me the others, to delight me. When I went to New York in February I took one along for Hugo. I placed it on our dressing table. When we had to entertain wealthy and aristocratic Italians I placed the doll on the mantelpiece. Hugo interpreted it as an assertion of the childlike spirit. His analyst said, "Let her have all the props she needs." The doll meant something else. It was the poem. It said, "This afternoon people are gathered together because of material interests, because they need each other to add to their power in the world, but they do not like or enjoy each other." It is a ceremony without iridescence or beauty that I rebel against. I will be hurt in the process. And I was. The Italian woman was cold and arrogant and I lost my confidence. The doll on the mantelpiece pleaded for mercy. The afternoon among the mature, the assured, the cool ones was for me an ordeal. It had the character of torment, judgment, an inspection, a duel, and I felt incapacitated. I felt vulnerable and unequal. I explained this to Hugo. It wasn't that I didn't want to help him, it wasn't that I shirked my responsibilities, it wasn't that I didn't want to please him, but that I couldn't, I was unequal to it. I lost my confidence in the world. It wasn't my world. I felt wounded by the arrogance of the woman, unable to hold my place, to assert myself. Hugo thought he had married a *woman*. I can be chic. I can look aristocratic. I have beautiful manners. But I am unhappy and strained.

I left the one doll on the mantelpiece and returned to the others. In my life with Rupert, they are not out of place. Rupert and I seek our pleasures, more humble ones; we avoid ordeals, we live by our wishes, we go alone to ski, we go to the movies, we seek those we like. But it is Hugo who bought me the dolls.

Around, around, around a circle of madness. Dependence. Rebellion. Rejection. Guilt. A childlike dependency.

I cannot grow in that direction. I cannot grow in arrogance, in a hard finish, in a gold-plated irony, impertinence or cynicism. With Dr. Staff I obsessively fought to be just to Hugo, to eliminate the neurotic obstacles to our marriage, to save Rupert from the tragedy of an impossible marriage.

"It is a most difficult decision to make," Staff acknowledged. I sat in the same room where I first came to weep over Bill's lack of feeling.

Back to Staff again, because once in Hollywood after Rupert left me, I sat on my bed weeping, and kneading and pummeling the pillows, repeating: "This is an illusion, this is an illusion." But when he came to live with me it ceased to be an illusion, it ceased to be a necklace of intense moments, and we fell into deeper and deeper layers. Daily living.

Our *rhythm*.

Hugo could endure monotony, discipline, daily repetitions, meals at the same hour. Every unpredictable change, every variation, disturbed him. After I cook and wash dishes with regularity for a week, if I hint lightly to Rupert: "I am tired of dishes. Let's go out to dinner," he is not only eager for a change, but more often it is he who will suddenly drop his work and say to me: "We're off." I have barely time to don my coat, the car is already pulsating, there is a mood of freedom, a breaking of bonds, of halters and harnesses, a sudden influx of speed and lightness. Rupert and I leap out. No obstacles.

Poor Hugo. I am hoping that he is now learning to live more happily without me.

The dolls dance, contorted by extreme stylization. In the mirror I see the bed that sheltered me in Louveciennes with Hugo, with Henry, with Gonzalo. One of the woolen sheets I used in the cold houseboat was stained with red wine, Gonzalo's red wine. But that has ceased to hurt me.

The present.

Rupert sighs over his endless calculations in his own room. He comes to mine to hear Brahms' double concerto. Or I help him disentangle his rebellions. If he wants to go to a movie he does not enter boldly to tell me, but stands at the door, ashamed, guilty, suggesting a movie as if it were a crime.

He responds deeply to tragic, human movies, the Italians' naturalness. He responds like an ordinary American boy to the charms of Rita Hayworth. He loves Westerns. In music he has infallible taste, but not in women.

SAN FRANCISCO, MAY 15, 1949

Que ma tête est lourde et fatiguée. No rest for me anywhere from awareness, insight, fantasy writing, analogies, associations. Writing becomes imperative for this surcharged head. I was happy when Hugo was in Brazil and there was no conflict. The day he returned and telephoned me from New York, tension again. Games and lies to gain time, to gain another month with Rupert. Two weeks left now, left to us. Rupert must take a job (dictated by his conscience), earn money and learn to fight forest fires during three summer months.

Hugo expects me in New York. He has planted flower boxes on the terrace of the apartment for my arrival.

Last days in San Francisco. Intense joys at night, in Rupert's strong arms, an electric orgasm, a caress that kneads the flesh, sharp, keen pleasures given by his active, fresh-skinned, fragrant sex. The smell of an adolescent. Nothing aged, *faisandé*, sour, and all of it light, readily evaporated, like a perfume. The mercurial silk of the body, it slips between your fingers for its aliveness. I never tire of feeling his neck, his shoulders, his physical perfections, the shape of his back, his stylized backside, so neat, so amazingly compact, so amazingly chiseled for vigor and speed. Such finesse in his profile, the shape and carriage of his head. All form and lines. Nothing has been carelessly designed. There is no imperfection. During his severe bronchitis he allowed himself to speak like a child at times, requesting, yearning, complaining. But once well again he recovered his role of authority.

He was born in the fantasy house of Lloyd Wright. He was raised with unorthodox people. He does not like conventionality. But above all, he speaks of the closeness we have and makes plans for a lifetime together.

Drugs. When it is intolerable, I reach for my French books again, saturate myself with the delectable Giraudoux, with the poetic analysis of Jouve. I rediscover a world so infinitely superior to America that I lose hope for it, for its crude literature, its crude life, its barbarism.

We are back from botanizing, just up the hill across the street. Rupert carries the shovel; I carry a basket for the flowers and a trowel. He sits analyzing and classifying the flowers. I have prepared Spanish rice. The back yard is wistful with the persistence of the drizzle. The flowers hang their heads. Some of them adopt the raindrops like dazzling bastard children, and up the hill with Rupert I found one that made me exclaim: "Chiquito, come and look at the unusual flower; do you want it?" The flower melted in my fingers. It was a raindrop, pretending, expanding in a bridal costume reflected from the clouds, spreading false illusory tentacles of white lace on the heart of the leaves.

The ballet of Japanese dolls dancing on the shelves looks down at me lying on the bed. At times I think of death. I can believe in the disintegration of my body, but cannot imagine how all I have learned, experienced, accumulated, can be wasted; surely it cannot disappear. Like a river it must flow elsewhere. For example, for days I received the entire flood of Proust's life and feelings, which has truly penetrated me, three times now, but each time more deeply—*this* is immortality, *this* is continuity.

The mockingbirds, the birds of California sing lightly, intermittently. At six o'clock the Spanish rice will be ready. Rupert will have finished placing his flowers in his scrapbook.

Once he confessed at night, two years after we met: "At first I thought you were impetuous and fickle, and that as soon as you had my love you'd go off. I was afraid of you."

Another time he said, "I was never altogether satisfied sexually until I met you. With the others it required an effort to adjust rhythms. With Janie it did not go at all. This is the first time that it is perfect."

Another time: "It's so good when it is with the whole self."

These statements give me confidence, but I lose it again when at the movies he raves over the cheap and obvious heroines, or when he meets Varda's girl of eighteen, and when I said, "Would you exchange me for Varda's girl?" he answered: "Only for one night and then I would forget her." I have allowed my hair to grow long, as he likes it, soft and barely curled, *très jeune fille*. He likes gay and sensual blouses. He likes to see my shoulders. He likes that I love nature while not being just a healthy, dull, stupid or insensitive girl.

He is proud of my writing, even if at times it causes him embarrassment with the uncultured foresters.

In his small bedroom next to mine, I hear him sigh. He is bored and tired of forestry studies. He wears glasses. I remember the first time I saw him outside of his lover's role. In love he was illuminated, resplendent. I saw him at the printing room where he was printing Christmas cards and was so surprised to find him serious, concentrated, shy and without luminosity. Sensuality illuminates him. But when he isn't all aglow with either desire or gayety, then he is anxious, strained, haggard (so much alike we are in this). At the foresters' dance, it was he who was out of breath from the folk dances, not I.

His only flaw: his temper. His tensions often become bad humor, and then he becomes critical, harsh. I can only use words applied to women for what he becomes: nagging, persnickety, finicky, and fussy.

Then he is the complaining wife and I the one rebelling against "details." He wants me to save 13¢ on gasoline. He didn't want me to have my hair washed at the hairdresser's, I should do it at home. There is only one good brand of mustard and I am expected to look around for it in various shops. There is only one good brand of coffee. He becomes hard to please. All his frustrations with forestry make him exigent, whimpering, and I wear myself out. At such times the redeeming trait is that he is fully aware that he becomes impossible (as a woman during her menstruation) and is ready to acknowledge it. When he goes too far I get depressed or rebellious, but he soon wins forgiveness.

He is ready to do anything, to make any sacrifice for the relationship. He takes pains to efface the wounds. When we went skiing in Yosemite I became neurotic and discouraged because I could not keep it up. After I said, "You'd better find yourself a wife who can ski," he replied, "Well, but then I'd have to teach her to make love as you do."

The Rupert *ordinaire*, Rupert the American boy is there, but then he suddenly transcends it; he is more than that, he is an imaginative Welshman. He is touched with genius at times, at moments with intuition, with poetry never reached by his companions. He is more sensitive and complex. He is unique, and everyone recognizes his personality. Among the foresters he is known for his folk singing and his guitar. At their parties he entertains them with grace and without egocentricity. He invites them to sing with him or he willingly accompanies a song he does not know, a singer who can't sing. Gently and without vanity. He moves me. When he is bad, it is eruptive, nervous, something merely to re-establish his exaggerated goodness the rest of the time, his control. Again I play the role of interpreter.

We have similar impatience. He scolds me for mine. But he loves that during the trip he never had to wait for me. I dress, make my face up, fix my nails and eyelashes, and my hair, all in the time it takes him to shave. And I can pack in five minutes.

Once in Paris I had a record of Erik Satie that I loved. I remembered it in New York and tried to find it. I couldn't remember the title. It was the ever-recurring song of remoteness, the one that appears in Debussy, in *Chansons d'Auvergne*, in Carillo's *Cristobal Colon*. It was a theme I wanted to hear again. It was the beginning of my new book I could not find.

Today sitting by the radio after breakfast I heard it and identified it. The other day driving to Berkeley I heard Debussy's *Sonate Pour Violon et Piano*, and again I wept and experienced the fullest, wildest sorrow.

I am invited out by Varda, by Ruth Witt Diamant, but it means leaving Rupert alone in his room. So I either refuse, or if I do appear it is only for a moment, and only for enough time to realize I am lonely in the world. I am not close to anyone. I am closest to Rupert. I am happy at home. I am happier alone with Rupert. At ease. Satisfied. The world is complete. Wherever my love is, the world is complete. Our true connection took place in Denver, on the sand dunes. I don't know why, but that lovemaking contained all we were, are, and would be to each other. It was a ring-like circle, it was soldering. There is lovemaking that has that definitive binding element. I felt it as such. Beyond lovemaking it was a marriage, because it gave us both a sense of gravity. Suddenly a man and woman discover the axis of the world. It revolves on this conjunction of male and female, the rotations of love become the rotations of earth, sun and moon, and gravity is achieved.

There is a sense of effortlessness in my life with Rupert because my feelings are with him; while he is working my love flows to his sturdy hands, to his warm-blooded skin, copper-toned when he is sunburned. Even when he is ill, his ears are roseate, his face has a warm color. Once during bronchitis, after I had made him perspire abundantly, I rubbed his body with Vicks, and his sex rose in excitement. He said, "I always feared this would happen in Harvard Hospital, or in the Army hospital, when I was washed or massaged, but it never did."

But it happened with my hands on his body. Excitement.

Return to New York, June 1949

Letter from Anaïs Nin to Rupert Pole:
New York, June 8, 1949

Darling Chiquito: The first nights here were like 100,000,000 years long. I felt better when I got your letter. That is all I need, to know you're well and still love me. I've thrown myself into my work day and evening. Not only reading manuscripts but writing on any subject, theme or item to prove versatility, and secretly investigating assignments with eyes and ears alert. I have hopes of seeing you one weekend in July, between the 20th and 30th if my publisher will let me attend the writers' and printers' conference near LA. I'm working for this, as it makes the three months seem lighter.

Dutton (and this is a compliment for you as well, my collaborator) thinks *The Four-Chambered Heart* is the best book I've done (it has more of a story to follow). Thursday they have the final conference. Following your advice, I also showed them the diary that they had earlier refused without reading it, but now they are laughing over it and getting interested. Oh darling, I'm trying everything, seeing everyone I should. Just a career woman now to fulfill our dream, and this is the dream I have when I can't sleep. In February, on our birthdays, we will go around the world before you settle down to forestry—one long, good, fulfilling voyage—and I am working for this.

Sending you money to deposit into my account, from sale of books. Or if you need it for Cleo.

Te quiero profundamente. Please do not burn or scratch for my sake, so I will have something to caress!

Tu Limoncita

June, 1949	Dutton rejected *The Four-Chambered Heart*
July 16, 1949	Return to Los Angeles
August 4, 1949	Acapulco
August 11, 1949	San Francisco
September 1949	New York

San Francisco, October 20, 1949

Father died this morning. The hurt, the shock, the loss, as if I had died with him. I feel myself colliding with death, breaking, falling. I wept not to have seen him, not to have forgiven him, not to have held him in my arms. He died alone and poor in a Cuban hospital. He collapsed Thursday. That is all I know. I received the telegram from Joaquín in the morning. I didn't want to weep. It seemed as if I would die with him. Then I wept. I felt the loss in my body. This terrible, unfulfilled love. Never to have come close to him, never to have truly fused with him. I envisioned him asleep. I wept. I had to meet Rupert, my slender one, my lover of women, but near and warm. I wept on his thin shoulder. He was tender and human. So tender. We came home. It is strange. Life continues. You eat. You clean the house, but the death is there, inside you. The loss. The absence, the truth you cannot believe, you feel it but you don't believe it, the pain attacking, dissolving the body. Guilt. I should have overlooked his immense selfishness as Rupert overlooked the great selfishness of his father. I should have sacrificed my life for him. Oh, the guilt. At other moments a destructive sorrow, the wish to die. The worst of me died with him, a craving for sainthood, the presence of madness, his madness. I fought not to be as he was, disconnected from human beings. I fought those who were like him, Henry, Bill, all the remote ones. I fought to be near, to fuse. From this death I will never heal. Rupert took me out to a movie. When I came home he sat in his room to work and I sat on my bed and sobbed. I can't accept his death. It hurts. I wrote to Hugo. I don't feel for Hugo anymore. It's the death in me, the unbearable thought that to have integrity, to survive the destructiveness of others, we strike out, harm them, we are revengeful. I wish I had been a saint. Joaquín was sweeter, yet he writes me: "I tried to get close and failed."

To work, to work. I feel the pain like a blow bowing my shoulders. Back in the pit.

Now I see the crime of loving young Rupert when I am closer to death and detaching myself from all he wants, all he seeks. Life with Rupert in San Francisco is coming to an end in January when he gets his forestry degree. It seems I have barely finished fixing up the apartment and we must leave it. Again to carry a trunk full of diaries to Ruth Witt Diamant's cellar as I carried two valises full of originals to a vault. Again throwing away letters, papers, manuscripts. Again meditating, ruminating a new book, gestating, again flying to New York in two weeks, unable to bear separation from Rupert.

I see this looking inward now as a great act of courage, for I have lived two years with Rupert on the outside. In the sun, in the car, active, a peaceful life outside, no great depths, except of feeling. The nights are deep with vehement fusions.

New York, November 1949

After months with Hugo this summer, I spent a month at home with Rupert and then had to leave for New York, called by a letter from Gore and from William Kennedy of Duell Sloan and Pearce, who will publish *The Four-Chambered Heart.*

Hugo at the airport. His kiss is different. It is not sexual. It is affectionate. He tells me he has lived like a monk. "But why?" I said. He wants me to feel guilty, wants me to feel badly. He has deep resentments. His patience, his gift of freedom is a pretense; his goodness is a pretense to hold my love. Hugo is an angry man. He was angry before he knew me. I have done much to make him angry. I know this. But Inge Bogner, his analyst, traces the anger to deeper roots. Even when she goes away on vacation he gets angry at her. His mother betrayed him by sending him away to Scotland when he was five, to the severe, fanatically religious Aunt Annie. He is struggling to exorcise this anger. He pretended goodness to win love as I pretended goodness. He feared desertion. But there it is. He greets me differently. No one is to blame. Something about him has withered. Full of gratitude, indebted for all I have, even for my happiness with Rupert, I arrive spontaneous and am met with a willful anger that is deep-seated and not caused by me, at least not originally. The original sin of the mother—for that I have been the scapegoat. So the kiss is kind, paternal, there is no fusion, no deep elemental tension. He is authoritarian with the porter. He commands the taxi. A part of me withers. The taxi drive is spent in a veiled reproach for my absence, and although Rupert too suffers from my absence, there is a difference. What shall I say? When your analysis is over I will no longer need a refuge. I haven't the strength for life in New York (true). He has had some birthmarks removed to be handsomer, to please me. I am touched, moved. When we get to his apartment on 35 West 9th Street, which I don't like, would not have chosen (the only beauty of it is a terrace all around with a view, air, space), he has a bottle of champagne, but when we are in the bedroom together, I have a moment of such anguish that I fear hysteria or madness. It seems to me that if I let myself be uncontrolled, I will instantly destroy my life with Hugo. This fear and the control I must exert constrict my throat, and for two weeks I had a cold that hampered my breathing. Anguish when he is asleep, and I am aware of the distance between me and Rupert, and there is the feeling that I have forced myself to come here, but this is mixed with a pity, an awareness of his struggles, his loneliness, his needs, his generosities, his good will. So I rush to Staff!

My relationship with Hugo is deep. With Rupert it is easier because it is not as deep. Staff has struggled to efface the image of Hugo the father, and as Hugo has been shedding the role, it has been successful. I see Hugo younger, less severe, more inadequate, more bewildered by life. I return home aware of Hugo's difficulties: he feared insanity (his mother is insane); he feared desertion.

Every morning for two weeks I went to Staff. Every night I had the sense of hysteria and of confinement. I could not bear to fix up the new apartment for our future life. I stalled. I took sleeping pills. With this I had to face intense activity with Kennedy, other people, telephone calls. An important friendship with Kennedy. Yes, love for Hugo, but no desire, no desire to live with him. Yet there is a fear of Rupert too, of an inevitable catastrophe. Only with Staff could I explode. Yet I cannot free myself of Hugo. He is part of my relationship with Rupert. Through Rupert I sometimes reach a Hugo who might have been. I reach the Hugo I first married and the first five years of our marriage. And I can understand Rupert as I did not understand Hugo. Rupert has the same seeking of responsibilities, the same conviction that to assume responsibilities is the role of man. Then the two figures begin to melt into one another. I wish I could feel towards Hugo as I feel towards Rupert. And when I envisage my break with Hugo I feel as if Rupert and I are two orphans, and I feel lonely.

But after two weeks with Hugo in New York I must leave.

The alarm clock. Hugo has to go to Dr. Bogner. He has done this more intensely, more thoroughly, than I did. It is his nature to be tenacious, obsessive. That he is fighting his resentment works in my favor. Because as he received me with indirect reproaches, or when I postpone furnishing the apartment, he believes it is his possessiveness that drives me away.

Millicent the maid is there, aging, withering, working now for the sake of her grandchildren.

My father died mad. He did not understand what happened to him. I want my suffering to be useful. I want the novel to teach life. I want the novel to accomplish what the analyst does. Without Staff I would have gone mad too.

I only wish I could have helped my father to die at peace with himself and others.

San Francisco, November 1949

I arrive at the airport at about six-thirty in the evening. It is dark, and, as usual, sharply cool, no softness in the air, the wind waiting to swirl, fog waiting to mantle the hills. Rupert hides behind a column, to surprise me, then leaps forward towards me and kisses my lips aggressively, hungrily, emphatically. The first time I had been away after we had begun to live together he said, "Never do this again. I suffered."

He has said each time: "I was lonely." I always think he will take advantage of his freedom, but he doesn't. This time he said, "I tried to enjoy myself, but failed so miserably. Went to a dance at Berkeley. It was so dull. After that I stayed home and studied." As soon as he has exams to take his face becomes pale, tense, anxious. His eyes are shadowed, his face drawn. In the car, with my valise in the back, and his dog Tavi between us, he kisses me hard.

Elation. Elation. Elation. He drives the big green Chrysler. I tell him about New York where I went ostensibly to help Duell Sloan and Pearce with publicity for *The Four-Chambered Heart*. When we reach home he lights a fire, starts to cook a steak. He opens a bottle of champagne. He shows me the big windows he cleaned. He bought me a present that will come later. I bring him a new book by his step-grandfather Frank Lloyd Wright, published by Duell Sloan and Pierce, a beret from the Spanish restaurant. News: how much Duell Sloan and Pearce is doing for me, friendship with editor William Kennedy, dinner with Charles Duell, people I met, my lecture at City College.

We went to bed early, to possess each other in the dark, his slender body like mercury between my fingers, his arms so strong, his strength pouring out like the strength of a cat, unexpected, vaster as it extends out of softness and fur, as it extends from Rupert's finesse and sensitiveness.

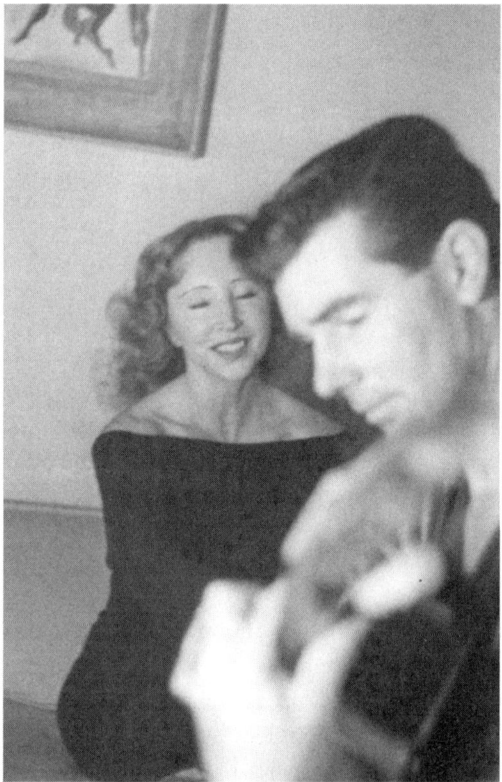

Rupert Pole playing guitar for Anaïs Nin

Sunday is a day of sun. He is working on a map he must design of the canyons behind Berkeley. So we make sandwiches and go out to walk through the hills. I wear my orange cotton dress from Mexico. It is warm. I am at peace. I am always at peace alone with Rupert unless thoughts of Hugo intrude. At peace, yet with a knowledge that devours me with anxiety, a knowledge of future tragedy. It is time, time I play with, time to allow Rupert to finish his studies, so he will be able to earn his living, time to live with him as long as possible. Staff said to lie to Hugo would be to gain time until Hugo's analysis is over and he has the strength to face my departure. But Staff also says Rupert is an aspect of Hugo, that Rupert is a Hugo without neurosis, without sensual repression, a Hugo without his destructive mother or Scotch aunt who beat him, a Hugo young and free. He is present in the relationship with Rupert.

But Staff did not explicitly say, "Lie to Rupert."

My feelings don't lie. What is a lie? Is it a lie when I leave San Francisco to fulfill Hugo's patient vigil?

Night, fulfillment, fusion. Yes, fusion.

NOVEMBER 10, 1949

Rupert graduates from forestry school

Letter from Hugh Guiler to Anaïs Nin:

New York, Sunday, December 4, 1949

There is no use coming back to New York until I work this thing out further with myself. I believe now the truth is, and there is no use concealing it from each other under a lot of words, that I have been angry at a whole accumulation of things in our relationship, and you have been too. We admire each other, we have pity for each other, but in our actual actions and attitude towards each other we have both shown that for the time being, at least, anger is stronger than the other emotions. As long as that lasts, we are going to make each other unhappy when we are together, and I for my part do not want to inflict this on you anymore until my anger disappears.

I appreciate the great effort you have made to solve the problem by capitulating (as you think it is) between the life you want and coming to New York. But every sign indicates that you cannot do this without a splitting conflict, even to wait until my analysis is finished, and will, on your part, in spite of every effort to the contrary, result in unconscious acts that show your own real angers.

And there is no need to fool ourselves that these angers on both sides are all out of the past. You began to deal with this honestly when you said there are certain sides of me you just don't like and have no feeling for at all. That is *today* and not the past.

I now realize we have always been under cover of one excuse or another, arranging to be apart a good deal of the time, except during the war years when we could not. The truth is we were not together more than momentarily and spasmodically during the years after 1928 when I took over the trust work in Paris and started traveling, with your approval and encouragement, "to preserve the marriage," you used to say. While I had the Trust Debt in Paris I traveled I suppose about six months out of each year. Then I went to London in January of 1938 and you took the decision not to accompany me, so I paid only weekend visits about once or twice a month over the next year and a half. We *did* not do this "to preserve the marriage," but because we were too unhappy living with each other all the time. I probably fooled myself about this more than you did, as I am sure your diary shows. The periods of being together were therefore also charged with exaggerated feelings in an effort to make up for what each of us thought we had been depriving the other of in the intervening period, or what we thought we had the right to receive because we had been deprived of something.

The greatest problem I have, and one that has created a big problem for you also—accentuated by your need to have someone dependent on you spiritually, you in turn being dependent in other ways—is my over-dependence on you. In this respect I have been like a child and now after fifty-one years of childhood, or reversion to childhood, I must have some time and learn how to go out myself, make friends myself without you, and to acquire a whole new attitude that is not at every turn simply another road around you.

You have asked me a hundred times: "Why are you so dependent on me? Why do you have no world of your own? Why don't you know what you want—colors in this apartment or anything else concerning our personal life? Why don't you express yourself directly instead of always through me? Why do I always have to be your soul?" You were really saying that you *were* my soul and were really asking: "Have you no soul of your own?"

All that was in part true, and I have at last awakened to it and all it implies. It has been a terrible burden for you to carry even when you said you liked carrying it and so often said that you were my soul. In the last year or two you have been trying to tell me that you could no longer carry that burden, and now I understand I really agreed with you when I took up the analysis, which represented my effort to carry my own responsibilities.

But then when, as a result of analysis, a soul of my own did start to appear and you began to see the shape of it, you were taken aback. It was not what you had imagined, not what you had wished for, or at least only in part, and it was then that a more serious withdrawal took place on your part.

Dr. Bogner has only last week broken the news to me that I have been deceiving myself into thinking that I am an artist. She says I am obviously primarily a businessman and only secondarily, and on the side, an artist. It came as a great shock to me, but I believe she is right. Much of my artistic endeavor was due to my despising myself as a businessman and feeling that I had to prove in some other way that I had a soul. But the business world represented reality for me and, to the extent that my artistic activities were done in the spirit of a flight from reality, and the forms they took could not be other than exaggeratedly remote, introspective and inhuman. Then on the business side there were corresponding tensions and exaggerations because such activities were under constant attack from within (myself) and from without (you).

And I will probably continue to keep up this combination of unenslaved, flexible business activities and making movies, as well as my general interest in art, for the rest of my days because that is who I am.

I am not going to take this opinion as final because I have found from experience that so-called artistic judgments often conceal neurotic lies.

The artist sometimes has something valuable to contribute and at other times simply sits behind his own kind of defensive barriers, except that he has the nerve to claim that they have something sacred and privileged about them that must be given special consideration. *Everyone*, I believe, is out for power and achievement in different ways, and you today, for example, are just as ambitious about your books as I am about my business. What is unfair, I think, is that you have tended to act as if your ambitions were in some way exercised for nobler and loftier aims than mine in business. That I now reject completely, and I believe you are honest enough, when you really think about it, to do the same. Childhood neuroses often compel you to act differently from what you really believe.

But you are what you are and certainly I am not the one to criticize your ambition to have a successful career of power and achievement, for I have nothing against that. I realize this furthermore is a structure that has been built up from your earliest days and that is something very real to you, and assumes an importance in your life so great that you feel you have to defend it at *all* costs.

Your behavior arises from a dissociation in yourself from one kind of business in order to carry on another kind, that the kind of business you chose did not feed you and that you therefore had to take from the one you dissociated yourself from to support the other.

The question you must ask yourself is whether you want to continue to be married to the person I have presented to you as my real self, whether you can continue in such a marriage without the unhappiness that has resulted from each of us keeping before us a false and unreal picture of the other.

But you see, darling, I have had a great shock, really from waking up suddenly and realizing that during my sleep I have been subjected to a long series of shocks, and I must have some time to gather myself together and gain new strength in myself, so that I will no longer be angry, as I will be as long as my confidence has not returned, which will take time after such a violent upheaval. You still write in the sense of being compelled to pay up for something, and I do not feel that you will be all right with yourself or with me until this has changed into something more positive; until you really feel that the two businesses (whether the two between us, or the two in yourself) are ready to go hand in hand towards a common goal, rather than one hand must pay for having taken bank notes out of the other.

For I am now completely disposed to accept the facts as we have discovered in each other, and any forcing at this time will only make it impossible for us ever to work out a relationship on a new and realistic basis.

I think it may be best for you to consider San Francisco as your headquarters and your stays in New York as visits only. As I get back into the foreign field I will be spending more and more time in Brazil and Mexico on business. We can then see how much time the demands of our respective careers permit us to be together.

We never had the peace that comes from being sure that each of us was accepted for himself and herself. We have been always in a state in which that self was threatened.

So now, Anaïs, I know you for what you are and you know me for what I am. There is no need for either of us to make the slightest demands on the other. When I get a little more on my feet I will not feel threatened anymore, and I have no desire to take away from you your individuality as an artist or a woman, or do anything but give you the fullest reins to your career. Let us expect little of each other and perhaps we will get something. And I assure you there will be no more ultimatums on my part if there are none on yours.

Hugo

Card from Anaïs Nin to Hugh Guiler:

San Francisco, December 1949

Dear Monkey, I think of you. I admire your great courage to be reborn as a new man, a damned interesting man. Please take care of yourself. Do not think harshly of me for expressing, or rather trying to find my real self. It was just as disguised as yours. I had to dig hard for it.

Saw *Man and Superman* by Shaw; remembered your having enjoyed it. I guess I found my match in you.

Your cat.

A WEB OF LIES

1950

January 1950
Return to New York; publication of *The Four-Chambered Heart*

Letter from Anaïs Nin to Rupert Pole:
New York, February 1950

Darling, you had the hardest task after graduating from forestry school, dismantling our home in San Francisco that we loved because we had each other in it, but that is only the first one and we will have other homes. I'm happy and proud about your good marks but not surprised. Your own concept of your capabilities and reality of them differ, as you see. It is only your faith and confidence that do not pass the test. I would grade you this way:

Personality—the most charming

Character—the deepest

Capabilities—the best

Confidence and Faith—Z, zero, the worst, the lowest

I'm full of confidence for our future, but the praise I get for *The Four-Chambered Heart* is not going to my head at all as they praise bad things equally, but among the pile there are a few understanding, sincere responses.

No matter how full, how productive the day, there is always one empty moment when I feel an anguish of the heart, and that is when I am aware of your absence. I know what the world gives is insincere and fickle, but what we have is like the sandstone mountains—fortresses. I work for us.

Write me soon.

My four-chambered heart is occupied by One completely. Limoncita

Letter from Anaïs Nin to Rupert Pole:

New York, Tuesday February 7, 1950

My darling, I'm concerned over the difficult thing you have to tell your family, that you want to marry me. If I were you I would not say too much—don't praise me, don't reveal the depths—I wish I were there to help you.

I have just gone through another hell—my brother Thorvald arrived on a stretcher from the plane, a hurt back in a cast and bronchial pneumonia, but thank god he is getting well and the hell is over. But I spend half my days at the hospital. My mother came down and I have to take care of her, besides all the rest.

I heard from Ruth the details of all the work you had to do, darling, which you minimized. I felt so badly. I heard even about the rain falling the day you left.

I await your letter from LA anxiously. I sent you two important ones there; I hope you get them.

Read the enclosed and please return it. All my reviews (except *Time*) are understanding and respectful.

Please tell me how you are, physically and mentally. Don't *fight* for me, darling. Don't be unhappy. We have a *rock basis* and no one can destroy it, but I don't want you to be hurt defending our relationship.

I feel as you did during exams: I am almost glad you weren't here, for I have all my mind set on my "job," a real career woman, first fulfilling duties—working—and imagining pleasure in March with you. I haven't even seen a movie or a play.

Write me soon. Your letters are my daily bread. I still risk getting run over reading them while crossing the street, also risk freezing as I forget to hold on to my coat or hood and stand on windy corners reading in zero degree weather!

Te quiero, te beso, tu calor me da vida. Tu A.

Letter from Rupert Pole to Anaïs Nin:

Los Angeles, February 10, 1950

Darling darling darling darling darling,

Miss you so much in so many ways. I too have been busy, but it's never enough and the nights are too long.

But all goes wonderfully. Finally got off from Ruth's loaded to the gills with stuff, looking something like a Park Avenue version of Tobacco Road, and of course accompanied by rain. Working like a fiend ever since here to get Perseus in shape and finally today my ad appeared, and what happens—*rain—all day*—perfect day to sell a convertible—only two people called and only one came. The ad is to run four days, however, so pray for a nice sunny weekend. Fellow today offered $1600 but my price was $1695. Am sure I can get at least $1650. (You'd never know Perseus—he's really, really sharp and gleaming. I think he's rather looking forward to showing off here in Hollywood.)

Now, have already bought our new car. It's a he and I think almost zoot but we'll fix that. He's just the opposite of Perseus, very fast and quick like Cleo. He has just the one seat with big compartment in the back and large luggage section that can be locked. He was born in 1936 but has the appearance of being very young. He's a little brash and needs quite a lot of toning down, but if we keep a firm hand on him I think he'll serve us well. Let's call him José. He cost $289 including license. Will spend another $250 putting a new motor and overdrive in him, then $40 for insurance, and we're set for transportation.

Much more to do here than I realized. Family seems to sense I'm going for good, and they finally asked if I might marry you. Said I hoped so, but that you had held back, wanting all to be sure. Mother seemed to be very understanding and approved more when I explained what kind of person you are and what our relationship has been. (Told her I had spent weekends with you, but not that I had lived with you at SF.) Lloyd I have avoided discussing you with, instead interesting him in other less controversial things.

The write-ups are wonderful, darling. Couldn't be more understanding. Finally they're beginning to realize what you're doing. Here is the Hartford one back.

My god!!! What a thing to go through with Thorvald. So glad he's strong and vital enough to snap back.

Take care of yourself my darling and don't try to do too much all at once, just enough and no more each day.

Till we're one again—R

P.S. No time to read Cocteau, but Mother said it's very amusing.

April, May 1950

First big tour of Mexico with Rupert—Veracruz, Minatitlan. Plane to Merida, Chichen Itza, Minatitlan, Tehuantepec, Oaxaca, Acapulco, stayed at Las Palmas.

May 22, 1950

New York; Rupert in forestry camp.

June 1950

Rupert begins work in Los Angeles National Forest. Anaïs in Switzer Camp. Anaïs in Clear Creek barracks. Back to New York.

August 1950

Mexico

September 1950

New York

Letter from Anaïs Nin to Rupert Pole:

New York, October 16, 1950

Darling Chiquito, I was just going to write you that *one* of the reasons why our relationship is so good is that you are always willing to make an effort for it (the other reasons are just natural, naturally good, effortlessly good) and I wanted to ask you what I could do, equal to your writing letters, which was not a pleasure for you. You never ask, or scold, or call *me* up; yet surely I must sometimes disappoint you. Promise me you will be as honest as I am, and tell me when I'm not acting as you wish me to.

You asked me something once, I do remember—not to be jealous. That I have worked on very hard. You won't have any cause to complain. But when I asked for letters, I feel a little ashamed and selfish; yet I must tell you I'm no longer ashamed, for it has released in you a genuinely charming and far from dull writer. You have the power to give a most life-like image of your life. I felt I had been at the beach with Tavi who was so jealous of the dog who went into water with you! I felt I saw you cut your father's hair with old-fashioned scissors. Darling, it is magical and abolishes in part the pain of separation. It's true, it becomes a way to talk and be near.

Now, my love…I don't want to be the problem of the unmarried woman to the Forest Service. The longer I stay the better for the tie-up with *Flair* magazine. I will wait for your letter. What if I come for your days off? Wednesday the 25th, wasn't it? I could have days off with you, and keep busy in LA till your next days off. Will take my ticket tentatively for Tuesday, arriving Tuesday night, unless you advise me otherwise.

All my love…A

Sierra Madre, December 7, 1950

After a long absence, Rupert's tall and narrow silhouette appeared against the lights. Tavi the brown spaniel leaps to meet me. Rupert's full and eager mouth. Always the firm, the tense and fervent kiss. Always under my fingers, his thin shoulder bones. Always the deep-set, large eyes. Always the sigh of relief, the exclamation: "Oh darling, it was too long." Tavi demands attention. Rupert is elated and disturbed. He looks distraught, tense.

The 1936 Ford has been painted grey. The lock on the door is repaired. I kiss Rupert in the car with joy. We always lose our way. The metal bags are in the back. They have made this trip so often.

The web of lies is so immense I get lost in it. But now, at this moment, I am happy in a piercing, burning way, which balances all the pain. Tavi, Rupert and I. Like this, we made our first trip across the United States, south and west. Like this, we go to Mexico, we go to New Orleans, we go to the desert, or to San Francisco. I always have surprises in the metal bag: a compass, a Spanish beret. We will have eighteen days together. In the metal case there is a new shirt, or a hammock from Mexico, or sandals, or a wallet of fur, or a folk song book. Rupert always has a surprise of another kind, usually something he built for our home, shelves or a desktop sandpapered and stained. We drive to our various homes. Now we drive toward Sierra Madre, an hour away from Hollywood, where we live in a Forest Service house and Rupert is a ranger. In the summer he fights fires, he patrols with a green car, he rescues people who get lost in the canyon. In the winter he works on flood control, and on Sundays he patrols. He grants fire permits. He lectures on conservation. He examines fire hazards.

We drive towards the mountains and left of the Santa Anita race track. We drive towards very old sycamore trees and a navy blue sign reading "Sierra Madre." Sierra Madre is a grand mountain behind our house. In the car, we climb. Tavi has his nose on my knee. The little car for two people is a shelter, fragile and a little rickety with tired springs, locks that do not work easily, a top that is difficult to lower or raise, windows that are not rainproof, and parts that break now and then from old-age maladies. But Rupert understands the car. He is confident and adept at repairing it. He is cautious in its care but reckless in his speeding. He is impatient in traffic, has to keep ahead of others, and curses the red lights and believes they are functioning only to frustrate him. He is always a little late and speeding, but he drives adroitly and has no accidents due to quick reflexes and decisiveness; his quick wits save him. Right there, in his care of the car and in his reckless speeding, is one of the million contradictions that form his constellated character. He meets me with fervor and emotional excitement, yet remembers to ask me all the task-master questions: Did you see about your naturalization? Did you find out about the divorce? Did you order the chair? Did you see the doctor?

About the naturalization: I began to use this as one of the myths to justify my departures. Americanization. Divorce. Jobs. Lectures. Magazine work. Publication of books. Christmas holiday with my family. Illness of Thorvald. Problems with the new book (*A Spy in the House of Love*). Disguises. Metamorphoses to cover my trips, my other life. The questions put by Rupert are answered with more lies. Only the passion and the love are true, so deeply true, and they justify the lies told to protect it.

This should be a joyous moment, a moment of finding each other again after I solved all the obstacles that pull me away. He does not know each return is a victory; each return has taken great efforts, great planning, great lavishness of acting in New York.

The dark mountains, the silhouettes of trees. Tavi is restless because home is at the top of the hill and we are climbing. I have evaded the solemn truths and emphasized the joy. Rupert turns to the left where there is a flagpole, a sign saying "government service only." The house is plain, standard stucco, green and huge, but it is among large trees and made graceful by foliage carefully and artfully cut by Rupert. Below is the valley, and at our left are lights as if Florence were spread through the pines and sycamores. From here, illusion is permitted.

I get out of the car and Rupert takes out a valise, a red hat box, a toilet bag and the worn, much-traveled grey suede and black leather handbag that, if spilled accidentally, would throw on the ground proofs of my deceptions—traveler's checks I can't explain, money, Cuban passport... But it is the bag I carry and watch over.

Rupert has cleaned the house, has filled it with flowers and winter bushes, greens... He lights the candles. His surprises and mine are exchanged. We are tense with happiness. "It was too long, darling. Too long, too long." Away from him I cannot sleep. Away from him I feel crippled, incomplete, not alive. It causes me pain. Pain in the body. The warmth of life, of the heart and of the body. It is about eleven at night. He has arranged not to work the next day so we can sleep in the morning if the telephone does not ring at eight o'clock with some tourist asking for information where to gather pine cones or where to find snakes. The bed opens on the French rose sheets I got when I sent for the belongings I had stored in Paris when the war began in 1939. Eleven years later, the same sheets from my life in Paris covered Rupert and me, the same blankets, and we dried our bodies with the same towels. On this bed Rupert does not sleep well without me. "You are my life, my all."

I believed him at first to be a volatile, elusive, mobile, mercurial character, restless and homeless, unfaithful and unattached. I was wrong. His first wish is for a home. Traveling is secondary. His greatest need is security of the heart. He spends all his time with me. He likes to go out with me alone. He does not ask other people. When I leave for New York he does not rush out to enjoy his freedom. He withdraws. He flows when I am there. A friend describing him while I'm away said, "He becomes automatic, and not alive. He has that 'where is Anaïs?' look. He looks schizophrenic." He comes to life now, his face alight, his smile dazzling. His hands are rough from rough work, but he knows how to caress. He has that sure, determined, even touch of knowing hands. He is a decisive, unfumbling lover. To slip between the sheets body to body gives us a joy we had lost. We make love hungrily and nervously. The keenness of it is almost unbearable. The sharp, clear resonance of skin and blood and nerves. Erotically we bloom, in a multitude of awakened cells, and the climax of pleasure is so prolonged, so far-reaching, that we both cry out. We hold on to each other as if to make the penetration permanent against all the separations demanded by life. I cannot leave again, I cannot leave again. This is so deeply felt, all through the body. I tease him because he has cut his hands and I want him to take care of them for his viola playing. I say, "I have a chipped husband." He has a touch of poison oak, but only a touch, not as in San Francisco. No more bronchitis either, but there is always lurking the possibility of fragility, of sudden illness, of the bronchitis that sent him out of the army, of the inherited asthma. There is that radiance of health easily destroyed by a vulnerable temperament.

The first day is carefree. We go to Hollywood for a movie. We have dinner at the Café de Paris on Sunset Boulevard where the waitresses are French, as is the food, and there is a miniature, duplicated Tour Eiffel, but where is the subtle sky, the animated face of Paris, the loveliness, the fountains and the beauty of the boulevard? Rupert's impression of Paris was unhappy. He was with the USO in uniform, sick and tormented by his wife Janie who did not love him. My fantasy about Rupert the great traveler is altered. Because he appeared to me in Cleo ready to cross the continent as casually as if he were driving from Sierra Madre to Hollywood, because he talked about travel, I had believed him a wanderer. "And I would be, if I did not have you," he said. So I am France, I am Spain, I am Italy, I am New Orleans, I am Mexico. "I am too sensitive to be a real Don Juan," he said, so I am all his women, too.

Our first day was happy. But the second day we have the problem of his family, Lloyd and Helen Wright. At first, without knowing me, they were fanatically, irrationally against me. They had no genuine accusations: I was a married woman, older than Rupert (they did not know how much older), an artist (and all artists are egocentric), and foreign. Finally I was presented at the court. Rupert believed I would win them. On Thursday nights we would go to dinner and to quartet playing. Cocktails set them both off into complete irrationality. Lloyd's brilliance of mind, I believed at first, I could connect with until I discovered him insane—sudden rages, rantings. Helen is psychotic, only hypocritically covered by her false goodness. Rupert is equally illogical, hostile, or else masochistic. Nightmare evenings—Rupert's mother jealous, petty and mean. Once I left weeping. After that I did not talk. Then Helen began pressuring us "to marry," meanwhile admitting she had not been able to like me. To prove I love Rupert, I must marry him. I had a responsibility. At this I revolted. On returning home I fainted on the doorstop (rejection by the parents *again*: mine, Hugo's, Bill Pinckard's, now Rupert's). Just before I fainted I said to myself: "*Je suis une femme fatiguée.*" After this, I refused to go to the house. Helen also said I could not return until we were married. Thursday became a liberation from the insane asylum—my one free evening to see friends who loved me, Jim Herlihy and George Piffner. Rupert at first rebelled against his family, against the split evening. But I said he must not break with them on my account. Their behavior, however, and my rebellion against it, has weakened the bond between Rupert and his parents. He realizes their love is not love, but domination. If he gives up forestry, they threaten to break with him. They opposed his first girl (an affair of five years) and his marriage (to a cousin of Lloyd's). His mother is obsessed with the fact that there is too much sex in my books.

The nightmare was partly over. I was over-affected and weakened by the conflict. I had been relieved to escape to New York, but now I was so happy to be with Rupert again. He accepted my refusal to be hypocritically "reconciled" to his family. He went for the music. I visited Jim and George, and we had a lively, phosphorescent talk. George had made a mobile, which he gave me. Jim had written a story. Jim, an aspiring writer I met three years ago, loves me. He cannot find with anyone what he has with me. We talk about this and books and Erich Fromm, psychoanalysis and religion. Rupert arrives around midnight. To many people, he gives the impression of moodiness. He is unpredictable and mystifying. He is either too gentle or too aggressive. He is at times strident and tense, or submissive and over-eager to please strangers. He does not like to share me. He sits beside me and rejoices because Tavi barks at my friends as if they were intruders. "Tavi," he says, "chase away the invaders."

He was drunk after Thanksgiving dinner and insisted on driving, could not relinquish control even when in so doing he nearly destroyed himself and me. About this need of control, I am helpless. It manifests itself in the choice of which food I should buy and which market, of which cleaner and which laundry, a car that I cannot have filled with gas or oil without permission, control over which friends are invited and at which house. One day I wanted to go to Hollywood to have my hair tinted. He asked me how long that would take. I said it was difficult to say, as sometimes one late person would delay me. About two hours. And then? One hour for a Turkish bath. "So three hours, not including the drive." said Rupert. "You leave at one and will be home at six," not allowing for delays, for walking between the two places, for a stroll down the boulevard, a glance at shop windows. Mad, I thought. This is mad. It brought me back to the first days of my marriage with Hugo—the first day when he insisted on going to the hairdresser with me and waiting for me; when I made plans without consulting him he was certain to change them.

There are times when this does not displease me, when it creates an eternity of closeness like a welding, like one night we left Kay and John Dart and Jim and George at the movies to return alone to Jim's room to make love, to sleep in each other's arms. But most of the time, I feel stifled. I have to explain and justify all I do. I have to ask for money. He forgets to cash his checks. He believes that by having very little cash in the house, one spends less. With what explosive relief I occasionally spend my own money, which is not really my own, but Hugo's, and with what gratitude towards Hugo. There is, then, Rupert's control of what I "earn" in New York during my absences from home.

I spend half of my day on housework (we are saving for a house or a trip). It leaves me half a day for writing. I wrote *A Spy in the House of Love*. Finished it in June. It is a book of 200 pages, a full-length portrait of Sabina. But on many days after housework I am too tired to do anything but write a few letters, read and take notes, struggle to repair the damage done by mismanagement of my books. Duell Sloan and Pearce folded up, so I was left without a publisher for *Spy*. Strauss rejected it, Houghton Mifflin too. Viking Press called it a romantic fantasy that would cause trouble with the censors. Scribner's turned it down. I feel the failure keenly. My other books were remaindered, so they will soon be unobtainable. Total failure. Should I pretend to die to reassure people that they can dare to approach my work without fear? Should I die so that my manuscripts should sell and my value in the market rise as a rare, lost object?

So after the homecoming orgy, after all the delights, the extremes of the pressures of daily life with Rupert—isolated, dull, prosaic—begin to weave a web that has all the suffocating aspects of a prison. The life is small, a small kingdom Rupert feels equal to manage. It is this knowledge that dissolves my rebellions. But after a week of housework and writing without hope of publication or recognition, I begin to contrive some form of escape. I dream of Paris. I dream of the artist life always denied me because I did not marry artists. I dream of earning $200 a month to be able to travel. But if I had

$200 a month, Rupert would put it in the bank to build a house in Los Angeles. I cannot see myself in a house in Los Angeles. Resentment against the vacuity of American life gnaws at me. I feel it when Rupert reads the poisonous *Time* magazine and listens to radio commentators. I dream of Italy, where the Italian edition of *Under a Glass Bell*, if not I, is traveling. Rupert shares in these fantasies. If his imagination accompanies mine in this roaming, his fears make him clutch at the kind of work he can perform most adequately, at a home and at me with a desperate need of stability.

The nights, though, are always beautiful. Each part of our bodies finds its nook, its shelter, its core of warmth. Even after reading *Time*, Rupert's flavor is something so remote. The American boy goes to sleep with the radio on. But when the lover emerges, it is a lover of consummate skill and fervor. The passion is an ocean large enough to dissolve the American boy until tomorrow, when instead of people, he will choose a movie, and then instead of Nathaniel West, he will read *Time* (having said that reading West was a task), which puts an end to any expansion of his reading. The American boy is there to stay (candy, pretty girls, *Time* and radio commentators), but the Welshman in him is a musician who listens to Beethoven with absolute maturity. He possesses emotional and physical depths, sensual depths; the mind alone is unawake. But Cornelia Runyon, the sculptor at sixty-five years of age, the woman aware of transcendence in stone, observes that Rupert is growing, maturing, while also observing my regression into youthfulness, greater physical health and sumptuousness.

There is always an apple pie to be baked for the American boy. If he were not so beautiful, one could be overwhelmed by the traits he has in common with his neurotic father Reginald, which are alarming, if not ugly. Rupert cannot throw away anything. He accumulates useless or worn things. He does not like to give. He is chaotic with his belongings. He loses and breaks and forgets. At sixty-five, his father keeps carbons of old medicine bottles, dirty clothes like a ragpicker, never cleans or washes his belongings, never throws away a paper, forgets and loses what he has accumulated…

On days when I have ironed, which I hate, baked a pie, which bores me, I feel virtuous and stupid, but Rupert is happy. He does not know that I am his mother in doing this, which appears like devotion, but as with my own mother, it is a devotion that hides the incapacity to love. Feed, clothe, tend as the mother does, but this is not love because it is directed at a dependent child and demands a return in absolute submission, a total surrender of distinct desires, different needs and mature love for others. Rupert eats the pie of which I am not proud except as I was proud at age eleven of having mollified my conscience and earned the right to read Alexandre Dumas for two or three uninterrupted hours. To draw the bath for a naked Pan is a delight. To open a bottle of beer for him is a pleasure, to feed Tavi, who has also a highly developed way to distrust one's conscience, demanding, with glistening, appealing, hungry eyes, even after a substantial dinner.

The evening will be sweet if only Reginald does not appear, always unannounced in his dilapidated car. The physical resemblance between Reginald and Rupert is very startling, but Rupert is a more sensuous and healthier edition. Reginald was given a woman's name at Cambridge, and his friendship with Rupert Brooke was suspect. Reginald has an aristocratic air, but now he wears glasses and he does not have Rupert's full mouth. He is asthmatic, from the age of five. He has all the neurotic symptoms that have been classified: masochism in food, obsession with his health, completely self-centered, breathes with difficulty, gives himself insulin shots while he talks, monologues incessantly and plays a constant comedy of consulting us, asking for advice, confiding, planning, and then doing none of what is suggested. His activity is void of meaning, direction or usefulness. He travels from one place to another in quest of relief. Now it is Riverside where he feels better being near the desert. Endless monotonous monotone discourses, free associations of dead impressions. His recollections of people are uninteresting because he never knows them or sees them clearly. They only exist in a tenuous relation to himself. Martha Graham was a woman he trained to act in a play when she was a young student. Esther Winwood was a woman he once took a walk with and whom he did not kiss. Famous theatre directors were men who rejected or produced his version of *The Idiot*. Charles Chaplin is a man who invited him to dinner one night and asked him for auld lang zyne's sake to coach his son on how to read Shakespeare.

Reginald wrote a play about Lincoln because with little makeup, he can easily look like him, and he can portray him easily because he has "Lincoln's compassion." His taste in literature is arrested at his contemporaries' early stages of growth. His responses are merely echoes of his Cambridge enthusiasm. The zombie quality of his speech is fatal. A death-ray, death radiations emanate from him. The static, stagnant atmosphere kills one's desire to give, help or talk because one knows it is a waste, a total waste. He will linger here, too long always, among the ashes he creates in the evening, get in his car that, like himself, seems incapable of reaching the next destination. He cannot be helped. He can only be served, washed, fed. He can only occupy a parasitic position in the family, whom he visits until people weary of his inordinate demands and escape from him. Now and then he arouses the protective instinct of a woman, and he feeds on it until the woman feels the zombie at her breast and that no life will come of this, only an existence as repulsive as a fish without eyes, with withered fins, who is less than a fish and only a little more than a stone, a static receiver of food who prowls the bottom of the aquarium.

At first I was devoted to Reginald out of an extension of my love for Rupert until his selfishness and madness frightened me, and I began to see him as a human tick. Now I live merely in dread of his appearing when I have friends of my own over and he reads them his play on Lincoln for two hours. Rupert repairs his car, gives him money and clothes, but I have stopped trying to get his writings published or even to get him to fill out his fellowship papers, which he could do impressively due to his Cambridge academic proficiencies. His blindness to others is complete. Decades after his divorce, he still goes to his former wife Helen for mail, for talks, while Lloyd stands there like a porcupine. To Reginald, I am a French writer who has too much sex in her work (as I am for Helen). But he likes my kindness to him, my warmth.

The choice combination of foresters (another sub-human form of life) and Reginald, or Kay and John or Alice and Eyvind Earle (Rupert's friends)—Kay a mediocre June, John colorless and gentle, Alice prosaic, Eyvind a second-rate painter who was a childhood friend of Rupert's—and the circle of a small, meaningless world is complete. I have to remind myself that if Rupert is thirty-one, I am living the life I led as a bride of twenty to twenty-five, before Paris widened and deepened and awakened me. Any woman could take my place and this life would satisfy her. But she could not satisfy Rupert because Rupert is not content with ordinary life. He has simply made me the luxury, the travel, the strange and infinitely varied flavor of his life. I am the possibility of other worlds.

One night, after the tumult and excess of lovemaking, I asked out of a lingering jealousy about an incident he had with a girl in the early days of our relationship after our first trip (which, naturally, was exposed by Kay), "You don't have what we have with other women?" And Rupert answered with great feeling: "Oh darling, *nothing* approaching it, *nothing* compared to this, it's all in *another* world, it doesn't count. Nothing like this, as big, as big." And he supplemented his words with an embrace so strong that it pained me. I know it is so, and I know this is the fusion I never reached with Hugo.

So the short, the lyrical, the intensely heightened moments of passion are isolated by a life altogether colorless, meaningless and limited, having no integration or connection with the nights. What I once considered an essential part of his character—the nomadic impulses, the quest of the marvelous and the strange—has weakened in him, and his main desire now is for a house built out of his own hands.

I wanted him to travel and see and know other lives before taking root in Los Angeles—I felt I would be a suitable guide to his other lives and that later I could relinquish him to the American girl who would match the American boy and read *Time* with him and fall asleep to the radio's barbaric lullabies. But when he sees the mythical young woman in the movies, in stories, in other marriages, he observes mainly how selfish she is!

Ruth had warned me: "It will be good for a few years." But four years have passed and we cannot be separated.

I was writing about the first week: one evening with Jim and George, one evening with Reginald, one evening with Kay drinking a bottle of gin, exposing her large legs up to her thighs with an ex-whore style, frequent references to her past lovers, and John, at twenty-six, hypnotized by Kay who is his first woman. During an evening at home alone I heard the train whistle and a pack of coyotes, with their thin, wailing cry, answering the train as if it were the call of another animal in the night. Tavi answers the coyotes with disquietude. The train and the howling coyotes gave me a feeling of loneliness and a hatred of the mountains and fields and trees that I cannot confess to Rupert, who delights in this space with its isolation and peace. Nature in Acapulco—sun, sea, jungle and warmth—seems festive and joyous, but in America it is the space of separation from life, it is the desert between human beings, it is a vacuum, an obstacle, an automobile route, that is all. It takes an hour to reach a movie, another hour to recover after being with people, weariness, when bed should be nearer. It is what has made Americans autistic, sub-human, unable to relate to other human beings, inarticulate. So the coyotes wail, and there is the awfulness of a nature that is melancholic and empty, monotonous and colorless, mistaking the train whistle for a lonely animal. Another evening of movies carefully chosen by Rupert, but usually a double fare, and to this he responds completely. The American boy responds to *The Loves of Carmen* of Rita Hayworth, laughs fully at the cartoons, but unlike any American boy, he is moved by the subtleties of *La Ronde* and *La Folle de Chaillot*. He is annihilated by deep tragedies of Italian war films. He is vulnerable, weeps over the death of *The Lovers of Verona*. And at this moment, I love him. No matter what limitations he has intellectually, he has emotional depth. So as we come out of the theatre, I am aware of his response to the desperate sufferings of Blanche, of his hatred of brutality and cruelty, of the fact that he refused to kill in the war.

In the movies sometimes I grow very cold, stiff and stupefied. I meditate on the art of writing becoming an obsolete art. Libraries are getting rid of books to make room for films. Publishers are failing one by one. The 25¢ books are succeeding but only because they are second-rate writing, ephemeral like magazines, easy to reach for or to throw away, not like the inexpensive French book that has a chance of being bound and kept. I think of the film I made with Hugo in Acapulco in August of an old shipwreck, the sea, myself, and movements I composed, and lines from *House of Incest*. In the movies I am aware that people are becoming more and more intellectually atrophied and that movies and television provide them with baby food—no need to masticate, no need to carve, no need to read a book with effort. People lie down on specially inclined chairs and receive the images. Speech, already inadequate in America, will soon disappear altogether, and the ability to derive significance from printed words will die with it. Rupert's distaste for reading and writing reminds me of the end of a world of writing, hastened by ignorance of writing in America, and my sitting here several evenings a week with Rupert at the movies is my acceptance, my resignation to a change in the human species as radical as its change from monkey to man, a devolution from man to automaton.

TWA Flight 34 to New York, December 1950

After leaving Rupert, I flew to San Francisco to see Mother and my brother Joaquín in Oakland. Last night, I could not sleep at first because I was in my mother's house, in Joaquín's bed that he relinquishes to a "guest," and I was tormented by a strong impulse to return to Rupert instead of proceeding to New York. This impulse, which urges me to return to Rupert, to the core of fire, the center of fusion, is human and tragic, for it runs in absolute opposition to what my wisdom and intelligence tell me. It is the irrational impulse, the primitive impulse that drives me to a body I desire, a hairline and neck that stir me, a hand that melts me, a mouth that makes its designs within my flesh, eyes that direct the tides of my blood, eyelashes that play on my nerves, a voice that commands my heart and haunts me in its absence, words of need and hunger that pursue me: "You are my life." I hear him rustling papers in his room while I am reading in bed, forcing himself to write forestry reports with the forced concentration of a child applying himself to a hated task—numbers, figures, statistics. His gravity gives him a false responsible air. People thrust responsibilities on him. He fulfills them adequately, so he gets more, but he hates it. His mother asks him to do big landscape jobs at a house she owns and rents out, where he spent his childhood in an American paradise on a hill above Hollywood, born of artificial plants and moving pictures. The house was designed by Lloyd Wright, and it is beautiful. We sacrifice Rupert's days off to this task and the fantasy of living in the house that he will inherit, but that I know I will never inhabit. Because my father was an erudite musician, I believed he would understand my particular form of music—my writing—but he didn't, and he didn't understand my life. Because Lloyd is an imaginative and original architect, I believed he would understand the architecture of my writing, but he does not.

Writing in the diary, I can condense a little of the elusive aspects of this mobile we call our life. And all the while I write, its aspect changes; I find that both my passion for Rupert and my anger at our petty life together distort the truth I seek. If Rupert, because of his neurosis, of his youth, cannot achieve the life we want, only the life *he* wants, isn't it true that I cannot achieve it either, that I am still dependent on others to feed, clothe, protect me, and that I therefore must accept what the husband or lover creates for me? I am still only stealing what I want, being unable to create it. I have nothing of my own. From my writing I received perhaps $250 a year, the advance on each book, and no more. I never get paid for my lectures. My records don't sell, and if they did, Louis and Bebe Barron, who recorded them, would not pay me, not out of dishonesty, but out of mismanagement.

The magazines reject my stories. Those who read me or are devoted to me are concealed from me, a secret society who will not buy the books. And so how can I speak of my life unless it is within the framework made by Hugo or Rupert? Rupert chose a profession before he met me. I did not know him when he was struggling to be an actor in New York (this while I was seeking vainly in Bill what Rupert gave me generously later). The first time Rupert and I were together we became lovers immediately. The second time he drove me out to show me a tree as other young men would accompany me to see a painting in a museum. This tree was beautiful, but it was an ordinary tree. There was also the painting of a tree by Eyvind Earle, his friend who painted many trees. Five years after starting out to be an actor, Rupert printed Christmas cards that sold successfully and kept him fed and Eyvind and Alice in a house of their own in a forest. But this painting of a tree was an ordinary painting. Like finding Rupert's hands stained by print ink and his nails broken and his skin rough, it touched me, I don't know why, when neither Miró nor the trees of mythology touched me. It touched me in the same way that two ordinary poplars did when I was seventeen. They stood as sentinels to the path into our house in Richmond Hill, and I addressed them as friends, conversed and sustained a relationship with them. There was, at that time, an Anaïs who could love an ordinary tree that was neither symmetric, nor exotic, nor rare, nor historic, nor unique. This Anaïs led a timid life under the protection and control of her mother, absolutely incapable of building any life at all, except one in writing, enclosed in a diary, nurtured on fantasy, derived of literature and entirely separate from her life on earth, which consisted of playing the role of substitute mother to her younger brothers when the real mother was not at home.

Anaïs was seventeen again when she met a Rupert of twenty-eight, whom promiscuity, an actor's life, college, or drifting did not mature or spoil, who was lost, defeated, but with his fantasies intact. He failed at marriage, and also, he felt, as an artist. And so together we began again with the tree he drove me to see, the first of many. He was on his way to study them, name them, to get a degree in the knowledge of trees, in the same Ford Model A in which we were going to cross the United States. He would go to college again for a forestry degree. In San Francisco, we were going to spend weekends visiting Big Trees. In Mexico, we were going to take photographs of the oldest trees in the world, two thousand years old. We were going to film cotton trees, orange jacarandas, palms, cactus giants, tequila trees, dead trees. We were going to bring back samples in our pockets. We were going to laugh at the obscenities of the Latin names for trees. We were going to make frenzied love under a pepper tree, make love under a big redwood tree. In the deserts of Utah, by the river, after a swim in the cold water, naked, after making love on the banks, in a place so primitive that we felt as if we were the first man and woman on earth, Rupert packed up a small, one foot high tender child tree from the forest and planted it at the edge of the river, the young tree of our relationship. The tree of life. Our adolescent passion—would it take root, bear leaves, bear fruit, bear flowers, harden, strengthen, become strong? At the moment, in that first year, its fragility, the tree, Rupert, his work, our relationship, seemed utterly fragile. I asked the name of the river. Rupert said, "It's called Dolores." Dolores, Dolores, Dolores, Dolorous. Why should it be Dolores?

The tree. The little one grew, at least within us. The roots grew strong, at least within us, wrapping roots that carried the vital sap between the two bodies. Anaïs of seventeen communicating with two ordinary poplars invested with mythological voices can live here in this little house of candor.

The other Anaïs, who moves at times in a bigger and more complex world, does so with effort and with difficulties.

When out of the bed of iridescent desires, I look out the window at trees that belong to a tasteless, empty, and homely America, to one of its communities that could disappear without depriving the world's reserves of either beauty or human life in their most developed forms. One that truly represents one of the lowest forms of life, one of emptiness in obese upholstery, void in comfort, a vacuum in functional plumbing. The cypresses that do not orchestrate the lights of the valley, cypresses with no history, no dignity conferred by the soul's convolutions, but only a community of robots producing robots, invading robots. Still, I look upon this from a bed that contains everything concentrated in one jewel, the princess jewel of sensual accord and ecstasy. Then the cypresses without history seem to be looking down not at an ordinary city, but at all the lovers, containing them all, extending them, concentrating in two bodies all the joys of the earth.

Two books were born during our life together. In San Francisco I wrote *The Four-Chambered Heart*. In Sierra Madre I wrote *A Spy in the House of Love*.

Rupert did his college work well. He had a four year job to do in two years. We had very little time for friends, for pleasure. He had so many examinations. I helped him with the typing, which was a heavy load, almost a whole book. We had a beautiful apartment on a hill. We had the Chrysler Hugo gave me in which I learned to drive. We had a fireplace in which Rupert liked to cook, to grill meat. Varda's painting and Eyvind's tree hung in the same room. We were very happy there in a different way.

I was deeply jealous and panicked by a very pretty girl who appeared. I felt uncertain of the future. I did not feel Rupert's clutchingness, although it was there, and for the first time, he expressed the pain caused by my absence. But he did not seem as possessive. Our only difficulties were a few scenes of jealousy from me, once when he stared back at a girl at a concert who had come up and planted herself before him, staring at him, and another time when he asked Ruth for a typist to keep up with his typing while I was gone and asked that she be beautiful.

The only times I wept were at a defect he has that I cannot accept: he is a fault-finder. After always putting the car in the garage, one day I felt tired and left the old Ford outside. Rupert immediately commented: "You must not do that as it might get wet and be difficult to start later." If I make the salad with lettuce leaves not cut as fine as some people do: "Salad must be cut small. Oh, you forgot the lime." One day the car broke down. Rupert blamed me. The garage man said no one could be blamed, that it was worn and would have broken down sooner or later. He gets irrationally critical, but always shifts the blame. I do not understand the meaning of this. If he can't find a book, someone has mixed them up—*I have*. This makes me nervous and causes me to lie when accused. He gets angry at the traffic. He gets angry at the movies if they advertise the wrong hour and speaks very loudly against the film—misplaced anger.

I do exactly the opposite. I seek to excuse or justify all he does. I never blame him. I know he carries an abnormal burden of guilt and the slightest addition makes it unbearable. I have tried to explain how I feel, but I've lost my confidence. Fearing criticism, I postpone discussions. He leaves the venetian blinds he took down on the floor. I wrap them up in an old curtain until we decide where to keep them. He says, "That's not good. I will put them in the closet. The curtains will get dirty." Of course, he also directs this perfectionism against himself. He treats himself as critically, as negatively. Hostility. To look for the flaw! My father did this. Hugo too. However, Hugo did not direct it at me, only at others, other women. Rupert loves me crazily, yet he also demolishes my self-confidence. When I left him at the airport, he noticed my low-heeled shoes. He said, "I like high heels with a fur coat." I don't *feel free*. I never feel free with him. "Your neckline is askew." Yet I know he is suffering at my leaving.

Suddenly, while planning a Christmas party, he observes the mediocrity of our friends. But they are his.

It's strange. Rupert's passion does not make me feel free or valuable. As the month passed I felt diminished, shrunken almost. As if the only moment of fulfillment were in the sensual fusion, but outside of that, I am not happy. I do not enjoy racing nervously to a movie. I do not enjoy so *many* movies. I do not enjoy parties when we go together. I don't know why. I don't enjoy my lectures if he is there. When friends come, he is not carefree. He is bound up in dancing, rigid. Why?

Early in the morning he is desperately sleepy. He craves each minute more he can sleep, so I bring him what the Mexicans call a "*cafécito*," a small cup of black coffee heralding a fuller breakfast.

When I leave him for New York, after the first stabbings of pain, after I master the deep impulse to return, then I begin to feel free and stronger. In New York I enter a larger life, and when I return I always return stronger, enriched, filled with confidence.

I am afraid to be ill with Rupert. The third week I wrenched my back helping him at gardening, and for several days found it hard to make the bed, empty the garbage pail, etc. One night I went to bed early after a hot bath. We had received chairs by mail order unassembled and therefore cheaper. Rupert was disappointed in the chairs (things are never as he imagined them). He spent the evening fretting. He turned the light on, awakened me to show me what was wrong. The word in Spanish is *majadero*. *Ay, qué majadero*, they always say about children. Fussing is the nearest equivalent—fretful. Fundamentally there is a great selfishness, which he recognizes. He only admits it when he speaks of children. On our first trip he talked about Bach's nine children continuously. Finally I used that as a reason for not marrying him—I cannot give him children. But then he exclaimed, "I don't really want children. I'm too selfish for that." I think he talked about them because it made him feel manly. It was bad for Rupert's manliness that a screen test revealed that he looked like an adolescent and could only play young boys' roles. He had no "sex appeal," they said. This made a lasting scar. Also, his New York stage notices emphasized his "boyish awkwardness." When he smokes his pipe and speaks sententiously, he is playing a part. During our first trip I was disturbed by some of his attitudes until I understood he was playing the part of an older man.

And yet I would turn the plane back if I could. For four years I have turned back, feeling elation, fever and delight at returning, impatient for his presence, to sit beside him in the car, with Tavi on my lap, to feel his strong hands. What I bring back is renewed faith in him, the passion to carry us farther. I return to my prison, understanding not only that it is a world in proportion to Rupert's abilities, but knowing too that in the larger one I am not at ease. It was a strain to meet Maxwell Geismar and his wife because they were so brilliant and so mature. It is a strain to meet Anthony Tudor, to go to Charles Rolo's parties and talk with representatives of Knopf, with older people of accomplishment.

Rupert's eyes twinkled at me with his joyousness. "We are so fortunate, darling. We have each other. I would give anything up for our relationship: my parents, or forestry. One month apart is too long, too long. Make it only ten days. Do your job fast and come back for Christmas."

Tavi wanted to climb into the plane. Tavi gets blue when I leave. They were driving on to see Rupert's family. He would play the viola not too exactly, but with fervor and brilliance. He does not practice. He has the temperament for music, the bravado and the impetus. He can be defined and described as Joaquín defined romanticism: strangeness added to beauty.

The plane is an hour late. Beneath me, while I was writing, the mountains and plains lay blanketed white, this West Rupert took me to, where aside from the Grand Canyon, the desert, the South, there was nothing to discover but monotony. In one day I fly over all these roads we traveled the first time for eighteen days to a life more in harmony with my maturity, my physical age, my achievements, my development. Yet for four years I have surrendered the more brilliant friends, the greater recognition I get in New York than I do in antiquated, provincial California. I surrender the care of the best doctors, the comfort, the luxury, the freedom from housework, the power, the possessions, and above all the love to whom I owe my life, all I am, my existence, and my creation, to return to Rupert. How has he bound me, enslaved me? I see him sitting in his bath, his slender, freckled shoulders, his dark hair and his eyes illumined at the thought of my divorce from Hugo: "You will be all mine."

A web of lies, lies, lies, necessary to this life. I am torn in two when I have to leave. Parting from Rupert, I always feel it is the last time, which I cannot bear again. Yesterday, listening to Joaquín delivering a witty lecture on Von Weber and Brahms, I felt the compulsion to return to Rupert. And then there is the fear if I return, I return without money. We have $200 a month to live on. I will have to take an ordinary job, which may bring us another $200 to *save*. I will not have the strength to work all day, to clean the house, shop, cook, iron, and live Rupert's life, not the strength—the strength. I am forty-eight years old. In appearance, I deceive everyone. I am alive and keen and inspiring to others. But I get so tired, so deeply tired. I cannot return, powerless as I am, to earn what we need. Fear. Fears of illness, of loss of energy, of inadequacy. Rupert expects so much of me. He cannot understand my economies of strength. To shut the garage door, to pull the hand brake on the old Ford seems difficult at times, to carry the laundry to the laundromat, to garden in the summer. I feel humiliated, inadequate. My impulse to run back is stifled. I got up at seven o'clock and was driven by Joaquín to the airport.

I could be happy with Rupert in that core of fantasy and sensual fusion that we enter at night, but I know that only one life will ultimately destroy me. I must make a decision I have eluded after years of lies and games, of living on a trapeze, of fear of falling in between, or of one love getting hurt; I have been incapable. I went for help when the divided lives became maddening. I crave peace, a choice, a simplification. Which one? Whatever I choose seems to demand a sacrifice I cannot make. With Rupert it is the *life* I do not want, with the certainty of tragedy at the end.

Arrive in New York. I will be here a month.

MY UNWANTED PRESENCE

1951

DECEMBER 1950-JANUARY 1951
New York

JANUARY 27, 1951
Arrival in Los Angeles

SIERRA MADRE, JANUARY 1951

Rupert's wild pleasure at my arrival. I was sick for two days with bronchitis. We swam though caresses, and clung all night to each other. He took care of me, warmly and completely. In the dark he said, "Separations are painful, but they make us realize how necessary we are to each other. What a life-giving love!" After two days, I got up to clean the house that Rupert had not been able to clean. Emerging out of an electric passion, a charged night, and having gained detachment, I can face the dirty house, the economies, Reginald's monologues, and Kay and John. Rupert, whom I have imagined *wanting* this life, reveals he does not want it any more than I do, but he does not know how to go about creating another. *This* is what he is capable of doing. So much of what one thinks, imagines, far away from the loved one, is false. How carefully one must compare it with reality, retouch it.

I found out that Rupert rebels against forestry and the dullness of the life while I am away. As soon as I return, though, he is content. I can see by the way he lives while I am away, he *stops* living. He eats monotonously, he does not bathe, change the sheets;

he loses his brightness and energy. I saw him come to life. And now at the end of two weeks, he is playing with quartets, he sings. And he has made out of his own hands the couch-benches I planned. At times I feel I am free of my love of Rupert. I see him in another world. I see the enormous areas of our relationship created by my playing a role. It may have been true at one time that in contrast to New York I wanted nature, serenity, an easy rhythm, but now I know that the only nature I like is the tropical one: Acapulco, warmth, languor, beauty and gayety. The Sun. But not California.

It may have been true at one time, after the infernal life in New York with the Press, Gonzalo, and Bill, that I wanted to return to simplicity, to a simple life with the One. But it is no longer true. I hate this kind of simplicity, its emptiness. I hate Rupert listening to "Invitation to Learning" (moronic and vulgar) or the commentators.

But as against all this, Rupert's face on the pillow in the morning, his sleepiness, his pathetic dutifulness, his tautness, his discomfort in the world, his rough clothes and finely chiseled body, his anxieties, his powerful, wiry embraces, his severities I no longer take seriously. Last night his face was illuminated because he was mischievously eating up the sandwiches I had prepared for his lunch the next day!

I think of all the human bondages, to a human being's voice, touch, warmth and trustiness. I could not harm him. But could I tempt him, marry him off? Couldn't I find the woman who would tempt him?

Days when I am happy to live out Rupert's life as he sees it: a couple who earns $200 a month (his earnings), which means that I must take care of the house (what I "earn" in New York is for our trips or for a house of our own) so I immerse myself in:

1 hour in the kitchen—dishes, cleaning, burning garbage

1 hour of 1 room a day—thorough cleaning, sweeping rug, mopping, cleaning pipes

1 hour of errands—shopping, shoes repaired, cleaning suits, tailor, post office

1 hour sewing or mending socks and underwear

1 hour for myself, bathing, care of face, hair, etc.

A little while for letter writing, reading if I'm tired, and then another hour in the kitchen to cook dinner.

After a week or so I hate the housekeeping, feel stripped and diminished, colorless and empty. No. I cannot live this way. Monday evening a movie, Tuesday Rupert plays with the Pasadena orchestra. Wednesday a movie. Thursday evening he plays quartets with his family and I see Jim. Friday evening a movie, etc., etc.

But then a moment of passion and all the discordances are effaced. I dream of the sea within us, the astonishing levels, variations, shapes, forms of matter, forms of life. The dream of writing the final book that will break my ostracism from the world.

I carry in my handbag a letter rejecting *A Spy in the House of Love* with insults, not politely, with condemnation of the "lie detector" character. Americans are barbarians. I am glad that my identification papers still say "Visitor"; even if I am a permanent visitor at least I am not condemned to stay here. I would like Rupert to live the artist life of Paris. I would like a life in Italy and the rest in the tropics. I want to die in the sea and in the sun.

I cling to the little things that make life so real and warm, when Rupert is sleeping and I bring him his *cafécito*. Tavi thinks he must defend the sleeper and he growls at me and wants to fight me off. Rupert smiles. His eyes are strange at times, not like a human being's but like the sea looking at you, nature, something without identity. "If I had not met you I would have continued to be wary of women, be a superficial Don Juan, but not happy, oh, not happy." When we are drunk he is lost, bewildered, tender. He smiles, his mouth is open; he could be easily possessed. His skin glows with health and ruddiness; his eyes are the sea, *not personal*.

And meanwhile the problem with his family deepens.

Letter from Anaïs Nin to Helen and Lloyd Wright:

Sierra Madre, 1951

Dear Helen and Lloyd: It was Rupert's idea, not mine, that if I gave you a chance to know me I could overcome your prejudice against us. I have tried, in spite of the fact that it was very difficult for me to have a good feeling about this attempt when your first words to me were: "You are not the woman we had dreamed of for Rupert," to which I tried justly to agree, telling you that was why we had waited to get married. However, I now discover through Kay and Reginald that your criticisms of me still continue, and when I examine them sincerely I find them so unjust that I can only conclude that the prejudice is still there, as much as before.

I gather this is what worried you: first of all I was a married woman. Well, now I am divorced.

Secondly: I was an artist and would not help Rupert stick to forestry. Well, I not only helped and took care of Rupert during his forestry studies, but encouraged and collaborated with him. He has not given up forestry for me. I have given up my artist life.

Thirdly: you keep saying I am not domestic. Well, I am not a hypocrite. I am not domestic one hundred percent. But I have been domestic and a good wife to Rupert. I have done all the housework and the garden work and whatever is expected of a Forest Service wife. I have done things I never did for anyone before, to save money.

Next: you still say I am a self-centered writer. Well, in the first place, if I were self-centered Rupert would not be the happy, content, healthy man he is now. I have continued to write because my writing means something to both of us. It adds to our life the kind of friends, atmosphere, and travel both Rupert and I need, and that is what has enabled him to concentrate on his forestry work. Without my writing, if we only lived on his salary, we could never travel or go to concerts or theatres. Rupert would have been unhappy in such a narrow life. If you can call self-centered the fact that I spent one evening at your house finishing a revision of my book, copying out a fragment for a magazine, and showing a passage to Lloyd with the human desire that you should understand my work, then you don't understand Rupert very well, because a mere hausfrau would not have made him very happy. You would have the right to say that if I had dragged Rupert into my artist life.

I never expected you to understand me, or really love me. But I did expect you to say as parents will: Rupert is happy, healthy, content. And to at least give up expressions of your prejudice to strangers like Kay.

Whenever there is unjust criticism it only means that the prejudice is still there. Therefore I do not see why I should continue to visit you if there is no sincere acceptance of me. It is utterly impossible for me to be where I am not wanted, knowing how you really feel, the snide remarks made by Lloyd about my trips when I have suffered from these trips and made them only to earn the extra means to go on happy vacations with Rupert. I am not happy in your presence knowing all this. I know you tried, but you must be aware of the insincerity between us. For instance, when I write you affectionate or admiring letters, you say I flatter you. When I give you my true opinion about something, you say I criticize you. Everything I do you have misinterpreted.

I feel that we have now had sufficient time to discover whether we understand one another. I respect Lloyd greatly as an artist and I thought he would understand me as an artist. I respected you greatly as a wonderful mother and thought that as a mother you would recognize my love and total devotion to Rupert and be glad of that. I have never once caused Rupert any pain or anger or disappointment. I believed this would be enough to create a bond between us.

Now I feel that it would be more sincere for me to stay away and to let you enjoy your relationship with Rupert without my unwanted presence.

Anaïs

February 21, 1951

New York; Peggy Glanville-Hicks has surgery.

New York, March 1951

A Spy in the House of Love was submitted to:

Scribner's
G. P. Putnam's Sons
Farrar Straus and Hal Vursell
Harper Brothers
Pellegrini and Cudahy, Coley Taylor
The Bobbs Merrill Co., Hiram Haydn
Macmillan's

Viking Press
New Directions, James Laughlin

Fragment "Donald" (from *Spy*) was submitted to:
Harper's Bazaar, returned
New Story magazine, accepted
Kenyon Review, returned
New Mexico Review, returned

Books translated are:
Ladders to Fire Holland, Uitgeverij De Driehook
Under a Glass Bell, Italy, Arnoldo Mondadori
Children of the Albatross, Sweden, Wahlstrom and Widstrand

Books published in England
Under a Glass Bell, London, Editions Poetry

Harper's Bazaar published a fragment of "Stella" from *Ladders to Fire* in 1947 but refused fragments from *Children of the Albatross*, from *The Four-Chambered Heart* and from *A Spy in the House of Love.*

Tiger's Eye published a fragment from two novels but is now no longer in the market.

Books are being considered by other publishers in Italy through an introduction by Mrs. Murray who represents Mondadori, as a personal favor and advice because Mondadori's list is overcrowded and will take years to catch up with my work.

Max Pfeffer is now my literary agent.

In France Serge Ouveroff is handling the books as Mr. Pfeffer's agent, and I am writing him for a report.

Copyrights returned to me on *Ladders to Fire* (E. P. Dutton)
Children of the Albatross copyright belongs to me
Under a Glass Bell copyright in my name
The Four-Chambered Heart copyright in my name

Letter from Anaïs Nin to Rupert Pole:

New York, Friday, March 16, 1951

Darling Chiquito, No letter from you today.

I won't inflict you anymore with emotional reactions to your family's behavior as I have quietly found the reason and can now be objective, and not care. It reminded me exactly of the destructive, hopeless, incurable, bitter attitude of Miller and Gonzalo, and how I tried to help cure them with no result except harm to myself. I hate war above all things, in the world as well as in families. I want understanding and love. It was good I came away to get a grip on my feelings. One never escapes pain anyway—when you get away from it, it follows you because life is full of repetitions. I escaped with you into a different world and met the same neurotic destructiveness as in your home; that's why I reacted as I did.

Please take my books away from your home. I don't want them there. I don't want their comments and opinions. Will you please humor me in this? Tell me how you feel, whether your strength has come back. Sleep a lot, darling. Our trip to Mexico won't be restful.

Te beso fuerte

A.

Letter from Anaïs Nin to Rupert Pole:

New York, March 18, 1951

Oh darling! I didn't mean to wake you up when I called! I calculated two hours' difference instead of three. Also I had to call when I was alone in the apartment. So sorry, darling. Your cold is still there, I could hear. You are right about a change of clothes. I also have to *leave* some things I won't need.

The most pleasant friendship I made this time was with Maxwell Geismar, the critic, and his wife. They are the best kind of intelligent Jews, very much like Ruth, but happily married and with children. She is his collaborator. We had a fine evening of book talk last night. He is engaged in a history of American literature. Lusty and humorous.

Love, I send you *Ladders to Fire* in Dutch, a rather pretty book they did and which is a success—why in Holland, I don't know. Is it the love of opposites? Can you see a Dutch maiden reading me? Still no money from Mondadori in Italy. Max Pfeffer, my agent, thinks we'll have to go and collect it.

You didn't say whether you got the plastic whiskey bottle and whether you wanted another.

About our trip: are you bringing the grill to cook out of doors and a few cases of soup for your anti-pepper wife? A few cases of milk too. I hope we don't go to the cold places! You need sun and softness, and I need you!

My list for Mexico with you:

Sandals (white, tan, etc.)

Walking boots

Grey raincoat

Travel suit—wide skirt, little cape, the blue grey one I wear with different skirts, with blue cotton shirt sewed to matching skirt

White Mexican shirt-waists

Black slacks if we must go on horseback, with your red woollies as mine have shrunk (if we go to the volcano). You might need a warm outfit too

White heavy wool sweater knitted by my mother, a woolen skirt you gave me

Peacock blue silk dress with black leaves design—our first dress—with matching scarf

White panties, bras, petticoats

Cotton dresses, *simple* ones: 1 navy blue, 1 orchid, 1 fuchsia

Purple bathing suit
Purple scarf for head with gold dots
Glasses in red leather case
Small sewing material box
Te quiero
A.

My friendship with Jim Herlihy is deepening. He is the best of all my spiritual children, the one who was temperamentally and intelligently more receptive, subtle and imaginative. At twenty-four he is productive, he talks nimbly and colorfully—his talk was more developed than his writing, but now it is infiltrating his writing. He would have been perhaps another competent, clever homosexual writer, but at Black Mountain College, where I went to read in 1947, he grasped at me, and I helped him to descend into the infernos and mines of buried treasures, to find emotion, where the gold vein lies, and he dug, he worked. But the relationship is very bold, equal, mutually dependent, and above all *elating* in our work world, in which we are lonely. He is my only friend-in-writing, my handsome, gallant Jim, and his moods and mine match in freedom of invention and ability for the mechanics of the modern mind. He has a mathematical, electronic, magnetic tape, jazz-of-angels mind. It has a quick beat and *fulgurance*; it is phosphorescent and elliptical, and full of the true relativities. No rigid absolutes. Liquefaction, not static!

He works at the Satyr Bookshop in Hollywood.

Letter from Jim Herlihy to Anaïs Nin:

Hollywood, March 22, 1951

Dear Anaïs:

I wrote your agent on Satyr stationery, telling him of my difficulty in procuring *Ladders to Fire* from my supplier in Pasadena, which should place you in the clear about its being out of print. Actually, I can't remember how the idea originated. We have just received copies (and sold them immediately, by the way) and have reordered likewise *Children of the Albatross*. I would have sent a copy of the letter to you in NY, but thought you would have returned by then.

I have put your copy of *The Four-Chambered Heart* in the window along with a display of your other work and some other "new writing"—Joyce-Miller-Kafka-Stein, etc. We don't have much of that, as you know. Am reading Maxwell Geismar and like it very much so far, even though I feel he overrates Hemingway. Lila [Rosenblum] and I listened to your records one night. I don't like the woman [Josephine Premice] with the drums in this *House of Incest*. She might do a fine job in the *Scenario* of Henry Miller, for some background sound, but it is disturbing with your reading. Also don't especially like Henry Miller's *Scenario*, but it might be good on film. He mentions you in his new book *The Waters Reglitterized*. Have you seen it? Also Berzon has a copy of the Obelisk *The Winter of Artifice*, which I'd like to borrow.

I got all that spring yearning out of my system for the time being (of course the trouble here is that spring comes to California a dozen times a year) and am beginning to work again. Lila is having a party Friday night (but no one is wearing costumes) and I may go to that. The trouble with my masquerade is that only you and Lila and I would wear masques, and everyone would be uncomfortable.

Anaïs, Pepe [Zayas] is coming to California on his next furlough, but I have a fear something is going to happen to him. He doesn't know how to kill and I don't think he can learn. I wish they would only choose those who are hell-bent on destruction anyway and leave Pepe out of it. This Korean War is the most ridiculous of all wars; everyone going through the motions and no one knowing why. I like your theory on the transference of explosions. It's the only theory that rhymes with the newspapers and the facts. Anti-Communism is only a militarist's hypothesis designed to disguise the real confusion. I say upward and onward with the explosions you describe of imagination and passion and illumination.

Love,
Jim

March 24 into April 1951
Mexico with Rupert

May 10, 1951
New York

Letter from Anaïs Nin to Rupert Pole:
New York, June 1, 1951

Work, work, work and wondering how long it will take. Articles are being prepared, and each week I stay means a hundred dollars more into our travel account, but I am wondering how long I can hold out. Now it is a week I have left. No letter from you yet. When I can, I will phone you, as if one is capable of talking only three minutes; after seven o'clock it costs only $2.50, and to hear your voice means so much. I am bringing back a list of long-playing records that we can study together. The best news I have is that I am at page forty-five of the last rewriting of *A Spy in the House of Love*; each day I do a few pages.

But the time is long, and Doña Juana is dead and her heart is in Sierra Madre; now it is only a shadow of herself walking down Fifth Avenue. I do want you to help me, while I am away, in an examination of ourselves: I want to find out the things I must do to make you happy, and I want you, if possible, to find out what makes you irritable, because later on, alone, I realize how my self-confidence gets low, feeling I do nothing right, or that I am not right for you, and I realize I sort of dread it when you are mad all the way to the airport, wondering if I am at fault. If while I am away there are specific things you think about, realize—will you tell me? It is better to face these things rather than let them accumulate.

Anaïs

Letter from Jim Herlihy to Anaïs Nin:
Hollywood, July 28, 1951

Dear Anaïs,

I wanted to talk about your diary but it is not easy to speak in the language of the sixth sense where multitudes are assembled. The idea of making sense even in a letter like this is something of a barrier, but I am determined to try.

You said you would be willing to risk my reading the diaries, and I am mostly disturbed by the fact you could consider that a risk. I would never read them while they caused you any discomfort or embarrassment, and those feelings would not disturb me. What disturbs me is that you can think I might, even conceivably, reject you on the strength of them.

Whether or not I ever read your diaries is inconsequential to the major point I am trying to make. The woman you are is the woman I know, understand, and love. What went before could be the greatest record of prostitution and murder on any level you choose, art, love, religion or all three, but they could never destroy one segment of my present regard for you; they could only throw more illumination on the magical processes that have made you what you are.

Love,
Jim

JULY 1951
Sierra Madre

Letter from Jim Herlihy to Anaïs Nin:
Hollywood, August 13, 1951

Dearest Anaïs:

I wonder if you know that you have shown to me and given to me in every conceivable way a kind of love that I have never known before in my life, and I am completely overwhelmed by it, don't know how to express to you how it feels and how more than grateful I am for it. It is not (as in the past with other kinds of love) that I am afraid of it, don't want to accept it, or am thrown into a sea of self-doubt (am I worthy of this, etc.). It is not a question of any of these things. It is a kind of shock, a kind of believing yet unbelieving. I really trust you and believe in you; so I know what you are giving me is real, is felt, is what it is. Yet, at the same time, it is the kind of love I have always believed in (and tried myself to give), but the kind that I have never found anywhere and had begun to despair of. When it finally appears, and appears so completely and so brilliantly, without complications or demands, I don't know what to do with it. I know that your love demands nothing of me except what I am; yet, of course, I love you so completely that I feel inadequate and want to give something else, something more and completely wonderful; yet I don't know what or how. All I know to do is what I would do for myself, to go to analysis and make myself healthy, to do my work to the best of my ability, and to be true to the things in which both of us believe. Of course what I am saying, in effect, is that I feel what you ask of me is only what I ask of you: that we not destroy ourselves through neurosis, and are consistently true to what you call the "true self."

Love,

Jim

Letter from Anaïs Nin to Rupert Pole:

Mexico, August 1951 [where Nin was vacationing with Hugh Guiler]

My darling Chiquito:

You were right (as always). When I got over the pain of leaving you with so much work on your hands, I began to feel the liberating purpose of the trip and to be happy.

I have my cousin Charlie Cárdenas' complete collaboration; he is very clever and has handled people even more complicated than the Mexicans—the Cubans. But he has set certain conditions that I don't tell my mother yet because of her health and that I don't tell Thorvald because he is neurotic on the subject of divorce. He bore up ten years with his first marriage because of a prejudice born of our own parents' separation. Also, he feels Hugo was a good balance to my "romanticism" and doesn't believe anyone else could be. Charlie hates scenes and quarrels and wants my divorce all done. He is convinced that I am serious, and he always believed in me in spite of his business associations with Hugo. So there is no pressure or drama, just quiet activity. I couldn't be more married to you than I am. All these legalities seem absurd.

Do write me, my darling. I feel sure it will be done twelve weeks from Monday. During the weekend nothing could be done. I believe I can stay in Mexico City.

Your *Mujer*

September 5, 1951

Return to Sierra Madre from Mexico

October 1951

Return to New York

October 8, 1951

Houghton Mifflin turns down *A Spy in the House of Love*

Letter from Anaïs Nin to Rupert Pole:

New York, October 22, 1951

My Chiquito: Last night even after an hour dancing in Brooklyn with Lavinia Williams' class of black girls training for a show, I could not sleep for longing for you. It sometimes hurts and is against nature. Yet, darling, you must help me not to run back to you before I have done what I must do. *If I succeed in my work I won't have to return to NY for the rest of the year.* Listen carefully: the regular publishers are gradually failing because the new trend is cheap books (they were too greedy). The policy of Signet to *reprint only* was made when they were afraid of being cut-throated by Big Publishers, but now the Signets are so strong that they are slowly seeking ways out of this policy. I suggested to Miss Porter of Signet that she add *Spy* to their list. Lila (who moved here) won't have a copy typed till Tuesday for her; I am working very hard and efficiently.

If this comes through (as you know I am not counting on this only, the manuscript is everywhere—Farrar and Houghton Mifflin and after that Viking, and others) I will get an advance of $2,000, which means no trips to NY for a long time. Help me to stick to this. As soon as you say come home, both heart and body come to life and say yes, yes, and the career and money go overboard. I will do all in my power to get back Friday, but, darling, it looks impossible if Miss Porter (who has also been reading *The Four-Chambered Heart*) needs *Spy* Tuesday. Pfeffer does not handle her. I met her through George Amberg, author of *Ballet in America*. At the same time Gore has been put in charge of a Signet anthology of new writing (to contain fiction, architecture, art), and will take a fragment for that.

So far I have what I earned, $500 *intact*, and have spent only what you gave me. We eat at Larry Maxwell's apartment, where I am staying. I have no rent (Maxwell feels guilty). Lila types for me in the evenings. I go three nights a week to Lavinia's dance class. I have had no parties, no theatre, no big evenings of any kind, nothing but *work*, except for dancing. I am working on an introduction to *Spy*; Geismar is working on one of his own. Friday night we compared notes; I will earn $100 for an article on Christopher Isherwood's new play, which I have been allowed to read ahead of opening night. This is all humanly difficult.

I know you must be lonely too, and I worry about how you are eating and sleeping, Tavi and the garden. But if I return with a Signet advance, you can start our house if you prefer that to a trip. Tell me what we have in the bank now, plus the $500 I have. I decided against sending it to you in a money order because it costs $4.75 and you'd have to go to LA and then to the bank. But if I get another $100 this week I will send it, having the last $100 for emergencies.

So much work that I have had no time for my immigration status, no time for anything personal, but no matter how frenziedly busy I am, there is always a bad moment when I realize I have been away for what seems like years and can't stand it one more minute.

Te quiero, te quiero, te quiero, A

Letter from Jim Herlihy to Anaïs Nin:

Hollywood, October 1951

Dear Anaïs: It is late Friday night.

I am delighted that you are doing so much in New York, seeing so many people and things that are impossible to see here. Rupert has not called and probably will not;

he often says he will, but that is just his way. I will call him perhaps next Thursday and invite him for a talk or something, but I don't think he will come. You and he looked so goddammed handsome together, like a prince and princess from a lavish illustration of a fairy tale.

(Is it wrong of me to write these things to you; no one reads this but you, do they?)

I hope you can do something on that end of the tightrope that will keep Hugo from expecting you so often; NY is good for you but the frequent trips are not. Make up something about a motion picture scenario; you can always say the deal fell through at the end. The going to and from must be a terrible strain. I must get some sleep, had only two hours last night. Your letter was wonderful. Please give my love to Lila.

Love, Jim

NOVEMBER 1951
Sierra Madre

DECEMBER 1951
Return to New York

THE TREE AND THE PILLAR

1952

New York, January 1952

The Tree--------------------->and<-------------------The Pillar
Meet

On one end of the trapeze there was a Tree.
On the other end a Pillar.

La Guardia Field. There was snow on the ground. Hugo was the tallest in the waiting crowd. He did not kiss me on the mouth. He bent down with tenderness. "How are you, little pussy? I was never so glad to see you."

A few months ago he greeted me less expansively. For five years he has been analyzed by Dr. Bogner. His withdrawn or brooding or sulking moods have disappeared. That was the way he controlled me, punished me and contradicted his verbal goodness. "Go away if you please. You are free," he would say, but his whole being resented giving me freedom. Now he smiled. He had been alone for a month. Most of his month was spent on business with Roy Archibald, married to Graciella Sánchez (Eduardo's sister), and my cousin Charles de Cárdenas (in Havana), so he is now part of the clan. He also does business with Thorvald in Mexico. So he drove up and placed my bags in a new Ford convertible, and, as always, began to tell me news of the business, the losses in investments, or the gains or hopes for the future. He now has an income of $1,000 a month of which I get $400 that I spend either on air travel or as "earnings" in New York that I deposit in the Sierra Madre bank as booty from my trips here. Hugo told me about the business and about Dr. Bogner and his various difficulties (no longer with me—we went through that hell together). After years of estrangement, we took up a terrible battle for truth, for our own rights, we tormented each other, and yet we also clung to each other. Once, while considering a separation, we walked around Washington Square observing all the "changes," the torn down and vanished buildings in which we had lived a part of our lives. The house on McDougall Street where Gonzalo and I had our first printing press, vanished; the old Provincetown Theatre, gone; houses on Washington Square where friends gave parties. And the despair at the idea of parting was so great our battles stopped. Hugo had fought to restrict me, and I to free myself. Imperceptibly, we were reconciled. Each time I come, he is more changed. The opaqueness, the sullenness, the coldness and anger vanished. He began exercises and also changed his body. He lost weight. He took up making 16mm movies. He was less obsessed with business, less angry at my trips.

We were driving in the wide, warm, spongy-springed car, soft-cushioned, silent. The radio was clear. We drove along the East River, passing by the new United Nations building. The feeling I had is that I was tired of my tasks in California, of my household duties, the endless petty rounds, and that all was not well with my body—I had a stiff back, a pain on the lower right side, headaches. As soon as Hugh was there I felt small again and I could abandon the reins. I abandoned myself to his care. He would say immediately: "You must get X-rays." He had already made an appointment with Dr. Bogner. Other times, if I return with eye strain, I go to the eye specialist—I feel I can. I feel protected. Hugo has solicitude, and concern. He told me about his health. In his last letter he confessed that in his friendships (men or women) he perceives roughness, a lack of consideration of his feelings on their part. He feels protected by me, and in another realm I am a good critic of his films, a good guide in the world of art. My friends have become the public for his films, as they were for his engravings. He benefits from my relationships with colleges and art groups. I have shown *Ai-Ye* at the Coronet in Hollywood. I showed it in colleges. We now are able to recognize in what way we gave to each other even if at the same time I rebelled against Hugo the businessman and my duties as the wife of a businessman, and even if he rebelled with jealousy of Anaïs the artist, he still made sacrifices as my husband. Today we can thank each other. It is he who has given me the fur coat that keeps me warm, the doctor's care that keeps me well, the objects that surround me in New York and in California. He bought me the calfskin bag in Mexico, the fur shoes in Hollywood, the dress I wear. It is he who pays to tint my hair so the grey won't show, for the vacations in Acapulco that keep me slim and firm-bodied. I owe him all, my writing too, an *objet de luxe*. His care, his work. We talk about his film showing in Hollywood. We came home, entering the apartment I designed, the wall-to-wall grey carpet, the blue-purple felt curtains, the fuchsia bed covers and couch covers. He bought the paintings, the Dan Harris, Alice Paalen, a reproduction of Chagall, figurines like Chagall made in Mexico. The apartment has a sensuous quality I like and that Hugo does not accentuate when he is alone. It extends its enveloping softness. Already I felt pleasure here that I do not feel in Sierra Madre. It is the Chagall setting, the richness of tones, the Japanese dolls.

Mail was on my bed table, publishers saying they will not publish *Spy*. "A romantic fantasy," says Pat Covici of Viking. "Brilliant but pornographic," says Putnam. Farrar and Strauss will not do it. Letters from éventails (I don't like the word FAN in America, which reminds me of an electric fan, and it has a flavor of Hollywood, so I say éventails). A membership card to the Museum of Modern Art. Announcements of Alice Paalen's exhibit. A telephone message from Thurema.

Hugo had a small bottle of champagne for me. Already I had that feeling of gratitude, of shelter, of a moment when I can let myself go and be helped, sustained, mixed with anxiety about time, the long time I have to be here separated from my other life. I emptied my valise. I have learned to live with few clothes, keeping light to travel. I have only two winter dresses, one for evening, two good summer dresses, two bathing suits, scarves, two handbags, and a few old dresses for the house.

The moment when Hugo made love to me I withdrew into darkness, for it is his act and I cannot respond. It is, for me, an act of thanks, of tenderness. No change in this—I cannot draw closer, or desire him, or respond. He is a friend, a brother, a father, everything but a lover. The first night, exhausted by the trip and contrary emotions, I fell asleep, and I slept late in the morning.

The second night I had anxiety. Time became enormously extended. In the silence I felt the great distance that separates me from my other life. I felt the pain in my body, and again an irresistible desire to return to Rupert. Then the days began to fill up—intensity, pressure, visitors, duties, pleasures, *The King and I* with Roy and Graciella, Eduardo talking about his stay in France and Italy. But a strange irony: all the friends I nourished with my tales of life in Europe have gone to Europe—Frances Brown, Bill Pinckard, Woody Parrish-Martin, James Broughton, Curtis Harrington, Kenneth Anger, Kermit Sheets—but not I.

And now when Hugo says we can go next summer for four months I do not want to go because I don't want to desert my other life.

In this life the horizons are limitless. I get in touch with France, Italy (where *Under a Glass Bell* is, as is Hugo's film), with the insight of Maxwell and Anne Geismar, with the ballet wisdom of George Amberg, with the echoes of Tennessee Williams' neurosis and creation, with the great gentleman of letters Victor Weybright of Signet Books, with Gore and his *Prince Malade* poses, his depression and absence of love, his devotion to me disguising the anger against his mother and sudden cruelties towards me when the two images are juxtaposed in his being.

Flavors and scents from many worlds. Hugo sometimes gets up at seven when he goes to Dr. Bogner and lets me sleep. As Jim writes me: "Whether you are Cinderella in the scullion (in Sierra Madre) or Cinderella at the Ball (in New York), the wand is in your hands, Anaïs." Of course, I never believe this. I feel controlled, dominated and pulled by my two loves at each end of the trapeze, and my ingenuity against catastrophe seems like paper umbrellas held over a precipice. At this end of the trapeze Hugo brings me breakfast in bed. It is eight o'clock and I see nothing but sky from my bedroom window, the curtains open now.

When Hugo leaves, I dress. I see Dr. Bogner and she unfastens the band of iron around my heart. I cannot make a decision. It would be forced. I cannot make a choice. I can only live as I live now in spite of the danger and the pain. Greater pain and greater danger would result from either choice of lives.

Millicent arrives and says good morning, and we exchange news. She knows my life and never blames me, whereas for others she is severe and religious. She does her work mechanically, but she is utterly free to come and go at whatever hour she pleases. Her hair is grey, and my devotion to her and hers to me have lasted for eleven years. "How are the children? Your health? Your eyes? Mr. Hugo got you glasses but you don't use them." She was jealous of the laundress, so now she does the laundry just to reign alone.

Now I am smartly dressed in a white woolen dress. Winter white. I will see Lila who shared, for a time, in the other life in California. Writing and analysis are our themes. A love that cannot be fulfilled for her because I cannot love a woman as Lila loves them. I will see Max Pfeffer who, since the death of his wife, has become completely irrational. I should break with him, he is bad for me, yet I can't, out of loyalty. Hugo will meet me for lunch and we will go to a French bistro or eat a shish kabob in a Turkish restaurant.

We will shop for gadgets, which he loves as children love toys. I will buy something at Brevoort where I have gone for eleven years. I will tell Dr. Bogner a dream. I will pick up a film copy for Hugo. I will see Louis and Bebe Barron, who made my records in San Francisco and now truly live a Village life on 8th Street.

One night William Kennedy, formerly of Duell Sloan and Pearce, came after interviewing me on the radio. We listened to the recording, and then I realized how Kennedy destroys all he touches by his madness. And he was my "editor" for *The Four-Chambered Heart*. We also looked at Hugo's film of zoo animals in Acapulco, which will be on television. We went to Harlem, and I danced the mambo wildly. Three evenings a week we study dancing with Lavinia Williams for an hour. She made Hugo lose his extra weight and lose his stiffness. She communicates warmth and joy even though she suffers from a lack of confidence. We do barre work like ballet dancers.

Lawrence Maxwell disguised his blindness and shallowness by having a bookshop but was exposed as a poseur who cavorted with dancers, actors, writers, who live a life he does not understand. I believed him to be devoted, and he is verbally, but in matters of money he has always been ready to exploit me. He keeps my books for speculation and higher sales in the future. Carter Harman I do not see because the impulse that once drew us together was unfulfillable then and caused too much havoc. His wife discovered it. It estranged them. When I no longer desired him, he came to me, but as music critic of the *Times*, the composer of ballets who sought to continue his marriage, he was unnatural and no longer glowing. He was an echo of my violent desire for Bill.

Hugo takes women out, but apparently he has no love affairs. I no longer think of it as a great tribute to me, but as an unnatural hostility to all but the one woman in whose love he believes. He does not seem to want anyone even when I am away.

Dr. Max Jacobson said I have no more anemia after having it for all my life. Hugo only has a cold now and then, small mishaps. But neurosis still torments us.

Christmas night was spent with unattractive people: a countess in a genuine damask dress, Charles Rolo the monologist (masturbations of the mind) telling me there are no great novels, having made no effort to encompass my work as a whole although he praised *The Four-Chambered Heart*. But he is included in the first number of the Signet anthology of new writing and I am not. I am not in the Museum of Modern Art series, not in the Poetry Center readings. It is not a neurotic fantasy of rejection. It is a very real, very opaque silence around my work. It is like my father who did not see us children, whose eyes never noticed except to scold or expose a flaw, a father who was either busy working or not at home, or who, when he was at home, read a book at meals and asked us not to talk at the table. Invisible children.

And that is why being the Invisible Woman of Literature hurts me. Dr. Bogner works, with subtle probings and subtle labor, to separate the facts from their association with the past, so that they stand as facts powerless to poison me. In New York you are confronted with your Man of Achievement problem, because here, among millions, in a robot capital, the matter of identity is essential to survival. Either you are someone, or you are a robot of a vast ant organization, and sink into anonymity.

A good month. I saw Victor Weybright again. He is not sure about *Spy*, he is wavering. I get a negative letter from Hiram Haydn. The telephone rings and it is Christopher Isherwood saying goodbye, not proud of his play *I am a Camera*, but glad of the money to go to England with and to invite more young boys to share his life. Tennessee Williams appears with Oliver Evans, the writer he protects. He plays a role. I can see today why I did not like him when I met him ten years ago, before his fame. I like his work and not his role, his utterly insincere voice. Oliver brings me bad stories, which he says were influenced by my stories.

Jim Herlihy is moving to New York.

Lila spent New Year's Eve with us at the Savoy. A frenzy of dancing, humor, genuine gayety, and above all this physical closeness, the currents between people, the reality of the body's life, the joy of dancing, the interest and tensions and attractions between man and woman. Hugo has become a good dancer. Lavinia arrives in white, dazzling and beautiful, but not believing in herself. She danced and held everyone's attention. Thurema came. I am pleased that Teddy, the seventeen-year-old spoiled star of the Savoy, a prizewinner, sought out by all the girls, suave and electric, *raçé*, courts me vehemently, of course. I laugh too, and say to Lila: "It's only the grandmother complex at work!" Hugo is dancing, smiling, a gay and carefree night. No need to drink or make efforts. At three o'clock, before falling asleep, I think of Rupert because it is midnight in

Los Angeles and by contrast the two lives are dissonant. He is having dinner at Henri's, the best and most expensive restaurant with friends of his family, older and uninteresting people. Then, of course, he will rage at the Ford not flying, stopped by signals.

Hugo is very pleased by my appearance. We are at peace. His shedding of "roles" has brought out a new Hugo I like. Humanized. *Present.* Vital. A little more and he will possess some of that electric charge I liked in Teddy that made me, for the first time since my return to New York, desire Rupert. Assurance, humor, the qualities of maturity on display at Woody's and Stanley's the next evening. Sparkle and ease... But this is not the adolescent sparkles in space, the fireworks that strew ashes. It is what happens when you conquer anguish.

At Charles Rolo's, the guests are intelligent and quick, but not deep. I see Luise Rainer, again married and mother of a little girl. Hugo talks now. He does not efface himself. He is joyous in company. He teases girls and is no longer jealous of the praise I get.

At the post office, where I go every day with a letter for California or a small present, the clerk, who knows me, wants to know who this forester is.

Charles Rolo reviews books for *Atlantic Monthly*, but it is Maxwell Geismar who truly flares up with enthusiasm over *Spy*. Rolo had reservations.

No one has given my writing the wholehearted devotion and active continuous service I have given to other writers. Miller urged me to write, inspired me, trained me; he gave very much to my writing. Gore did too. Gonzalo only when he printed. Hugo gave the most. No, I was wrong, I *have* been given devotion. I forget this when I am still walking the streets with an unwanted *Spy*. Gore gave me practical devotion, Henry artistic, Hugo human, Gonzalo a physical service not born of faith in the writing; he did not have that.

Today Hugo feels more secure as an artist. He can give big parties alone. He has friends of his own. I believe in his films. They are poetic and very tender and human.

He fell in love with all that I loved in Mexico. Acapulco is my paradise on earth. Hugo filmed it all.

Last night I was treated by the members of the Living Theatre like a celebrity. I wanted to laugh when one said, "If I call up, your husband won't say no? I know that Steinbeck's wife had to protect him against too many visitors."

I gaze at shop windows but I don't buy because in two weeks I will be at the other end of the trapeze, and there all the money I have is needed.

On mornings Hugo does not have to get up early, we sleep until nine when Millicent brings breakfast with the mail. This, to me, is the height of luxury. The phone rings. Ex-lovers who do not forget. Even the one in Paris years ago who made love to me in an elevator. Or Hugo's family, the mother insane, on their way to England. Friends from New Orleans.

Larry Maxwell says, "There is a letter for you from California." By a system of personal chain reportage Larry knows all I am doing.

The black and white calfskin is wearing down after four years, so Hugo gets me a leopard belt—the head has its eyes closed and retains its moustache. I send my children in Hollywood (Jim and George) cologne for their amorous life. They have mentioned a new erotic décor in Hollywood: black sheets. So our yellow ones here and the coral ones in Sierra Madre seem bourgeois now.

Charles Duell pursued me vehemently during our year of partnership. I was truthful and sincere in my refusal. But he turned away in anger, especially after failing as a publisher. I wanted at one time his beautiful wife for Hugo, but her figure was too matronly and my fantasy bore no results. I still dream of a perfect wife for Hugo; then I will be sad but resigned to a fate I deserve, and I will go away to the other end of the trapeze.

Hugo Guiler (l), unidentified man, Anaïs Nin

At 35 West 9th when you ring the chimed bell, the white door opens on a white square entrance room carpeted in grey, with mirrors on the wall. The telephone is ringing. Millicent is ironing in the kitchen. You can see into the large salon, its walls almost all covered by curtains from ceiling to floor that deaden sounds; the grey carpet softens footsteps and makes the deep fuchsia-covered benches around the room the only warm, rich tone, a blending of a masculine color of neutral grey and a feminine color of fuchsia. People are entranced by the colors and textures. The solid color is a wonderful frame for heads.

The telephone is ringing so I shed my fur coat and answer. It is Wifredo Lam, negro-Chinese painter, protégé of Picasso, in New York for a week, from Paris, en route to Havana. His voice is plaintive, anxious, and requesting. He expects that Hugo (Hugo still playing the role of protector) will help him sell his paintings. He needs to show proofs of his activity in *Cahiers d'Art*. He elaborates intellectual constructions and all his cohabitations take place in space, not on a level of human gravity. Before me he wants to shine only with meteoric lights. As a human being he stands like a Giacometti statue, abstract and distilled in violent contrast to Teddy Brown, the negro of seventeen who says all he has to say with dancing, whose body is charged with fireworks, a magnificent agitation of a million particles and cells. Every negro who imitates our abstract mental language serves to betray its absurdity. Unconsciously Lam presents us with an intelligent burlesque of our theories, concepts, and analysis. The formulas and the jargon. So he cannot dance. He is the painter of white ghostly puzzles subjected to dissociative forces.

My reading from *Spy* on Sunday, arranged by Ivan Davis in such a childish, ineffectual way, was rescued from total failure by the efforts of Lila, Hugo, Lawrence Maxwell (Ivan was sending typewritten cards that were not even prepared ten days before the reading).

It was a shabby place, like some ex-burlesque hall, without the humorous shabbiness of rococo European places. It was too late to back down, and many wanted to hear the new manuscript that Bobbs Merrill, Houghton Mifflin, Viking, Farrar Strauss and Young have rejected. I wore the same old black jersey dress pictured on the cover of *The Four-Chambered Heart* because it is a dancer's dress. It reveals the figure, uncovers shoulders, while swirling and moving in rhythm. I presented an outline of the design of the novel and read fragments of it.

There were about 100 people, of them 80 friends. No official figures, no invited celebrities (no William Carlos Williams, no John Cage, no Oscar Williams, no publishers, no Laughlin, no critics, no Charles Rolo)—but *friends*—deep, kind, loyal friends. Anne and Maxwell Geismar, Lila Rosenblum, Lawrence Maxwell, Woody Parrish-Martin, Louis and Bebe Barron, Stanley Haggart, Lavinia Williams, Eduardo Sánchez, the Davises, the Kennedys, Max Pfeffer with two admirers, Thurema.

The sincerity of the response, the rapt silence, the stirred faces, the words of praise. I know by this the work was right and deep. The reading itself was praised. It enhanced the writing, made it more comprehensible. The danger of poetry, said Geismar. Some truths were crystallized in the outline, even for Hugo: "I understand it better." Everyone was moved. I was happy, in good form. I felt what I read. I was happy to be told I looked beautiful. The change in Hugo too, healthy, roseate, shedding a Jupiterean glow, no more jealousy or envy, a certitude of his own value. He is no longer grey and withdrawn. He looks and acts serene, generous, free. He keeps me, but he plays the host, at ease, accepts compliments, performs introductions, enjoys what there is to enjoy.

Ironically I have to cover a "loss"—the reading cost me $25! Ironically the celebrities went to the Living Theatre opening of Rexroth's *Behind the Mountain* and were forced to admit the play's stupidity.

The absurdity of my position in letters was made clear to all that day. I am in a private world, recognized by very few. Suddenly I find my humor, due perhaps to Dr. Bogner. She has me examined physically, and X-rays showed no illness, there was no anemia, no cause for the pain in the abdomen, which I believed to be a tumor, no cause for the pain in my back. So we have to accept I am presenting the symptoms of my father's illnesses: sprained back, abdominal pain—the twinship continues.

Every day Hugo and I drive up together to Dr. Bogner, to X-rays, to errands, to a coffee and doughnut shop, to see Rollo Williams' new lighting miracles on Madison Avenue, to see *Jungle Headhunters*, to see Alice Paalen's painting exhibit, to have cocktails with Eduardo, and to make new friends: Frances Keene and her husband. We go to Brooklyn to dance with Lavinia.

The telephone rang after the lecture. The Geismars were moved and understood me better. Lawrence Maxwell says, "I worship you." The telephone rings again. Paolo Milano, the great natural comic and the author of the introduction to Viking Press's *Dante*, discoursing on me and refusing to speak of his own writing. "*Il y a du vrai et du faux en vous, une naïveté fondamentale. Tout est si jeune en vous.*" [There is the real and the false in you, a fundamental naïveté. Everything about you is so young] I finally obtain the secret underlying his buffoonery: his hidden writing. We quarrel in a friendly way; he does not believe in the poetic novel, or in psychoanalysis. But he is delightful and whimsical, elated, and a true mimic.

Reaping emptiness and impotence from Rexroth's fatuity, we re-write a play, a better one at the Barrons', and order Hugo to be the messenger, to deliver a message behind the window of their recording room, a mime's desperate attempt behind the glass of a soundproof room! An image out of the past, out of the dim years of his absences. Hugo was absent while we lived together. I am absent now, intermittently, but so much more present when I am here. He is happy.

My dreams reveal that the other life is cramped; its only flow is erotic. Its beauty is that of the night; the day is ruled by the car, movies, the house and garden, and impossible people.

The coffee at 35 W. 9th is made by Hugo more often than by me. He expresses the need and desire to take care of me. He is vigilant and devoted. I have made an enormous effort to redress this situation, not to be spoiled or pampered. I seek to establish a rhythm. He does not believe I have been a bad wife. No one will believe it. Hugo has felt loved, not deserted or estranged. Such a fast pace, no time for hair washing or manicures, just quick Vapon shampoos and self-manicures. Manuscripts to deliver (Jim's novel), books (Geismar's for Mondadori)...

Letters from James Broughton in England, Curtis Harrington in Italy. Woody Parrish-Martin brings presents from Italy. Talking about me as his literary godmother to a woman fashion artist who was amazed to find a "young woman." I say, "Your original expectation was closer to the truth!"

Dr. Bogner exposes the discontent with Rupert's life. *The room is too small.* Rupert and Joaquín become interchangeable. Joaquín was the thin child with big eyes who came to my bed when there were storms.

At a Rorschach test I draw whimsical figures, a dancing girl, a wistful boy, a humorous cat, and write a whimsical prose accompaniment, but my reaction is the fear that Dr. Bogner may think I am crazy.

"On the contrary," said Dr. Bogner, "I think you have a very subtle and very accurate way of distinguishing between fantasy and reality."

TWA flight 93 en route to Los Angeles, January 1952

Kathryn Winslow cannot sell my original manuscripts in Chicago for $50. Someone offers Gore $1,500 for the manuscript of *City and the Pillar.*

Hugo makes a plan to go to Italy for the film festival where his film *Ai-Ye* was shown last year and his new one may be. Hugo says, "Why do you go away when I like you more than ever?"

The gifts one makes at Christmas also contain messages to be decoded. One leopard is cut up to supply a leopard belt given to me by Hugo, a bracelet and earrings of leopard given by me to Lila, a belt for Rupert from me. Hugo wanted a lighter that shows fluid in a plastic holder and two miniature dice floating in it. A gambler within the functional necessity of fire!

And when the telephone rings again it is Gore who wants to take me to a chichi party, where I find a cocotte's apartment, a cocotte of the 1800s, and a Balinese shadow theatre, not human beings. So I leave early, and I leave him in a homosexual world that shows none of the splendors of ancient corruption but a deep freeze participation that seems to follow—too long a stay in incubation. In other words, the greatest proportion of America's population is a breed of artificially nurtured infants who will never reach maturity, symbolized by Truman Capote. Gore himself is "bored with sex and its monotony," and his work is perishing from leukemia.

Twenty-five years too late, America is discovering surrealism. The American fear of reality is so great that they not only feed on ersatz substitutes, but also on synthetic matter, on preserves and mostly on the food and pottery and ornaments placed in the antique tombs for the delight of the dead.

They can't wear the Hindu saris, or Siamese silks, but rayon acetates; music must come from machines, the theatre is on TV, books come out of automatic boxes.

Stop, Anaïs.

America is destroying itself. I don't need to analyze its self-destruction. Zombies of civilization. The process of zombification is apparent to all now. Critics are writing about the necrophilia in literature. What irony.

Useless anger. I have never been able to love America, never.

Half of one's life is too much to spend in a country one does not love. You don't love a plumber, an electrician, a microbe hunter, a fabricator of gadgets, a man who, when given a piece of wood and a knife *whittles* it away, a mechanic. The negroes gave America its only art: dance. The Jews its only intelligence: doctors, analysts, scientists. The Americans plunder the fashion designers of France, imitate, borrow, steal. But aside from science, engineering, construction, mechanics, they utterly cannot contribute anything to creation or humanity. The natural beauty discovered on the trip with Rupert only exposed, by contrast, the unrelatedness of the architecture and the life of the people to the canyons, the deserts.

It is bad to seek reasons for not living. It is always a personal reason.

I am on the plane. At seven this morning I was lying in Hugo's arms. It was raining. He was troubled by my departure. I was also. I developed a swollen throat. I did not want to leave. I felt if I stayed I could forget Rupert as a moment of intense fire and beauty, of fever and fusion but not happiness. Yet once more, I return to Sierra Madre.

Six-thirty in the evening. I return to a human being, to Rupert, to his needs, his given self, to my promises, to desire, but only to him. The life I do not respect. With Hugo now there is serenity, and comfort of the heart. When I am charming or witty, he is pleased, but I feel no pressure to be. So many barriers have vanished; perhaps the sensual one will too, when he ceases playing role of father, when he regains the virility of assertion. His indecisions, his wavering, vacillations, and permeability have made me aware of his softness. The only hardnesses were the stubbornness, the withdrawals, the anger that he practiced. But the nervous virility of decisiveness and affirmation of direct desire he did not have.

Letter from Jim Herlihy to Anaïs Nin:

New York, January 1952

Dear Anaïs,

The theme of your new writing is exciting and wonderful. I've read the thirteen pages you sent and have put them away for you. I think it's a good idea to send them to me; so many things can happen on a trip, and why take chances? I am so anxious to see what the book itself is going to be. It looks like you are going to work on the relationship with Rupert. True? I'm not going to comment at all on what you send me, but just hold it for you, as I don't want anything I say to have even the slightest effect on what you will do. But, as usual, the writing is beautiful, and I read it with the greatest of pleasure. Last night and this morning I tried to push myself through Djuna Barnes' *Ryder*, her first, and had to give it up in despair. I think one of the significant differences between the two of you is that you are readable. Another is that you are doing a better job, a much bigger one, too. Of course I realize there are few who've gone as far as Barnes, and can well understand why you think so much of her; she is fearless, also, and plunges into waters that would drown the naturalists. But I really don't see what it is in her that you identify with, apart from the courage you both have.

I had dinner with Hugo early last week, and one night we went to the Savoy where he is looking for dancers for his 42nd Street film. (I suggested a title for it: *Top of the World*, which is a nickname for 42nd Street.) I haven't heard from Hugo since, but we had a fine evening, danced and watched. I love the Savoy.

I'm glad you're working. People who wonder how you can write so beautifully should know how much time you give to it, how devoted you are to it.

Love,
Jim

JANUARY 24, 1952
Return to New York

Letter from Anaïs Nin to Rupert Pole:
New York, Thursday, January 31, 1952

My love:

Got your letter yesterday on your weekend at home.

I'm writing you two letters today in case you go home for the weekend, but will also phone you Sunday.

My job is secure because the UN is so active and I have a general knowledge of other countries. So, darling, I got my ticket for Feb. 17th so as to be there for your birthday.

If you want a party for your birthday you can plan it. But, my love, I ask you one favor, *please*, for me, this time. Get the maid in for one day before I come. I arrive so tired, as I did last time, and dream of a clean house. Also it takes me a while to adjust from career to housework. It is worth the $8, believe me. I wasn't able to clean before I left and I don't want you to do it. When I work to earn $400 it seems little to ask to spend $8 on housecleaning. Don't refuse me that. It means a lot to me, more than you can ever guess.

How I wish we could go to Mexico in March! We have earned being together and carefree! I dream of the beach and you very, very close.

A

Letter from Jim Herlihy to Anaïs Nin:
Detroit, February 1952

Dear Anaïs:

At home with my family.

Had a letter today from an old friend, Dorothy Styles; she said something which deserves repeating: "Acceptance of your stories will always be much less noisy than opposition to them." I think you would do well to remember this. I know from personal contact that you are considered, artistically, a phenomenal success by many people, and it would be false and wrong of you to "accept the fact of failure." It is by no means a fact. I will say that you have not reached as many as you might like to reach, but you must realize you have no idea how many you *have* reached. I, for example, have never written to an author to express my feelings about his/her work unless I had known or met them previously. One of the major reasons that you question the value of your work is that you have had more contact with the noisy opposition, the crude, empty-headed, frightened, pigeon-hearted, chicken-livered, the sick, than with those who have quietly accepted and in their hearts thanked you for your work.

For many reasons, some of which we can guess, you have reached a kind of intermission during which the people in New York do not wish to publish you. It is only accurate to look upon this as failure if your whole life is based on their standards; otherwise it doesn't make sense. I have a feeling that you have fallen into the trap of comparing yourself with other writers, like Vidal, when actually each of your careers is unique. For good writers, real writers, bestsellerdom is an accidental state that should have nothing to do with their energies. It would be wrong for you to assume that because you have not produced a bestselling book and therefore do not have publishers clamoring for your manuscripts, that you have failed. For the love of the little gods and the big fishes, do not be afraid to continue in your own way any more than you should be afraid of departure from it. My chief concern is that the binocular vision, artist-woman vision, of Nin is being affected from the outside. I don't care ten francs what or whom you write about or how, because my belief in you, personally, assures me that you can only produce, in any terms, in any language, fine and beautiful work. By all means write the final book as you suggest you might, as if it will not be read here; if necessary, trick yourself into believing that no one will read it. I remember in one of your pamphlets you suggest this trick as a method of attaining a certain freedom from fears of censorship. It is easy to see why *Spy* has been turned down. You know as I do that it has made an unpopular statement; it has said that the love to which a human heart must be faithful may have many faces. And to whom are you saying it? To a world that is being slowly and tragically destroyed by the conflict of its legends with its realities. Now can you tell me that the failure is yours? Your opposition falls into two categories. One is the type of person who destroys himself in a greedy effort to use the power of love as though it were a household utility like the phone, to be summoned by dialing and hung up at will. He never realizes that he is the instrument through which the power flows. You tell him that his genitals are a transmitter commissioned by a power bigger than himself, and of course, in his frenzy, he doesn't know what you're talking about. The other category consists of human beings who destroy themselves preserving the myths of their grandparents; you tell them that their sorrows and failures are not their own, that the dead must be buried to bring other loves to birth, and they claw at you for sawing their crutches in two. You think the failure is yours?

You mention failure and I shudder; but I have thought about it since your letter arrived yesterday, and when we are together in New York we will talk on and on about this until I have shown you the mistake. Let me go through *Spy* with you, coldly, objectively, and try to find what needs to be removed or added to make its values more accessible to the idiots. I suppose you should tear this letter up so that no one will ever say to me that I accused Anaïs Nin of being a metaphysician, but secretly I will admit that you have struck some eternal chord inside me that makes even good jazz sound like Chopsticks.

Love, Jim

P.S. My best wishes to Hugo.

Flight 95 TWA en route to Los Angeles, February 17, 1952

On February 15th I was with Hugo for his birthday. But his birthday came at the end of an unhappy month. When I arrived (after only a two week absence) I found him tired. In spite of the fatigue he persisted in taking three dancing lessons a week and began to struggle with his film and its mechanical difficulties. He was angry, irritated, frustrated by the mechanics. He got emotional, he overworked. Then he fell ill with sciatica. Bad nights and pain. On the way to the doctor he caught his finger in the taxi door and endured more pain. His nail had to be removed. With all this he was depressed. On my own I had to confront continuous rejections of *Spy* by publishers (most recent one from Macmillan), complete exclusion from poetry readings, from all critical estimates, debates. Total invisibility and failure. With Dr. Bogner, I worked on this, unearthed rebellious and terrible anger. Appalled by them. Still busy repressing anger. Frances Keene forced me to break with Max Pfeffer (now completely pathological, having lost his balance after his wife's death and his daughter's marriage). In an effort to rise above the pain of neglect I worked on an article on the "Necessity of Symbolism" in *Modern Novel*. Reworked it.

Nursing Hugo: he had to be dressed, bathed, accompanied, both of us truly depressed, and then Dr. Bogner got ill. Hugo had barely recovered when our month together ended and Rupert began to prepare for my return.

Meanwhile, during the process of objectifying with Bogner, I had reached detachment from *life* with Rupert, not from Rupert himself. But I realized that I have repudiated *all* of our life together, that it was not for me and I was playing a role to please Rupert. *All* of it, his love of the countryside, his love of living away from cities; I like to live in cities when I'm active and to go away completely when I'm exhausted. I hate middle-of-the-road places, commuting, half-city, half-country. I hate the hours spent driving. I hate dull people. I hate driving two hours to see a movie. I hate his profession—working for government. Graver still is his dream of a house in Los Angeles. His American boy's love of pretty people, of America itself, and a total lack of internationalism. I hate his parents who are acute neurotics with bourgeois lack of awareness of themselves, who pretend to be artists but have bourgeois prejudice against true artists. One by one, every element of this life was thus negated. Nothing was left but the moment in Rupert's arms, the moment of fire and frenzy.

With Hugo it was the opposite. I like everything about him, the life he made, his treatment of me, his artistry in film, his psychological courage, his depth of vision, the harmony between our struggles and of our orientation, his intellectual development, his evolution towards wisdom and mastering neurosis, our stark honesty towards each other, the fundamental respect, the mutual interests.

When I see Rupert again his many human elements will soften the picture of our life together, but basically all of it is distasteful to me, and destructive. Of course, that is no basis for withdrawal, for Rupert would only say, "I will give up forestry. I will do whatever you want. The relationship means more to me." But that would be a role on *his* part, merely an exchange of roles. And I know too well what he genuinely wants.

Hugo was disturbed at my leaving. My only justification seemed weak: exhaustion, impossibility of relaxing, unbearable tension in New York. For this is a *part* of the truth. On the plane, flying away from New York I began to relax, flying towards an obliteration of all that seems so important in New York, towards a provincial, stupid California. Nothing tremendous awaits me.

I am tormented by pity for Hugo and Rupert. Only Hugo gave me a deeper love. When Rupert struggles to write a letter because he finds all writing difficult, he does it badly and with great effort, and I get angry when he offers excuses like a child: "I was busy," but he does not for one moment identify with how I feel. To make this clear, I have to stop writing him letters and torment him, and then he sees. If I say over the telephone I am tired, he answers that he is tired too, never any pause during which he feels *my* tiredness. His love is selfish. Yes, this selfish love he has given me wholly, entrusting his happiness and life to me, absorbed as a child is, not separate, dependent, but not to be depended on. I am his balance and his reality and his connection with life. When I am ill, the balance is disturbed, as mine is when Hugo is helpless. I can't bear the exposure of my helplessness in a sick Hugo.

I have sounded the depth and power of Hugo's love often enough. I am preoccupied with returning it. I want to surrender Rupert, but how, how? I have grown detached. I see him objectively: possessive, insecure, self-centered. At thirty-three, that is how one loves. It is the extent of his love. Hugo and I have gone farther.

I had to learn, however, to surmount my guilt towards Hugo because it created a wall against my tenderness and compassion. This wall is dissolving.

I began by writing two books for two lives. They were to be separated by twelve hours of air travel, thousands of miles, two volumes unrelated to each other. Only in the simple, white, rugged, modern-furnished office of Bogner did the two meet. The alternate design. But not here. As I wrote, the images began to overrun each other. The boundaries were not as clear. At many points, my feelings flowed from one into another. In an effort to control pain, confusion, conflict, I begin anew. The first three weeks of each life I am more or less tranquil. It is the wish of transition that disrupts me. And timing. How to leave Rupert at the right moment (not during an illness, a crisis, a critical moment), not to leave Hugo when he needs me. To arrive when Hugo wants to work on the film, to leave *after* Hugo's birthday and arrive in time for Rupert's birthday, the 18th of February. Rupert's vacations and Hugo's vacations, crises to be resolved at Bogner's in time for each. Time inflicts pressure on my nerves and on my imagination, and what I cannot foresee makes my calculations frightening (Hugo's illness, Rupert's sudden orders to go to a camp where I can't be, publishers' delays). So my alibis do not function, the creation of "jobs" as my *raison d'être* for traveling. I can't bear this tension anymore.

At first my feelings were with Rupert. The image of Hugo, retracted, severe, kind but withdrawn, was an image of duty, not of love, but today I feel for him and feel less for Rupert. For Rupert, I have a feeling of human responsibility, of tender duty now, of another kind. How can I free him? He flatly does not believe in analysis that would detach him from me as it detached me from him.

Hugo, I discovered (because he finally exposed it), contained a youthful Rupert afraid of life. He deposited (as Rupert does) his troubled dreamer in me, the restless traveler, all the burdens of his own fantasies that cause him unease or guilt (the love of travel, irresponsibility in the practical life, the pursuit of pleasure). Both Rupert and Hugo lured me as would a troubadour (two guitars, two singers, two inarticulate pasts), but then they both equally set about the solidities with exaggerated thoroughness (a concealed inadequacy manifested openly through me, as I am unquestionably unable to be the builder of economic structure). Hugo played a role to please me and to touch all the weaknesses in the other that he could and then disguise them from the world's eyes.

Endless goodness

Protectiveness

Reassurance

So many falsities—when I deserted Hugo for the sake of my life in Paris while he was in London, for evenings out, he took up art as obsessively as Rupert took up his viola.

Anyway, Hugo began to reveal—to manifest the Rupert I pursued—distress. A struggle to master his life. Anxieties. Confusion. Conflict. The armor had dehumanized him. As the armor dissolves, the revealed human beings bear a likeness to what I finally understand I am weary of: my constant comparing or opposing them, these two faces of my divided body and soul struggling to be made whole. This cleavage I cannot continue to live out. It takes superhuman strength.

Now I understand my obsession with orderliness—to counterbalance a deep, dangerous confusion. Two lives, two lovers, threaten my sanity.

When enormous shocks endanger you, you cling to small objects. The hostess recovering after an airplane crash observes she has a run in her stocking. Her mind could not absorb her own near-death or the death of thirty passengers. I no longer have the irresistible impulse to fly to Rupert. When you learn to avoid traps, dangers, suffering, destruction after much experience, you learn that the *pleasure* of desire is like the pleasure of a drug: it ultimately kills you. Out of passion I have not yet seen a beautiful life created. It seems to attack couples who are not fitted to create a life together. It seems to be born of illusion, and therefore I cannot create human life, only destruction. Rupert imposed on me his ideal of a domestic, outdoor woman, which I am not. (Could I be his mother? She is partly crippled by a rigid back, almost deformed.)

Halfway through the flight towards Rupert, I ought to be telling of the past month, not of the future.

As soon as I arrived in New York, Hugo worked on the new film. It's the most poetic one he has done. We took scenes in Acapulco of a shipwreck, very unstudied, as I walked in and out, avoiding all the cliché poses, which was, in part, suggested by the opening passages of *House of Incest*. Hugo also handled the camera in unexpected ways. I suggested the superimposition of water, which created an extraordinary myth, never done before.

Meanwhile, I am utterly defeated by the negative reactions to *Spy*; eight publishers refused it. I began to rage. Everybody is getting published except me; Carson McCullers, Paul Bowles, Tennessee Williams, and Truman Capote are reigning.

The problem is this: these writers have written fantasy and describe poetic situations in plain, naturalistic language. I have telescoped the outer and inner reality with a special poetic phraseology, always a phrase that has a *double* meaning. There is a transmutation—the external and inner are *one*. You are a spy in the house of love, a cape can also be a flag of adventure, a dress is becalmed as feelings are; it is more than a symbol, it is the integration of the two into one meaning within the object. It is a house *and* a prison.

Anyway, whatever it is (relativity of truth), they don't like it.

Max Geismar is *moved*, but I doubt if he could say why as clearly as he did with Dreiser.

It hurts.

It shouldn't hurt. Talking to Hugo in a restaurant, I consider total abdication. I started to weep with a deep sense of loss, the loss of a beautiful language I evolved that contains meaning as well as aspect. Sitting in the restaurant, the image of myself giving up a writing nobody wants appears like a vast fracture of diamonds sinking into the sea. A great loss, I honestly believe.

There are precious words (yes, I know, the word *precious* is today an insult) that have taken many lives (all of them mine) to infuse with irreplaceable meanings. No one else can do what I have done. I know that because it took the utmost of a spiritual vision allied to the utmost sensuality, to clothe in flesh such deep meaning, and it took a *life in hell*, and many lives of painful explorations, and it took even a dangerous sojourn in the worlds of madness and the capacity to *return* to tell what I have told. Centuries of civilization, too; it took birth, tradition and aristocracy of blood, it took freedom from economic slavery (Hugo) to give me my integrity; it took a body to live it out, a soul willing to burn.

Anyway, Hugo cried too. And I cried over the negro problem in *Cry, the Beloved Country* and wondered once more at the people who sacrifice their human life to create constant proofs of the eternal for the other life: cathedrals, pyramids, works of art.

Meanwhile, the homosexuals are ruling the arts and mechanics of writing. Everyone is so preoccupied with the acceptance (or rejection) of homosexuals on moral grounds that they overlook the only essential basic problem of homosexuality as a symptom of adolescence, a retarded maturity. However, they are not to blame. The entire American cult of the adolescent is responsible. He is a pampered schoolchild of Puritan parents and therefore content with schoolchildren's sexual activities with those of their own sex. But why should they make an effort to mature when all around them maturity is confused with aging and American literature?

The cult of the child produced the type that pervades American letters—arrogant, narcissistic, intent on destroying the parent as all adolescents are at seventeen when in a struggle to assert their own identities. This is in harmony with an adolescent incapacity to love, admire, respect, or evaluate. All of these are phenomena of adolescence.

The true degenerates are not the homosexuals, for being homosexual, but those who by a process of stunted growth continue to exhibit at fifty all the symptoms of awkward, aggressive, dissonant, unstable adolescence.

An older woman seeking a lover is humiliated by a gigolo (homosexual dreams of punishing the mother for her sensual desire, which a child considers as a betrayal to himself). Love between girls, as in college dormitories—adolescents are reconnecting childhood situations, the imitation of the father (lesbian), identification with mother (homosexual). Identification and imitation are early, undeveloped phases of love. The breakable pseudo-marriage comedies these couples enact are no more than a rehearsal for maturity, but how can we condemn it when our idolatry of youth and parody and shame of maturity persist? (It is only recently America has discovered that mothers and grandmothers could still enjoy a love life, to be beautiful and desirable.)

In literature, writers of seventeen, unless they have the genius of Rimbaud, can only write like the sons of Hemingway, the sons of Faulkner. It is unfair to expect more. It is also unfair to publish them until they have achieved their own *identity*. Every young writer is a derivation of a mature writer, but these schoolroom exercises should not be published, nor should they be reviewed by classmates. The production of campus magazines is not for adult consumption. The mature readers are fed baby food. It is absurd to publish echoes of Henry James and then to demand that they have the wisdom and depth of whom they are imitating. There was a time when the Europeans spoke of childlike Americans as a source of charm and ingenuousness of a young country. But these children today are more like delinquents, and both our glorification and our severity are equally exaggerated and disastrous.

Meanwhile Hugo is there to love. He has lost his stiffness. Altogether he has come alive after five years of analysis. His skin becomes warmer in tone. He had been truly *absent*, truly withdrawn. It was not an exaggeration when I entitled one diary "House of the Dead." He had been so severely *repressed* as a child. Puritanism and severity. Rebelling against his parents for his rights, to marry me. And then, sensual life crushed him with guilt. Bogner has spent the last five years pursuing a man in a cavern; he was out of contact with all but me, and ours was so tenuous. It is strange that this Hugo—vulnerable, passionate, emotional, of whom I only caught glimpses—was the one I sought in Rupert. Rupert was open; he gave me this self without guile or disguises; he admitted fears, insecurities, inadequacies. When Rupert plays a fatherly role it is never to cover the adolescent. Hugo, to cover the adolescent at twenty-five, played towards me but one role.

Now I understand my sadness the day Rupert moved in to live with me in San Francisco—because it was not only Rupert, it was Hugo at twenty-five years old whom I saw for the first time as he *was*, not as he pretended to be. Hugo admits today a vast edifice of pretenses, different from mine, a mask of passivity, of negativity that was a tortuous labyrinth of evasions as any built by a woman.

Poor Hugo. I feel now the most immense compassion. Not as free, or as natural as Rupert. And I, at twenty, took his role seriously, never knowing what he thought or felt, baffled, finally ending up being the only one who cried, laughed, decided, talked, revealed.

Hugo was immured. And I was blind to that aspect of him. True, when I came home at midnight and he was already asleep, he did seem childlike and tender, but in the midst of sleep only, and if he awakened completely, it was to say with mock severity, "You are late!"

He was so enmeshed and immured that only through painful and painstaking analysis and my rediscovery of how a young man feels through Rupert's openness, was the young Hugo revealed. But even today how different it is to know him! We wanted a dog. We wavered between the kind of dog Bogner has and the kind I talked about, a spaniel, like Tavi. It is through the absence of individual desires, likes and choices that I unfortunately established a domination that did not make me happy. I have resented this *indecision* in Hugo to the point of feeling it was not virile. I associated decisiveness with virility; it still gives me anxiety. He has no assurance, no certainty. What a long travail Bogner had to do. Yet he has a strength of another kind: the courage to confront his neurosis and struggle with it for five years. Strength to persist in his marriage when so much of it was destroyed by neurosis. Strength to persist with the bank for twenty-five years when it meant such a strain. Strength to endure me. Endurance, doggedness. But what he lacked was decisiveness of thought or act—and the act of thrusting I associate with virility. His way was indirect, passive, circuitous, Machiavellian too. To dominate me not openly, but by guilt, to control me not openly, but by sulking, by depression.

It is incredible how little human beings understand each other. And these people dare to say all has been written! They dare to uphold novels written in the distant past, when they would not go to a doctor that old, or drive a car that old, or study sciences and engineering of that period.

Sierra Madre, February 1952

Coley Taylor of Pellegrini & Cudahy calls the lie detector "vague and confusing" and Sabina "boring."

Letter from Anaïs Nin to Coley Taylor:

Sierra Madre, February 1952

I was not angry at your frankness, and everyone has a right to his personal opinions. However, I find that under cover of "honesty" and "personal reactions," you expressed a lack of human courtesy and a limited insight. The whole cause for the deterioration of publishing and writing lies precisely in this lack of literary objectivity and this substitution of unskilled emotional reactions to writers. It is you who are bored, who failed to see the continuity or the revelation of character. Maturity in evaluation consists precisely in examining your inner subjective reactions so as not to inflict them upon writers as criticism. It does not harm me because I am a veteran, but your so-called honesty harms young writers. Your letter was insensitive rather than honest, destructive and irresponsible if it had been addressed to a beginner who believes that publishers are impartial, objective, mature critics, men of taste capable of evaluating writing.

Anaïs Nin

Western Air Line, en route to New York via San Francisco, March 16, 1952

Anguish sometimes meets me at the plane, or is present at departures. I never know. A month ago, anguish and guilt filled La Guardia Airport because Hugo had just recovered from a bad bout of sciatica, because he rebelled at my leaving, because his weak state made me feel compassion and desperation too. Other times anguish travels with me to Los Angeles, if Rupert has been ill or lonely. Today it did not torment me because in three weeks I will meet Rupert at Miami and we will have our vacation together. Also, so many times boarding the plane, so many painful departures finally dull the feelings. One cannot always tear or rip; one ceases to feel the breaks. On the way to New York I will visit my mother, so old, so old, and Joaquín, and sometimes I cry: it is intolerable, I must choose one life, one love, I can't go on. To save myself from such gigantic waves, cyclones, catastrophes, I concentrate on the little things that do not hurt. It is raining. Yesterday Rupert and I drank a zombie at the Beachcombers, which was a fabulous drink, without after-effects, just elation and *la ronde, la ronde*. Hugo has written me voluminous letters. I look down at my orange cashmere coat, soft and beautiful and warm. I look at my white wool dress bought by Hugo, and a leopard skin bracelet, earrings and belt given to me by Hugo.

We are not flying yet. I am not gone yet. Rupert is standing in the rain, watching me take off. Rupert's voice and the feel of his thin shoulders and haunches in my hands stay with me in the folds of my clothes. My image of Hugo is never this possessed or desired. Hugo is always visible but not felt except in terms of compassion. Rupert stands now on the shiny wet asphalt and all I can think of is how disturbed I was when Hugo sent me a book on sex. He has been investigating, reading, questioning. Why? He could not learn from me, and that injured his pride.

I remember attempting to transmit what I learned. But later this ignorance suited me. It closed all the areas I did not wish to enter with Hugo. Now he writes me he wants to explore them, with me. At this point should I not confess that the reconciliations, the remarriages, the rediscoveries, the reunions are all possible except the sensual one? That I cannot return to Hugo sensually? I do not desire him. He has lost me irrevocably in this realm. I can only find his quest tragic, too late. Just as my finding Rupert too late is tragic. I ask myself, is this the greatest act of gratitude for Hugo's love, what I am doing, or is it truly a crime of dishonesty? If I freed him, would he find what I found, a sensual marriage, and should I surrender now, having made every known human effort to return to him and failing at this ultimate marriage of the senses? What woman was ever caught between two such ultimately destructive marriages, one in which I must pretend a physical desire I do not feel, another in which I risk all the sorrows of an aging woman loved by a young man, desertion, and the end of illusion?

Dr. Bogner waits, waits, as Hugo waits. Would he love or hate me for the truth? What would the truth create? What would the truth destroy? There is always one question one cannot ask the doctor. The doctor examines, probes, guides you into your own insights but will not answer the ultimate desperate question unless you can answer it yourself.

When a conflict is worded simply in the form of a question, you are only being a child again, asking a superior guide, "What shall I do? What is right?" The doctor never answers. The doctor is the sphinx. Such an answer is only made to children. I am a woman of forty-nine; I cannot be a child. Yet I do not know what to do. When Dr. Bogner examines my life with Hugo, she finds a good marriage of maturity and works at removing obstacles to a sexual partnership. When Dr. Bogner examines my life with Rupert, she exposes the illusion that sustains it and reveals the greatest mystery in the entire universe: that an illusion can nourish, sustain, and feed with the brightest of all flames a sensual marriage until it appears stronger, more unbreakable than the marriage of two people who have *exposed illusion*, vanquished it and *know each other truthfully*, having thus reached the possibility of *real* love, not romantic love, a *deep human* love based on friendship.

Illusion welds, burns, and fuses bodies together and produces *passion*. The truth then, is that true love does not seem to create passion. The truth of Hugo, which I respect and admire, does not arouse desire. Rupert does, even with all his unformed character, his wayward childishness, his whims, unbalances, neuroses, his errors, his weaknesses and inconsistencies.

What should I do for Hugo—set him free? How should I repay his goodness, loyalties, and generosities to me, his patience and his forbearance? Not for myself, since this has suited my twisted and broken self to live as I have, but for Hugo, for *Hugo*, who gave me all he had to give, who is fumbling in the dark, almost reaching the truth. He has had no help in this exploration, *no comparisons*; he has known no other woman—does he know that I have spent all but five years of our early marriage eluding him, not wanting him? Will he now pursue the truth until he senses it? He writes so sincerely, so heartbreakingly: "I realize I know nothing about you, that if I failed you, it was through ignorance."

Those who lack the courage to face the truth often are protecting themselves from the unbearable. Hugo is slowly approaching the truth he did not dare to find or face. Very often I felt that Dr. Bogner did not believe I should be the one to tell Hugo, that the discovery must come from him.

When the marriage was repaired, a friendship established, what remained unsolvable was Hugo's own quest for a passion I cannot give him.

Letter from Rupert Pole to Anaïs Nin:

Sierra Madre, March 1952

Querida

Do hope you got to NY all right. Storms all along west coast but only trust you escaped them as soon as you headed east. At any rate, after reading *Night Flight*, anything in a DC6 should seem easy.

Rain, rain, ever since you left but it's left everything so clean I've really enjoyed it. Very cold now too so glad you picked this time to be in NY.

Farther than I thought to Miami—about 2,900 miles, which is about seven driving days at moderate speed—so I'll have try to get off Saturday or perhaps meet you in Florida Saturday night instead Friday as planned. At any rate I'll try to be Mexican and just take this one easy, not too much close planning.

Keeping looking at map in front of me, seeing where you are and where I am, and where we'll first be together again. Much better, this both leaving home and meeting in strange foreign places, much better than waiting and wanting you so much to come back to our home. In a little over a week now I set out to find and to keep my true wife.

Till then—*te quiero siempre*

R

New York, April 1952

When I left Rupert three weeks ago we planned for his vacation in April. We were going to explore a possible job in Puerto Rico. He was going to drive to Miami and I was going to meet him there to fly with him to Puerto Rico.

On the way to New York, I thought: my trapeze is working, I have not fallen off, the two lives are kept separate, and I retain my sanity. But when I arrived, Hugo was not at the airport. What he had believed to be sciatica was actually a slipped disk or ruptured cartilage in his back. He had been in bed two days, and the doctor had ordered two weeks flat on his back. When I arrived, I took over a nurse's duties, endless rounds of cooking meals, serving them on trays, connecting the electric razor, fetching pipes, buying tobacco, pipe cleaners, newspapers twice a day, running to the post office, typing his letters, buying books and magazines, looking for his comb, etc. Fortunately he is not in pain, just when he walks. Two weeks passed. My compassion was defeated by Hugo's exaggerated demands. He indulged in *constant* demands. He refused a nurse. I worked hard with Bogner, delving, delving, above all dissolving guilt, but what a struggle to change my feelings towards Hugo.

The day came for the visit to the doctor. He was not satisfied with Hugo's condition and advised an operation. We saw another doctor. He said an operation would only be 60% successful, and Hugo was not bad enough to resort to this, so we could try two more weeks of traction in a hospital bed at home. By this time, I called up Rupert: "Please don't leave yet, I am delayed by work. Meet me next Wednesday at Miami instead of Sunday." As if he guessed that Wednesday I was going to delay again, he sent me a telegram:

March 31, 1952
Phoenix, Arizona
Anaïs Nin, care of Larry Maxwell
44 West 12th Street, NY

Arrive New York Friday night will help with your work. Have fun. Let's do our waiting together. Nowhere you can reach me so can't say no. Cancel plane ticket get money equivalent. All goes wonderfully. Desert riot of color. José impatient and in fine fettle. *Je t'aime toujours plus.*

Rupert

He was on his way! At first I was panicked and trembling. Now comes catastrophe! The situation of a nightmare!

But I quickly called on the "underground" that helps me live my double life: Lila, Lawrence Maxwell, Jim Herlihy, Millicent. I telephoned Jim, trapped by his family in Detroit: "Come and help me." Then Maxwell's where I am supposed to be staying: Larry will tell Rupert I am waiting for him at a hotel. Then Lila and Jim will entertain Hugo Friday evening when Rupert arrives. Hugo falls asleep early in the evening. But this cannot last. I could not bear it. Without guilt, fear of tragedy, punishment, failure, these can become games of chess. Only the guilt creates anguish. Today, with Bogner's help, I am ready. She shrugs her shoulders, denies tragedy, and I almost gaily face the difficulties. After all, Hugo's state is not serious, and I must merely make great efforts to protect them both.

Rupert in José, driving, driving, always impulsive and unwise, obsessional and headstrong, and Hugo on his hospital bed, in a cheerful room full of sun and sky, well-cared for by Millicent and me; I gave him a Siamese cat today.

I lie in the salon, alone. Hugo has visitors, six filmmakers discussing "society" and its problems.

Spy is in the hands of Random House.

Analysis almost gay today. Bogner: it's a matter of organization ("Take the tragedy out of it, Anaïs"). Tragedy is guilt, the fantasy that my life will end catastrophically, like my father's.

I am not my father. Yet after he died, I fancied myself in a tomb. I felt my head on marble or stone. I feel his long hair as mine. He left a diary that Joaquín destroyed.

I count the rarity: a day of lightness.

I count the rare days of peace. The rarer days of joy. Sometimes I feel I am losing my battle against depression, but today I feel courage. I think of the pleasure I will have being close to Rupert again. Perhaps in two weeks Hugo will be well, and perhaps I will be able to go to Puerto Rico.

This meeting of Hugo and Rupert in New York is the one I have avoided for five years. Why should Venus turn against me now? What labor with Bogner, what an effort to find reality, to confront and expose the fantasies. She questions everything, to untangle my life from my father's, to pursue the traces of guilt everywhere. Why was I ashamed of the Chrysler Hugo gave me, which I allowed Rupert to sell? I cannot *take*. I am ashamed. I do not have a right to pleasure, possessions, luxuries. I am proud to have reduced my belongings to two valises of books, one painting, one rug, one bed cover.

Poor Hugo, his hair almost all grey, his body heavy and fat for good now, the deep frown between his eyes hardened, impossible to erase. His oscillations between demandingness, severity, indecision, chaos, passivity, confusion. (They are like Rupert's oscillations between criticalness and impulsiveness, between irritability and passivity.)

Both Hugo and Rupert lose their belongings, mislay, confuse, forget! Bogner said to Hugo: "It is atonement, self-denial." My method was different: I didn't lose or mislay, but I gave Henry and Gonzalo all I had.

Now it is spring in New York. My dresses are few, but beautiful and smart and interesting. My bags are always ready. I own nothing superfluous, not a ribbon or a scarf I don't wear: the better to fly with, my dear!

Toujours prête à voyager.

Rupert drove straight to New York in five days, once driving all night. Impetuous, anxious, too. It was all planned: as soon as Rupert phoned Larry he would be told I was on my way to the Fifth Avenue Hotel, room 1620. At 6 o'clock Larry called me. I went to the hotel (around the corner) and prepared for the greatest crisis of my duplicities.

It was the first evening I had left the house since Hugo's illness. Hugo was uneasy, but he behaved exactly as he has through the years of our marriage. The night before he had said, "You must go out. You have been shut in with me for six weeks, you must go out. I will be all right."

Rupert arrived pale, tired and very tense. I made him take a bath and have a drink first. And then I told him half of the truth—about Hugo's accident and helplessness and Millicent sending for me in a crisis, Hugo's bad psychological state, etc. I pleaded eloquently while at the same time showing Rupert my love and passion for him, my sympathy for his disappointment, but I realized that he was actually *relieved by the truth*. He took it well, generous and compassionate. We went out to dinner and a movie, *Blithe Spirit*. The ex-wife haunts the second wife's house. I said Hugo was like the ghost, and Rupert said, "But a needy ghost." For this I love him. We returned to our room and sank into burning caresses. As we fell asleep, I said, "You are generous, and I love you for it." I pressed no decision on him. I made him see how torn I was between duty and love. At dawn I stepped out of the room, and at six I was home to answer Hugo's call. But he received me brooding. Of course he had not slept well. He had asked for me at three. Jim had answered I was asleep. He was angry. I nursed him.

I met Rupert at the Museum of Modern Art. We walked down Fifth Avenue. That evening we went out again, to a Spanish nightclub and to the *Jour de Fête* movie. Rupert himself had decided it was best for him to have a look at the job in Puerto Rico alone.

The Sunday after Rupert arrived was the worst day. Millicent was away, and I could not leave Hugo. Rupert was leaving for Miami and I could not see him. Jim was not available; he had gone to Woodstock. Lila was not free. The desperation of it! Why? Why? Anyway, it was Sunday. I have always hated Sunday.

Finally Lila came, to please me. I saw Rupert and we had lunch together. And after that in his hotel room we made love wildly, and with such passion that I felt now I can marry him. I can marry him because I have tested his love for five years and it is still deep and strong. I can marry him because in this crisis he behaved like a mature man. I can lean on him in a crisis. His confidence in our relationship amazed me, and for the first time I realized how much it means to the *other*. His doubts at the moment would have only caused three people great suffering. His confidence simplified the situation. I was able to let him drive away alone in his little Ford, with sadness but not desperate sorrow. Rupert drove away, right here on 9th Street, a few doorways from Hugo's house, and I returned to my nursing job. Jim had prophesized I would lose him. And if, not to lose Rupert, I had been forced to desert Hugo in his moment of utter helplessness, I would have hated Rupert, myself *and* Hugo.

That Sunday was over. The next crisis would be when I *could* meet Rupert. Days of nursing. A few visitors, and Jim the only point of lightness during the day, like the moment of dancing after days of crawling. The weights pulling downward on Hugo's legs. They are only the concrete image of the weights in my life with Hugo.

But at end of ten days of traction, the doctor said he was not well enough and advised us to continue until April 22nd. Rupert continued his trip alone, driving away with my summer clothes, my beach clothes, and I never went back to anything more difficult than this care of a Hugo I do not feel for, for whom I only have tenderness and a sense of duty and gratitude. The worst of the illness was not only that it demanded of me all I do not have to give, patience and time, but that it aggravated Hugo's defects, as if magnifying his love of being waited on, catered to, served, of having constantly lost objects found, of having errands done that were not absolutely necessary.

I was in hell, longing to be with Rupert, feeling so torn and divided. Now I am hoping to be able to leave the 24th when Rupert will meet me at Miami. Hoping to see Bogner every day. I got rid of the pain of defeat as a writer, but I can't make my life *whole* or my love single.

Strangely it was during Hugo's illness that I felt most definitely that the care came out of compassion, but was not spontaneous; as I dried his body after the bath and bandaged him I did not have the feeling of passion I had when I took care of Rupert. Rupert's mature behavior also placed him in Hugo's role and made of Hugo the "needy ghost."

My bed is in Hugo's workshop. I hear Hugo in the bedroom rattling papers, smoking, reading. I almost fell off the trapeze. Rupert is not enjoying his trip. He has repressed his rebellion, I know. He hopes this will bring on divorce. I am immensely tired.

Jim Herlihy helped me. And Millicent above all, who stayed all night the second night of Rupert's visit, devoted, understanding.

April-May 1952

Met Rupert in Miami; drove to Los Angeles; returned to New York

New York, May 18, 1952

It was during Hugo's illness that I was able to make a decision. I cannot tell what made this decision possible. If it was that Hugo's illness aggravated my feeling of imprisonment in my marriage, if it was that Hugo's illness demanding my continuous presence made me irrevocably aware that I could no longer bear to live as his wife, or if it was that the illness emphasized Hugo's characteristics, which I have never adjusted to, accepted, or shared: his exactingness, his slowness, his fussiness with details, his earthy, unliberated mannerisms. Or was it because the danger of losing Rupert made me fully aware that my true life was with him? *With Bogner I faced the disastrous truth: I do not love Hugo. I want to separate from him. But I am afraid to be crushed by guilt.*

All I know is that when cornered, driven to extremity of anguish and conflict, I could not choose Hugo, but Rupert.

Jim speaks of Hugo's oldness, too old for me. But he was always old. He was old at twenty-five. He was deliberate and cautious. He studied economics. He was cautious with women. He was withdrawn. He had only one friend who was a mystic and outside of mundane life. He studied the guitar. He led a pleasureless existence. He accepted tedious duties. He played golf. He was shocked when I suggested he walk hatless in the summer night. He did not know how to live. He was a kind of invalid. And now, characteristically, when he dances, he dances too intensely, his rigidity is broken, his back is strained. He chose the conservative cure, not the quick operation. Nothing that he does is for freedom or for joy.

Whenever I speak of him, I condemn. Bogner reminds me that Rupert has similar traits, that he is restrictive and duty-ridden. But Rupert dreams of a carefree existence. Not Hugo.

(I always write about Hugo as if he were in the wrong because I feel I am in the wrong for not loving him. Always feeling I should love him, that he has taken care of me, but that he has been an obstacle to what I most wanted in life, freedom and passion.)

So Hugo symbolizes a static life, more acutely now, more obviously, a slower rhythm, such an ironic and painful truth. It is at this moment that I realize what I have refused to see: that I do not love Hugo, or wish to be with him. That at night, in his apartment, I am still awake expecting *life*, missing *life*, disconnected from *life*.

Why *now*? I cannot bear to take care of his body. I cannot bear his clothes, his habits. Everything drives me away from him. At every step I have to struggle with guilt. It seems wrong not to love him; I feel like a criminal. On the other hand, in Sierra Madre, I feel that I might cease to look upon my life with Rupert as a crime against Hugo. Why should it be a crime not to love? It seems unjust, unmerited on Hugo's part. Half of me sees him compassionately. In his awkward gestures there is a tenderness that is revealed in his Mexican film.

Since I am so caught in guilt, in forcing my love, I listen to an objective third view of Hugo by Jim Herlihy. Jim is twenty-five, handsome, mobile, intelligent, talented. When Rupert informed me of his arrival in New York, I telephoned Jim who was imprisoned by his family. (Between love affairs, between jobs, he makes crash landings at his home and then cannot get away.) His father was going to make him deliver telephone books for $50 a week. And anyway, we had a pact to call on each other for help. I called him up and said, "Jim, instead of delivering telephone books please come and help me take care of Hugo and I will share my allowance with you. I need you. Rupert is on his way here. Millicent and I are exhausted."

Jim came. His atmosphere is playful, but the core is serious. He came and very lightly, very deftly became the understudy for my role, so that later, when I decided I would meet Rupert in Miami so that he would not drive back to California alone and feel utterly deserted, Jim could take over.

Hugo accepted this as naturally as if Jim had been his intimate friend. He used him as a secretary, to run errands, to entertain, to repair things. Hugo bought him a cot worth $10 and thanked him, but when Jim borrowed a tie, Hugo wondered if he would bring it back. Jim was amazed at Hugo's expectations and demands! Jim found Hugo a sweet man, lovable, but tedious and self-centered.

I struggle with a handful of images of Hugo's character, seeking probably a justification for not loving. That is the error. There is no need of justification. As Jim put it, "He is not the man for you." We are not suited to each other.

But the situation aggravates the guilt. Hugo is handicapped. Why didn't I face this long ago, act long ago, when he was younger and had more resiliency, more capacity for making a new life? Because every impulse I had, every emotion, every desire was restrained by terror, terror of Henry Miller and his cruelties (and his betrayals with other women), terror of Gonzalo's wildness and betrayal (with Helba), terror of life.

Hugo was the haven.

And terror comes from being dependent, at the mercy of another, vulnerable. This is what denied me freedom, pleasure, and all I have missed.

Today I can no longer control my desire. I want a life with Rupert without the suffocation of guilt. I also want a life with Rupert without terror of his youth, his impulses, his enthusiasm for other women, his future betrayal.

The power of guilt is what almost drove me to madness. I left Hugo in care of Millicent and Jim, with their consent and approval (I had told them I had to visit my ailing mother). I met Rupert in Miami. We had a delirious night. He had prepared for me a basket full of surprises, gifts from Haiti, Jamaica, Puerto Rico. "Because you could not take the trip, I wanted you to have all the flavors." All the gifts were thoughtfully chosen, ones I loved. Exotic sandals, a jewel box of the finest wood, wooden glasses and an Indian velvet belt embroidered with silver flowers.

He was disappointed because I was pale. It rained in Miami and our morning swim was cold. Rupert said it was time to drive back to Sierra Madre (I had promised Hugo I would be away only a week). We began our trip with the basket of presents, the unused beach clothes, a suntanned Rupert with a new considerateness. Why? Had he feared to lose me? It seems to me that he is kinder. The open road again, which seems to be the motif of our life together. It is when I like Rupert best, on the open road. I get infinitely tired from the driving after eight hours, but he pushes on. Now he is eager to get home. He wants his home. He is only intermittently nomadic. I would like our home too if it were in Europe, not sunk in the oceans of a tedious American atmosphere, uniform and like canned fruit, so externally perfect and flavorless.

We were in the small Ford, in the sun, the top down, stopping to visit monkey farms, tropical flower farms, alligator farms... Stopping between Panama City and Pensacola to lie on a salt-white sand beach, bordered by purple heather and a purple sea with white snow fringes, wavelets like froth and lace at the edges of silky waves. Always there is the telephone call to be made to New York and the vision of Hugo lying on his hospital bed with traction, cords pulling down his legs, painless but binding, of Jim there giving me absolution to continue the journey, and the tense, firm lovemaking at night. Rupert's eyes glistening with infinite dissolutions, and when I asked him what he was thinking, he answered, "Oh, my work, and where will it take us, and us, and whether there's anyone who has a relationship like ours."

Later: "The owner of the hotel in Haiti has a French wife, and she reminded me of you just a little, but she was not as beautiful or as interesting."

Bogner says that I am an accountant, that I keep the strictest Ledger of Guilt with precise mathematics she can hardly follow! I stay home for several weeks, sacrifice invitations, to stay with Hugo so that I may go away for a week with Rupert. A week. I count the days. On Sunday, as we drive along in the sun, I can visualize Millicent, who has sacrificed her freedom, bending over Hugo's demands. Or Jim longing to go out and writing me: "My real life begins at eleven after I leave Hugo asleep."

On the seventh day we arrived at Sierra Madre. It was warm and sunny, and there was so much to do to rearrange the house, to weed the garden! And I could not tear myself away from Rupert. So I asked for and obtained a few days to rest from the trip. Hugo told me it would be madness to return tired. I accepted a week. It was a happy week. There was so much to do, and Rupert was passionate and elated and he leapt into his job, and we had a race at night, after the movies, to see which one could get into bed first. This was a happy week, and in the Ledger of Guilt it was written that I had a right to it, that I had done intensive and wearying nursing. But because Rupert's free days came on the weekend and I wanted those three additional days with him, then I fell conscious-stricken. And those extra three days were *stolen* by exaggerating an earache and a bleeding sinus brought on by wind during the drive home; these three days were clouded. I ceased to respond to Rupert's passion. I was frigid and ceased to enjoy the house, garden, beach, Tavi, the sun… *I was dead*. Dead from guilt, by guilt, of guilt.

This was so clear, so exaggerated, so blatant, that I was fully aware of it. And my next thought was: I cannot bear this living like a criminal anymore. I must separate from Hugo and marry Rupert and stop feeling I am *stealing* my life from Hugo.

The impulse not to return to Hugo became stronger. I had to force myself (only because of his illness) to get on the plane. Hugo is lying on a hospital bed. He needs me. Millicent needs me. Jim has been there for eighteen days.

I told Bogner: I have made my decision. I need to live my life with Rupert.

And I took up my duties again.

"There are safety measures against danger," said Bogner. "Yours was division. Divide the loves, divide the writing, divide everything for safety measures. It is your only way of achieving balance."

"But that is cowardice, fear!"

"No. Life does present real dangers. Every human being has to learn safety devices."

If I had married Henry Miller, I would have been destroyed. If not entirely so, then Helba and Gonzalo would have finished the job properly.

My manuscripts are returned by *New Mexico Review*, by *Kenyon Review*, *Harper's Bazaar*, *Partisan Review*. All the doors are closing against my work. It hurts.

René de Chochor, a young handsome Frenchman, now acts as my literary agent. When I wanted to try a new publishing house, Ballantine, he said I couldn't because I must not antagonize Signet, and Signet's anthology is nothing but publicity for the books of authors they intend to reprint (the public doesn't know this). Signet pays

Charles Rolo double for writing a piece of "criticism" that praises Mickey Spillane and Simenon (Signet authors). Politics—*c'est nauséabonde.*

Letter from Rupert Pole to Anaïs Nin:

Sierra Madre, May 1952

SUBJECT: Her absence again

My darling, that plane looked so dark and lonely standing there waiting to carry you off. Sad trip home with Tavi especially glum. Lots and lots of work since then. Good for me, as long as I have to work I would rather keep going hard, and then if I'm really tired at night the pain of the lonely bed is so much less. These long days help too—I can work in the garden, or on signs or on our furniture till almost nine o'clock, then just get paper work started when it's time for bed.

The place is beginning to look really beautiful. What a change since last May. Only wish we'd planted more flowers.

Do hope you got Eduardo's apartment and that you're not trying to do too much the first few days.

Our relationship is so strong now I have no uneasiness about your absence, no doubt in anything you do, only a sense of utter emptiness, a feeling that all that makes my life rich and full has slipped off into the darkness like your plane and is hiding from me high in the clouds waiting for you to bring it back.

Siempre tu hombre

R

New York, Thursday, May 28, 1952

4:40 Dr. Bogner

8:30 Dylan Thomas play at YMHA

Everyone rushes to hear Dylan Thomas' *Under Milk Wood.* It is Village gossip in nursery rhyme, beer and pub humor—childish. And he looks like an overgrown gnome baby.

Our decadence—Williams, Capote, Thomas.

Decadence of poetry and passion. It is infantilism.

A day of rain. Another one of Hugo's copper plates polished. Letter to Rupert. Enjoying what I have instead of regretting what I do not have.

Gestation for a new book...

To Bogner: "I am afraid to read publically again, for the last time I read at Circle in the Square, only friends came. It was not full."

"You are easily discouraged."

I wonder.

I tried so many things. I looked up the woman who was once married to Hugh Chisholm and now works as fashion editor of *Vogue.* She loves my work, has read all of it. We have lunch together. I showed her *A Spy in the House of Love.* I suggested a series of descriptions of women dressing from different books. It would have been amusing. Proust on dresses, negligées.

Nothing came of it.

A woman who reads me with deep interest, Lillian Libman, now working for Constance Hope, offered to manage me, but when I call her up, she is too busy, she is out of the office, or raising funds for the Metropolitan Opera.

New York, May 29, 1952

10:00 Bogner

5:00 James Merrill

6:30 Theatre—*Misalliance* by George Bernard Shaw

New York, May 30, 1952

Errands

4:00 Drove to Anne and Max Geismar's

My prison… Hugo's recovery so slow. Today he is in traction again, which means helpless. So I telephone Rupert (who expects me next Sunday), clean the rug and work at Hugo's apartment while I dream of returning to Rupert.

It is Jim and Dick Duane who cheer me, who take me out. Dick is new, so he must be described. He has black hair, a turned-up nose, warm smiling eyes, a warming smile, a nimble figure and a beautiful voice being trained for nightclubs. At twenty-two, he has had experiences of travel, love affairs begun at age of fourteen, and a beautiful woman's knowledge of being protected, "kept," managed, etc. He is dressed with utmost chicness, wears perfume, but he has been beaten by thugs and knows the gangsters who rule the nightclubs and exploit entertainers. He is an echo of Pablo and Albert, not as serious as Albert and handsomer than Pablo. He is full of devotion and exuberance and playfulness. We accepted and loved each other instantly. They included me in their love affair. Dick may become another Sinatra.

Scrub, scrub the grey rug with the newest chemicals so that you are permitted to imagine your arrival at Los Angeles, a tense Rupert always nervous at my arrival and departures, an elated Tavi, a fragile, dangerous old José and the night, the beauty of the night with Rupert.

Dream I

I am standing on a narrow island, similar to Fire Island. I can see the sea on both sides. Suddenly I notice that it is covering the island, moving forward and not receding. I can see the shore of the mainland is being covered by the tidal movement. The other people are not identifiable. In desperation I look for a way to escape. I find a sandy, rough road that leads to the mountains. We sit hunched, watching the island being submerged slowly. An old man without teeth is talking through pressed lips (Reginald?). I see there is yet time to rescue some objects from the house, so I go back for all my Mexican scarves.

Dream II

Rupert, Frances Keene and I are in bed together. Rupert is making love to Frances, and I am very unhappy. He is enjoying it and saying how good it is after being sexually frustrated.

Dream III

I am in bed with Gonzalo and making love when Hugo turns on the lights and sees us in the mirror. Hugo sobs and I collapse.

Dream IV

I am sailing down the Seine on a coal barge with Rupert. I am wearing slacks, and I feel free, like a bum. A man seeks to lie beside me, whose identity I don't know. I say to him, in order to discourage him without showing it is I who wish him not to touch me, "My mother will see you. You'd better move away."

Bogner points out: the boat is free. The attitude is free. But I am not. My mother is not visible. I have incorporated her into myself. *She* will put an end to the man's advances. I am not carefree.

I have to handle a desperate irritability with Hugo. I cannot handle his illness like a temporary handicap. It seems to me to be an extension of his entire temperament. It seems that he has always worn a brace and walked slowly, that he has always dropped things, and has never been able to find things, has always called for Millicent or me, has always been unable to hammer a nail or paint a flower box, that his clothes have always looked limp and unpressed, his room has always been stagnant, that he will never have the aliveness he has *never* had.

Now I better understand his obsession with money—he is helpless and needs a staff of people to work for him.

My entire nature rejects him, from the smallest to the largest habits; I can only see what irritates me.

He snores.

He has insomnia at four every morning, reads until seven and goes to sleep, so no matter what time we get up he does not act fresh or rested. His breakfast must be elaborate, and just so. Toast must be buttered before the egg is placed on it, the coffee has to be just so... Every time he gets into the elevator he has forgotten something so I have to wait with my finger on the button. His main activity is misplacing objects where no one could guess. If he calls the liquor store he is sure to forget one item so that Millicent or I have to go out for it. If there is no spaghetti in the house he won't dispense with it. He must have it, and that's another errand. Finances are arranged so that money is never there when we need it and everything is paralyzed. Millicent needs it, the household needs it, I do, he does. He has an elaborate system to frustrate us all! He takes from Jim but does not return. It is I who share my allowance with Jim because he helps me.

Hugo inhibits all my efforts to cook by showing no interest in anything new: we eat chicken and lamb chops, chicken and lamb chops.

He wastes food, lets things spoil. He never knows of the newest theatre in the Village. As soon as I return I find out about it and then he goes there.

He never hangs a picture or beautifies the home. Whatever he buys is a gadget for some of that American obsession to diminish the power of the hand, an automatic cigarette lighter for the car, etc. After a few tries the lighter burns his suit, which he then puts in the closet where it will lie for years.

He is still, after four years, technically deficient in his moviemaking, has no ingenuity, no gift for mechanics, just as he buys the heaviest suitcase, the heaviest "portable" radio on the market, chooses the wrong restaurant, or monologues without variations or color or emphasis. When he *should* take the lead, he doesn't. In Acapulco when Annette Nancarrow got in her car with her two children, we were caught in a deluge and the car stalled in a yard of water. Hugo (who knows about driving) was passive. He demands the *efficiency of others*. His own defect in his handling of objects was symbolized in his buying a defective houseboat that ultimately sank.

He stumbles and fumbles about, hitting his head while grilling meat, setting fire to the paper under the grill, redecorating a simple room into an overcrowded, stuffy one, the opposite of casual. In the one room we have for entertaining in the apartment he would put a dining room set. The bourgeois and the conventional in him are incurable.

Everything he touches takes on that inanimate quality; I struggled so he would not dress like an old man.

But all this is wrong. As he is, he could please another kind of woman. *I am still trying to justify my non-love.*

His kindness and selflessness camouflaged all this, created a smoke screen. For twenty-eight years I could only see the kindness. He gives me this, he gives me that. He protects my life. But he never gave me *life* itself, just the care. If he had entered *life* with me when I began to seek it (in Paris), I would not have sought other relationships. He sulked. If only he had opened the house to people. I was made to feel that every natural wish was unnatural. He did not *share* my wishes. To this day my anger at his traveling with a Baedeker travel guide still lingers as one of my sins against him. He did not love life. He loved me in place of it.

Six or seven echoes of a past drama are not enough to create a relationship, yet they do. And in love the same transposition takes place. The only reason why I had such a sensual attraction to Gore was because he came when I had just lost Bill Pinckard. Gore was Bill's age, and like Bill he wore a uniform, was a writer, and he had the same rich voice and the same full, sensual mouth. They both had that pale, frozen quality that tempts my warmth, challenges my passion. This alone explains why a few years later when the reality of his character finally conquered the illusory one, the desire disappeared, and today I cannot understand how I could ever have desired Gore or considered a life with him (especially when he says he doesn't like people who are too sexually active, that he likes a minimum of gestures).

This illusion even existed in the relationship I considered the most solid of all, the one with Hugo, because we clung to it. It was based on Hugo's *roles*. He played the kind, young father. This was fraudulent. He reveals the opposite: he not only acts like a child, he has become acutely egocentric. He has no feeling for people themselves; he only sees them as objects to be won over. When I invited the whole cast of the Circle in the Square players to a party, his only preoccupation was he would not be able to show them the *Ai-Ye* film.

His permissive (unconsciously possessive) persona was a role, but analysis and his illness have destroyed it.

Illusion begins to weave its trap as soon as some facet of the person's character (including the role he plays) corresponds to a fantasy another carries, a wish or a need. The conflicts begin as soon as the real character shows its opposition to the fantasy of the other (like Hugo's lifelong opposition to my way of life, his incapacity to share it).

Hugo gave in to my need of a kind father. I gave in to his fantasy of a Japanese wife (obedient, docile, as opposed to the arrogant, independent American woman he still hates). But we were both frauds: I wanted pleasure and freedom, not servitude. He wanted total, exclusive devotion, but not from an ordinary selfless woman; he also wanted the artist. The Hugo I see today I don't love.

Yesterday, the party was my wish. I saw the troupe act in Tennessee Williams' *Summer and Smoke*. The producer, José Quintero, told me he read my work three years ago in Woodstock, and it was an initiation to his new life. Hugo begins by saying he will make the punch, and since he has given parties before, I decide to obey. I buy what he tells me. I remind him a dozen people are coming, but he is sure he knows. He buys *one* bottle of rum. The party is in full swing when after only five people have drunk the punch, it is low and weak. We have to telephone for more.

The apartment was beautiful, like a stage setting. The party was joyous. Geraldine Page was utterly beautiful and as interesting as her role, fully sensitive and aware, full of shadings and delicacies.

But when they went away I hated to be left with Hugo.

Bogner says I hate the *traction itself* as a symbol. I hate the weights tied to cords, from the feet and from a belt around the waist. I hate them as what I most hate in the world, to be bound, and I cannot look at Hugo's illness but as a part of his character. Why is it I have turned against Hugo so much? His self-centeredness, his willfulness. It is not he who gives Millicent three days off when she has a stiff back.

I'm appalled at the hatred! I can hardly bear to kiss him goodnight. I lie in my bedroom and feel lonely but no desire to go to his room. He can no longer comfort me, or protect me, or reach me. I feel pity for him at times, but that is all. I feel mostly that he has weighed down my life, and by not sharing anything with me has made it appear a child's whim. Even in Acapulco, no spontaneity or enthusiasm of his own. Always a weight to be dragged. With all his permission to go and live, he has been my ball and chain. I feel like the Siamese cat when she leaps about the room and wants to run away, chase birds on the terrace and play the role of a mysterious jungle cat.

Why must I part from Hugo with hatred?

It is possible that all this is *a case against him because I could not bear the guilt of leaving him*?

Dream: Geraldine Page appears in California as I am lying in bed with Rupert. A little while later I see them in the sun; Rupert is sunbathing naked.

New York, May 31, 1952

Cleaned and lacquered copper plates.

Cocktail for Bill Nims, Jim Herlihy, John Weldon, Curtis Harrington.

Royalty statements from Duell Sloan and Pearce:

For six months ended January 31, 1952

THE FOUR-CHAMBERED HEART forty-five returns, forty-eight special editions sold. Royalty earned: $8.42 Balance unearned: $107.28

UNDER A GLASS BELL thirteen regular editions sold, one foreign. Royalty earned: $4.05

CHILDREN OF THE ALBATROSS six regular editions sold. Royalty earned: $1.65

Total balance unearned: $101.55

New York, June 1, 1952

10:00 Dr. Jacobson

11:00 Dr. Bogner

Errands, bank, sale of surplus books

Cocktail

Evening.

I said to Bogner, "After I drove to Sierra Madre with Rupert, I had to take care of him because he was ill, clean the whole house and unload the car. As we had bought many breakable things, there was much to carry, unpack and put away. Yet the first time he was up, he said he would take the laundry to the laundromat because when I took it I paid to have it dried, and bringing it back wet would save money (60¢ or 70¢). But I told him I was already overburdened, not to give me an extra burden (wet sheets are heavy to hang out and we had accumulated much laundry).

"I know he does not intend to lack consideration for me. He is obsessional and self-centered. He felt we spent too much on the trip and that we must begin to save."

Bogner asks why I cannot be firm about such incidents. What deprives me of this is my secret feeling that *if I were stronger* I could do it all, and the shame for not being stronger makes me unable to assert myself. *Also*, there is Rupert's fanatical need to be always in the right, and to be obeyed. He wants to control me, even in the smallest matters. I must use his kind of soap (which smells of kitchen soap). I must like spicy food (which I don't like).

Last night I felt, perhaps, we are always forcing others to be what we want, need, imagine, and we never forgive them for being themselves.

Dream: I am passionately desirous to be with Rupert. We have nowhere to go. I have just left Hugo and I have been bad to him. Rupert and I try to make love in a field but find it is the back yard of a house and the family is watching us. We decide to go to a hotel, but there they try to shut out Tavi. Rupert returns joyously saying that the hotel will accept Tavi.

My impatience and irritation with Hugo are very strong. The same traits I endured with lovers, I resent in him. Why? Gonzalo snored. Rupert loses and forgets things.

So I'm bad to Hugo before seeing Rupert, independently of my relationship with Rupert.

This becomes clear.

I relate to Hugo in the same terms others relate to me: in terms of need.

This need is what I regard as my weakness, and I hate my weakness.

So I am angry with Hugo, but Bogner modifies the over-simplification. To need does not exclude love.

Anaïs, a selfish lover.

The need itself, being the state I most resent in myself, is associated with my life with Hugo, Hugo's presence. It is the *need* I resent. And it has deeply colored my life with Hugo as to present all of it as constraint, duty, obligation, responsibility (as with parents), eliminating all elements of pleasure, gratuity, spontaneity. I always said Hugo held on to me, but didn't I too hold on?

But why do I revolt against Hugo?

I have always revolted.

I revolted against Miller's friends, against Gonzalo's destructiveness. I'm in revolt against myself.

Peggy Glanville-Hicks. She appears frail and small, but she is physically sharp and incisive too, with a presence full of nervous energy and accuracies. As she talks, her focus is impeccable, her language subtle. Quick-witted and graceful. It was enchanting to find someone with such a luminous structure, a complete inner city of definite values, living and feeling only at the core. I fell under her spell. I sent her my books. She locked herself up one day and night and then wrote me. I think she understands all. Her letter and her words rescued me from the despair of so many doors closed against me.

I wanted to see her alone, but Hugo was there.

Among illuminations on music, on people, the character of Paul, she repeated that

I had explored a new territory, that I had said what seemed impossible to say, that I had raised the novel into the realm of the poem.

She invited us to visit her in Jamaica.

I found it difficult to write her, because faced with my own kind of diamond facet, I felt a cognition of light, two people reaching altitude simultaneously: there is a silence. She seems more certain, more able, more capable of navigation while still repudiating the insight of analysis.

"Who was Paul in *Children of Albatross*? Was it Paul Bowles? I know him so well I was sure it was him, as he was at seventeen."

Anne and Max Geismar. With them, it is another atmosphere. Earthier. A house. Children, dogs, garden. Earth and mind. But not subtlety.

Max is slow and laborious. His face is aged with anxiety, though he is younger than we are. Anne is small, vital, assertive, but with a humor made of thrusts, honesty like a child's, all the truths flung out, comically, but they are tragic truths. Anne and Max have reached a high point of irritation in their marriage. Max dreams of a free life like Balzac's, or the characters in Russian literature, and Anne seeks fulfillment of her intelligence by collaboration with Max on his books. But Max is modest, self-effacing and not as famous as he should be. I respect and admire his work. Even when I do not see writers as he does, he is solid and truthful and sincere, and you accept his interpretation as a work of fiction with a validity of its own. He is truly a novelist who makes novels of his studies of writers. His work reads dramatically and is often better written than the writer he handles, enhanced by his own interpretive imagination.

The four of us have a vigorous interplay. Anne's humor is a kind of courage. Max is warm and soft. He is not quite contemporary, and certainly has no perception of the future of writing. He belongs to earthy, prosaic, Germanic America. Anne's eyes are more open.

They should have revered their roles, and they would have been happy. Anne should have been a man and written the books. Max should have been a mother, and a wife.

I see her face on the Mayan sculptures, the lost Hebrew tribes.

The humor converts the anxiety. But it is in the air. They drink too much. They are cut off from the sparkling life of New York by their life in the country, by home and children.

They belong to a period I did not know (I was in Paris). He was encouraged by Edmund Wilson and was a friend of Max Lerner and the leftist intellectuals. When he writes about the young writers he does not know what to say. They lost a "world," as we lost our art world in Paris, and have not found a new one.

New York, June 2, 1952

12:00 Bogner
1:30 Peggy Glanville-Hicks

New York, June 3, 1952

12:00 René de Chochor. Discussion of hopeless *Spy* mess in Paris, *New Story*

12:30 Lunch with Herbert Alexander, Business President of Pocket Books, assistant, Max and Anne Geismar, René de Chochor
Dinner with Anne and Max

New York, June 4, 1952

4:40 Bogner

5:45 Café Brittany, where a friend says, "Hugo is marvelous. He is so complete. And he loves you so much!"

New York, June 5, 1952

11:00 Bogner

Feel free, at ease, open, confident.

Went to see *Paris Review* for a job. But it's a struggling little magazine, so I ended up offering my help.

Bogner understands that the diary has saved me, that it was my truth and my reality. But now I also see how I related to people. Taking the best, I called it, and rejecting the rest. But with lovers, friends, it was effective. It is why I did not like, want, or need Henry's white trash friends or Gonzalo's destructiveness. But I fought with Hugo. It was a permanent life and I was trying to live with it. The rebellion was active. I also ran away from Hugo's complete self and into partial loves. Always partial.

I have reached a new honesty. It is not pleasant to face the fact that I did not love wholly, accept completely, but always partially. I see it all clearly now. I can live with Rupert's desires, dreams, fantasies, directions. I can live as a forester's wife, have a home in Los Angeles, accept his adolescent patterns.

Moments of joy. An open window on windblown bushes, the cat leaping in, joyful and intense. Serenity. Hugo reads Proust.

Herbert Alexander says I'm a female Proust. Anne and Max get electrical shocks from the diary, life transfusions. I'm told I'm more beautiful in New York. And I then I remember the life in California. No, not life. It is life with Rupert on a desert island. Poor Rupert. When I made fantasies (that could become true) of Rupert acting in Italian and French films (he could be a Gérard Philipe, the hero of *Lovers of Verona*, a Louis Barrault), at breakfast or dinner time, to enliven our present life (the hikers, the horseback riders, the youth that pass by all look like dairymaids, cheese vendors, milk-fed products, like the road ads and magazine covers nauseatingly standardized), Rupert thinks of all the obstacles.

At Black Mountain College, Richard Lippold, who was teaching there, fell in love with Jim Herlihy and said his next large work would be dedicated to him. In 1949 he created *Variation 7, Full Moon*, and whether Lippold intended it or not, I saw in it a portrait of Jim. It is the perfect irradiation of swift and slender threads vibrating in all directions. It is a tower of antennas. And to this transmission tower I confided the full radiation from the diary.

Jim reads the diaries avidly, and starts an answering rhythm in the code of today's language, and it is in his youthful, perfect receptivity that I measure the life-transmitting power of all my life and work. Jim says, "It is the only book I can read that gives me not only life but the knowledge of how to absorb experience, the chemistry itself of love and art perfectly welded and perfectly told. In volume 40, I love the interplay between all the relationships simultaneously, Henry, Hugo, your father, Allendy, Artaud, and the audacities, the courage."

His words are so volatile, so full of improvisations, that I cannot retain them. It is in talk that he scales all the musical edifices. His writing is constrained by comparison. In talk, he reveals this complete psychic wave receiver and transmitter of all forms of subtle messages.

We meet at the Museum of Modern Art, on a subtly hot afternoon. I wear the light fiber shoes I got in Yucatan with Rupert, a chartreuse handwoven skirt from Vera's at Cuernavaca, a black cotton blouse. I carry a wicker basket and wear a wicker crown and veil over my hair.

Jim always says, "How beautiful you are," and by that he means to tell me the elation I cause him, the lift he feels, which he also gives me. With the greatest of ease, we gain altitude. Whether we stare at a Giacometti portrait and both see Rupert's body, or at a Duffy who makes the darkest night airy and transparent, Jim's talk, febrile and highly colored, seeks to throw back to their source the waves of illuminations he has been devouring, each one to be returned to its inception, its creator, but enriched by the absolute receptivity.

Jim's receptivity is closer to me than Max's. Max is too earthy for me. It is Jim who is my spiritual son. I experience the pleasure of fecundating, as I did when I lived with Henry.

Some of the questions hurt me. "How could such a relationship (with Henry) ever be destroyed? What destroyed it? Will I find out in the other diaries? You know, I believe you know more about love than anyone in the world. Here is the great work of our time. Yet you are not praised as you should be. You are castigated—why?"

We sit in the Café Rockefeller Plaza with iced teas. We sit at White Horse Tavern at eleven o'clock, still talking, after attending a party so incredibly mediocre at Travis Lee's that I called it a crash landing.

What Jim's writing will become, I don't know yet. He is handicapped by the false virility of American action literature. He has difficulties in plunging inwardly. He is further handicapped by a sense of taboos, a reticence about his homosexuality.

He gives me elation. I also feel like working when I return from our feast of words.

Through the growing mists of the last Martini, I tell him, like one last invocation,

"Jim, above all do not be trapped by what you *need*; seek what you truly want, not what you *need*."

James Leo Herlihy

Today, I telephoned Rupert, the artist, the poet, the musician, voiceless, wordless, submerged in a trivial and ordinary life. What does he want of me? To be plunged in a larger life, sorrows, experiences? If so, why does he cling so to the shores of his little life? How can I sweep him into anything while he clings to his present life?

"If we had ten thousand dollars, said Rupert, "I would begin to build our own house."

I asked, "Here in Los Angeles? Without first seeing the other places where life is at its richest?"

By contrast, Jim says, "When I get money from my book's publication, I will go and buy that castle in Mallorca you told me about."

Sierra Madre, June 1952

When I returned, Rupert was thin and haggard from poison oak and not eating well. A week later he looks rested and relaxed, healthy again. There is no doubt that he is in great need of me. Tonight he did not want to go and play viola with his family because it is one less evening together and we have been separated too much. I lie in bed alone. I hate the silence, the coyotes. I would rather be in a city, in the Village.

But I am rewriting *Spy*. I started angrily at first—everyone was against the fantasy, the lie detector (Sabina's conscience). Either I sink now, or I tell the story anew without the help of fantasy. Now I am interested. Half of me, after analysis, is willing to make an effort to be clearer. I do not want to be silenced, to be blockaded. In poetry there is depth. But there is also the danger of misunderstanding.

Now I am less angry. I am interested to see if I can simplify the design and yet keep the richness.

Sierra Madre, June 20, 1952

A night of lovemaking, and if not lovemaking just the bodies sleeping together, the warmth and silkiness of Rupert's skin, the contentment. I woke up bubbling with gayety, rushed to the typewriter (Rupert was asleep) and worked *con allegro e vivace* on the new version of *Spy*. At first I was shocked at the universal dislike of the lie detector personage, angry too. René de Chochor said he should not be a personage, even a mythical one. It is Sabina's guilt and should be inside her. This corresponded to what I was learning from Bogner, the projection of guilt onto others: the policeman, father, confessor, husband, doctor, analyst, critical friend, or art critic, creating this hallucination of *condemnation in the eyes of others*.

Sabina, being primitive and subjective, would see all of this (as I do). But the novelist…

I began to simplify the design, to incorporate the guilt, to reabsorb the lie detector, to take out the fantasy, and to fill out realistically. Now I am no longer angry. I feel that poetry is mystery—if you want to draw close to human beings you cannot speak only in parables. I have raged at the wall growing between myself and others. I don't want to be alone, exiled, cut off. I wept at being isolated, at the blockade of the publishers. But then I began to wonder how much I was responsible for, that my expectation of miraculous understanding was childlike. I pondered on all that Djuna Barnes did not tell us, on all that Proust left out, and on what Henry James did not reveal. I realized how much I had not told. There is a feeling of *protection* that is derived from *mystery*. In poetry and the myth you are always able to escape from a definite accusation.

Elusiveness might be *fear*.

Evasion would be a safety measure.

You avoid detection, revelation and punishment.

This truth came clearer through my condemnation of homosexual novels because they do not tell all, they do not *reveal*, they evade all the truths. Jim Herlihy and Gore Vidal do not tell the truth because of the fear of incrimination.

Obviously I could not write more about Sabina's marriage because it would lead to the revelation about mine to Hugo—I could not tell all.

It is an intricacy of design. Sabina would see guilt as a living personage following her and taking notes on her actions. But one must know that only Sabina saw him, not the rest of us.

This is the first separation I have made, an objective separation of elements entangled within Sabina. I don't know if this is growth as a human being or an artistic regression, but I must try. I have often enough longed to join the two, the woman of the diary and the artist.

When Rupert woke up I was making a parody of my second version: Mickey Spillane, Mae West, James Cain style. I made him laugh, playing it tough.

Cut out the fantasy, I kept saying angrily. But the only true doubt that finally made me rewrite the book is the knowledge of all I did not say.

There is subjective identification with what Dandieu calls the primitive's and child's emotional participation. When Sabina randomly telephones the lie detector and invites him to track her down, inviting pursuit (as the criminal does), the lie detector becomes a reality.

Bogner examines my anger and anxiety when I am asked to explain myself. I expect intuitive, miraculous understanding, or else I'm disillusioned and don't want to struggle to make things clear. The *neurotic* expects this.

Once Bogner challenged a statement I made, that the development of the modern novel should be like the unraveling of a character in analysis. She objected to this on the basis that it was only the *illness* that was examined during analysis, not the total personality. I was immediately disturbed by what she said, not because I failed to see the accuracy of it, but because until then I had taken it for granted that Bogner *understood* my work, which may not necessarily be so.

At eight the alarm clock radio begins to play Mexican songs. Through the curtain of muslin painted with yellow gouache given to us by George Piffner, no sun shows because of the tall trees surrounding the house.

But in the faint yellow light I see Rupert's face on the pillow. He is very sleepy and lazy in the morning. He only moves to throw his arms around me. I get up one minute before he does, so that I can comb my hair and brush my teeth, powder lightly, redden my lips. Then I get into jeans (properly weathered, stylishly faded and dirty à la California) and a sweater, to make coffee. Rupert is not interested in breakfast. He looks somnambulistic. "I must have coffee instantly. I feel weak and cold until I have it." We sit by the window in the kitchen, where we can see the road, the hills beyond, the Forest Service office, the beginning of the road leading to Mount Wilson. I can see the valley; on certain afternoons the valley looks blue and I imagine Acapulco beyond, ocean and mountains, particularly if the sunset is fiery. I have a house and dishes to clean, errands, signs to paint: "No Smoking," "No Fires," "Closed Area," etc.

At the post office I read Hugo's letters, in which he is gentle, wise, understanding. No sign of his present egomania or his stubborn, sulky, resentful ways. The good Hugo of the past is there, only now I no longer believe in that self, because it was a role. Today it is not that. Today he is completely self-centered.

Whatever he is, he haunts me. He haunts my life with Rupert, particularly in sensual moments, when I feel that I didn't give this to Hugo. And *I wish I could.* I feel it is a tragedy, that I cheated Hugo. I want to believe that Hugo did not inspire this, did not summon it forth, that he has a responsibility in this too. But why does he haunt me? Why can't I get free of Hugo? I am not free. *It is like a debt.* I owe something to Hugo—*I failed to give him myself.* No doubt he is in part to blame. He did not give me himself either. He concealed the greater part of himself. He desired me, but he did not give me his thoughts, his natural self. He did not even know how. He was *psychologically* blind, and still is.

Did I try to say indirectly, by my art: this is who I am?

Today, at least, I am happy when I forget Hugo. Here with Rupert I am healthy. I am no longer jealous, fearful of every girl. I sleep deeply, easily. I can be awakened by the coyotes at midnight or the boy scouts at six but I fall asleep again. I do not lie tense and anguished as I did in New York. I cut the grass. I water the lawn. I wash my hair. I sit in the sun painting my nails. Even when Reginald comes, I have a cure: I work on a rug, and I let him talk about his intestinal vagaries, the color of his feces, his liver, his Lincoln play, repeat his old monologues on Shakespeare and Ibsen… He should be in an asylum, actually. He is gently delirious. He talks about his past. I work on the rug. Rupert gets irritable and depressed. After Reginald leaves, Rupert plays with Tavi on the rug, like a boy, plays roughly and wholeheartedly.

Hugo was never open, never spontaneous. I never knew what he felt. He withdrew.

Why can't I live my life with Rupert alone? *Perhaps it is because I cannot desert anyone.*

But with Bogner I learned to overcome the complexes I would carry from one life into another. For example, both Hugo and Rupert are exacting and demanding, not easygoing. I resent their criticism and commentaries. I never ask Hugo or Rupert to cook a certain dish in a certain way and none other. If Rupert or Hugo is doing something I do not come to see *how* he does it and suggest a better way, the only way! Bogner explained that Hugo did this because he himself had long ago rebelled against established order in a such a negative and destructive way (chaos in his belongings, confusion in papers) that any loss of control, carelessness, or inefficiency in another makes him anxious: both he and Rupert need others' organization. It is their own carelessness they fight in me. It so happens I am extraordinarily organized. For example, Rupert is particularly delighted with my sign painting. I have a steady hand and I don't smudge. His delight is caused by his own inability to paint—he is impatient and careless. So it has nothing to do with *me.* If I did it badly he would be hyper-critical (his inability *plus* mine causes the anxiety of inadequacy).

Now I understand this.

But I began to not care; it is their problem.

I have been exceedingly critical of Hugo's practical inadequacy. He posed as a banker. He assumed leadership in the practical, economic basis of our life, yet he failed in it (he speculated in Paris with borrowed money and indebted us for years). True, he reached a high position in the bank, a good salary, but he used to say himself: "That's because I'm a good judge of men. I surround myself with good workers. I know how to make others work." When he finally made some capital (which was due to Archibald, his partner), he promptly set about speculating with it unwisely and impulsively and lost almost all of it. It was I who insisted the largest share should be in bonds and in the cautious hands of an advisor.

I have never had more than a month's allowance in my pocket. His "budgets" were pessimistic and always filled with errors. I see now I hated this because it added to my incapacity for making money, making me feel utterly helpless. *We hate to be betrayed in our needs.*

Letter from Anaïs Nin to René de Chochor:

Sierra Madre, June 22, 1952

Dear René: when I received your letter Thursday I spent three days thinking it over, rereading the *Spy* manuscript, in all honesty and with care. Believe me, there is nothing more I can change without betraying the inner story as I wish to tell it. Sabina cannot return to Alan with a confession, and I make this very clear, because he loves only one aspect of her. Her talk with Djuna (whose presence I explain clearly: they had met before in Paris) is the only way to reveal the nature of the truth I want to point out. Any other ending would be the classic return to the husband, to an unsolved problem of a new kind of sincerity, which is to recognize the roles people play in regard to each other. I cannot change a word of that ending. I sacrificed the fantasy of the lie detector, simplified the design, made the sequences more obvious. I also clarified, in general, Sabina's motivation, but that is all I can do. I cannot at this point pretend to be a naturalist—I am exploring the inside, and as you well know, here the ploys and denouements are quite different.

If the novel fails now, well, *tant pis*. America is not the place for the poetic novel anyway. I'd rather sink with it as it is and retain my feeling of integrity. I am being true to a new form that will evolve out of a new relativism of character.

Anaïs

Letter from Jim Herlihy to Anaïs Nin:

New York, June 1952

Dear Anaïs:

Your letter today is tucked away at 256 W. 73rd Street. First of all please believe me, I am very happy, happier than I have ever been over any sustained period, and there seems to be no way to convince you of this. I have enough objectivity in this situation of helping Hugo to last for both of us, and when I have an hour free I'm going to sit down and write you a devastating letter. I'll say nothing now, except this: I see very clearly that nothing you can possibly do will save Hugo from unhappiness, whether you act out of guilt, love, pity, or whatever; you must live your life and free yourself, and I never have been more certain of anything than this; you have absolutely no cause for feeling guilty. When you feel like that and act out of it, you are responding to legendary moralities and not to reality. You are now a big girl, and are maturing; it's time to leave home. Naturally Papa is unhappy, but this is not your fault. I wish I had the time now to go into some of these details more thoroughly. I love you so much, Anaïs, and I have observed for a long time the fact that you are tender, conscientious, kind, and loving by nature. But the Catholic part of it is atrocious. Please, for Christ's sake, take care of your duty to yourself, just this once; and whether or not you feel called upon to return to NY sooner than the end of July, that's up to you, but do not do it out of a sense of guilt and obligation. You have *no debts here*. Also, it may come as a shock to you and perhaps puncture slightly your ego, but Hugo is doing quite well without you now. What he needs is deluxe service and companionship, and frankly, Anaïs, you are a damn fool to give up any more of your time and energy and devotion to what he can either learn to cultivate in friends, or buy.

The important thing for you to know is this: *I am not burdened*! I would feel perfectly free to walk out and never come back again, if I thought I wanted to. Actually, I enjoy being here most of the time, and I can get time for work, plenty of time—I spent thirteen hours last Saturday afternoon and evening, on my own, typing. There is no reason for you to feel that my liberty or my freedom is being sacrificed. After all, if it weren't for this, I would have to go out and earn food money, but now I take my meals here and am comfortable and without tensions or needs, and you know that I am very happy to perform a few little jobs now and then that will earn the right to enjoy this freedom I have. The traction is no problem to me. Any time I want to make a plan for the evening I'll simply tell Hugo that Millicent will have to stay or that he will have to spend the night without traction. You know, don't you, that the doctor said he could do without any traction at all during hot nights. Two nights so far he has gone to bed without it, and Saturday I took the prop out from under his bed so that now it lies flat, and looks much less medicinal than before. He is getting much better every day—he went shopping at length the other day, and was going at it steady for about nine hours yesterday with no ill effects. You seem to feel that this is some kind of a hell for me, but you are mistaken. I like to feel that I am earning my room and board, and that is exactly what I'm doing in the simplest way possible. It just so happens that I would move heaven and earth for you if it would make you happy, but in this circumstance, I am doing absolutely nothing for you that is not benefiting me just as much.

Now about this unpleasant little subject of money: I have hidden away the item you sent last week, and also the little check from this morning's letter. What I intend to do, if you approve, is this: I'm going to live completely on my slightly undependable income from the gov't, and from Hugo. Actually, when I think this thing over, I'm amazed. Why should you help me when it is Hugo that I am helping? If I have trouble with the gov't checks (today two checks came at once, amounting to $50), I will tell

Hugo that I am having trouble and ask him for some money. Chances are this will not come up, but if it does, I feel at this point I would be perfectly free and justified to go to him quite openly about the whole thing. I think this is a slightly delicate period of your life financially and I want you to have as much as possible in reserve for emergencies. So I'm keeping the $100 hidden for whichever one of us needs it first. If I have to spend it I'll let you know, but if you need it, you say so instantly. Is this all right with you? If it is, just tell me quite honestly, whether you think it would be all right to go to Hugo. I see no reason why I shouldn't if any slight emergency should arise. I have done and am doing a good job for him, and slowly he begins to realize just how good!

I want you, Anaïs, to let me begin to deal with Hugo separately from my relationship with you. The reason for it is this: he must learn to *evaluate friendships and services rendered* in a realistic way. If I need help and decide to ask him for help, he will, or should, be very glad to give it. If not, I'm going to be extremely cool, and my relationship with him will come to an end for the simple reason that he will not have done his part in the thing. You see, Anaïs, he has no idea that you have helped me, and I begin to see more and more each day that what this is doing is simply building his ego to the extent that he believes he is one of those *special* people for whom others render services out of awe, admiration, or something. This is poppycock and rubbish. Relationships are two-way affairs, and I want to make him realize that, if I can. If this situation becomes pressed between us, and I decide to stop helping him, I think you should trust my judgment about it, and allow it to happen. Doesn't this all make sense to you? Please don't think any more about Hugo being your responsibility while you are in California. *Hugo is his own responsibility*, and at the present moment I feel strongly impelled to do what I can to make him realize this. I want you to let me do it. Unless of course, I am not thinking clearly about it, in which case you must point that out to me.

You know, you act like one who thinks she is the first woman in the world to ask for a divorce. I am beginning to wish you would get it over with! Thank God you are beginning your schedule of work; I'm terribly sorry you are swamped with housework. Please *demand* for yourself the time for your writing. You are a great woman, and a great writer, and you have absolutely no business with dust-cloths unless for a few minutes a day. The heavy stuff, never! Every time I imagine that you might possibly, even this morning, be at the typewriter, I feel a tremendous excitement and anticipation. And you must not feel that you are alone. As long as I live I will be devoted to you and to your work, and I will possibly one day be in a position to help you by making people sit up and take notice of it on a larger scale. There is no ceasing of wonders, and anything, literally anything, can happen—but one thing is certain: something will.

Love,
Jim

Sierra Madre, July 1, 1952

I have been back with Rupert for twenty days. At first I was keenly happy, a physical happiness. The first week we celebrated our reunion, and every outing, a movie or a dinner at Café de Paris, seemed festive and magnificent. And then, slowly, mysteriously, the life began to bear a resemblance to my life with Hugo. Rupert (it is not a hallucination) begins to behave like a younger and more charming Hugo. I think I am a victim of a dream. Hugo once came in and found me cooking spaghetti. He leaned over my shoulder and said, "You did not put enough water in the pan." Rupert arrives and finds me cooking spaghetti and says, "You must put more water in the pan." When Jim and I hung up the terrace awning in the wind, a hard job, just before a party and got ourselves all dirty and had barely time for a shower, Hugo came to see, and all he found to say was: "One of them is hung inside out." When some furniture arrived here at Sierra Madre, the bookcase had to be moved. To avoid having the books on the floor, and as Rupert was overworked, I set about making a temporary construction until Rupert found time to set up the bookcase (a heavy job, but I thought the tidiness would relieve him of feeling he had to set it up immediately). When he came home, all he had to say was: "You didn't distribute weight right, the shelves are sagging." So the next morning I spent an hour correcting the sagging. Then he was annoyed because the present arrangement exposed a shelf he had no time to paint.

Even though I know he feels guilty because he feels he should have set up the bookcase, the repetition of such incidents still depresses and angers me.

My memories of similar situations stem from my father's criticalness, which made me feel humiliated and diminished. Bogner fought to make me realize this was not directed against me but against themselves. *They must throw responsibility onto others.*

I can throw it all off for a while, but then I begin to feel unworthy, inadequate. *I can't hang on to my own opinion of myself.*

Yesterday I was angry.

Before going to sleep he kissed me. When I get angry he acts like a child seeking forgiveness. He does not say it, but he tries, with charm and a kiss, to reconcile me.

It takes Kay Dart's visit and her extravagant praise to cheer me. "Oh Anaïs, you're not only a genius, brilliant, and beautiful, but so human, so warm, so giving, so gracious, and I always feel 'charged' when I see you. I love John, I'm happily married, yet I can't live without seeing you! Nothing takes the place of our talks."

It is this diminishing that Bogner describes as a reversion to a child status. In this I have made little progress. Three weeks after talking to Bogner and feeling strong, I now feel depleted.

When I'm elated about writing, I have to sit through a meal listening to three commentators! When I'm elated about some symphonic passage from Proust I have to listen to Rupert reading aloud from *Time* magazine. The full irony of escaping from Hugo's will to Rupert's tyranny!

If echoes create false relationships, how much weaker will the love they create be? The *points* of resemblance will be enough to set up a chain of responses. One response (from sheer power of habit) will be enough to awaken the neighboring nerves and create the illusion of a total bond. If the currents of love can be interrupted by certain grooves of resemblance, what hope is there of escaping from repetition even if I change?

I have changed profoundly since the first time I met June Miller twenty years ago, yet June reappeared in my life with Kay, and Kay, as well as June, responded to me in the same way.

Kay has the same very white dazzling skin, the same Amazonian proportions, and in the paleness the eyes burn. June was more beautiful. Kay is marred by fatness, by an automobile accident that gave her false teeth, by a scar on her cheek from a blow on the jaw given to her by her first husband (the jawbone was broken), yet dressed in black, her voluptuous handsomeness shines. But the character is the same. Now I can understand my response: an echo, and Kay's life is like June's. But why Kay's attachment to me?

Is all this in *my* vision, these analogies, these interpretations? If June had found a kind man (certainly not Henry) as Kay found the saintly John, she might have bloomed this way. The fundamental difference is that Kay is June exposed, June confessional and truthful. Henry would have had no mysteries here. He would have known everything. I wonder now whether one can say "I have given myself" if one has withheld the truth of one's self. More and more, I feel that if I did not give Hugo my physical self, he in time denied me his emotional self, in the sense that he concealed all of what he considered to be his "weakness," his fears, his childish longings… He played a role (a father role). I wonder now what we did give to each other. Not very much. A *façade*.

I have spent a week enduring Rupert's irrational behavior: high irritability, explosiveness, injustices.

So I began in a state of half sleep to yearn for a kind and undemanding Hugo, then suddenly I awakened fully with the shock of a new realization: the Hugo I need *no longer exists*. He was a good, silent Hugo, selfless and self-sufficient. That was a *role*. The real Hugo today is just like Rupert. Analysis and illness have unmasked a demanding, exacting, dependent and wearying Hugo. It was having these two lives burdening me that drove me into desperate revolt recently—two children and no husband.

To Rupert:

Beware, my darling, of self-destructive, negative tendencies in you, for as you know, when we harm ourselves we also harm the one we love, and you unconsciously have harmed me. Try to see this objectively. It's no good saying you won't do it again. The help is knowing *why* you do it and then when you understand the mechanism, you will be able to stop.

If you continue doing this, then you must become aware of its destructive effect on me. You are getting rid of your poison by injecting me with it, so that I feel guilty, inadequate, diminished, and unhappy. The result of your preoccupation with your own guilt to the exclusion of the *other's* similar problem is that I feel unprotected, lonely, and *unjustly* treated.

You also have guilt for the presents I make you, and instead of enjoying them you deprive yourself of enjoyment by finding flaws in them.

Let's stop *blaming* the other. You see, I don't *blame you ever.* If the brakes are bad, *you haven't had time to fix them.* If that day I had been seriously hurt on the parkway you would have felt responsible, yet I myself would not have blamed you. I want you to become aware of this big reservoir of guilt you carry, which causes you (in self-defense) to throw blame onto others because you can't bear to add to it.

You said, "I could shoot you for having my jeans sewn up!"

You blame me for getting your jeans sewn up when you know that you never remember either to get enough jeans, or to get them fixed in time. I didn't even *know* your other jeans were shrunk or useless. You *know* that you are disorganized, and you fear I should say, "But why didn't you buy other jeans?" You know you can't have just *one pair* of good jeans and that at some time or other it will have to be washed or repaired when you need them.

Case of the floor polish: When I ask to use a floor polish that is easier you feel badly because you feel that is your job and that I am indirectly reproaching you for not having done it. Actually you have no time, but you should not refuse me, as you do, getting an easier polish, or insist that I use the one that requires two operations. Then I feel you are not protecting me or saving my energy and that you are being selfish in insisting only one polish is the right one.

Causes of quarrels: When the axle broke you blamed me. Actually, you are so fearful of being blamed or reproached, that before the other person does anything, you make a self-defensive jump and accuse. You can't bear being accused. A broken axle is no one's fault, actually. Behind this lies your uneasy feeling about having sold Perseus, the fear that I should say someday ask: "Why did you sell it? Why don't we have a better car than José?"

The result of the throwing off the blame to save yourself is that you are unaware of its effect on me: I can't bear being reproached or blamed either, and I know I'm not a very good driver, so when you said it was my fault I believed it and felt awful. This blaming others, you see, turns out to be a selfish act in the end. Let's divide responsibility. In this case there is *none.*

These notes on quarrels helped Rupert to understand. He returned tired and gentle. We had a happy week. Museums, quartets, a swim in the neighbors' (Campions) pool, relationship with Christie Campion (six years old) who says today, "I will be *your* little girl." Movies. Dinner at Café de Paris, on a terrace, on Sunset Boulevard and the movie *The Wild Heart.* Long letters from Jim telling *all.* A day with Kay in Hollywood helping her to find a job. Pickwick Books asks for more *House of Incest.* Hugo is working on his film.

Sierra Madre, July 1952

It was not Rupert who offered to trade in my fifteen-year-old typewriter on which I could no longer type adequately. His obsession with economy does not prevent him from erratic, sudden impulsive extravagances, like buying a book we can borrow from a library. I feel that my life with Rupert would be intolerable without money of my own to combat his enslavement of my time and energy.

I am deeply depressed by this *control*. I asked a workman to come and fix the lawn mower, which was too stiff for me to push. Rupert caught him and sent him away ($2.50 for adjusting it properly), saying it belonged to the Forest Service, when he knew I was doing this so I could be able to cut grass when he is on a fire crew.

He has chosen a cleaner in Arcadia, a laundromat farther away. If I listened to him I would spend my whole morning on errands. Of course I cheat; I go my own way. I save time, come home, work on my mailing list and get an order for several books each week of $7.50 or $10.

I have grown to dread his questions, his displeasure. I have to justify whatever he discovers I have done. By buying the non-polishing wax, one operation, I buy my liberty. This is what creates my gratitude for Hugo.

Anaïs Nin with Rupert Pole's boots, Sierra Madre

Sierra Madre, July 15, 1952

I have made a discovery that puts a different light on my feeling of housework being wearying to me. The doctor believes I had, as a child, rheumatic fever, and that what I believed to be attacks of flu (sore throat, aching bones, fever, fatigue, difficulty in breathing) are actually attacks of rheumatic fever. And I was washing windows, kitchen walls and waxing floors! My longing (seemingly capricious) for warm, dry places, is all explained now. My aches when I was eleven and thirteen—in the diary *mal aux jambes*, fatigue. I considered it a great sacrifice to walk from school, 91st Street to 72nd Street to save 5¢ to buy my mother lilacs.

Letter from Jim Herlihy to Anaïs Nin:

New York, July 1952

Dear Anaïs: Tomorrow Hugo and I are going to the zoo, and because you took your turn at relieving me of guilt, I'm going to spend next week reading and at the museums of modern art and natural history.

I'm sorry, Anaïs, that I must tell you Hugo has still not once asked me if I needed anything; it is incredible to me that it has not occurred to him to do this. He even told me once in conversation about the nurse who wanted $11 a day, which he felt was outrageous, but it never crossed his mind that my help has saved him hundreds and hundreds of dollars, and that I have given him certain services that are purchasable. I'm certain he feels no qualms about asking me to do anything for him, even on a moment's notice, no matter what I happen to be doing at the moment. You know, Anaïs, it occurs to me that you must have been his conscience all these years, that you must have secretly paid his debts in thousands of ways. You know that I tell you these things only because I want to show you how it seems to someone who is relatively an outsider. I am sincere, though, when I say that I don't mind this and that I'm really enjoying greater freedom now than ever before. And so you must not think for a minute that I am unhappy about the arrangement; I want you to stay as long as you like, not that I don't want you here, you know that, but because I think you have a debt to yourself that is much, much larger than any to Hugo. Please remember that if I felt I was being compromised, I would tell you—I know you believe I am possibly over-considerate of you, but I wouldn't lie to you about something as important as this might be. About that money, I'm going to put the checks in the bank until I need them. Hugo lent me $15 in advance of the arrival of my gov't check, and I'm simply going to borrow more if necessary and not dip into our secret money until the emergencies arrive. I did expect him to say I needn't return the money, but he didn't. I want you to see this clearly, Anaïs, so that you will be in a better position to evaluate what you call your "debt" to him. Hugo is a good businessman, and just as you carry your artistry into your living, so does Hugo carry his "business" into his living. I think that the sentence I just wrote is an important one and I want you to think about it, and read it again. He is incapable of a simple "gesture"; they are not gestures, they are "grandstand plays" and extremely calculated. When Christina Guiler, his aunt, died, he sent a five-dollar bouquet, and then told me on two subsequent occasions that he was billing his mother for it, and also billing her for the cable in which he informed her of the death. I was appalled. And I see this so often; for example, he is giving Len Lye film in return for his services in designing the titles for the picture, and I have never seen such a contrast between the extreme care of deciding how much film to give (when he talks it over with me) and the bravado with which he hands it to Lye. On two occasions we went out to the movies with the plan to stop on the way home and have dinner at a restaurant; the first time he decided he wasn't hungry and we had a hamburger, the second time we stopped at the Captain's Table where he ordered fish, and when he looked over the menu, he suggested I'd like a hamburger steak. You may not know these things, because I would imagine that he takes great care to disguise them to you. He has just written a letter that he showed me, a letter to you about *Spy*. I began to quarrel with the last paragraph, in which he said that neither of you have progressed toward facing reality, even though the book would seem to indicate that you had, and in which he said that we put a statement of our sins into a work of art as if it exonerated us from the sin, and we could go on living it. When I quarreled with this, he said, "I simply have to tell you that it's true, and that's all there is to it—we'll discuss it more another time." Or, in other words, "I have the answers, the discussion is ended." He says in the letter that he came to represent reality to you, and in another part, that you fled from reality. I did manage, Anaïs, to point out that there are certain facts, unalterable, about reality, from which a human being has not only the right, but the duty, to flee. Reality, I said, includes a great deal; it embraces all the existing orders, social, economic, climactic, emotional, and if we don't flee the insuperable, the insupportable, we are nothing but cowards!

I am truly sorry that you don't have the freedom you require in either place. If I could only feel that you were wrong and that your desires for freedom were irrational, I would like so much to be the one to point them out to you; but always your bondage is the prison of others' neuroses, and their fears turn the keys on you. Keep your banner high, Anaïs, and always realize, as you seem to now, that freedom is not a sin, it's a right!

Please tell me this: can I write you at General Delivery with absolute freedom? Do you have to read the letters at the post office and destroy them before you go home? Or do you have the time and place to take care of your secrets? I would like to know this.

Hugo said in conversation that he might possibly postpone his trip to Venice to August 10, depending on whether or not the film was ready for the Festival, and whether or not the directors of the Festival write him that they would be willing to view it at this later date. I hope he doesn't postpone, but if he does, I thought I might warn you in advance that if you want to stay longer, possibly into August, in Sierra Madre, that you might begin preparing Hugo for it now by telling him that you have been either exhausted or ill, or both, or that you have to go to the dentist or something. He was not at all put off or irritated, it seemed to me, when you postponed your return to the end of July, and I must tell you, as part of the duty of one of the many members of the New

York Magic Company, that you can milk the situation bone dry, because I believe he is in a high mood and will accept what you tell him. He does not seem to have suffered at all from the suspension of his analysis, and he is very busy and happy and even elated over the shape the film, its sound and titles are taking.

Love,

Jim

Letter from Jim Herlihy to Anaïs Nin:

New York, July 1952

Dear Anaïs:

I think you must actually put a few hundred into a car, invest in some freedom out there. Movies and radio and *Time* are not enough to keep you writing. You know the prison aspect of the life does actually have something to do with the writing energies, how they are diverted; this I believe. We write under such circumstances because the bars remind us it is impossible to find our excitements elsewhere, or a release from tensions in a world that is closed to us by distance and barriers. I'm glad you've accomplished a lot, but I do wish you had more of the kind of companionship you really need; I wish too that I were there to offer it.

Hugo is fine. His spirits are high. I'm giving up the apartment on 73rd Street. I don't want the place alone, not now when I will be having Hugo's apartment on August 1st through September. My rent is up the 23rd so Hugo has said I can move in entirely with him and perhaps help him get packed. I don't like to bring this up, but I do wonder if you plan to go to Europe, Anaïs. Or do you think you'll stay out there another month or two while Hugo is gone? Hugo is filled, as you say, with the film. I like it, by the way; it's beautiful and sad; I suggested we call it *Bells of the Atlantide*, because the Barrons' music suggests something of this quality, and the whole action might take place on such an undersea continent or *nativity*, which offers a certain irony when associated with the crucifixion-like shot of you on the plank standing with your arms outstretched. The picture did make me sad, but I want to see it again and think about it some more. You are beautiful, of course, and your movement is wonderful, like a trained actress-dancer; I wish the film were longer.

Don't worry about Hugo. I keep him in hand and do not permit him to impose. He is basically kind, though occasionally thoughtless, and I straighten him out now and then, which he seems to like, and we get on well. I help him give dinner parties and entertain, accompany him to movies, spend an hour or two talking with him each day, put him in traction about five nights a week. He is practically well, has been going at a tremendous pace lately. The bed will probably be sent back the end of this month.

Do you feel that your "decision" still has its original strength, or have you become wearied by "movies, radio and *Time* magazine?" These last few weeks have taught me a great deal about your problem. I have a very similar one: of finding a world that will be big enough to hold my heart and my goddamn mind. Wouldn't it be simple to be brainless, healthy, and contented? Maybe we can find some way of keeping these two parts of ourselves alive simultaneously, though I certainly have nothing to offer on that score now, just the hope that things will settle into a more complete pattern.

All my love,

Jim

Sierra Madre, July 1952

The meaning of art:

First, I failed to bleach the dark brown walls of the house lighter. Then, having been bored by 24 hour duty on the 4th of July with streams of cars passing, empty faces, Rupert's activities, roadblocks, signs, homely fireworks, and a visit from a drunken, sloppy, bawdy Kay, two homely young men, a diffident John, the trees, the sight of Sierra Madre, while Rupert sang I fixed my eyes on Varda's painting. It was as if I had stepped out of my life into a region of sand with tiny crystals, of transparent women dancing, airy dresses, figures whom no obstacle could stop, who could pass through walls but remain accessible to the imagination that escaped the confinement of the brown-walled room, four walls, small screened windows, duties, restrictions, labor, a waste of one's time and strength. I ceased to think of myself as a caged animal pacing in a fever against limitation, and wanting the impossible, for I acquired in these moments of contemplation of Varda's painting the certainty that such a state of life was attainable.

The abstract tree is indispensable to man, as nourishing as the tree in the forest of human life, as necessary as the human tree. It is the guiding lookout tower, the indication of an existing oasis, of the hidden treasures lost to man, which he would otherwise cease to believe in, and consequently not be able to find.

With Varda's painting I can find what the cedar trees and orange bushes have not given me, because they only contain the present and no long-range vision into the fullest expansion of man's farthest-flung treasure hunts.

Physical beauty deteriorates in one's eyes as the character of a person emerges. One of Rupert's most beautiful physical attributes is the narrowness of his face that sets off the largeness of his eyes. But as time passes and the pettiness and narrowness of his character constantly manifests itself, the limitations of his insight superimpose themselves upon the narrowness of the face, which appears less beautiful as it becomes associated in my mind with not only his narrow range of thought, but with his father's small, shabby habits.

Letter from Jim Herlihy to Anaïs Nin:

New York, July 1952

Dear Anaïs,

Your letters have arrived through Dick.

Hugo says you might be coming back to New York the end of this week or the first of next. He is busy with exciting new developments in his film and will probably not get away August 1st. I don't think he's made any preparations other than renewing his passport. We are getting along very well. We talked Sunday about his authoritative father-like tone when he talks to me (and you), and he was very understanding and willing to see it from that point of view.

I want you to know your letters are perfectly safe. I have most of them hidden at 73rd Street, and when I can't get down there, I give them to Dick, who puts them in a secret letter box that he is holding for me. I'm awaiting the arrival of the envelopes and will get the enclosures out of the "locked Pandora's box" at 35 W. 9th and mail them very soon.

I'm worried about your traps. And I don't think you should blame yourself for getting into them. I am beginning to feel, however, that you must think very clearly and surely before you let yourself in for the one in the West exclusively, for you do have much more freedom in New York. I only wish that your lives could all melt into one. Love, work, money, play, all in one place. Maybe it will be possible that all these can exist together soon and you won't have any more traps and cages to contend with! Do you think we can arrange a secret talk next week when you are in New York? Hugo is worried about the fact that you might have rheumatic fever.

Dick and I are staying here at 35 W. 9th during the hot weather, sleeping in the bedroom; the traction bed is in the studio.

I hope you aren't being tough on yourself because of your dissatisfaction. Remember that *none* of us could be very happy completely alone in Sierra Madre, and it is only too true that Rupert does not supply *all* of your needs. And I'll tell you something else—if you decide to remain in California, I'm going to take a place that's not a million miles from you. I think Dick wouldn't mind living in Altadena, or somewhere within shouting distance, and the quiet would probably suit me well, so long as I knew I could talk with you without any trouble.

Meanwhile, write me when you can and know that I love you very much.

Jim

En route to New York, July 26, 1952

Yesterday, the day before leaving, I tried to remember everything to make it easier for Rupert, to clear the icebox, wax the floors, order, cook and cut Tavi's meat, water the garden deeply, weed the last patch, paint the last sign...

At four o'clock Rupert came home. I said I would like to go swimming in the pool next door. He said we had the bookshelves to finish; then after a while he said, "OK, to hell with the shelves. We'll have a quick swim and finish them later."

It was 90 degree heat. We got into our bathing suits. He began to look for his terry-cloth kimono. I said, "I took it to get washed. It was very, very soiled and I wanted you to have it clean for the pool. Only I didn't have time to call for it. Reginald came, then you came home. I was hot and tired from weeding, so I let it go. Here is a big towel."

Rupert got into a fury: "I don't want it washed! Washing shrinks it. Never send anything to be washed unless I say so. I'll wash it myself," and on and on. A completely disproportionate anger.

More than angry, I was appalled, frightened. It reminded me of Gonzalo's explosions. The injustice and irrationality of it. We went to the pool. I didn't stay long. I was filled with bitterness. I returned home. Reginald was still there; I couldn't control the weeping.

When Rupert returned I had closed the bathroom door. Tavi was anxious and licked my hand. Is this the cruelty I fear and cannot free myself of? Is it Rupert who is made to feel such harshness so keenly, or I? Rupert found me. Kissed me vehemently, kissed my eyes. I am afraid that my sorrow aroused him, as it used to arouse Gonzalo. Did I imagine this? He kissed me over and over again.

Because Reginald was there, I fixed dinner. The heat was oppressive. We worked on the shelves all evening. We replaced the books. Rupert turned on the radio and listened to the moronic convention speeches until one-thirty in the morning, and then I talked. I told him I could not take such scolding, that if I were like Kay and drank, talked too much, wasted my days, left the house uncared for, I could understand. But I was doing a great deal, a great deal that I hated to do, out of love, and I would not *allow him to scold and nag.* I told him the scene about the kimono was irrational, unjustified, even incredible. He is not aware. He was sincere. He was brought up on such harshness and irrationality from Lloyd, so he does not give it importance.

But it is important to me. It's *destructive.*

He said, "I can't be like you. You are good. You never criticize. I can't do that. I am not that way. You should nag *me.* It would be constructive."

(Seeking the angry parent!)

I explained: "We have been nagged and ostracized enough. That's why you have no confidence. I could destroy what confidence you do have in a week if I acted towards you as you did towards me."

In the dark, he grew passionate. I recognized the passion and the irrationality, as in Gonzalo. He cannot distinguish between just teachings (such as how to start the car in the morning) and the scene about the kimono.

Well, Anaïs, you're in for it. All you will achieve is that Rupert will seek to *control* this irrational fussing, ill temper, without understanding what it means.

The passion, the promises, the wild caresses, the begging for me to treat *him* the way he treats *me*, the masochistic-sadistic primitive reactions, the fact that *I can't do this* nor will I accept it being done to me—all this will be the death of our relationship. It will get worse (it already has). Rupert is very neurotic, and our relationship is making him more so.

He is so unbalanced, either too tender or too harsh, too kind or too selfish, too yielding or too stubborn.

In the face of neurosis there is absolutely *nothing* one can do.

Even under the most ideal circumstances (Acapulco, for example), he makes himself unhappy. He lost his money and felt desperate, he was angry when the movie broke down, he hated to be overcharged, or this or that. Was he truly happy in Acapulco?

When I finally rebelled and talked to Rupert about his fault-finding, he failed to understand its effect on me, my effort to find the cause of it, and said in his usual psychological blindness (consisting in *repressing* whatever presents a problem), "I won't do it again," just as he failed to understand the destructiveness of his family's attitude towards me. I was in distress. For what always creates anxiety in me is the doubt of my own sanity. I always question myself: am I being over-sensitive, am I exaggerating? This weakens me. When, besides this, Rupert is completely unaware of his actions, I feel lost, as I did with Gonzalo. I have occasionally wondered whether Rupert is sane. I wanted something he could not give me. I could not lean on him for a moment. *I felt alone*, unprotected.

I wanted to weep but didn't. I was harsh with myself. Well, Anaïs, you wanted Rupert's aliveness and passion. He is an adolescent. An adolescent can't protect you when you are in distress. Now you know what it is. You are alone. No Hugo to turn to—no one.

He left me with a passionate embrace. I am glad to be alone and resting from his selfishness.

New York, August 11, 1952

When I arrived in New York this was the situation: Hugo was almost well. He walks normally, not too fast. He cannot bend down or carry packages or weights.

He was trying to finish the film for the Venice Festival, which is August 20th.

Hugo was defeated by the technicalities of the film just before his illness. When I left, the film was complete except for smoothing and polishing—technicalities. Immediately Hugo turned to Len Lye, who, being an artist, did not give him technical help, but superimposed his abstractions over Hugo's film so that by the time I returned, the film, simple and clear at first, was almost entirely obliterated. The Barrons were in despair but found that the slightest criticism made Hugo angry. So when I returned I was the one who had to say, "Your own film was perfect before Len Lye's abstractions. You should have confidence in yourself as an artist." Hugo was angry, but I soothed him and we continued to work. Slowly, we rescued some lost passages from the original concept. The Barrons created a very original electronic score. The film began to emerge. The abstractions were better integrated. But how we worked! Hugo leaned on Louis technically. They stayed up all night. Bebe and I gave out and fell asleep all dressed. At six in the morning I got up and made breakfast.

Hugo withstands strain amazingly, but his temper is worse than ever. Bebe feels he has changed.

I help. We get up early. I go on errands. Jim drives me almost every day to Flushing, where the Kodak factory is. We have no visitors. We work at Len Lye's workshop and here at the apartment tonight. Tonight Louis went on vacation with his family. Both of them are exhausted. So Hugo has a new "crisis" and calls Len.

On July 29th I appeared at Immigration for a preliminary examination to become an American citizen.

Rupert's letters beg me to return. "I am lonely. I want you back." His letters are full of promises. "I am fixing the sprinkler so you won't get wet anymore."

Between these two relationships I have one island of peace, and that is with Jim. It is the perfect relationship. Jim dreams of how it would be if he were not homosexual, but I warn him it is perfect *because* we don't have the love problems.

During the rides to Flushing, Jim and I unburden ourselves.

Dick has become jealous—he opens Jim's letters, he asks where he is going, he telephones him, he argues. He tries to control Jim's dress, his friendships. "You must give up the poor artists." Jim is estranged from Hugo after taking care of him in my absence because Hugo places everything on a business basis, talking in a commanding tone so that Jim feels like a "secretary" or a "servant." Hugo gives ungraciously, and not generously.

Sometimes I am aware of my immense debt to Hugo for all he gave me, and of my guilt for having lovers, but recently I have been aware that Hugo gave me material things and protectiveness as substitutes for the essential, vital elements he did not give me: aliveness, presence, sensuality and pleasure.

Guilt makes you hate someone. I hate Hugo most of the time. Now and then I feel compassion, but something about his set jaw, clamped mouth, tense face and manner antagonizes me. He is never genuinely humorous, or easy-going, or joyous.

It's an obsession with me, to *justify* my leaving him. Jim thinks *everyone* and *everything* justify it.

Jim and I plan escapes from control and nagging. I know when I return to Rupert I will be happy for a week and then fall prey to petty, childish tyrannies.

En route to Los Angeles, August 20, 1952

Three weeks of Hell.

It is not the work that was hell, but rather the complications, all due to Hugo's complex and confused mind. He would make changes to the film and confuse the printers. He made errors and had to send for Louis Barron. Finally, broken down by fatigue, he admitted to his inadequacy, and then I felt compassion and rallied to his aid completely. It is hard to help when you have no faith; I know Hugo's self-sabotage too well. One night at two in the morning I awakened with anguish. We had an almost satisfactory print, but I knew he would make changes. I begged him not to, or else to give up the Venice Festival. He worked all night, and I got up at five to make breakfast. Out of exhaustion we stopped opposing each other and reverted to the old tenderness, the old relationship, which means I showed weakness and exhaustion and gave in to his way of doing things. Up at seven, errands at the film lab on 54th, to a film supplier carrying equipment, trips to Flushing with Jim, irregular meals, work in the evening, and the final print too dark. Hugo, who is technically unskilled, attempted a job too difficult for him and ended up directing others to do it, putting pressure on Len Lye, on Louis, on Jim, on me.

When a man is honest, resentment is disarmed. Hugo's terrible inadequacy was the reason for his aggressive, willful marshaling and controlling of others, and he fully admitted it. From this moment on I resumed my loyalty...to the weakness. My rebellion subsided. The last few days were given to work.

Now it was too late for me to go to Venice. I was already away from Chiquito for three weeks; so, by an incredible feat, for Hugo had bought my ticket to Milan from an agency, I had to persuade the airline to cancel it and then to go on to LA without letting him know. I finally got Hugo off with his film (so necessary to his ego) and eluded his plan to have me follow a few days later with a more perfect print. My "underground" helped me again. But those who help me have a feeling of being helped by me, loved and lavishly protected in return.

Before Hugo left, in the chaos and tension, I lost my wallet one evening: tickets, $750 in cash for my trip, traveler's checks, my passport and Rupert's letters! I didn't realize this until the next morning. I became hysterical *for this reason*: If I lose my money, then all is lost. I have a feeling I must hold on for both of us.

Hugo then became very forgiving: "Because I lose and forget everything, you see, I feel sorry for you and know how you feel."

We went out in the rain, to the police station, and then to the Italian restaurant where I had dinner with Jim the night before. And there was the wallet! The Italian waiter added a human phrase: "If you didn't discover the loss until this morning, then you only suffered for a few hours!"

Hugo had, at last, a spontaneous gesture. He gave the waiter $100.

The last day Hugo spent most of the night at the laboratory. I packed for him. We looked once more at the print.

Poor Hugo, poor Hugo, poor Hugo.

And now I go to the same pattern in Sierra Madre, the same design and same neurosis, with only one great difference: it includes passion.

Sierra Madre, August 24, 1952

Our estimate of people is in terms of our needs, in terms of the role we arbitrarily assign to them.

Hugo's *pretenses* of being an effectual man added to my anger. His admission of inadequacy disarms it. He is as faulty as Miller, Gonzalo, or Rupert, but he pretended to be better, stronger, more powerful. My anger—I called it hatred—has gone. I think of him as he truly is: psychologically blind, inadequate in the world, inadequate as a lover, confused, uncertain, upheld by willfulness rather than true strength.

The day you have compassion for the *father*, you are mature.

Sierra Madre, August 25, 1952

Rupert and I recovered all our passion and happiness this week.

While I was in New York, he built me a dressing table. He was passionate and intensely happy. He spent his three weeks working on furniture, seeing only the people who come to see him.

Heat. Peace.

Movies. Café de Paris. Martinis. Garden work in the sun. Beach.

Joy at night. Acute and lyrical.

Sierra Madre, August 31, 1952

Hugo (under the pseudonym of Ian Hugo) is in Venice with *Bells of Atlantis*, inspired by *House of Incest*.

I am not there.

I gave that up to be with Rupert. We sit now in the room full of the furniture he made, with my "ideas." Rupert is playing Debussy on the viola with two young male violinists, and a young male cellist. The violinist's wife sits near me, writing letters. The split of my two lives is acute, and I have to make so great a mental effort to coordinate them that I had to let Jim compose the cables announcing I could not join Hugo because I could not get a travel permit. (The permit I did not receive is in this book.)

Jim calls himself the Spy King. I call him Intelligence Service, Underground, etc. I will never forget how he helped me and how intelligently. He asked me to marry him when I reach the age of seventy, or at least at the end of my sensual life!

As Rupert sits there and we have once more established the communion of mouths, of a high-strung sensuality, I see superimposed images of canals and graceful boats and all I have lost floating in the large water-green of his eyes, laughing; his radiance is greater than all the possible beauty of Venice. There is nothing sadder in the world than places that have a sensual beauty, such as Acapulco and Venice, visited without one with whom to share the love these cities arouse. Acapulco was a caress on the skin, a preliminary to other caresses.

How quickly I recovered here, deep sleep, sun, the garden, the emptiness of the life and people. Peaceful.

My compassion for Hugo is no longer sharpened intolerably by any feeling of self-blame. It is not my fault now that I see and hear him from afar as over-willful, resentful, demanding. There is no longer, as I once believed, a distortion of my own vision. Even for this I always blamed myself. Have I made him angry? I deserted him!

But long ago, his character, for which he is half responsible, drove me away. He did not bloom psychologically, or expand with me. Everything that happened was caused by *both*. We are both responsible, and both to be forgiven too.

Every one of us, as D. H. Lawrence said, is dangerous to other human beings. Hugo's constriction stifled me. My desire for pleasure angered him.

Sierra Madre, September 1, 1952

This morning lying open on Rupert's desk was a poem from a girl violinist referring to her hangover, a kiss, Rupert's beret forgotten in her car…

I began to shake and tremble; when Rupert came I questioned him. "Oh, it was nothing. After the quartet we sat in her car and she was very high, she talked and asked for a kiss"—which he gave her. "Of no importance." She repulses him. (She is actually coarse-looking and stumpy with hairs on her chin!)

I can't keep my balance, not for this incident, but for what it presages—if even a girl he does not like can get a kiss from him.

He gets angry because I have promised I have faith in our relationship and I show I don't. I get angry because I repeat that *all I have asked of him is to be secretive and clever so I won't know*. Why didn't he destroy the silly letter? Why does he have it on his desk? But the *shock* is there. Immediately I think: I wish I had gone away with Hugo, because that is one pain Hugo never caused me.

I think of the time Jim asked me for a kiss and I turned away from his mouth, risking the loss of his friendship, because, as I said, a kiss on the mouth is for lovers.

My happiness and confidence crumble. I love Rupert less. I work desperately on letters and sending manuscripts, on attaining the freedom that would enable me to run away from Rupert or Hugo. What I crave at this moment is to be where I am not cut off from the world, to find another thread of contact. Neurosis resembles a spider web. It creates such a fragile contact with life that the slightest shock destroys it, and with it life.

Then an hour later Rupert was sent on a fire. I slept alone, hating the solitude. No escape, no world to go to.

Midnight. He is back, exhausted. He wants me to lie beside him until he falls asleep. I am still shaky inside, but convinced once more I cannot break with Hugo.

The last rejection letter from Knopf was another shock: "This is Anaïs Nin's best book, but the novelty has worn off. We can do more for a new writer."

I bought all the remaining copies of *The Four-Chambered Heart* from Charles Duell, and he writes to ask me what we can do about selling them.

Letter from Jim Herlihy to Anaïs Nin:

New York, September 1952

Dear Anaïs,

Magic Coordinating Center still in operation, but our offices have moved. Still no worries, however, as real magic is seldom affected by place. One needs simply to stretch his tentacles; also the telephone is a great help in keeping things under control.

Dick has not stopped talking about your letter in which you mention Rupert's very slight infidelity and your response to it. He is really comforted to know you act the way he does in these matters. As for me, I'm seldom jealous unless the lover is flagrantly indiscreet.

Love,
Jim

Sierra Madre, September 1952

Such irony. With Rupert I can't bear the married life, and Hugo is in Venice, at the Lido, meeting interesting people, being interviewed about the film I helped to create.

I fuss about women and Rupert's flirtatiousness. He fusses about picayune things—constant supervision and control. I can't even make a rug by myself. Rupert makes a design for it. I can't feed Tavi a canned meal that he likes just as well. Control, control, control. I end up lying and concealing what I do. The doctor in Sierra Madre finds me extremely low in calcium, which could bring on arthritis. This weakens the nerves and brings on the crying jags that I have and had very seriously as a child.

I love to hear news of the world, of Hugo, a bigger world. Rupert is happy in a small world (with Anaïs, of course).

I think I would like to make films of my works with Hugo.

I started to fill in the diary that Kay will sign as hers, not only in hopes of making a success as a Spanish realist, but as a supreme prank to play on a stupid world.

There is an interesting relation between the old-fashioned dictionary definition of neurasthenia (neurosis)—weakness of the nerves—and Jacobson's research on the lack of calcium in those with an artistic personality.

Dr. Martin: when calcium is low in the blood, the body takes it from the nerves, and leaves the nerves frayed and *exposed*.

I plan to leave my body to medical researchers. It may help them to prove that if I had been more balanced in my physical alchemy I might not have been an artist, just a happy woman.

The feeling of weakness that haunts me and has driven me to seek protection from the bourgeois world—fear of breakdown, mental and physical—may have an organic cause.

Sierra Madre, September 10, 1952

Rupert is at his family's for music. Now, at eight o'clock, I sit in an Italian pizzeria next door to Coronet Films, alone with my diary. The people I could call up, alas, do not interest me. They are victims of the Great Standardization, and although restless, bored and even rebellious, they are doomed. They can only escape by drinking, or by reading or seeing me. As Kay says, "Oh Anaïs, you are a shot in the arm." But I am tired of being a medical stimulant. Also, I run out of supplies. A rich interior life that you cannot share begins to fester. For the artist, bourgeois life is hell. The artist must live according to his own inner dictates. I never had the courage.

The life I wanted: Varda's life, on a ferry boat in Sausalito, with a sailboat, all made with his own hands, without money. He makes a little by teaching at an art school, but he does not need much. He wears jeans and has enough for red wine. When he invites friends, he does not hesitate to serve only fried potatoes and red wine. But the fries are exquisite and cooked picturesquely in an enormous frying pan (from the flea market), served in enormous spoons (flea market). He is the sublime ragpicker.

If only I could have loved Varda. But he repulsed me physically, and I didn't like his *madness*.

Rupert is bound, obsessed with security as Hugo was—first a home, a piece of land.

For me to have the life I want, I would have had to have recognition and acceptance from the world, whereas this year I have had more rejections than any human being can endure.

An unbearable reality is Mother aging, dying very slowly before our eyes, Joaquín enslaved from the age of fifteen to forty-four to her care. Reality is Hugo traveling alone because I can't love him as a lover, or feel free in his presence. Reality is Joaquín and I yearning for Europe. Reality is Rupert's neurotic fear of being like his father, an irresponsible artist, shiftless, chaotic, depending on his old age pension of $75 from the California government.

And then comes art, the ridiculed, persecuted art. The great mathematicians lose themselves in intricate calculus, the astronomers in space, the scientists in chemical discoveries, the doctors, chemists, and inventors can all take flight and say they will return with a remedy, a gift for humanity, a discovery, a cure, an evolution—and the artist?

hunger
disease
separation
loss
torture (whether by the Nazis or by the self as Van Gogh)
death (in life or after life—just the same)
disintegration
deterioration

Rejection letter from Stanley Kauffmann, editor of Ballantine Books in which he calls me "an intensely private writer."

Sierra Madre, September 15, 1952

The people who came to see me, attracted by my work, do not interest me. I feel compassion for the poverty of their lives, for their hunger, for their boredom and restlessness. I see their human lives, and it does not seem like life to me.

I am lonely.

Today I stayed home alone. Read. Wrote letters. Watered the garden. Brushed Tavi's hair. Did not write because now I am plagued by a new form of illness: it starts with difficulty in breathing, a congested chest, aching bones, a slight fever. I have no energy. A wasted day.

The highest moment was remembering Yma Sumac...the voice, the face, the body. The voice has all the richness, beauty, and range of a Myth Woman. It makes her more than a woman. And added to it is the beauty of a legendary figure. I was swept off my feet. For once Rupert and I were welded into one admiration, one fervor. He ceased to be my lover. I looked upon him as half of me, the male half, and wished he would possess her, for me, since I as a woman could not reach her. When some figure is great, in art, in beauty, one transcends the personal and rises into passion.

Strange miracle caused by a great value.

All evening I drank Martinis, a new pleasure.

My mysterious relationship with drink. Either I could not tolerate it physically or rejected it psychologically—I don't know. It used to harm me, like poison. Either I grew healthier, physically, or I no longer resisted its effect, which I feared and hated, or a combination of both. Anyway, scotch harmed me, and wine. But vodka and gin did not. So I became addicted to Martinis. Rupert makes them perfectly. Then I released my humor. What the neurosis had destroyed, humor, was suddenly released. With Martinis come relaxation, dilation, enjoyment, humor and irony.

I believe that what I have feared so keenly, and resisted in drink, was the same feeling that overpowers me in Acapulco—non-caring, detachment, irony, drifting, passivity. It seems to me even now, that I could drink myself into insensitivity. *I would cease to struggle.* And I would go to pieces. Evidently I am fully conscious that the destructive tendencies in me are strong and to be watched. However, all it takes is one Martini a day, or a few at the Mocambo, to forget the vulgarity of the place, the most vulgar nightclub in the world, the head waiter peddling and enforcing drinks on those crowded near the bar waiting in vain for a reserved table, drinks when you can't even stand, or hear the singing, and when the first one we rashly ordered was spilled on our dresses by the jostling!

At least there is this difference between Anaïs and other women. When I behave neurotically (as I reacted to Rupert kissing the violinist), I know it, I acknowledge it, I face it, I combat it, I am honest about it, treat it like bronchitis, an illness. I made it very clear to Rupert what I suffer from, my one defeating, devastating fear, and how he could help me defeat it. So much analysis, so much honesty, and still, at Rupert's enthusiasm for pretty girls, or his flirtations, I shake, tremble, suffer like a shell-shocked soldier at a blown tire. I reenacted for Rupert the *echo* of traumatic phrases: my father's passion for *la jolie*. Rupert's similar reaction. A pretty girl on horseback passes by, dismounts, sits on our lawn. Rupert leaves his lunch to go and pretend to be helpful.

He understands. And because of our talk, he expressed his own greatest fear: *to be a failure.*

I know it is fear that prevents him from attempting a bolder, bigger life, as an actor, as a nightclub entertainer, or even as the lover of a beautiful and wealthy woman. It was paralyzing fear that drove him to seek a more modest life, an easier career, a woman who sustains his faith, guides him, strengthens him.

To conceal your weakness (fear) from the loved one is an error. If you have to pretend to the loved one, then you might as well not live together, but live like Varda on ephemeral love affairs.

I was very kind to Gonzalo's wild jealousies! I never tormented him...I tried to help him. They were unjustly founded for ten years. And even then, the affairs I sought were to escape Gonzalo's hell, not out of passion for others. Gonzalo drove me into them, as I might well drive Rupert away if we lived exposed to temptations that Rupert cannot resist. That I know. He can't resist because his weak ego is involved. It flatters him. He enjoys conquest even when the woman repulses him. It is not real, but just the same he could have an affair on this basis: exacting to his narcissism, just as my father ruined his second marriage over a woman he did not want but who had challenged him by refusing him, which made him wonder whether he was growing old, losing his power, and so he was determined to conquer her only to prove he was not old, he had not lost his power.

Not owed even to my father's love of beauty, but to his need of conquest is my mother's misery, the loss of a father I loved, the loss of a musical world, an art world, Europe, a crippled childhood, a violent transplantation to a country I hate, the loss of my languages Spanish and French, of my people, the loss of my confidence as a woman, my neurosis.

So much due to what I believed was my father's interest in pretty women!

No wonder, as I explained to Rupert, that a pretty woman is for me the announcement of catastrophe, a fire alarm, war, death, destruction.

Letter from Anaïs Nin to Jim Herlihy:

Sierra Madre, September 1952

Dear Jim: I see you are disappointed that nothing miraculous happened after the success of your play *Moon in Capricorn*. But that is New York, and quality and even success are difficult to direct, to crystallize. Have you no agent? In this cold-blooded war between the artist and the salesmen (not the public), you need an agent.

Hugo's letters from Europe, so glowing, so fulfilled in understanding by others, in the delicacy of relationships, in the abundance of individuals, have made me homesick for Europe. With this, I have a greater and greater awe and respect for those like yourself who persist in their quality and development against so many odds and with so little help from the environment. I do respect you, James Herlihy. It takes guts to be anything but mediocre and middle-class crass or a gangster in this country. The high average of low level is staggering.

Knowing Hugo, you realize the date of his return is unpredictable, but already he is not returning September 25th and will be in London until September 30th. He is now staying with a relative of mine in Paris in a sumptuous apartment, but shivering cold.

How far off do you sit from the sun lamp, and what is the maximum? It is doing me a lot of good. All is well here. I have worked out most of the problems with Rupert. The trouble is I was too gentle and too subtle. Now and then I get mad, and I find it works better. My flare-ups intimidate him.

Tavi is eating his lunch with his license medal tinkling against his plate. Soon Rupert will drive up in his green fire truck and ask for beer. He will have lunch and discuss the movie we will see. A little anesthetic Martini will float me through.

Don't lose patience with New York. You are the kind of person they will be kind to; your quality is disarming because it's disguised in charm. They can't bear it straight. But they will recognize it more readily in you, I predict.

Love,

Anaïs

Sierra Madre, September 21, 1952

I am learning to laugh

to float
to forget
to be carefree

The one pain I cannot bear is the failure of my work. Rejections on all sides. Ostracism, but there is private, sincere devotion from individuals.

I yield to the Martini's glow. It has helped me to
laugh at my past selves
laugh at jealousy
laugh at much that once hurt me

SIERRA MADRE, SEPTEMBER 1952

Humor. The theme of this year. Discovery of humor. I am weary of emotion and tragedy.

Letha Nims is dark-haired, with Slavic features, is voluptuous, with unexpected dimples in her cheeks, has a disarming smile, but a direct, lurid glance. She is humorous and sharp-witted. Bill Nims is soft, gentle, objective. He handles her sudden excesses gracefully.

Hugo's letters have awakened all my restlessness, my longing for Europe and Paris. Rupert is too earthy for me. When the conversation soars, he always speaks of prosaic, trite things, incinerators and forest fires... I blush *for* him as I once blushed for Hugo. Rupert's physical charms blind everyone and he is forgiven, but he is boring. His talk is boring. He is either pedantic, or obvious, or trite, or petty, or else utterly irrational.

I lie in bed, tired after our late night with the Nims. I have surrendered what I once held precious: lucidity. Lucidity was pain. With Martinis, I do not even remember our talks. But no talks here are remarkable. Anesthetic, that is what it is, a blurring of the edges, a stunting of the memory.

Rupert, my vehement lover, crushing me and my breasts, holding my hips with his two strong hands, my vehement musician, why can you not be mute? He talks in opposition to poetry, to all wisdom.

The sprinklers are the fountains of Alhambra, spraying green-grass tiles and a cocker spaniel, emotional, hyper-sensitive, a dog you cannot scold or ask to sit in the back of the car or to eat alone, the long-eared dog who sits on queens' trains in Spanish paintings. Rupert is a disguised Prince of Wales, the true one whom the world has never met, and I am, or was, the writer of distillations and elixirs of life. Our passion is the flower that only blooms at night, wildly then, charged with our wiry, nervous, stylized extracts of passion, condensed, potent.

Kay reads diaries 31 and 32 and almost says, "Throw away your arty books." She likes the untransmuted stuff—I meditate, plot, deceive. Having been hopelessly cast-typed as abracadabra, I will reappear under another name in my plain realism—the diary. (Dear diary, it isn't you who are plain with realism until I change it into surrealism?)

The bedroom is as festive as a Mexican basket. Christie Campion, my occasionally adopted child, gave me ten of her watercolors from which I made a panel, covering a wall between two doors.

The only anxiety is that since last Thursday, my mother has gone to bed ill; but for each other, alas, we died when I married, we died when I ceased to be her child. At my first flight out of the nest my mother cast me away forever.

There is nothing more tragic in the world than the walls of China that grow between human beings, and the real priest is the one who dissolves them.

Kay is as large as her magnificent displays of emotion, as her abundant drinking, luxuriant dramatizations, avalanches of talk. As a chaotic specimen, she is superior to Thurema or June. She is perpetually intoxicated, heaving, swelling, expanding, dissolving, weeping, sighing, mimicking.

Her hair changes color; originally it was dark red-brown. It is strong and thick. It always looks uncombed. She arranges it, and one second later it looks disarranged. Her skin is very translucent, matte white, her eyes a burning fawn color. Her vision is slightly defective, only it should not be termed so, for the slight deviation of her eyes corresponds to her natural absence of emotional focus. She has lived as children paint: the door leans to the right, the windows are asymmetrical, the trees slant as after many storms, dogs and children stand as paper cutouts. She cannot keep an even keel, or a secret. She cannot ever break her impulses. She has to reach the bottom of every bottle, the bottom of every relationship, the bottom of despair, and she is sorrowful when the night ends, her friends fall asleep, the gin has evaporated and not a single drop more of affection or lust is available.

Her shoes wear out five times faster, her dresses tarnish six times faster, her hairnet tears instantly, and when she color-rinsed her hair, she left indelible stains on the four walls and ceiling of our bathroom. She is the champion glass breaker, drink spiller, and utterer of all that should be censored or reserved. She is of the race of burlesque queens who insist on quoting poetry now and then, who insist on idealization and tender treatment. She has a Rubens body, a pioneer's language, and still carries in the folds of her large voluptuous dresses a little girl who likes flowers, perfumes, and jewelry in the Woolworth manner. Living in Europe never altered this taste acquired from her Midwest bourgeois origins, and her only rebellion came out of alcohol, in striptease habits and language. The uncontrollable emotional climate, in the style of Dostoevsky—shame, repentance, despair—prevented her from becoming a great actress. She has a gift for extracting the maximum drama out of her past, out of her return to America loveless, her caged life as a daughter of a schoolteacher, her "psychotic fugues," her work as a nurse, her lesbian-tinted camaraderie with other women, her car accidents, her devastating reactions to Rupert's taboos (to prevent her from being here to see me every day), her father's recent death. She spends her time confessing to John, winning absolution, and immediately accumulating new reservoirs of guilt like any good Catholic.

Rupert controls her invasions. One cannot have orgies of talk and emotion every day!

Kay loved Rupert, desired him, but her massive bulk and its preponderance to floods, invasions, earthquakes, and volcanic furnaces repulsed him. A man must feel hesitant to sleep with a twelve-armed, twelve-legged goddess whose vast sensual caverns could delight an army. Rupert resisted her flank attacks, feeling the ocean itself was surging around him, and that the undertow was profound. She was prepared to hate me. But when she saw me she loved me. She loves me more today than she loves Rupert, although she would still like to possess him. I have always loved these outsized women on a magnificent scale, who are rudderless and such scintillating failures.

All of us, warmed and kindled, nevertheless make a swift gesture of flight when she telephones: can I come now, can I come tomorrow, can I make dinner for you? One's instinct is to say no. She is lush and prolific like the tropics, and like the tropics, absorbing. All this I say, resisting like the others, yet knowing that by a strange irony, it is I who have seized upon, overwhelmed, and possessed Kay by giving her the diary. Both Kay and John are so responsive, so vehement. She read, wept, was overwhelmed, haunted. At first we had plotted that she would adopt it, sign it, say it was hers, because it would not harm her, and under this disguise I could overcome the obstacles that prevent me from publishing it openly. But when she read it she said, "That would be like saying I painted a Da Vinci or an El Greco. I can't do it." Honest, truthful Kay saying, "Compared with this, my life was tawdry." Kay, so tumultuous, sensual, rebellious. Her religious gratitude for my saying what she had felt. She relived her own life in a different light.

Her gift to me, in return, was to renew my confidence, my feeling that the diary may yet bring me the freedom I crave. *I can't bear the drudgery anymore*, the 365 meals to cook a year, the 1,000 socks, the broom, the waxing, the window washing. I can't bear it anymore! My love for Rupert has condemned me to this.

Kay's fervor and John's sincere respect have given me the impetus (once more!) to make a prison break.

The truth is I hate Sierra Madre, the people, the lives they lead. I hate the life we lead. It is mediocre and filthy and dull. Last night, music at the Rosens'. The level of the conversation was 1,000 feet below animal life, the narrowness and awkwardness below all possible measurements, mostly prosaic, almost totally devoid of imagination. Their worst sin is that they don't *wish* to know other lives. They are ensconced in their gopher existence, and when you tell them of other places they almost invariably say, "I prefer hamburgerism, automobilities, drive-in weddings, and good homemade syphilis, Goodrich sprinklers, piethrowing humor, telwithoutvision, robot men American made, women untouched by human hands like the bread, the absence of miracles and chromosomes."

After one Martini I was delirious: American civilization is functional, purely functional—bridges, water closets, conveyances... So out of boredom they drink gin to anesthetize themselves. They can't bear what they have created. Then the gin stupefies them so they turn to jazz. Jazz wakes them up, makes them feel alive. Gin comes from England, so all in all they have created nothing but a purely functional world.

Either this functional world has caused an atrophy of the mind, or America is congenitally moronic. The ones I like, I like as human beings, but *never* for qualities of mind, perception or wisdom. I can't bear to live here anymore. Once should never live in a place one hates so deeply. I regret every hour I have spent here. It was wasted, meaningless, unproductive, uninspiring. But how, how can I reach the life I love, with Rupert, and be free of chores, no longer a servant?

Saturday I went to visit Mother. Found her weak from amoebic dysentery. I cared for her. She improved. At last I was able to express devotion, tenderness, to see her purely as a human being. Even to sleep at her side as I did when I was a girl (at sixteen, when I asked for a bed of my own, there was a scene), to hold her hand and let her be my child. I suffered from pity, the revolt against death, but was cheerful, until I got back and wept in Rupert's arms. So strange, Rupert standing naked in the dark (he was in bed and I got up to go out and walk, ashamed of my tears); he rushed to the door, turned off the Beethoven music that had disturbed me, and held me. He is silently compassionate. And later we had the passion that brings me back to life.

I find life tragic and unbearable. Now I seek forgetfulness. I would never have created the work I have if I had not had that terrible *awareness* that increased the sense of pain; I never tried to escape. I looked, I felt, I responded. But at last, at forty-nine, I'm tired. I tried to escape the awareness. I drank to fall asleep. I drank on the plane, quietly, enough to stop being aware. I drank last night. I am drinking now. Compassion, for Joaquín so tied down, Mother in bed, shrunken, tired. Thorvald is rough, tactless, without tenderness. Joaquín so tender. Rupert so tender. I lie alone. I didn't want to go out with Lloyd, Eric and Rupert to a concert. It was my mother's aggressiveness, possessiveness and tyranny that built a wall between us. But at last I could treat her tenderly, and not as a daughter. I lie alone reading Hugo's letters, answering them. There is what I call a deterioration of my faculties, but I wonder. This diamond awareness is suspended like the mystic clairvoyance of the Eastern priests—no alcohol, no drugs, no impairment of the seeing faculties. Oh, god. What a painful destiny. Meanwhile all around me, human beings sought and found forgetfulness. I didn't. I gazed, listened, recorded. Now I am tired. Too much pain. Too much. No wonder people turn away from my writing, an incisive and searching scalpel, the surgeon Anaïs operating without the use of anesthetic. I think I have earned my rest from awareness.

Letter from Jim Herlihy to Anaïs Nin:

New York, September 1952

Dear Anaïs,

Your letter at 35 W. 9th rec'd.

The Barrons are angry with Hugo. Bebe said on the phone that he has been writing and cabling them orders from Italy about the film print and she said they feel exploited. But I told her she should simply send a bill for their services and then she would no longer feel that way. I explained that Hugo is honest and pays his bills, but is not thoughtful and forgets. Also, they need money now and Hugo has put off paying them, according to Bebe, and they are also peeved about that. I don't know what to say to them except that Hugo will make necessary adjustments when he returns. Bebe has a clip from *Variety* on the film. Glad it was a success. As you know, the Barrons are very fond of you. It is only Hugo they are angry with. Bebe, too, said that his analysis seemed to have made a monster of him. I think she is only temporarily angry because they are low on cash, and because they're terribly busy, too busy to go the airport or film labs. I thought you might like to give Hugo a reminder about their money, perhaps in some subtle way; I don't know why they just can't write him and tell him they need to be paid; but I think Louis is a little backward about it.

You are a wonderful twin, and your letters are beautiful.

Love, Jim

Letter from Anaïs Nin to Jim Herlihy:

Sierra Madre, September 1952

Dear Twin: Let me reassure you quickly about the Barron situation. You did the right thing in warning me, as this is the only way I can neutralize Hugo's lack of feeling for other people, and if you had not written to me I would have believed that Hugo had taken care of them. This way I may salvage the relationship. He is fond of them, he needs them. I don't know what makes him such an egomaniac at the moment. I sent them $100 on account for immediate needs. But if they call you, tell them the idea did not come from you so they won't think you told me what they would not let me know. I was frank about Hugo's expectation that they would add it all up and ask him. He expects people to be direct and to speak in terms of money. The Barrons usually say nothing and then get furious. I bet you they won't write me and say what Hugo owes them. In a few days I will send another hundred. Of course, we are saving Hugo from suffering the consequences of his attitude (loss of me, of you, of the Barrons, of other friends, of helpers).

What I have worked out with Rupert is that he now knows the cause of my jealousy (my father's silly love for every pretty female caused me to lose everything I had) so that he no longer feels it as an effort to control him, but a fear he must help me with.

His control I found the cause of too, and so I no longer resent it. I laugh at it. I make fun of it. When he broke a glass the other day and we had company, I clowned and covered my ears, saying: "Watch, everybody, it's coming, I will get the blame, listen..." And he did blame me, but could not keep it up because everybody started to laugh, and he ended up laughing too. Whoever can laugh first is saved, and usually one can make the other laugh.

Love, Anaïs

Sierra Madre, November 1, 1952

The time has come to return to Hugo, and I have no desire to leave Rupert. I have learned to navigate alone through the moment when I have to face a crisis alone, the moment when Rupert cannot help me. The moments I can't bear, the aspects of my life with Rupert I can't bear, I now endure with anesthesia, a Martini. These moments of rebellion against the empty life, the dullness, the crassness and prosaic American way of life, which hurt me like a compressing shell, like being cast in too small a mold, I have no remedy against. But still, I do not want Hugo, or closeness to Hugo, or a bigger life with Hugo. He is like a distant brother now. His entire trip to Europe was not seeking love or pleasure, but triumph, power, with his artist self this time. I feel compassion for him, but no closeness to what he seeks so desperately. And yet the Sierra Madre life I can't bear. Rupert is too afraid; he needs security, or the safe adventure.

When Kay inherited $20,000 from her father, she wanted to sell her house and orange grove and go to Paris. That is what I would have done. But John and Rupert talk about how to make Kay's and John's life secure on the inheritance, how to invest it...

But in spite of this, Rupert's efforts and fears touch me. When he realized I had not written all summer, burdened with housework and gardening, he tried to help me, but not by giving me a maid once a week, but by doing the work himself.

I prepare 500 pages of the abridged diary for de Chochor to see if I could make a new start under a new name, open new worlds, as I feel absolutely ostracized in America as Anaïs Nin, the esoteric writer. I must achieve freedom from this life of servitude somehow.

Now I lie in bed. Rupert is practicing his viola to play with a new group. I have three French novels at my bedside. On the "blurb" paper band around the French novel is printed: *Il faut toujours voyager, toujours vouloir être ailleurs*. The credo of the romantics and the neurotics but also of those who do not wish to be buried alive.

Sierra Madre, November 4, 1952

Rupert fights off Kay and her possessiveness, laziness, drinking... I am usually more indulgent. But the other night she arrived drunk, and her behavior repulsed me. She becomes sticky, enveloping everyone like an octopus, drinking from other people's glasses, smoking their cigarettes. Her dress was up above her knees, her lipstick smeared, her mouth obscene. A blurred, inchoate mass of flesh. What I saw this time was the carnivorous appetite to touch, hold, caress, eat. Suddenly I saw her ugliness; it was not only a repellent destructiveness, but an infantile jelly, living by suction. She did everything she could do to make herself repellant. I gave her a chignon because her hair was always straggling and taught her how to pin it on firmly. No sooner did she arrive than it tumbled and she began fixing this already soiled and matted piece before everyone. Then, surrendering, she deposited it on the plate next to where Rupert was fixing drinks. I gave her the best French cheese, a delicacy, and she fed it to Tavi, threw spaghetti on the rug for him. Meanwhile she used the voice and gestures of a three-year-old—a little voice, candied gestures. She then proceeded to tell me that Morton Levine, who interviewed me, does not like my writing; she attacked Letha Nims, interrupted Levine, tried to sing Rupert's song and couldn't, never attaining burlesque, so no one could laugh but rather felt ashamed as if she had displayed a soiled diaper. We have charity for this, but this time I felt none. I knew this will be followed the next day by abject apologies, but I knew this was Kay too, and the other Kay, when not drunk, is merely controlled.

I am tired of children of forty. It is without grace or beauty to be infantile at forty, weighing two hundred pounds. Parasites and failures who are capable of something else, but who are too lazy, too undisciplined...no, it is because they feel impotent and useless that they destroy. Kay's only activity is destruction.

I understand now that it is up to me to create an interesting life here. Rupert can't, does not dare. He feels he was a failure as an actor and fears bohemianism. But to call Kay a "bohemian" is an insult to bohemianism.

Rupert is changing, maturing. At a more sophisticated party at the Campions', the results of our talks appeared in his defense of modern painting.

But the other night, frenzied by hours of radio election speeches, by Kay's behavior, by the awareness of stupidity of my life with Rupert, I felt I couldn't bear it another moment. I have to get away from here.

November 1952

Return to New York

Letter from Anaïs Nin to Charles Duell:

New York, November 10, 1952

Dear Charles: When I last saw you I brought you a card saying that *The Four-Chambered Heart* is indefinitely out of stock, and you said it was a clerical error. So I left with confidence that all was well and the machine would function smoothly. I hoped you were joking when you asked me not to become a competitor and discouraged me from buying back my own books. I didn't intend to set up shop, you know. My business is writing. I got the books for friends, for European publishers, for Christmas presents, or for movie producers or for whoever could help me or was genuinely in need of the books. Now, I find that the Satyr book shop ordered four copies of *The Four-Chambered Heart* about the time I left Hollywood, October 5th or 6th or thereabouts. Here it is November 10, over a month later, and the order has not even been acknowledged. I don't like to bring details to your attention. If you tell me who is in charge of distribution I will write to him. But I do want you to know that what I brought to your attention is harming both of us, and I want to know whether I will have to attend to the distribution of the books myself. You seemed to be desirous of selling the remaining two hundred copies that you have in stock, but how can you do it this way?

I did not call you again because after we talked I realized in what a deep way you failed me. You treated *The Four-Chambered Heart* like the ephemeral seasonal fiction, not like one of your art books on dance, not like one of your long-range faith, of continuous or permanent value. For a few hundred dollars, so little really, you revealed your identification with the usual conventional publisher. It was a matter of convenience, balancing books and storage space. It was very naïve of me to believe you had a vision of their future value. My work will sell as long as Wright's architecture or Graham's dance, yet you could not see that. So little money involved, and such near-sightedness. But this is on another level, and I am only concerned now with the functioning of that selling machine. At least if human faith and vision are out of order, they can't be repaired, but selling machines must work. That is all I ask.

Anaïs Nin

New York, November 14, 1952

The physical pain of separating from Rupert makes me feel that I cannot endure it. I will break with Hugo and stay with Rupert at all costs. I thought of this in the plane. Hugo is very strong now, successful, self-confident, having won security as a businessman and recognition as a filmmaker. He is swimming in a big life. He won't miss me.

But from the moment I unpacked my valises in the light, spacious and graceful apartment, every object and incident conspired to lure and enchant me. White walls, sky, openness. On the table packages of French books from Hugo, announcements of gallery openings, theatres, dancer friends' shows... A big package containing two beautiful Italian dresses. The telephone beside the bed. Millicent's care. Food already in the icebox, money for Martinis and the theatre. My first errand was to the bank for six months' allowance all at once. Jim and Dick effusive, dancing around me. Then Hugo's arrival from Europe, a healthy, triumphant Hugo, amorous and talkative. Ten minutes after he arrives he wants me in bed. He is a friend for whom I feel neither passion nor distaste. It was a gesture of affection. We talked about Italy, France. *Bells of Atlantis* was described by Abel Gance as the first true film poem, and he compared it to Rimbaud's *A Season in Hell.* (I once described *House of Incest* as *A Season in Hell.*) Magazine articles on the film. Ten people to send my books to. *New Story* wants to do *Spy.*

I feel strong and quiet. I have helped Hugo settle down, paid bills, had lamps repaired, changed light bulbs, answered mail, seen Dr. Bogner who finds me well. At night if I can't sleep I take a Martini and think of Rupert. Now I think of him as one for whom I have to create a life. We talked about how fears narrow life, how anxieties cause shrinking and withdrawing. My child of the brilliant, eager eyes is waiting for me to create our life.

The days are filled.

Lila is transformed by an analysis that gave her the strength to go to Alcoholics Anonymous and cure herself.

With Bebe and Louis there is a good collaborative friendship now, solid and very fecund. He has acute ideas on technology, science. She is musically gifted. The electronic music they composed for *Bells of Atlantis* was the third part of a perfect triangle of images, sound, words. It is poetic and abstract.

Eduardo, just out of the hospital, pale, worldly, elegant, suave, cool, unentangled, dispassionate, tender.

Hugo is obsessed with filmmaking, and yet, in the middle of this, when he began to describe the preparation they had made for my arrival in Venice (Hugo, James Broughton, Kermit Sheets, Curtis Harrington) and my cable saying I could not, he suddenly wept quietly and added this divine phrase: "I'm weeping, I believe, for what you missed. Analysis believes one can weep for no one except for one's self, but I don't think I am weeping for myself, really, I'm sure it is for you."

After this I could not sleep. At dawn I took a Martini and floated into a fever and the nightmare of being only half a wife to Hugo. But I am beginning to feel less guilt. If Hugo had needed passion as strongly as I did, he would have pursued it, as I did. My guilt was greatly due to my imagining his deprivation of the passion, but it may be that he truly is more tranquil, and has substituted a quest for achievement and power for sensuality. He needs to rule. He does not want to owe anyone anything: he wants to pay. His obsession is not with love.

Is half of Anaïs better than the whole of some other woman? Hugo has to answer this himself.

Jim came, recently devouring volumes 31, 32 and 33. Devouring truly. The effect on him was explosive. He had been losing interest in reading, his eyes would close, he would fall asleep, but he ravenously read the diary until four in the morning and became delirious. I tease him: "You dope fiend! I shall have to ration you!" "More, more," says Jim. "It is incredible. It is beautiful. It is the most alive thing I have ever read. It is the *greatest* of all works..." and raves, recalling this passage, this phrase, with utter sincerity, truth, depth.

This exultation of Jim's (with poor Kay's inchoate but similar reaction, in her case alcoholic fervor) gave me something I am absolutely seeking, the integration of the two works (as I am seeking the one man, the one love) into one work. I read over the volume I gave to Jim; I am myself disturbed.

La science est faite pour rassurer.

L'art est créé pour troubler.

I feel a strange thing. Every now and then, from the age of twenty on we announce pseudo-maturities. Now I am a woman. Now I am mature. It may be relatively true, or true in part. Certain aspects reach maturity. But this year I reached one that permeates mind, feelings, acts, and work with more evenness. I matured politically. I matured musically, and humanly. I owe this to Bogner. Anxiety was choking my growth and limiting my interests.

Letter from Anaïs Nin to Rupert Pole:

New York, November 22, 1952

It is almost as if we wanted to communicate by way of the movies. As I had seen a *very* dark projection of *Los Olvidados* in a very poor film house in Mexico, I went to see it again around the corner, and was again overwhelmed with horror. The artist does not lie. It is only that he condenses, telescopes many incidents together and makes it so strong a dose, almost too strong for a human being's endurance, and yet, darling, I do feel that it is by visiting hell occasionally that we keep alive our gratefulness for heaven, and our compassion for the doomed ones.

I used to fly from the radio (like it was castor oil), but now I am grateful to you for having matured me politically. I find I understand politics and can listen intelligently at the UN. Poor Chiquito! I didn't take to radio speeches. I guess bringing up a wife is a tough job!

Will phone you Sunday.

Your devoted

Pez Vela

New York, November 23, 1952

A winter evening. All of New York's exhibitionism in shop windows, orgies of luxury, orgies of glitter, stimulating envy, desire, hunger. Home, surrounded by lush curtains and bed covers, an orange negligée with a wide belt of leopard skin, there exists the illusion of a deep, great luxury that I can create. I am watching dinner cooking while Hugo dictates letters to a secretary. I have just talked with Jim on the telephone. He is living out his life in his twenties, covering up his deep longing to be a child and a woman by allowing Dick to be both for him.

He sustains me at this moment when the world of publishers, reviewers, and other writers ignore me. Kimon Friar does not invite me to his radio program "Magic Casements." I have seen so many writers obtain the praise I do not get: Carson McCullers, Kay Boyle, and now Isabel Bolton. I have been snubbed many times by James Laughlin in particular. I am excluded from contemporary anthologies, Signet, New Directions, Perspective and Richard Aldridge's anthology too, from all collections of short stories. Not one big important critic has made a thorough study of me. I have had no devoted publisher. I can't fill a small theatre when I read. The bookshops won't carry my books. Anthony Tudor choreographed Auden's *Age of Anxiety*, weak and pale compared to my work. Martha Graham ignored me. The Museum of Modern Art ignores me. And yet I know I am one of the great forces in contemporary literature. I know absolutely now, that I am as great a force in new writing as Djuna Barnes, Giraudoux, Anna Kavan, Virginia Woolf, Genet, Rimbaud.

It is a desolate and lonely feeling. I can arouse a sacred fervor, a feverish worship, a fanatical response in a few, but I can't break through to the world, the immense world, in France, in Italy; it seems to be every artist receives love and praise but me.

And so Jim speaks now in a secret, fervent way about a life-giving, passion-giving work flowing into his veins. What can I do? I can't publish the diary, my best work. I don't want recognition when I am eighty like Colette, arthritic, a mummy.

And later the world will wonder why I held my personal, intimate life so precious. The world gave me nothing, no salary, no decoration, no presents, no homage of any kind.

So last night, while Hugo revised *Bells of Atlantis* with Bebe and Louis, I invented a tapestry made out of a bamboo shade and pieces of colorful textiles collected here and there, read of Genet and felt that if he amplified the work of Rimbaud, he also wrote nothing by variations on the theme of lust, cruelty, jealousy, evil—the criminal poet who told me what Rimbaud did not tell. For this ultimate truthfulness about his own knowledge of evil, I respect him. People should respect those who dare to go all the way on any road they take. But most people prefer the Étoile, to merely look down five or six avenues and never to the end of any one of them. Cowards all. Miller did that for America, but for an America tone-deaf to anything but guns; only gunshots wake them from their moronic lethargy.

Letter from Anaïs Nin to Rupert Pole:
New York, November 25, 1952

Darling, I'm so sorry I awakened you. The reason I call you then is that after that hour the circuits are always busy. It is my lunch hour and usually I have to wait in line for a free booth at the drugstore. Usually I start a call by waiting 15 or 20 minutes in line, then waiting for a free circuit. I snatch a coffee and sandwich in between and get you about two o'clock when it's time for me to go back. This time no waiting, and poor Chiquito half asleep. It makes me long to be there beside you in our warm bed.

I am so sorry we could not share the Cinerama together—that's an *important* experiment—the illusion of reality created by three projectors on a vast rounded screen is so strong that the audience *screamed* with terror at the roller coaster picture, and you feel you are *inside* the speeding motorboat. I had to write it up, otherwise it is impossible to get tickets.

Monday citizenship. We were herded into a courtroom, kept waiting for four hours, treated with very bad manners as if were all ignorant and illiterate and given a speech going like this: "I don't know where you come from or what you were before, but now you must behave yourselves. This is the best country in the world, and USA citizenship the greatest privilege granted to you. Be grateful for it."

Anyway, you now have an American wife! I will get a diploma in a few days, by mail, and immediately ask for a passport so as to be ready for the next trip, as getting a passport takes time.

De Chochor has hopes of getting *Spy* to Avon.

You haven't told me what the doctor is doing about your stomach. I'm glad the sun lamp helped you, darling. Did you get a thermos and do you drink something warm for lunch?

Te quiero más—your new, American wife

Letter from Rupert Pole to Anaïs Nin:
Sierra Madre, November 1952

My darling

I received your wonderful letter today telling of all you have been seeing. I feel so much better when I think you're doing more in NY than just working, when I realize that much of your work is interesting and that you make good contacts for your writing too.

The terrible thing is that when you're gone everyone takes pity on me and keeps asking me out, but I'm so bored I only want to stay here and read and practice and get some sleep (very tiring physical job now).

So tired. Must say good night, *mi pez vela*, and hope that you'll not jump off when I let the line slack a little—the line will stretch to a star if you wish—just so I can always reel you back to your true home and *tu hombre*.

R

New York, December 2, 1952

As a result of my efforts Jim's first story was accepted by Aldridge's anthology, a book that will reach millions. Such celebration! Jim's delight. He has been writing for five or six years. We all went to his place to drink a Martini together—Dick, Bill Noble, and two neighbors. Before Hugo arrived, Jim suddenly put his arms around my hips, pressed his head against my hips and stomach and said with passion, "Oh, I love you, Anaïs, I love you." I saw Dick was frightened by the passion in Jim's voice, the abandon. So I caressed Jim's head like a mother, stirred by his fervor. And thus we celebrated the beginning of his life as a published writer.

Jim, drunk, kept repeating: "Before I met you at Black Mountain I was ready to commit suicide. When I met you my real life began." I strengthened the past in him. I tried to weld his inspired talking to a direct, plain style. His style became richer and the lyrics quickly more original. I'm proud of him. He was utterly sincere, he worked hard, he was receptive, flexible, persistent and now capable of direct and warm gratitude. I never *over*-praised him.

This underlined my failure to help Gore. I had no influence whatsoever on him. He took nothing; he is very ill, living in utter fantasies, megalomania, lost, and I can't help him. The contrast was violent. I can't bear Gore's venomousness.

Bogner: "You identified with Gore when he was frozen, frightened, shaky, wounded."

This power of empathy frightens me. I wanted to marry Gore, live close to him. Today this appears like madness, the ultimate self-destruction.

Activity. I love this. Hugo in another room with filmmakers and film distributors. I am in touch with all that is created in experimental films, the ballet world. Writing. I sent *A Spy in the House of Love* to *New Story* in Paris today. It will be published in the spring. Now I feel like working again. Two years were wasted on American publishers, a fruitless quest for one intelligent or sensitive or imaginative one, not for me, but for my work.

At eleven o'clock I close the tall, long felt curtains. The room has a velvety texture while the snow falls outside. Hugo is taking a bath. There are French plays stacked on the night table, a Martini. The day has been full. Curtis Harrington, who at twenty-five has already made one memorable film, has been talking about the French filmmaker who proclaims that writing will become more important for its condensation (rather than negligible, as it is here) for film. The distilled phrase will become a necessary element of film. Good writing in films is rare. The dialogue in *Kind Hearts and Coronets* is unusual.

Then Brand Sloan, filmmaker and distributor, tells us about his feeling that film is one of the many facets of "literature," branching from it, dependent on it. He is making a film on Varda. I think with sadness of the emptiness of life in Sierra Madre. Alcoholic Kay, frightened, the passive John, the humdrum Campions, Reginald who is like a dusty attic full of yellowed ideas, the isolation from all creature activities. Curtis brings pollen from France, rereads me and rediscovers me. Everyone is working. It is a beehive of activity and discoveries and pollination.

Chiquito, Chiquito. Sometimes I think that instead of considering the divisions and splits as a disease, one might look upon them as merely bigger and more difficult syntheses to make.

Just as Hugo and I finally combined our clashing obsessions, his with money and mine with art, finally ending in a combination that required his money, my creativity, and himself as artist (and to the artist in Hugo I was a good wife).

Perhaps my interest in the film world may bring to Rupert a bigger life in which his particular beauty could be used in art films; he could be fulfilled too. I know it means risking the loss of Rupert, because the world and other women would then possess him, but this dream is the one I first made for him that will bring him the romantic life he does want (if he didn't, he would not have loved me, but rather a suburban, unimaginative woman).

An ordinary woman might not have made Hugo any happier, might not have helped him to fulfill his dream of creation.

Letter from Rupert Pole to Anaïs Nin:

Sierra Madre, December 1952

My dearest, sweetest (well, most of the time) Spanish wife,

So, so tired—*mon dieu, quel, quel jour*—too fabulous to try to tell you about now. My father, June, and June's few-months-old baby who is allergic to everything and who June is sure is Reginald's, and a completely mad Russian character named Malya who is taking care of the baby, all arrived and informed me they were staying here for the night to go on to Hollywood (and San Francisco) today.

I said no!!!!! Simply but firmly that I would take them to a hotel but they couldn't stay here, so they agreed to go on to Hollywood, but it rained like hell when they left so they only got as far as Arcadia and arrived at the Aztec Hotel carrying bags, bottles, and what have you and took over three rooms.

June, the baby and Malya arrived here at seven this morning to give the baby a bath and have only just left, joined by my father at four and Kay and John at five—such a madhouse that I thought we were bohemian!!

Malya (who used to be an opera singer) sang Russian songs to the baby, and the baby alternately looked like the reincarnation of the Dalai Lama and cried bloody murder—and June talked incessantly about my father and love and Quakers and India and Gandhi. I finally escaped to the garage.

You sounded good on phone, at least till I said I wasn't alone, but from the above you can see why.

All my end-of-month reports are still ahead of me, so goodnight, my beautiful Americanized Spanish wife, who is all the music I shall ever need or want. Hurry back—music has only empty sounds without you.

R

Wait till you see your Christmas tree; *you* have to make the decorations!!!!

New York, December 8, 1952

Jim wrote a story called "Jazz of Angels."

"Jim," I say over the telephone, "write me some more Jazz of Angels." Jim, quick-witted, nimble, alert, is the one I can talk to in writing language. I say "rhythm" and it means as much to him as to me: contemporary rhythm.

Last night at the Downbeat, Candido, the Cuban drummer, drummed himself into an orgiastic frenzy, his legs around the drum occasionally lifting it from the ground—such violence! Max Geismar wrapped his leg around mine and he smiled, a humble, timid smile, a man who has not been fêted, who does not live in the present, who is a serious historian of literature. His work does not give him joy. They are, he and Anne, highly humorous and aware, but unhappy. I like them together, as a couple. I don't respond to his desire. I don't know how to discourage it without being cold or cruel. I wish he would not make me say it. The sparkle between the four of us is so evenly distributed, and his desire unbalances it, introduces anxieties and guilt.

Jazz of Angels… Rupert writes me lyrically now, about me being all through his music.

Christmas is in the air.

Gathering presents, buying my ticket for Los Angeles, telephoning Rupert. I have *always* spent Christmas with Hugo. I would like to give one to Rupert. I have less guilt and shame for my desires. If Hugo had been a man of passion, nothing could have prevented him from seeking fulfillment, as nothing will prevent Rupert. Hugo was not interested in interplay with others and, until now, was not even too greatly interested in friendship.

But today he receives the jazz directly, the friendship directly, the pleasures, the praise, the recognition.

TWA flight en route to Los Angeles, December 11, 1952

Rupert said over the telephone: "You *must* come back!"

Hugo, after our good month together, always becomes destructive when I leave. He is still the boy who is in a fit of rage, destroying the red kite he most loved.

I spent three whole days Christmas shopping, to find surprises for Hugo. I prepared a Christmas mobile hanging from the ceiling, and under a Swedish angel are chimes that turn under four candle flames and tinkle merrily. I left so few things undone. I bought presents for his friends. And because of his back, and because he tires easily, I waited on him.

Yet on the way to the airport he looked grim and tight, and he began to express anxiety about the bad weather for flying, and I have said many times on such occasions: "One has to trust the airline's weather reports. Bad weather here does not necessarily mean bad flying weather." I have to face the fact that I cannot leave in peace and freedom, that Hugo resents it and will always resent it. I have to accept his bad humor, his revengeful mood. And not mind.

We had our irrational quarrel, because he still, after years of analysis, does not sleep well, and last night after giving him dinner in bed, another present of a Japanese black lacquer teacup and tray, and lovemaking, I found him awake and asked him about what worries and troubles him. He answers: "The problem of Cornillat and Wyss." This problem of Hugo's indulgence and affinities with Cornillat, a crooked adventurer, a neurotic, even pathological type, has haunted our life and endangered our economic security for five years. He allows Bogner to probe but resents it when I do. I said, "Don't you think it might be constructive to dwell on the fact that making movies will allow you to have your own adventurous life?"

Millicent and I sat eating our lunch together in the kitchen. She said, "I had a hard time getting used to Mr. Hugo's ways when you first began to travel, but I'm used to them now. I keep thinking he's no different than my children, always asking for this or that, where is this or that, and fussin'."

"Goodbye, Anaïs," said Jim. "What a rich month you gave me; you fecundate me."

"You do too, Jim. We have a writing language. You *answer*, you know; one wants to be answered in one's own language. Whatever I gave you to read I feel you take up and improve on, continue or prolong my thoughts."

Hugo, curiously, I see now, had his own language, the *opposite* of words: engraving and film, all visual. That is what made him so impenetrable to me.

It's like a Greek living with a Spaniard, a Spaniard living with a German.

Every human being becomes destructive if he believes himself wounded or attacked, and I become destructive with Rupert when he is so obvious about his interest in young girls. I become destructive with Gore when he humiliates me, when he walks with Curtis after the ballet and I hear him say, "I could have been a ballet dancer, I was very good at it, but I couldn't bear to touch the women." Or: "After the ballet you should see the cars with rich men at the stage door waiting to scoop up the boys, while the ballet girls have to go home alone," like his fantasy in Antigua that the students having a fiesta were homosexuals, when everyone in Guatemala knows the girls are not allowed on the streets alone. I went out that night to challenge Gore's fantasy and found myself not only among students desperately seeking to dance with me, but saying poetic, vehement, fervent words of desire, becoming so demonstrative that I was forced to re-enter Gore's house and barricade the door against them. After I went to bed in my own room, in the dark Gore allowed two boys in, and I heard them refuse his advances and ask where his cousin was (he had said I was his cousin); "We want to see her."

A white world outside the plane window. Clarity. Clarity. Recently I could not bear the white expanse of my lucidities; I sought anesthesia. Last night, after a quarrel with Hugo, I drank; I did not stay awake in misery. I was able to sleep for an hour. The realm of constant awareness I tried to live in was as difficult to bear as the states of grace of Catholic saints or the states of contemplation of the mystics. To see, to hear, to know all. In the process of becoming more human I have been able to descend into inchoateness, into lethargy, into smogs and fogs of the mind. Some links, some bridges, sustained or maintained by great effort, are slipping away from me. I see now what a critic meant when she said *Winter of Artifice* was *unbearable*—there was no refuge, no pause, no rest, no escape from the awareness. A diamond lodged in the head, the unblinking eye of the clairvoyant. But altitudes wear out the heart. As the white clouds pass me I think of this state between New York and Los Angeles in which I sit alone and belong to myself...a neutral area, a bridge of sighs, white sighs; when I come down again I will resume my humanity. I took flight from a bad night into whiteness.

I wonder why the analysts fought the diary. Lila said fervently, "Oh God, I'm glad you are writing it." This is my life's work and I must attend to it.

I had to take my shoes and stockings off, soaked by the rain on earth. The large airport umbrella almost carried me off across the landing fields. I carry *Spy*, in its final version.

Lila says, "You tend to split everything into various fragments to divide your work into two kinds of writing and then to pit them against each other. Your greatest difficulty is in integrating. It is true that a book can seek the flow of life, but still the novel sought to integrate certain episodes, not to capture fragments."

But we live in fragments. The design is only revealed later.

But, being a writer, Lila says, "I just think of the diary as a *different* language, as one thinks of film, dance or music."

The diary and art. Was I trying an impossible integration? Is it as impossible to integrate my passion Rupert and my husband Hugo?

High above, every large form of life seems possible, at 30,000 feet altitude and in pressurized cabins! Returning to New York the last time, a month ago, I had begun to feel free of pressure. I had to learn not to mind Rupert's criticalness. "It is not against you. You have to learn that most angers and attacks are not against you, personally."

If I were to write to Henry, I would say: I am now a forester's wife—not legally—I don't like to be legally anything because it means *à perpétuité*.

If I were to write to Jim, I would say: There are times when as a forester's wife I answer "Paris branch" because I am so bored with Sierra Madre. Sierra Madre is a community that has been antisepticised and anti-insecticided beyond recognition. It is made up of the healthy American life, which means pool fraus and picnic fraus, variations of the hausfrau.

From one to four, oblivion from a bottle. But the mind persisted in its activity. I thought I must make some of my lies true, such as the alibi for this trip, that Lester Horton is doing my story "Rag Time" in the modern dance.

Anne Lye says my work is a goldmine for filmmakers. I don't want them to discover me too late.

Now I have a desire to see Rupert, to hold him, to sleep by his side. But I have no desire to get into the life there.

Anaïs, make a wonderful life in California. So I took addresses of jazz places from *US Confidential* and found places in Redondo Beach, and New Orleans jazz on Western. At an art gallery I chose Gil Henderson, but not for the quality of his painting, but because of his dreaming a life one can't reach. One grey day we visited Lloyd's glass Wayfarer's Chapel, and it was beautiful, on a hill high above the sea, but Lloyd himself is narrow-minded, fanatical and destructive, violent like a white Gonzalo.

There is Christie, next door, a child of poetry, an elf, but secured to earth by her parents. Christie says, "Anis, Anis, look, today I am a cowboy." And I bring her mobiles to make, and hang up her free and joyous paintings. But already she is taught to "trace" her drawings, and the Catholic school dresses her in a uniform. Her mother worries about her fascination with my dresses, my Japanese dolls, my mobiles, my talk.

The clouds have vanished and with them the shadow of the plane, which was traveling below us, and, depending on the depth of the clouds, it would often come up towards us, growing larger and closer.

Now that the clouds have dissolved (and I remember writing to Jim and Dick about the many *vacancies* I had seen among the clouds on my last trip), I see rivers, fields, mountains. I see neon lights and car lights. I see a map of a great nation that was misnamed. It should have been called *Woolworth*. When nature presents a noble, vast spectacle, such as the canyons, the desert, Mr. Woolworth takes care of merchandising it.

I dream of saving Rupert, of revealing his beauty to the artists who are making films, of giving him a wonderful life, of giving him the life of passion he dreams of. In short, to give him his dream.

Twilight. I know what Rupert is doing at this moment. He is tidying the untidy, chaotic house for me. He is late. He is bathing quickly, trying to listen to Chet Huntley and other commentators, drinking beer (because it is cheaper), nursing poison ivy on his legs. He will have rings under his eyes. He will drive tensely, impatiently. He will be misinformed about the plane's arrival and miss me. Or he might stand, brooding, with Tavi at his feet, his eyes in shadow, and his eagerness kept leashed.

It is strange that as I fly towards Rupert and focus on the passion, the flame, the electric sparks, the life itself, the greater expanses, the international landscapes, the universal worlds of art all recede, and I focus on a dollhouse. I think of Rupert constantly calling my attention to a bare mountain, to the fire-path, a fire break he patrols, and my controlling the desire to say, "It is not beautiful." America the beautiful is as unstirring as its pink and healthy children.

Nightfall, completely now.

TO DO
Send a set of diaries to Jim for safe keeping in New York
A set of diaries to Sierra Madre
Originals to be copied to Sierra Madre
Put originals copied back into safe in LA

Sierra Madre, December 17, 1952

Dinner by Henri Charpentier, the famous chef taught by Escoffier, in a motel house, where he presides dramatically over an unsurpassed banquet and monologues incessantly of his dialogues with Queen Victoria, Jim Brady and the Rockefellers, his shenanigans at the age of ten, and all the *Ulysses* inventiveness of a French Joyce in the kitchen, whose sauces are made of poured words, flavored anecdotes stirred with an enormous spoon-fed ego. Servant, then flatterer, then tyrant, then title-giver, then assertive of his own nobilities and distinctions, he immerses us in a fading world of vainglorious memories, humble bromides, moralization, and the woman who keeps him says, "He is unusually wound up."

Like all the people greatly concerned with the galleries of the past, painted and sculptured heroes of the halls of fame, he does not see who is there to listen, who might be, for all his astigmatism, a present-day Jim Brady, a descendent of Queen Victoria, a future Rockefeller, or at least contemporary variations of the same themes of human personality. All this is because his memory reverts and remains in the scenes where he played an important role. There is, listening to him, Letha Nims, who resembles Dolores del Rio, who is ironic, mocking, humorously acidic; there is Bill Nims with the soft eyes of tender men who live slightly up-tilted at the corners like autumn leaves that are never able to open completely before the inclemency of weather; there is Kay, sumptuous, florid, a shoulder bare in an orange blouse, her blouses always seeming about to slip off, her eyes burning, her hair now in a permanent, tidy after the stormy critical hangover of her last drunk; there is John, timid and well-behaved like one still obeying firm and gentle parents; there is Jack Powell, tense, willful, sophisticated, and probably cruel to his Latin wife from Panama; there is Rupert at the head of the table, a princely and radiant host.

A few hours earlier Rupert was gathering pine cones and mistletoe at the top of the mountain for the ladies. I feel I am losing some of my artificial plumage and iridescence from New York. The climate of nature in place of the art life does not elate me. But Rupert is so joyous and proud of his Christmas tree, of his first Christmas with me, and our passion burns.

We spent the evening wrapping presents for his family.

The manzanita Christmas tree was decorated the very day I returned from New York with a collection of presents.

Is part of the incurable guilt I feel due to the fact that I owe Hugo all I wear, my trips with Rupert, the vacuum cleaner with which I clean Rupert's home, the warm fur coat, the care of my hair, nails, the doctor, the dentist, the rest I can have, my book being published, in short, *everything* that I am, everything I developed? It is good to tell myself that I have replenished and returned all this in other forms, that Hugo *could* do as my other men did, take all I gave him and share it with other loves, other relationships? I wonder how it would affect my guilt if I could overcome this dependence so that I would not feel all I have was given to me by him. Would it make so great a difference if I had bought all the charming little gifts I discovered for Rupert and his friends out of my own efforts?

Sometimes I feel lonely for Hugo, but all the moments that could give me pleasure with him seem marred by his temperament and his "oldness." The nights are ruined by his loud snoring. Homecomings are always deflated by his anxieties. Serving him tea during his bath before dinner, because of the absence of joy, becomes a duty. I don't know why, but these same moments with Rupert are usually joyous, full of teasing, playfulness, pranks, elations. Our disagreements are insignificant, not bitter as they are with Hugo. Hugo's anxieties continue, and from afar they seem greater.

At a party recently, lost among unidentifiable people, the moment an attractive woman came in (I did not even see her fully but out of the corner of my eye), I could hardly continue socializing. My anxiety had awakened. The rest of the evening was merely an evening to suffer through. Even while drunk and immersed in the music, I was aware of every movement made by Rupert and the red-haired actress. Rupert's naïveté and obviousness did not help, of course. He found her and her husband an "interesting couple," when actually the husband was a six-foot lump of flesh who coaches football at UCLA, a bore. (Talk about the humiliation of the artists, there is nothing more hermetic than a football coach. They can only talk in cave man language.)

I have to live with this illusion. It is incurable. I return from New York full of strength from analysis, full of confidence, feeling beautiful. Just before we left for the party Rupert said, "You're so goddamned beautiful." And when I said, "Why goddamned?" he said, "Because you're a temptation, and there is no time for lovemaking, we have to be on our way." And ten minutes later, I suffered from the constriction of fear, a panic of the body!

The next day I had a cold.

C'est la même chose.

At least I'm proud of one thing: I did not reveal my condition. I did not spoil Rupert's pleasure. In the middle of the party he kissed me on the neck. To reassure me?

The Peace Dove

It all began with my catching sight of a Swedish peace dove carved out of paper-thin wood, with an iridescent quality of dew. It was tied to a wall, not flying as it should be. I bought several for very special poetic Christmas gifts, gave one to Ann Lye, left one for Hugo to give, brought one to Rupert, and to Lloyd. A symbol, Mr. Freud would have said. You wish to make peace with Rupert's family. You know Lloyd would understand the symbolism. Peace upon the world, and upon families (neither being truly possible). So we arrived one afternoon while Lloyd and Helen sat having cocktails. There was a fire in the fireplace, Martinis on the table, and I felt the mood was auspicious.

Lloyd did like the peace dove. Immediately, it must be hung over the fireplace, under the diffuse ceiling light. Immediately Helen must rise with her limping, aching, arthritic leg dragging to find thread. Immediately Rupert must bring the ladder from the kitchen and climb up and change the bulbs, rearrange loose wiring. Lloyd and Rupert do not agree on the way to hang the dove. Lloyd says his way will make it rotate now to the left, now to the right. An argument develops. Rupert gets stubborn and angry. The thread breaks. The peace dove falls. I pick it up, uninjured. Lloyd says he will hang it up properly. But the thread breaks again. His wrath flashes on Helen. "Why did you give me such thin thread? If that's what you sew my buttons with, I can see why they come off all the time!" At last the peace dove is hung according to the mobile principle of Lloyd Wright; Rupert's hands are now dirty, Helen's hip hurts her more acutely, and the peace dove is bathed in indirect lighting. Lloyd wants a flock of them gyrating, and while there may be symbolism in everything, there is no peace anywhere!

Letter from Jim Herlihy to Anaïs Nin:

New York, December 1952

Dear Anaïs:

Something I came across in today's reading from Journal 34 made me decide to write you in spite of the fact that I am not "in the mood." Something you said about the main object of your journal being not to forget, not to omit, to even write badly. You have no idea what an important document your journal is, Anaïs; to me it means more than anything I've ever read in my life. And in that little ship I truly intend to sink the Holy Bible, Dostoyevsky, Lawrence, Shakespeare, and all the others, because this is the most entirely un-dehumanized book of them all. Many great books have unmasked certain or even large areas of human deceits, but in nothing I've read have I felt that the purpose itself had such a purity and unity apparent in every sentence.

I suppose one of the things that's kept me mute, or comparatively so, is the fact that I have been in a certain awe of this journal ever since I began it, and feel it was somehow disproportionate to its value that I should comment on it thoughtlessly and quickly or unbeautifully; but the moment the thought crystalized, I was deeply ashamed that any such misgiving could have stopped me even unconsciously. I don't want to make you unhappy by saying that I am in awe of you—you know this is not the case. It's just that you have made something beautiful that, as you said yourself, was not intended to be a work of art, but more of a by-product of your living—call it what you will. Now I happen to believe that it is a work of art, but this should not be a frightening thing, or even respectable. Stravinsky said that the trouble with music appreciation in general is that people are taught to have too much respect for music: "They should be taught to love it instead." And you know, Anaïs, that I love you far too much to be in awe of you. They are contradictions in terms. And I also think that I don't make any separation anymore between you and your journal. You and it are one to me. In certain instances the journal has transcended, gone ahead of you, almost as if the awareness with which you had written certain parts of it was the awareness of a drug addict, or one whose integration was so perfect he must be dead and gone to heaven. But I think that's fine. Like in *Spy* when you talk about the high moments, I might be afraid I had lost you to the angels, that my friend had gone to a world where breathing itself was a pure state of beauty—I might be afraid of that if I didn't know instinctively as I read it that you have written here a description of the potential of man's spiritual existence. This is something that I have always felt distinguishes the artist from all others who engage in crafts. They assume from the beginning that man is an angel in trouble; they write or paint or carve or whatever about his troubles, but they never forget that he is an angel.

(I think I just said something beautiful. Did I?)

This letter may seem heavy, but actually I am elated, very happy today. This is not very humorous, but humor is sometimes a form of hysteria that overlays unhappiness. I am not humorous today—I'm happy and that's better. I walk down the street and proclaim wild wild wild and strength strength strength, and love love love.

From Jim, your twin.

Eric and Lloyd Wright, Rupert Pole; Leona Weiss, Helen Wright, Hausi; Anaïs Nin

DESIRE WILL BUY ANOTHER AIRPLANE TICKET

1953

January 27, 1953
Return to New York

Letter from Rupert Pole to Anaïs Nin:
Sierra Madre, February 1953

SUBJECT: Microbial Miseries

Strange, darling, I knew something was wrong with your last letter—it was too good to be true, too fast and too fine—henceforth I shall take all your written *pronunciamentos* on your health with my usual amount of salt!! Got up early, gargled with soda, then mouthwash, then whisky, stood *à la tête* for a full ten minutes, then tried a little opera and in fine voice, waited for your call—no call—but just as well because I'd rather spend the money on Acapulco or a binge at Vegas. But the point of all the gargling was to convince you that I'm hale and hearty again. I have lots of strength from taking it easy and cleaning out thoroughly, and the cold only flirted with the chest this time, just a little over the weekend and didn't really try to live there.

Do take it easy, love. The first week away is always your Waterloo because of the sudden change of climate and because you try to do too much. You'd better buy some more of those warm boots and some hot little mittens.

Strange, I just happened to be listening to a random station driving in the car when a doctor started to talk about diseases. I was all ready to switch him off when he began talking about anemia. I listened carefully and was amazed to hear him state that anemia often produces two secondary symptoms. The first is an isolated and completely unaccountable fever (remember your fevers)—they're not serious, and not rheumatic as that other Dr. tried to diagnose them; they're definitely caused by the anemia plus a general run-down condition. The second is pseudo heart trouble. Anemic persons are often very conscious of their hearts, he said, and every now and then their hearts seem to "act up." Their troubles are often diagnosed as heart murmurs, but these are not true murmurs, and the anemic person has nothing to worry about (at least about the heart). It is the anemia that causes both the fever and simulated heart trouble. The anemia itself, he claimed, is tied up with general health, proper nourishment, but above all with elimination of waste material. All anemia is caused to some extent by improper elimination, by accumulated wastes, and this may sometimes be the only cause. He sounded very intelligent and matter of fact and didn't seem to be selling anything—and I believe him—so no more worries about the strange fevers or a tricky heart. But let's get those bowels movin' gal, and probably you should drink more water. I never see you drink water!!!

Goodnight, my love
Hasta muy pronto
R

Letter from Anaïs Nin to Rupert Pole:

New York, January 1953

Darling Chiquito: I am so happy you wrote me about the meaning of our relationship, because I had been feeling blue and guilty, when alone, for my "rebellions." You know, my love, I always looked upon the gift of "life" as the most precious of all our possessions, second to love, and one that most people abuse and do not value. I looked upon life very much as a work of art in itself, something to be created, beautiful, expanded. For the sake of this I have always been rebellious against waste, or destructive people, alcoholics. And I was afraid I had made you uncomfortable sometimes. But looking back I feel I owe to this relationship an interesting life and not let it, by passivity or too much acceptance, become uninteresting.

I know you *feel* the same way. I know you make sacrifices for this. I know that. But sometimes you're more tolerant of people than I am. I love this trait in you, but I also think if we don't have courage our whole life could be smothered by the Kays, those who live off others… So forgive me. The only time I have been weak in this is when people are in real trouble—then they have a right to take up our time. So, since I was feeling a little guilty about my efforts to free us, for a life of our own making, I was very happy to read your letter. I don't want my rebelliousness against mediocrity to ever make you unhappy. I suppose having lived a "couple years" longer than you, I know now that compassion sometimes can be self-destructive. I carried it to the point of self-destruction, and I learned that it was a sin too. As the Hindu philosopher once said, do not hurt others, do not hurt yourself either—both are sins. A tightrope to walk, isn't it?

Don't worry about the cold. I have rubber rain boots and the two coats (felt and a big black one), and with a scarf over my beret, they work fine.

Te quiero mucho y mucho

A

PS: Darling, About the Mexico trip. I just got a letter from Annette about the Hotel Jacalito. It is 50 pesos a day, 10 pesos extra for breakfast. I suppose that means with maid service. Trouble is I don't know what to answer because we don't know the date. We can't commit ourselves.

Letter from Anaïs Nin to Rupert Pole:

New York, February 9, 1953

Your voice sounded cheerful, darling, although we both made a mistake in dates according to our wish-fulfillment, and it is farther away from Feb. 27th than we figured. It seems like years. Sometimes I get a desperate impulse to quit and jump on the plane. There is always a bad moment before going to sleep, of longing and loneliness and *seeing* you so clearly like a vision, leaping into bed always ahead of me but never ahead of Tavi!

Now I will tell you what you want to hear. I got my passport. An honest-to-goodness American passport. Shall I get visas for visits to Mexico or Guatemala together with you in LA? Send me a list of all you need from the film supply shop.

I feel so lonely and cut off and far away without your letters, but I guess that is one way you will never change. I think now it is really a complex and not natural. You have certainly five minutes for me, and that is all it takes. It makes me very sad sometimes, I must confess. Also don't you realize it makes *me* feel like not writing, and that to me is estranging and creates distance and makes separation seem stronger than the love, like big deserts stretching between us, deserts of silence? I hate silence. It is like an absence of communion.

You share so much with me when I am there, so little when I am gone.

A

Western Union cable from Rupert Pole to Anaïs Nin:

February 13, 1953

Anaïs Nin, care Herlihy: 256 West 73 St.

Feast of music playing every night. I'm trying for permanent group for summer. I know I've been miserable correspondent completely unworthy to receive your beautiful letter, but you did take in a Mexican husband knowing well his faults and his love. Only four more weeks and we will wander again together with love.

Rupert

New York, February 1953

In January, on the plane from Los Angeles to New York, I could not sleep well because of a sharp pain in my hip. For years, almost once every year I had gone to some doctor and said, "I have a pain here, in the right ovary." He would examine me and say, "There is nothing." I would return to Dr. Bogner a little ashamed, thinking as I did as a child: *J'ai une maladie imaginaire*. This time, the pain pierced through my sleep and I said to myself: I must do something about this.

I went to Jacobson, who sent me to a new doctor. He found a tumor, so large that it may have been mistaken for the ovary itself. I went to another doctor. He felt the tumor. To the second one I said, "I want to be operated on as soon as possible." He chose Friday, the 29th of January. I did not let Rupert know. He would get anxious and try to call me for news, or even come to New York. It would create complications. I couldn't have feared death, for I made no preparations such as I always intend to make about the disposition of the diary. Thursday I entered the hospital. After Hugo left at nine o'clock I felt the loneliness, the stark humiliation and danger. The nurse shaved me, which saddened me. I still did not know I would be cut. I thought the operation was going to be done through the vagina, or wanted to think so.

Early Friday, at six o'clock, they put a homely white shirt and leggings on me. The New York University Hospital is dismal, but medically good. I had a little room with two windows. In extreme illness I get very passive, obedient, child-like, trusting. I surrender to others. The trip to the operating room, which I know so well now, was, as usual, accomplished in half sleep, half fatalistic submission. The anesthesiologist was the last person I saw. I felt sorry for them having to get up so early and told them so. Then I heard her say she had to give me ether instead of an injection because my blood pressure was too low. I hate ether. But she helped me by saying: "I will take it off if you feel uncomfortable. And first of all I will give you oxygen until you see how easy it is." I was so grateful that she helped me, was not an autocrat, and after two whiffs of oxygen I gave in, but I held on to her hand. Mercifully, at the second whiff of ether I was unconscious. How long I don't know—it is like death—total absence. And hours later I heard my name called—Anis, Anis—it was the nurse. But Hugo's voice called me and I made a greater effort to return. The feeling of distance...I saw Hugo's face. I saw the doctor's face. I asked, "It wasn't cancer?" A useless question as they didn't know yet, not until after the laboratory tests.

I had a big bandage over my stomach. My first shock was to realize that I had been cut open, that I had another scar, one more flaw. After that, *pain*, pain and sleep. The night nurses ghostly, but so kind. Days of weakness, pills to get to sleep, injections. My hands were blue and painful from blood transfusions and dextrose because I could not eat. It was as if I had committed hara-kiri.

Visitors. Hugo's kindness, the old Hugo as he was before, bringing me a Japanese kimono, slippers, a new nightgown.

On Sunday, feeling so weak that it was an effort to talk, I telephoned Rupert as usual, pretending, acting, and he could not divine the truth. He thought I had been a little remote, displeased by him, perhaps.

I wrote to him as if nothing happened.

Jim and Dick came. Lila, Larry, Ruth Witt Diamant...

Weakness...weakness. But now they make you walk the third day, slowly. So I made friends. A girl whose leg was in a cast after being knocked down by a car. An old Russian professor thinking the hospital was like a concentration camp.

No strength to read or to write. Pain. But I slept at night. After nine days I could go home. I wept with joy to be safe and sound again and at home. So grateful for Hugo.

In convalescence you are once more in a cocoon of stillness. You have not even the strength to be restless. Every day there is more strength. I am horrified at the scar; I feel humiliated.

Hugo so kind...there, always there, when the truth is that he is weak, troubled, filled with fears, in need of help. Terrifying. *The most difficult thing in the world to do is to admit and face the weakness of the one from whom you seek protection.* This is what I have had to do, and to *help* him.

My illness only truly lasted ten days...extreme weakness. But soon I started to be active. The tumor was not cancer.

As the physical scar heals, I become aware of the psychic illness once more: the fact I cannot face is that I am a failure as an artist.

I cannot resign myself to this, because like Hugo, I cannot bear failure or rejection.

Hugo had to pay for the publication of *A Spy in the House of Love*; he tried once more to protect me from the truth. Poor Hugo.

Today he started to make love to me and couldn't. This happens occasionally (it happened to Gonzalo). This, together with his completely irrational behavior with the film (the best print he got he wants to lay aside because he can't face the Museum of Modern Art, fearing defeat), gave me anxiety. I felt in this state he should not be driving to see a business friend in New Jersey. I had a bad premonition. I went out to stop him. He had come back. I said, "I feel you must not go today." Then I went with him, to exorcise the danger.

I sit at a bar now—only five people, Sunday—and like all American places, it is joyless, dismal. I'm deeply depressed. I was angry with Rupert for writing so little. I telephoned him. I said I could not bear it. Then once more I tried to explain to Hugo: "We are both obsessed with this need to succeed as artists. My only cure is to run away. Let me go and get sun and peace, and forgive me; I am not running away from you, only from our two sicknesses."

"I am very sick," said Hugo. It is as if his whole life depends on people liking his films. I don't understand either why I should care, lose sleep because the Four Season Book Shop does not like my writing and refuses to sell my records, or because Wallace Fowlie writes a book on surrealism and poetry and comments on the poetry in Miller and not a word on me, or because Kimon Friar "forgot" to come by one evening.

Poor Hugo—both of us are tormented by this need to win praise, love, understanding for our art. Why? Why? Why?

Today I don't know what gave me this sudden fear that he would drive out and hurt himself. I feel for him, the defeat of his sensuality.

Letter from Rupert Pole to Anaïs Nin:

Sierra Madre, February 20, 1953

Love!!!

So terribly depressed after your phone call. It's my own damn fault, and excuses don't help, but one thing you must realize, my darling (I had thought you had accepted this after all the trips and all our talks, but I see now it's something deep in you that I should have been aware of and more sensitive to), that when I don't write it doesn't mean I don't love you, it doesn't mean that I've forgotten about you, it doesn't mean I'm spending all my time with some willowy blonde, it doesn't even mean that I don't care enough to write. At the worst it usually means that I'm working hard, that I've been forgetful about getting the damn stamps and envelopes and remembering to find a mailbox, and that it's getting near the time we'll be together again, and I've forgotten how much my letters (or the lack of them) mean to you.

I did write two letters recently, one Saturday night before you phoned Sunday and one Tuesday night. One was mailed Tues. night and the other Wed. One should be there by now—it's possible the post office intercepted them as I couldn't find envelopes and had to use official forest service ones, used an air mail stamp that didn't cover the official cost and it is remotely possible they might send it back or even refer it to the F.S.

Love, it's more difficult for me to write than you, not only psychologically (I'm always afraid the letter will seem dull and poorly written to you), but physically. At lunch time I'm either way back in the forest with no paper or at the office where there are ten or twelve people sitting around and talking, making writing impossible. Then I'm not free to get out all day the way you are, nor can I dash off a note or buy stamps or envelopes or mail as easily as you.

Have rarely been as tired as these last two weeks—so much music, perhaps too much—but I do want to become a really good violist and playing is the only way. It felt better to splurge while you were away than when we wanted more time to do things together. I come home, fix dinner, try to straighten the house, and fix lunch for the next day, then practice what we're playing that night, then go out to play till 12 or so, home at 1 dead-tired, back feeling broken, and repeat same the next day.

Then Lloyd and Mother are broke and have to borrow money, so they're desperately trying to sell the lot below the Griffith Park house. The wind there blew down many trees, so I have been working there with a rented truck on days off to clean the place up and make the lot look bigger. Also have to do all repair work for the tenants who live in the house now.

Then all the daily stuff of keeping the house going, keeping Tavi going, income tax, insurance bills, etc., etc. Have to fix my car up for Mother and get Eric's car ready for our trip. Believe it or not, there are two *Times* here now that I haven't had time to read—often don't even get to listen to my commentators anymore.

Haven't seen Kay or John, or the Nims, or anyone.

Love, we decided together how long you'd stay before you left here. The reasoning was we need the extra money for this longer trip and it was better to stay a little longer this time, while you're already there, than to have to go back right after our trip. I hope we can be together all summer after the trip and not go back until next November.

I got my passport. I went to the dentist. He made a horrible thing that fits in my mouth at night and keeps me from grinding my teeth—are you happy??? No diarrhea since I gave up coffee.

Sierra Madre fire whistle just blew in brush region, so had to get out there—thank God it was just a tractor on fire. Very cold here now with very strong winds, very bad for fires.

I still do love you, every part of me loves you even if I do get Mexican and forget to reaffirm it with letters.

Su hombre Mexicano

R

Letter from Rupert Pole to Anaïs Nin:

Sierra Madre, February 1953

Querida Limoncita

So good to hear your voice again, you sounded so well, but you seemed a tiny bit cold, disappointed; was it because I said I felt wonderful? My love, my only love, past, present, future, I am terribly lonely and unhappy whenever you're gone, and I usually sound so down when you phone. Then you say you're worried about me, so this time I decided to sound happy to help cheer you up, and what happens? Did it cheer you up? No! You only sounded sadder and sadder, possibly because you wondered what was making me so happy!! So, my darling, I can't win. Next time I shall be sad again.

But sincerely, love, I'm awfully happy and looking forward to our trip. It will be our last by José, to real *tropical* jungles.

How much off can you get on film (movie and still color) at Hugo's place? I can only get 10% off here. We're going to get pictures this trip.

To the beach yesterday; it was so warm I had the top of the car down and my shirt off all the way down. Sand was lovely was but water impossibly cold.

I don't know when I love you most, *querida mía*, when you're away and I realize how empty, dull, and meaningless life is without you, or when you are here, warm, vibrant, close to me and giving me life and love.

R

EN ROUTE TO LOS ANGELES, MARCH 1, 1953

The sun illumines what I write. I left a tender, forgiving Hugo, not angry anymore at my leaving, because this month, during the physical weakness that threw me completely under his wing, I was able to reverse the tides and open myself to his needs and difficulties with utter sympathy. Before this my guilt was so great that I could not allow myself to understand Hugo. When you have great guilt all you can think of is that if you admit the guilt the other will again demand that you surrender. We got from religion the false sequence that guilt means wrong-doing, that confession means atonement, penitence, which ultimately leads to reform, or a return to the original state. So, not wanting this, we erect a defense; the guilt becomes the defensive war. But now I know its true evolution. Guilt is self-censorship; to become free of it means to accept one's self as one is, and the reality of one's acts. To be free of guilt means one is free to understand another's problems. I never had to give up what I could not give up by force. I had to accept myself, and therefore Hugo, and have sympathy for his difficulties. For example, Hugo feels a wife should be there all the time. When I leave he feels deserted. I feel the compulsion to leave, for many reasons. I cannot act otherwise at the moment. To admit my difficulties *and* recognize Hugo's, or the pain I cause him, is what I was able to do for the first time.

I once used his many flaws and weaknesses as alibis for my leaving. I permitted myself an accumulation of irritations, and finally I had enough explosives to push off. But now I feel his flaws as human, pathetic. And I see mine too. I can bear to look at them. Whatever Hugo is, I am fallible and defective in other ways. I am more volatile, more peripheral, I escape, I live split lives, I live by deception, roles, impersonations, duplicities. But in our distortions we are both "possessed." The effort we have made to put an end to distortion has been courageous. What Hugo's role hid was a mutilated man whose instincts were literally crushed by a cruel aunt who beat him (particularly for sexual licenses).

I once saw Hugo in terms of what he had failed to be, in terms of my selfish, weak need of a father. Now I see him as like all the young ones I helped so well to gain strength, on whom I lavished compassion and protection. In terms of his evolution, analysis is like an electric shock treatment; it throws you back into childhood to reconstruct the personality. You can't reconstruct it without a past. You re-evaluate the past so it will be not an incubus or succubus but a sturdy base to a structure.

Hugo *has* been retracing the unstable, the stuttering, the fears and obsessions of adolescence, the megalomania too, the tyrannies and the irrational confusions. I could not help him because I feared helping him meant surrendering my life as I must live it. But this is not what helping him meant. It meant understanding *him*.

He felt my understanding; he felt that I was equally driven by forces outside of my desire in the sense that they are shaped by the past and not by me today.

For example, I look at others with my own eyes. I evaluate them by my own set of values. But when it came to looking at myself, I looked at myself through my *father's* eyes. I judged myself by *his* standards, which I do not believe in. In his eyes I was not beautiful; I had flaws. All his standards were superficial, vainglorious, purely external.

Hugo decided, while I lay unconscious on an operating table, that our quarrels did not matter, that he did not want to lose me. I decided that in spite of his many difficulties, he gave me a true love, big enough for me to trust as I never could trust Rupert.

Convalescence. Such utter weakness that you lie like an animal, playing possum, or hibernating. You are only aware of clean yellow sheets, blankets, radiators steaming, the ceiling mobile, food on trays, a haven, a shelter, gratitude. Adrift—every current is stronger than you.

With Bogner I went back monotonously to a loss of beauty (the scar), dreams of jealousy of Rupert's flirtations, a dream that Hugo is a woman.

How fully she explained the divided lines. At each end an obstacle drives me away. At each end, I bruise myself against a fear and run away. I do not leave of my own accord. I run away. The fears spring up, barring the entrance at both ends. At Rupert's end, it is the fear of jealousy. At Hugo's end, other fears or barriers. The Wall of China. *The years I lived with Hugo alone* were death for me, because of his silences, negativities, submersion, repressed states. But it is no longer true. The other torment connected with New York is that life there is primarily concerned with achievement, activity, creation. The constant chess games of personalities are all played in terms of this is the playwright of the season, this is the actress of the moment, this is the writer of the newest books, this is the composer from Paris, the representative of the Greek section of the UN, the television director, the filmmaker, the distinguished X, or the notorious Z, or the toast of the town, fêted by *Vogue* or *Harper's* or the critics, always men or women of achievement; the others are not there at all. And so all my wounds are reopened. Kimon Friar says, "I have to earn a living at Circle in the Square readings, and so I have to have big names like Tennessee Williams, Lillian Hellman, Arthur Miller. I cannot afford to not have a full house." He may have heard that I did not have a full house last year when I read from *A Spy in the House of Love*. Just as Hugo feels deserted when I leave and feels he needs me there continuously, I feel incurably rejected by the world, that I have not won the place my work deserves.

At this critical point the analyst cannot help, because the analyst's task is to question which element in the work estranges me from others, which lack, which neurosis, perhaps, dictates a work not easily understood.

I have created a fluid, flowing life in the sense that I had to live out each fragment of it, each detour, ultimately ending in a deeper synthesis than those who accept ready-made patterns.

As Hugo's problem is desertion and failure, mine is failure and rejection. Whoever voices any of the many categories of rejection, I can hear. What of those loving, accepting, understanding voices?

Do you hear them?

Or do you only hear what hurts?

There are some human beings immune to joy and who react only to pain, such as Artaud. But I think I am being saved. I was one of the doomed. And without Hugo I would have been.

After convalescence, I felt detached, detached from friends, activities, parties. I felt detached from Rupert too. I am not looking forward to our trip together. I do not like travel by car—too much driving, too little leisure or enjoyment. I hate sitting in a car for so many hours, arriving windblown, sunburnt, tired everywhere, to dress and wash quickly and rush out to see things. My heart is in nothing I do. The last talk with Bogner was on the strain of divided lives—always at least two (diary and novels, two homes, two men), unreality and loss of strength because I cannot integrate.

But when Peggy Glanville-Hicks says, "There is a synthesis in every line you write. There is no need of a final one in the old classical sense. Continue to be fluid; continue to flow," I feel she is talking about the kind of life I have chosen, its immensity, its many extensions, fullness, that its integration must be in every moment, in every fragment, that there must be truth and wholeness.

We have learned the separate functions of all the parts of the body, but we do not know how they relate to each other.

I have learned all the separate functions of our emotional being, but I do not know how they can be integrated.

Relativity. Time. These are the secrets. We relive different ages, or karmas, as they say in the East. All of them related, extended. I may stumble upon the secret of our unconscious in which there is no time, and past, present and future are superimposed.

We set up a false rational man. We had to rediscover the denied irrationality and control it. It can be controlled. But we need good deep-sea divers, we need adventurers, we need explorers.

Synthesis and integration are sometimes mistaken for absolute assertions; there is the danger in conventional summaries.

Sierra Madre, March 2, 1953

Au ralenti, en veilleuse. I do feel dimmed and slowed down as if the motor that once pushed me no longer works. Is it convalescence, or a new state of being?

There is too much to synthesize. Peggy was shaping geometric figures with her hands to express the need of limitation. I was amused by the comedian who did a take-off of an orchestra conductor "boxing off" the flowing music into squares. The emotional life cannot, perhaps, retain the old forms it once used as molds any more than music or the novel can use the old structures. There must be a new architecture for our lives, and works of art as well. At one point no one knew whether Debussy had merely lost his way and dissolved. Now we know he was discovering the fluid quality of emotion, just as Alban Berg has discovered the language of our *nerves*.

And now, in writing, where do I go? Which way, from where?

Relativity is the key word. Flow.

Is it only in America that there is such a denial of emotion?

The diary was held together by me. The novels? In whose consciousness will the whole appear? Shall I be there as Proust was, but invisible…as a catalyst?

I divided myself into several women.

Dream: I had an engagement with Thurema Sokol that I failed to keep. Thurema reproached me bitterly, so I finally agreed to visit her. Then I found her surrounded by very large but tame lions. I was amazed that they just sat about, decoratively. Then Thurema showed me a newborn lion. It was astonishingly small, without fur, and it had a pouch like a kangaroo.

Dream: My handbag with all my traveler's checks was on a roof too high for me to reach. I appealed to a little man for help. He suggested I drive a bus along the house, and from the top of the bus he would reach for the handbag. I drove the bus and he reached for the bag. I could not stop the bus, so I let it slide on its side. When I looked around, the man was gone. I finally tracked him down to a house and found him reading aloud from my childhood diary he had found in the bag. I greeted him and his listeners and asked for my bag. The man was evasive. The other people were ironic. I was astounded that, having read the diary, they could still treat me so badly. I began to realize they did not intend to give me back my traveler's checks. I pleaded with them to no avail. Anguish awakened me.

Mexico trip notes:

Saturday, March 14, 1953

Left Sierra Madre noon
Phoenix, Ariz. nine

March 15, 1953

Left Phoenix (Superstition Ranch) at ten
El Paso seven

March 16, 1953

Insurance, AAA, etc. Left at noon
Camargo at eight. Stayed at El Baco

Dear Anne and Max: Your Escapist No. 1 Doctor of Philosophy of Europe, Bachelor of the Arts of Europe, Master of all Europeon territories, is writing you while driving at 75 mph towards Mexico. "When one is hurt one travels as far as possible from the hurt," wrote a writer we three know far too well and other people not well enough. Purple cactus, mountains shaped by nature like Aztec temples, and children who think Woolworth toys are a supreme delight. All this, and the contemplation of different kinds of troubles, such as droughts or one's best lamb killed by a foreigner's car, destroys the germs of the ego from which we suffer. Why did the ancient artists not care about personal recognition and accept anonymity? Probably because they believed in celestial models, as we don't. Anyway, here the ego simply does not flourish. The climate is unfavorable. There is no respect for achievement, only for charm, wit and other direct and perishable products. Mexico has no writers. Words are used for fiestas and courtship only.

Of course, one does not get cured immediately. While waving back at the peasant children, I have written twenty pages of the new book.

Left March 17, 1953 at nine in the morning

Juarez Restaurant. Party of American tourists bewildered by a waitress who did not speak English, saying: "They can't *talk*!"

After Chihuahua, on the way to Aguascaliente, a little roadhouse with good rice and chicken soup, good eggs, black beans, good tortillas, crisp.

Politeness is the best currency, more important than money.

Cocotillas.

Do not buy solid rubber shoes—too hot.

Canteens with water necessary.

Plenty of 1 peso pieces for tips—they have no change.

To carry perfume, which may spill, put in face powder. It evaporates, leaving face powder perfumed.

Oil and cologne are basics.

Wonder how they die, those who are buried by the roadside.

Windowless sepia adobe house, box-shaped.

Zacatecas—cone-shaped granaries.

Motel Indios—17 kilometers from town.

Dust towns.

Mexico City.

Friday, March 22, 1953

Rest at Tehuacan, pool.

Saturday, March 23, 1953

Vera Cruz—shrimps sold at café and eaten off a piece of toilet paper.

At market girl ordered brains. Butcher took animal head off hook and shook brains into her market bag.

Square, cafés, marimbas, band, guitar and songs all at once. Women with fans and red dresses.

On way to Jalapa. Even tombs are painted in joyous colors—laundry blue.

Waiting for a ferry, a Mexican lies asleep on seat of truck.

March 24, 1953

On the way to Cuetzacualto.

Waiting for the ferry to Jalapa. Beer stands under old sheets. Trucks waiting. Little boys seeking to earn a peso.

Purple waterfalls.

Next to huts—rocks are painted yellow, green, blue for decoration.

Mexico has a genius for discomfort—shower next to water closet. Thinnest towels.

Ceilings are low to bump foreheads, beds are inclined to spill you, closet has nails to catch on clothes, the mirror is stolen from the cabinet.

There are stones carved and laid by artists who are the priests of the religion of beauty, which outlives all other religions. Slaves, artists, sculptors, painters; we no longer know the identity of the hierarchy.

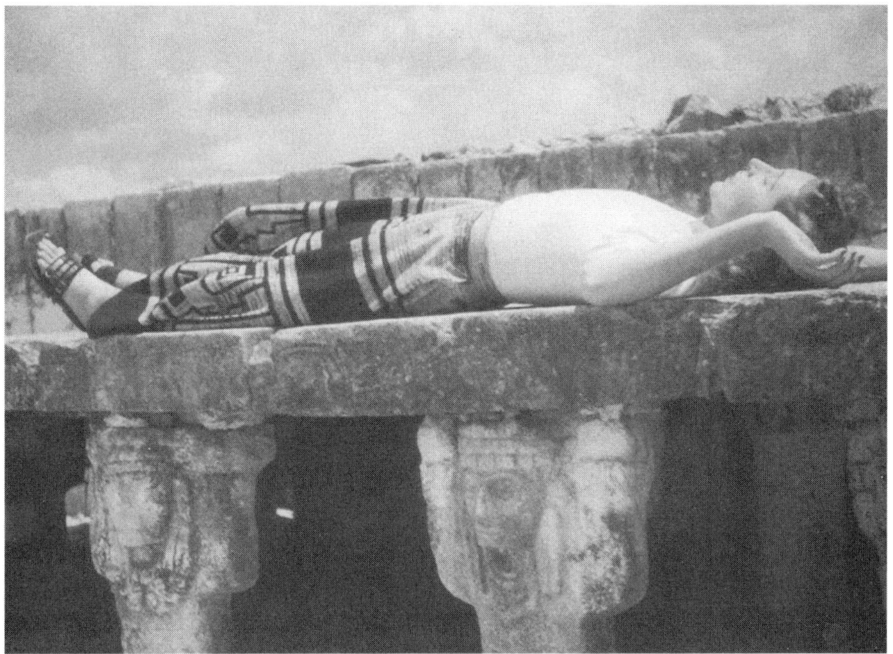

Anaïs Nin at Mayan ruins in Mexico

New York, May 19, 1953

When I returned after spending eight weeks with Rupert, I found Hugo had had a relapse from spending hours cooking a Balinese dinner, and from dancing. So I leave a Rupert barely recovering from a bad bronchitis I nursed the last week we had together (and I was already thin and anemic from too hard a trip) to put Hugo in traction again at night. But there are changes. Hugo has quietly become aware that the more helpless he feels (as during his three months' illness), the more acute and exaggerated his authoritarian manners and his demands become. He cannot accept care, yield to care. He feels humiliated. So he acts the tyrant. His needs turn into commands.

I was ready to tell Bogner that I want to live with Rupert, who at least admits his needs, acts the child rather than covers it up with pretenses. I am tired of living with Hugo's pretenses.

Bogner patiently resumes the work of examining not how Rupert or Hugo feels, but how *I* do. The trip of seven weeks of which four were spent in hard driving, eight to ten hours a day on difficult roads, eating badly (the food in Mexico is the worst in all the world), sleeping, sometimes badly, in rooms either noisy or without curtains, or with beds sliding sideways, or insufficient covers, turned into an ordeal, a marathon. I was ill in Campeche with a grippe. At end of the trip Rupert collapsed with one of his worst bouts of bronchitis, so I had to nurse him, drive the car through a five-day sandstorm, and not at my own natural pace, but urged by Rupert to go as fast as he goes, 70 or 80 miles an hour, which made me tense and afraid. All this because Rupert's will is inflexible (being connected to his virility—if you can't tame or control your wife, you are not a man) and because I don't dare assert too strongly my "weakness" as I am ashamed of it.

The doctor found I had lost five pounds and was back to a low blood count of 63% (90% when I left).

So the first objective was to take care of Hugo, give him breakfast in bed, help Millicent because Hugo's demands when I am away wear her out, and get my strength back.

Emotionally bound to Rupert, finding it wrenching to leave him, yet fully aware of the distress of the cramped life, his eccentricities, irrationalities, caprices, and—I must name it—his selfishness.

I'm assailed by dreams: a small house with Rupert, dilapidated, airless. An old man dying of asthma with an artificial respiration device (Reginald, the potential neurosis of Rupert haunting me).

So you feel, Anaïs, emotionally bound to Rupert, but you are aware that he harms you. He refuses you a maid once a week although you contribute as much to the household as he does. He has anxiety and guilt about money. He demands a great deal of you. He wants everything his way, wants you to make money but also be home. His neurosis causes you suffering.

After a few days of Bogner's probing (which always begins by eliminating any "decision" in favor of one life or another), breakfast in bed, no housework, I picked up.

I slip easily, naturally into my life in New York.

It could be a marvelous life if Hugo had stopped speculating and losing his capital. When I returned he said, "We must go easy." So I immediately was careful.

Then this morning three shocks.

He gave *New Story* $1,500 to publish my book, and they spent it irresponsibly on a magazine, so my book is not published; Hugo has entered into other speculations and they have failed; then yesterday: we go to a cocktail party, meet a mediocre engraver, and Hugo buys three engravings with a great expansiveness and flourish, spends in in five minutes $60 for something we don't want after refusing a few hours earlier massages that the doctor advised for him and for me.

I feel, Dr. Bogner, that what I really want most is not to feel dependent, helpless, or to be a victim of both men's neuroses. I know they have them. I accept it. I have my own. But I want to feel strong and free within myself, not dependent on either Hugo or Rupert. I want to be the builder of my own life. Then I won't feel anxiety.

I can accept Hugo's weakness as long as I don't feel that it drags me into a life that should be carefree and isn't. I want to be able to watch Hugo's "speculation" as I would watch a gambler or an alcoholic without feeling he is destroying both of us. That would help him more. I want to be able to watch Rupert's tantrums, anxieties, without being drawn into them.

I want to earn my own money. I want to own my share of Hugo's capital that he is endangering. I want to be able to guide and build my own life.

I feel *frustrated.*

Every frustration comes from seeking to impose on others *your* desire. Hugo was intended to build our life while I built its interior meaning.

He failed because although he built its exterior freedom, he is unable to surrender his vice, the illusion of *greater* wealth, the great American virus, which is poisoning his enjoyment and mine. No money to make movies, but his adventures in the world of business have squandered the equivalent of three or four movies. Hugo always thought it was his weakness I resented. It wasn't. It was mine. At the same time this is the reason why I cannot collaborate with Hugo in his business life—*I do not believe in it.* I did not believe in the bank that demanded not only all his time, but mine too. I did not believe in the National City Bank who pressured its employees into buying National City Bank stocks with money borrowed from the bank, and then when the stock crashed, forced its employees to "pay back" the loan, which was beyond their income, because it looked bad on the books, and this forced Hugo to seek help from his mother to whom we paid back a *huge debt* over a twenty year period! I do not believe in any of his business ventures or the American illusion of wealth he pursued. I do not believe Hugo has a flair for this.

I have a right to separate myself from Hugo's obsession with business. But as soon as he reproaches me, I feel crushed (while at the same time acknowledging, with tears in his eyes, how much and how deeply I help him with his films, his engravings—preserving his copper plates from corrosion, clarifying his confusion on the new 42nd Street film).

Business has only given me anguish and a restricted life. The money he finally made through "relations" was only due to Archibald's twenty years' experience.

I have a similar problem with Rupert's forestry. It too demands much of me (the telephone rings very often, people ask for information and help, I have no privacy in my home, and we get such a ridiculous salary of $250 a month while on 24-hour duty for five or six months every year).

So I dream. We try to sleep in a house open to the public. I beg for Acapulco.

Or I dream that I am pregnant.

Or I throw myself suddenly into the struggle to be financially independent.

Or I sink into depression when the doctor finds me anemic and not responding to injections.

Anne says over the telephone: "Diaries 31 and 32 are *marvelous*." Max is more articulate. They understand it cannot be published, but on the strength of it, wouldn't someone protect my work, my present work, and help me to produce more?

"It is tragic that it can't be published, for it is all that one feels *behind* your work. It would be more understandable to the world. You should be more ruthless."

Books that I loved and read carefully during my time with Rupert: *Beethoven* by J. W. N. Sullivan and *Really the Blues* by Mezz Mezzrow.

There are extremes, not only musically but philosophically. One, supreme awareness, and gaining altitude by suffering. The second, forgetfulness, and gaining altitude by moments of fever, ecstasy. The first defines the role of art. The second, the role of opium, drugs, drinks.

Changing altitude after the episode at the hospital was what I achieved by these two books, and by the sight of Chichen Itza, the Mayan city. Climbing the pyramid with fever and chills, but climbing, away and upward from the ten days of physical pain, the feeling of being near death, and the mutilation of a scar.

Wrote a little in the car until fatigue, strain, and finally depression silenced me.

When we returned from the Yucatan, I was too weak to realize what I had gained: detachment.

Bogner objectively crystallized and reinforced this, about my work and the neglect I suffer, about Rupert and Hugo.

Activity

Got a handyman to carry away the rotting flower boxes

Telephoned for mineral water bottles to be called for

Cleaned all copper plates of Hugo's—100 of them

Bought jeweler's rouge downtown

Tickets for Dylan Thomas play

Got hair retinted

Lunched with de Chochor, discussed how to repair damage, misappropriation of funds by *New Story*

Wrote John and Kay

Mailed books ordered

Bought blackboard for engagements

Took *Ai-Ye* back to distributors

Read Jim Herlihy's friend's manuscript (terrible, cheap and sentimental)

Made dinner for Dr. Wyss (one of Hugo's bad investments)

Saw Capote's *Grass Harp*

Saw Martha Graham dance

Tried to get into *Paris Magazine* uselessly

I always create space and order—air and lightness

Bought stamps

Altered dresses bought in Mexico—too severe at neckline

My costume in New York is: a white princess tailored coat; a white Grecian sculptured dress; a white hat with two slim abstract birds in flight and a veil spangled with rhinestones.

"Aren't you afraid the birds will fly away?" asked a painter.

"No. I fly off first, myself. They follow me."

Parties. Exhibits. Letters from Ruth about Europe. "I could stay here forever." Annette Nancarrow, alone, created the life she wanted in Acapulco. But the man she wants is *here*, so Annette is here.

I telephone Rupert, but I can't write him anymore because he doesn't. He killed my letter writing.

The hour I love most, and was always saddled at, is twilight. You dream of the evening and what it will bring. You cease the day's upright effort, you recline, or bathe in perfume, or dress for some event. I love *bridges* best of all. Taxis, planes, the diary, the hour of dress, the in-between hour, the only moment in which I exist alone.

I no longer *suffer* from Rupert's absence. I live my larger life hungrily, the one I cannot enjoy with him, and I am repulsed by the thought of returning to a lover who is petty, who insists on penny pinching, on "retreats," and all the negative forms of life, who is adolescent, who gives me ecstasy at moments, but not happiness.

Lila and I judged Tennessee's play *Camino Real*. It reveals his sentimentality, sadism, frustration, chaos, vulgarity. It is destructive, gangrened. Every value is ridiculed—poetry, romantic love, woman—all because he cannot write about the theme of his true obsession: a sordid sexual life, composed of prostitutes, promiscuity, immaturity and no love. Why does everyone overlook the immaturity that characterizes homosexuality? Pepe told me what I suspected: "I had an affair with Gore. It's unbelievable, he is a baby, sexually, absolutely underdeveloped."

Bogner insists that my choosing one life, one man, will not solve the division within me. Such an act, made arbitrarily, has no meaning. I would have to amputate part of myself to live a married life...that is all.

Integration.

All I have achieved is to live out both branches fully, at times smoothly, joyously, with shorter moments of guilt, shorter moments of anguish.

Poor Hugo. He suffered when I separated from his business activity. At last I am able to explain clearly: it harmed me. It threatened me. I lost faith in it.

Hugo and I sleep as late as we want and rarely make any appointments early in the morning. I almost always awaken cheerful, gentle, happy, a trait Hugo still loves, admires and envies. Almost never do I awaken angry or depressed. I greet the day like a party. It is only later, at the end of the day, when I will yield to depression. But I like the morning, the promise, and I feel the newness of the day. I expect a good day. I like the dark felt curtains. I like the view when they are open—sky and only the tops of the highest buildings. The smoke and soot will only assert their presence later, when the windows are all open, or we try to get a sunbath on the terrace. New York offers the most evil of all environments, the heat of the Congo, the dampness of Saigon, the cold of Annapurna, the smog and fog of London, the wind of the Texas flatlands, the dirt storms of northern Mexico.

Breakfast made by either Hugo, me, or Millicent, is served on a tray. Hugo reads the paper. Then telephoning begins: business, friends, filmmaking, or the writing world. We coordinate our engagements so I can go with Hugo in the car. I see Bogner, the doctor, run errands for Hugo or the house or our work. At the end of the day I am not quite as light. I should have been celebrating the birth of *A Spy in the House of Love*, but instead Eric Protter has misappropriated the funds and is on "vacation" in the south of France and does not even answer letters. In the mail, letters from friends (Ruth Witt Diamant, James Broughton, Claude Fredericks, Curtis Harrington).

Hugo cut out a picture of a sculptured Grecian dress from a paper and said this will suit me, so I went to see it, and now I wear it. He was unable to show *Bells of Atlantis* at the Museum of Modern Art.

I laugh to think of all the *respect* I get when respect is not what I want. "*Too* distinguished," whispered a girl at the *Flair* office when I was introduced as a distinguished writer.

Americans rush to coronations in England but cannot bear true spiritual or artistic aristocracy. The infantilism of Truman Capote's cloying sweetness pleases them.

Chinchilito telephoned! It is as if Don Juan remembers to telephone at least once a year. Asking obliquely, politely, suggesting a meeting, but I say the place (mine) is subject to sudden invasion. He understands. Laughs. He will soon sing at the Metropolitan.

Jim and I have a rapid jive language of our own. His last novel is well done, firm, but occasionally he transcends direct action and practices what I call the equivalent of jazz in writing. He has rhythms and flashes of insight the others, Gore, etc., do not have. I am always elated by his presence. There is quicksilver in him, a lightness. On days of anguish he looks pale, rigid, and becomes ironic (often with Dick) and cutting. But not with me. We talk about the diary, his work, our lives and relationships. But I cannot accept his friends, Dick, John Weldon, Bill Noble, all the Jims he does not like in himself he has transferred to them. I like what he is with me.

Martini hour again.

White dress, white bird hat, and to the theatre with Dr. Wyss of Switzerland, Hugo's underworld business associate. Why don't they admit openly they are pimps, gamblers, alcoholics, gangsters, under the cover of "business"?

The most tragic moment in human relationships is when we are given to see accidentally, by a ravishing work, or in a moment of crisis, the image that the other carries within himself of us, and we catch a glimpse of a stranger, or a caricature of our worst self, or a total distortion. My rebellion against the business world was perfectly justified in my case, because it was antithetical to the artist's world, and of all the ways to achieve security (food and shelter) it is the most dismal because it produced an atmosphere in which I could not exist. Hugo's many failures to succeed in such a world caused me harm and intensified my desire to withdraw from it. Hugo saw my resistance as a denigration of the businessman in him only because he himself, in his own eyes, was ashamed of the pursuit of money.

I never made him ashamed of this; I tried to make him use it to attain our artist world, to create an artist's life, rich and interesting in meaning.

But after all these years, to see so clearly the distorted image of me in Hugo's mind hurts me. It was as if Kay Dart, for instance, read my diary seeking the complete story of our friendship and found only a page I had written in a mood of impatience with her drunken behavior one evening. She would be totally ashamed, horrified, to see only the one photograph of a drunken Kay while she believes that I, of all people, understand her, know her deeply.

Hugo, besides, seems to have most artfully concealed from me all the feelings, the human feelings that might have touched me, moved me, endeared him to me. He did not do this willfully, because of all the human beings I have known, Hugo was the blindest psychologically, blinder than any stupid or ignorant man, because his culture and intelligence were used purely to disguise his lack of self-knowledge and insight. This is the secret of why he never arouses protectiveness or compassion. As did my mother's aggression, he has repelled tenderness.

It is strange that the helplessness, awkwardness, inefficiency, chaos and unawareness that are so marked in Hugo, combined with aggression, authoritarianism and willfulness, cause others to react with hardness and a lack of tolerance merely because he has successfully smoke-screened the fallibilities that could arouse compassion. He challenged others with his pretenses and did not inspire tolerance, but rivalry instead. He never disarmed himself, and an armed man does not arouse human love.

Today I see him, at moments, as a human being.

Of course, it is also possible that I did not want to see a Hugo as helpless as Henry or Gonzalo or Rupert, because then I would need one human being to sustain me. I do not believe I could have borne then the knowledge I have now of Hugo's own self-destruction, naïveté, blindness, errors…

I never built a shell around myself.

My only defense has been flight.

Je n'aime pas les crustacés.

Louise and Bebe Barron

I met them in San Francisco. Bebe was both dainty and voluptuous, with black hair and a delicately rounded face with large eyes. Louis was small and self-effacing. It took me time to realize how much they knew about the arts and sciences. Louis is a specialist in electronics. He concealed his learning behind a hesitant manner. Working on recordings together (at that time they were making records, and they had asked me to do some reading for them after hearing me), a friendship grew. They incited me to read all of *House of Incest*, which I was hesitant to do. I did my best reading for them. Hearing it played back also forced me to work to improve my readings.

But they had no capital, no managerial drive, and the records sold slowly. I received about $45 and that was all. Now and then they say, "We owe you money," but I don't ask for it. When they came to New York they set up a sound studio, and Sound Portraits became a profession. They made sound tracks for films. They became Hugo's friends as well. Bebe has taste and flair as an artist. She studied music and filmmaking. When Hugo made *Bells of Atlantis*, they were responsive and helpful, became collaborators. They had already absorbed *House of Incest*. It inspired them with an electronic score for the film that complemented it with beauty and strangeness. It was an unusual collaboration, with dedication, fervor, sacrifice, and selflessness.

They felt that we had encouraged their creativity. Today we heard a piece they composed for Paris. It was light, whimsical, and full of rhythms. John Cage, on the other hand, using the same principle, created a harsh, chaotic, disintegrated piece. Louis and Bebe will go very far in this development.

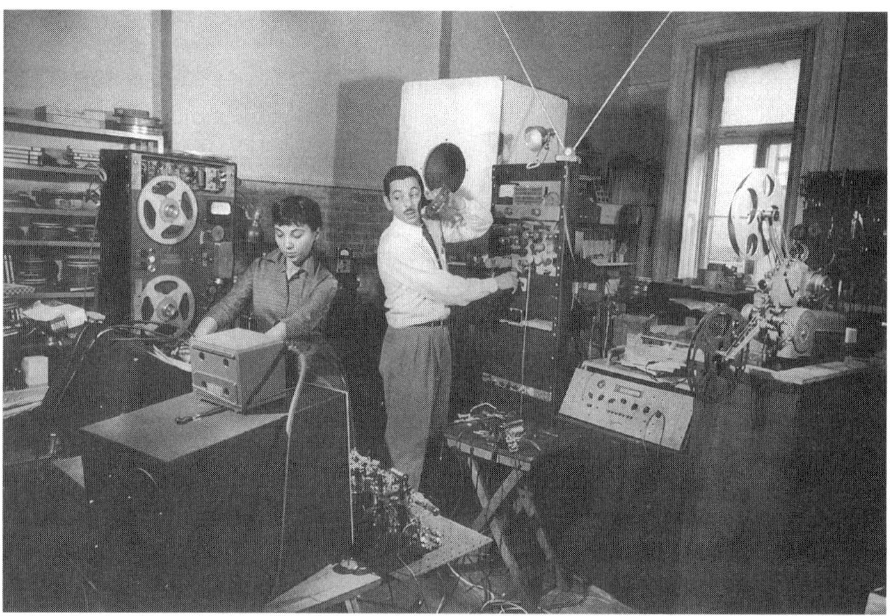

Bebe and Louis Barron in their studio.
Photo: Walter Daran

All these innovations originate in France. How much better it would be to live at the source, to watch them being born, to participate in the experiments.

Sometimes it maddens me to have lost my birthplace, my roots. I do not belong here. I belong where art is *born*.

But with Louis and Bebe there is an easy, fecund relationship. They work intensely; they live a varied, chaotic, flowing life.

New York, June 8, 1953

I took the train to visit Anne and Max alone, for the sake of the new territories opened up by the diary that we wanted to explore together.

Max wants to live out all the experiences we are discussing. But Anne and I want a vigorous study of the trap I'm in, and between the three of us what we arrived at was to present the diary as a fantasy.

We spent our lunchtime condemning the limitation of the abstractions I made in favor of the naked truth, then deciding the naked truth could be read as a total fantasy.

By the end of the lunch, we were all ready to believe, or shall I say disbelieve the diary, and we had prepared our defenses for the lawsuits started by various men involved in my fantasies, such as Henry Miller, who would swear he scarcely knew me.

Max sits in the garden having very obvious erotic fantasies, Anne extracting them and I encouraging abstraction because I cannot respond to them. He is too natural for me. He admits quite sincerely that he does not understand or care for surrealism or poetry in the novel.

Actually he represents both the full development and the limitation of the American literary product.

All the departures from naturalism he fails to follow, although he is willing to admit that the naturalists do not necessarily give us reality. He finds reality in the diary, even though I often give as much space to the dream as I do to the incidents.

It is strange in his case because he does not lack imagination. As I said to Anne, "Now let's tell Max that he has invented the writers he has studied."

There has always been, in my life, a series of ponderous and deep Germans whose seriousness has attracted me while also causing me distress.

It is the relationship I hear in Debussy's sonata for piano and violin, in that the violin, like a bird, attempts desperate ascensions, and the piano by its denser substance does not allow the complete flight to take place. It asserts a ponderous body that the violin seeks to transcend.

Thus my ties to the earth have been manifested by my ties to Henry Miller, Otto Rank, to Jakob Wasserman, and now to Max, while I was equally tied to the poets, to Djuna Barnes, Joyce, the surrealists…

Now I feel that if I can partake of both these divided symbols, that if ever I can integrate all these various developments into one, if ever without destroying a single human being in the process, then I will be an artist of a new category.

Max's mind was not on solving the problem of how to publish the diary. He got dressed in the period costume of the country gentleman, in shorts, offered his legs to the sun's promiscuous rays. However, the sun is more selective and discriminating than we think. There are some legs that the sun frowns upon and does not tan with graciousness. Those are the legs of the people we don't happen to desire.

We should not usurp the rights of the sun and decide which legs should or should not be exposed to suntans or to fires of desire.

It was very arrogant of me to decide that Max's legs should not be exposed to the sun, merely because, after all, I am not the sun.

It is true that Hugo, with whom I profess not to be in love, is the human being for whom I made the greatest sacrifice of all: my life as an artist.

What kind of love is that?

But there was today in our chess game *à trois*, a more vital vigorous interplay than *à quatre*.

I have learned when to loosen the keys of my guitar so that the strings won't snap.

Max stares continuously at my breasts (as if they were plentiful to begin with), and his hunger is so apparent that I am glad it is not sun season, and nearly time for me to go home.

I said, "If a system is corrupt, such as the literary system, how can we go on with our work without taking a militant step to take power in order to impose certain values? It is as in politics. If it threatens the survival of the human being who has not been militant, then is he forced to become militant?"

"Max must continue with his work," says Anne wisely.

But meanwhile it is Richard Aldridge, and not Max, who is given a position of leadership and power (as editor of *Discovery*, as a much-publicized young critic). And Aldridge is truly an adolescent critic seeking to give final status to adolescent writers, some of whom, like Gore, are not yet born. There is a word for the love of the dead, but none for the American love of the fetus.

At this point I could see everything clearly, as if I, and not Herzog, had climbed Annapurna without the loss of gloves, fingers and toes, and remained there a few minutes while the sun went down and it was time for the train for New York. The journey could have been made in a jet plane, for my thoughts took such a detour that my body got to Grand Central ahead of them.

The detour was around Joyce.

There lies the secret.

Max felt that realism has masqueraded as reality, so it would be just to let reality masquerade as fantasy.

I came back tired, because I felt that with them I had been on the point of reaching this miraculous fusion I have sought so desperately between diary and art, between naturalness and abstraction.

At home, I mix vodka, ice and lemon juice, and abandon the trapeze of marvelous stunts. I watch Mitou, the aristocratic Siamese cat arrange her limbs in a manner suggesting a total absence of tension.

New York, June 9, 1953

Noon	Bogner
1:30	Dr. Neumann
2:30	Letter service for Hugo
6:00	Dinner at home
8:00	*Maya* at the Lys Theatre Café Society, and Bonsoir cabaret with Dr. Wyss and Hugo

Everything falls into place.

For the first time I am able to say to Hugo quietly, without deep disturbances, anger at myself, or fear of his reactions: "I love my life with you, but I also need my life alone. This is the worst I have to tell you."

Hugo's answer was that it was better to be told this as a fact and not covered by excuses (lectures or trips, etc.) that made each departure a shock. It is good that we admit it does cause him pain. He does not need a life alone. But he recognizes that I expressed this need before we married, when I told him I did not want to be a wife, but a mistress.

I try to point out to Hugo what he gained by my absences: he made friends of his own; he learned to be a host, a good cook, a sociable man. I accept wounding him because I also have made sacrifices for him. It is now clear that the abstract work was created to protect Hugo from the truth and that if I had given the world my total self it would have responded as Max and Anne did.

Everything falls into place: the absurd contradictions and splits in life and in work. I understand the relationship with the airy young men (the unusual, the remote, non-human relationship with a distant father who was a volatile, airy being), and the necessary relationship with deep, serious, earthbound men (my reality).

I understand my comfortable relationship with women (no danger), the mother having been the stable, fixed point of loyal love.

Hugo's fixities were necessary, his density and absence of volatility.

All my irritations are gone. I accept myself (my own ideal of a wife prevented me from this, my own ideal of a woman) and Hugo (my need, unrecognized and against which I rebelled), but as Bogner pointed out, I myself had weights on my feet, the weight of guilt, and I could never have lived the life I wanted—the weight was in myself, not the men.

Now I see everything clearly. I see distinctly that I want to be with Rupert but that I reject his life. That I want to be with Hugo and that he may, in the end, turn out to be the greatest romance of all my life; if only I could recapture my original desire for him. Is such a thing possible?

Desire will buy another airplane ticket, desire will pack a bag once more, desire will lead my steps into a life I detest, all of it, from the small, difficult-to-manage rusty car, to a place and house I don't like, to mediocre friends who create nothing, to the sterility and emptiness of California. Rupert's body, face and passion are able to create a moment of fire, a moment of altitude, which is a trap and does not extend into the rest of our life together.

New York, June 10, 1953

10:00 Dr. Jacobson

1:53 Train to Hartsdale to visit Everett Ball and Jane Eklund

Sliding from a doctor to a play on a whore's life, *Maya,* from a walk in a Texas plains wind along 8th Street to the most comical of all shows I have seen in New York at Bonsoir, full and wild laughter, then back to the doctor's office, fermenting (am I pregnant with a book again?), from there to visit Everett Ball, the only writer I noticed in *New Writing.* One is always grateful to one who causes admiration because it confirms that it is not a catatonic condition towards writing one is suffering from, but simply the absence of good writing. His is rich and transcendent and poetic, but alas, he is married to feet of clay in the form of his wife, six feet of physical perfection but no flame, with a limited vision.

They are both writers. Old house, new baby, spaniel puppy, ice cream in the garden, good talk. Everett almost refers to the "poetry" in my books, the beauty, but half an hour later asks about the missing elements.

Coming from one who writes very much as I do, I answer truthfully. He has seven stories going around, a mischievous glance, quick and with a shade of mockery—sprightly, and a slight tinge of the exactor's affectations.

An amusing encounter, because when I telephoned him about visiting us in New York, he said, "You may not remember, but we have met. I know Rupert too. We met at Eyvind's."

Immediately I had to think of how I could solve the problem of their visit or meeting Hugo, but it was solved by their inability to come to New York because of their baby. So I did not have to mention Hugo. I try never to involve others in my deceptions unless I am truly cornered. I have not yet met anyone unwilling to help me at crucial moments. If they don't go to California to live, then I will tell them.

The afternoon in their garden was weighed down by the presence of his wife's health, the baby, the ice cream ritual, and I felt that perhaps if she had not been there Everett Ball could have discussed the essence of my work and not its absence of materiality.

I reached a pause with Bogner. Giving Hugo facts (I need my life alone) freed him of anxiety about the unknown, the hazy worries. Will I be able to give Rupert facts? If I could, it may also free him of guilt; he must have guilt when he refuses me what I need. Guilt produces anger at the one who causes it, a self-defensive anger.

In Sierra Madre I identify with Tavi, the spaniel. In New York with Mitou, the Siamese blue point.

Rupert worries about Tavi growing old. Tavi's jealousy, emotionalism and delirious love. Rupert loves to have him there, gently scolding him when he is sleepy or lazy.

Hugo underlines the resemblance between Mitou and me. The nose, the sleekness... People comment on the resemblance. Mitou reacts to Hugo as I do—comes for affection, warmth, lies with him. At other times she is detached, indifferent, refusing Hugo's caresses. Hugo says to me so often: "Why aren't you content to be beautiful?"

Both men take great care of their animals, Rupert with mock severity and rough games, Hugo with exquisite thoughtfulness. Hugo never puts Mitou away to sleep without first caressing her and putting her into a good mood.

I identify with Tavi getting old and play with the idea of going off with him so Rupert will be spared the actual loss.

In Sierra Madre I feel less beautiful in comparison with California standards and also due to Rupert's response to ordinary prettiness.

Well, Anaïs, if you don't like Rupert's life, change it. Get Rupert free of his neurosis.

At least you *do* like the life you and Hugo made together, the variety, the richness, the fullness of activity.

Now I will go back and write the finale to all the other books.

How can I make the characters clear? How can I now remove the veils? How can I enter another territory, in a different tone?

Falsities are created by a change of focus due to a change of mood, the betrayal of the truth by the lapse of time. Memory is a great betrayer. This diary proves above all the absolute failure of memory, its distortion. I can prove this by the fact that I find in it scenes I had forgotten, feelings that shock me today that had been successfully repressed later.

As Jim reads, I read with him, and I am surprised, startled. The only true courage I have is to *feel everything*. I do not always act or dare to live out my decisions, but I experience them emotionally to the fullest. I don't believe that if I had lived a complete life with Henry, I could have lived our relationship any more *fully*; I did go through infernos several times. The only thing I have ever refused is to marry my various lovers. I thought it was fear, but now, with a greater honesty, I wonder if it wasn't merely the knowledge that there was more to be lived, other loves.

When I finished writing the very human, simple, sincere *Winter of Artifice*, when I wrote the corrosive, fantastic *House of Incest*, I was not yet satisfied. I still had something to say. And what I have to say is really distinct from the artist and art: *it is the woman who has to speak.*

When I call for Lila at the AA office, I find her typing hundreds of letters in answer to enquiries from troubled alcoholics. And she tells me Gore's mother volunteers there occasionally and that she is kind and charming. What a sudden change of focus, away from the monster Gore created, when I took his side and accepted his image of her. At this point I am able to suspect Gore of distortion because I have seen myself distorted in his eyes.

During the second part of our relationship (dating from my departure with Rupert), Gore changed from a frozen, sighing, lamenting, pitiable figure of someone very ill, to a malicious, bored person spreading death rays. Nothing that I ever said to Gore penetrated him. Only my pity. And nothing was born of our relationship but destruction.

My last image of Gore is a languid, sluggish young man of twenty-seven who seems lifeless and withered.

In the rigid framework of bourgeois life, a whim, a caprice, a fantasy takes on the resemblance of a tragedy. I know that my presence in the Geismars' life is a danger to Anne, that she has controlled her anxieties by controlling the relationship, and *I helped her*. I kept it shared, balanced. When I was leaving for the station, Anne offered to drive me because she had shoes on and Max was barefoot, and one of them had to stay with another visitor who had come.

I help her because I like her, because I have no desire for Max, and because his desires are too transparent and adolescent. I don't like that kind of honesty, which is truly a lack of tact and consideration.

Max seemed defeated. Why? Has he realized I do not respond? Or is it that the formal arrangement of his life leaves no space for such whims? The artists have created a life in which such whims can take place without damage, a house with many doors and open windows, flexible designs. During chaos or fiestas, infidelities are unperceived by others.

I hate bourgeois life more than any form of life on earth.

The longing for Paris grows immense.

The next few days Max talked over the telephone about having to go back to work (he has just finished a book). The refuge, the withdrawal.

I am transmitting to them the fever and restlessness that the lives of Henry and June first caused me. *A fever to live.* When Anne came to our lunch with Herbert Alexander, she and I had coffee afterwards alone. She said her marriage to Max had been like mine to Hugo and that when she arrived in New York that morning, she felt: "I haven't lived at all in spite of Max and the three children."

In the unconscious lies not only man's demon (as we feared, the primitive, the instinctual, the uncontrollable forces of nature), but also this free, large, expanded figure of his myths, the great figures man has loved in Beethoven, in Einstein, in painters and writers of stature. Man's love of these figures betrays not only his dream, but the actuality of what man has achieved.

A crucial talk with Hugo let me see this. "When I was born, my father was away at work in Puerto Rico. I had my mother all to myself for two years or so. Then not only did my father return, but my brother Johnnie appeared too, and I had to share my mother with both of them. This was the end of unity, a perfect cell, a swimming in my mother's love as in a sea. I was deprived of my element. It was like dying."

I said, "And that is why then, when we married, you tried to make a life *à deux*, excluding the world."

"Yes."

"But you know you could have had that exclusive love from other women, the fiercely possessive one, such as Thurema or Ruth, who would have been there all the time."

"Yes, I know. My first entanglement was with a woman who was exclusively the mother. As you know, I shied away from her. As you also know, I went to see her a few years ago and found a wife and mother and nothing else. Sure, I didn't want what I had with my mother, what my mother and father had together, but by this time, in my early twenties, I had also developed other needs, intellectual needs. A woman had to be intelligent. You had these *other* things. You were a better combination of elements."

It is quite possible that this cell with the mother is the one we always seek, not with the father, because it *seems* unbreakable, the strongest bond. I feel that I sought this with men as erroneously as it must be for a woman to seek to possess another *as a man*.

This is probably the secret of Jim crying out in one of his letters: "What is this passion I feel for you?" Knowing it is not sensual, yet so powerful.

Humorous fashion of the moment: short, boyish haircuts, huge Ubangi earrings, and crinoline hooped skirts. Amusing image too, of the sleek model with heavily painted eyes (a fashion in Paris fifteen years ago), wearing a cotton dress and carrying a country basket.

Letter from Anaïs Nin to Rupert Pole:

New York, Thursday, June 11, 1953

Darling Chiquito,

The last week is always bedlam. I couldn't write. I had a visit that will amuse you, the way it happened. The only good story in the *New Writing* anthology, I felt, was by an Everett Ball. I sent him one of my books with a few words of tribute. I got a phone call from him saying: "You don't remember, but we met. I know Rupert." And he invited me to visit him, his beautiful writer wife, baby and spaniel at Hartsdale! She had heard me read. We had a good afternoon all about writing.

I went impulsively to look at a beautiful sport jacket for you, couldn't resist it, never noticing it was a Mark Cross, and that it cost $135! Very sad because it was made of the same raw, hairy, primitive silk as my black Italian dress, in a natural champagne color, material from India. And I wished I could get it for you. You will have to be contented with my good intention to get the best jacket for the very best quality man. I always think of you in that way, as deserving the very finest quality in all realms.

New York is hot, humid, like any day in Calcutta.

No sign of Hugo, who is traveling.

Te quiero mucho

A

Sierra Madre, June 18, 1953

When the two lives stand apart and are opposite, I can balance them. It is when they weld by resemblances that I get lost. When I arrive in New York I have to unclutter the apartment first of all, throw out the old magazines, the empty bottles, the worn-out clothes, the discarded gadgets Hugo collects and then no longer uses. When I leave, the apartment is alive, the objects have life. The mobiles work and the candelabras have candles.

When I return to Sierra Madre the same trash awaits me. Rupert never throws away anything. The broken plate he will someday repair (and never does), the torn old shirts, the *Time* magazines. The house is cluttered. I make it clearer and lighter, but Rupert impedes this activity and rescues useless objects out of the garbage can. This haunts me and brings the two men into a focus that distresses me, of father and son. Millicent says, "Don't give Mr. Hugo any more tables or shelves, he will only clutter them."

I have to give Rupert an explanation of why I threw away my ten-year-old fur boots so completely worn inside that they tore the skin of my feet or tore up whatever socks or stockings I wore.

A drama brought about by my request for a maid exhausted me and depressed me. Not again! I can't fight once more for independence, and suffer the guilt attending my rebellions.

I spent one evening with Kay and John, and one at Lloyd's. Lloyd is very sweet to me now and has ceased to mistrust me, but I do not trust him. He is tall and heavy, with a high florid skin, a Chinese cast of features, the small eyes almost closed, with either a merry look or an angry look. He has the fair skin of red-haired men, freckles, long white hair, large ears. He has an expression of emotional vulnerability, but stronger than this are the anger and aggression. He treats everyone angrily, insultingly. He will start talking poetically about Mayan architecture and midway swerve to a diatribe on politics, ending with sputterings of rage. It is a drama of great frustration, of a man overshadowed by the greatness of his father.

Sierra Madre, June 1953

This time I did not have the wild, frenzied desire to be with Rupert. I feel he has slowly smothered the passion by seeking a domestic wife while I sought to live out with him only the heightened moments of adventure.

Today he is a young man full of anxiety about our not being married because it might be revealed to the Forest Service, and he is a young man who talks too much when people come for the special purpose of meeting the writer Anaïs Nin, or who asks for homemade apple pie because it is better than the one from the shop, or who passively accepts a new government law that we must pay rent while actually the place belongs to the government and strangers can use it like a railroad station. The garden is government property and requires special care (inspections now and then of the home and garden) for which we pay now!

But, and this is what always disarms and castrates me, Rupert cannot do better, and he cannot do better because his anxieties are too great when he attempts other professions. He even suffers when he is asked to prepare a television program for the Forest Service.

If I truly loved Rupert, for his own sake, I would see first of all that he gets analyzed, and then he would also be free of me, his passion, and realize I am not the wife for him.

When I arrive I am always elated by the emotion of seeing Rupert, and he is irritated by all the difficulties. Last night he had been notified that the plane was arriving earlier so he had to rush; he arrived highly irritable. I always say, "Don't spoil my homecoming!" He raves and rants at the airline. I say, "Next time I won't let you come to the airport. I'll just come home on my own." His pleasure has become anxiety—I was calmly waiting for him. He was afraid I would not wait. I don't understand all this; the tension and anxiety destroying the pleasure. Finally we are home. "You are looking mighty pretty; the leopard and white make you look Russian."

Tavi is frankly joyous.

In the dark, passion. Recovery of the bodies, repossession of every part of the body, each one seeking bodies, both equally slender and nervous and electric. Rupert was beside himself after possession, kissing my eyes and saying: "The only good thing about your going away is that it is so good to have you again. Your return is so wonderful. It is so wonderful when you are back!"

If only I can keep my high mood; if only I can keep my altitude even when our evening begins with Rupert killing a mouse with a broom, eating synthetic Spanish rice (all ready to cook in cellophane) and a Martini in a thermos, tasting of a tin cup.

My heart is affected by making the trip, and I am fighting off a cold brought on by the barbaric air conditioning on the plane, pages of books and hair actually blown about by cold air; so I lay in bed this morning until eleven, unpacking in between. "You look vital and well," said Rupert, and he looks so frail and so young compared with Hugo.

Kay calls me up: "I left my handbag with my driver's license and glasses. I must come and get them!"

The house awaits my care.

I shy off...

I hold on to my precious egg of joyous expansion...to not lose it...

Rupert asks gently for a mincemeat pie. Tavi has been bathed in honor of my homecoming, but not brushed, and he molts on me and on the rug.

I pasted the novels together so that I can see what has to be done for the next symphonic movement.

Rupert says, "Isn't this so much better than an apartment in New York? There is space, air, and quiet."

He is happy.

The inner music starts again, not from witty songs at Bonsoir, not the plays on Broadway and streams of visitors, surprises, not from Annette in New York pursuing a new love, Peggy so divinatory, Bill Nims so soft and tender, music not made of motion, variety, flow, not from talks with Bogner, with Jim, with Lila, with Hugo reading Proust, but from Rupert's body, his slim, stylized, neat, compact, graceful body in his

Ranger's olive green. Rupert sits listening to commentators, but I do not hear them. All the watery reflections of Venice lie in his eyes, and his eyes, so heavily fringed, seem like a piece of Venetian gold and green damask.

Sierra Madre, June 20, 1953

The next day we got into work clothes and went off to garden at Black Cat Drive, Helen Wright's property, because gardeners are too expensive. The house will someday be left to Rupert, and Helen gave him a present of $300 when she sold part of the property. So we owe her that. But it is hard work for five hours, and I'm exhausted and so is Rupert, his face so thin, rings around his eyes and his voice strained, short of breath. I cook dinner for Lloyd, who is alone, and then there is music later, so today no writing. I lose my mood. I feel as if the earth, so overpraised by people, is stifling and only fit to throw over dead bodies. Too much earth places you six feet under.

Gain altitude!

Sierra Madre, June 27, 1953

One more attempt to persuade Rupert to let me have a maid one day a week. He is stubborn. When he is out of arguments, he reminds me of the need for economy, to which I answer, "But I bring money into the household and I should have a right to decide how I spend it." Then he says, "I will do the housework myself." "But you have too much to do, and seeing you do it will make me feel extremely guilty and unhappy."

He gave in, ungraciously, when I accused him of short-sightedness, that the writing I wanted to do might liberate us financially. Now I have to find a maid, and that, in Sierra Madre, is a problem.

But I decided suddenly to let the house go, to do the minimum as a hausfrau, and this Rupert accepted because he himself, when left alone, lives in chaos and dirt.

And I worked.

First of all, I reorganized the novels so that the sequence and development of characters is infinitely clearer. I slashed and reshuffled scenes.

My mind is clearer than it has ever been. I feel sure, steady and integrated.

I worked on rearranging the diaries, taking an inventory of all my work. If I do not write another word, I have produced something to be proud of.

I feel coordinated, and about to solve my major problem.

But first of all, order.

I lie now on the chartreuse couch watching dinner. Rupert is watering the lawn. He said, "When I was so unhappy in New York, I felt I wanted to get out of doors, do something useful, but now I realize I can't live in isolation either, without a city, music, movies."

But yesterday we spent our free day with Lloyd at the beach, and then Rupert played in a trio. Tonight we go to a wedding of one of the foresters, and Monday Kay and John.

But I have not lost what I gained in strength and firmness. Rupert's passion for other women is the same, but I am no longer jealous. I am detached, and I find myself free of jealousy, a marvelous victory.

When you hold on to your own true character, people cannot interfere with your growth. There is something restrictive in Rupert himself, but now he does not have the power to stifle me.

He lies asleep now, but the radio is screeching news. If I try to turn it off (to work—I can hear it all over the house) he awakens! And wants it on!

But he listens with touching hunger to my "fantasy." First we get liberated financially. Then we go to Europe where he will act in French and Italian films (where they will appreciate his sensitive beauty). Having appeared in those, he will get a U.S. contract. Then he will have all that he wants. A boat. Women. A house of his own.

What I do not say is that then my creation of his life will be over.

I do feel that if I leave Rupert to this life with the woman who will fit in it, he will always have the longing, the curiosity for the worlds he sought to grasp through me.

At the beach yesterday I was watching a group of young people giggling and teasing each other. I felt that Rupert, though thirty-four, should have been with them.

I told him, "I was trying to imagine you at twenty, giggling and teasing."

"But," said Rupert, "I was never twenty years old. I did not fit in. I was, at fourteen, talking about mysticism and philosophy." I knew it was true. I see him today, with young people. He is not playful or humorous, but pompous and solemn. He lectures to them, advises them.

Actually, it is only with me that he becomes playful, carefree.

I was able to turn off the radio! Rupert sleeps. His freckled back bare, suntanned. When I first knew him it was rough too, and I initiated him to the use of olive oil. Now it is smooth and almost as silky as the tender skin of his belly and thighs.

He has a very white skin, pink cheeks, ears, mouth. Hair only where it should be, arms and legs and sex, nowhere else except a few on his chest. I cannot follow with my eyes the line of his back to the slender waist and the full, firm backside without feeling a wave of desire.

"We won't go to the wedding," said Rupert. "You are right. One should not do anything one hates to do. You must not force yourself. I feel better already, just having decided not to go. It weighed on me all day."

Work, work, work, work, work.

Sierra Madre, July 1953

"End to the Tree of Life" would be the title of the story of the men and families sacrificed by an underpaying, exploitive Forest Service, to preserve trees that are in turn burnt by a man who wanted to get work as a firefighter. The forests are ravaged by man and protected by man. The drunken firebug at the bar says, "You think these trees are beautiful, do you? Look at them well. They won't be here tomorrow." Idealists have gathered in the Forest Service, good men who have a dream rather than a lust for money or personal comfort. Their wives live in isolated and shabby places, shacks with outhouses, or trailers. They can't take jobs, being too far away from civilization. They raise their children on scraps.

FLW (as Lloyd calls his father) is the god of the household. Lloyd has not been able to grow in this atmosphere. The architectural magazines are filled with FLW's work, with tributes. What was a justified battle of the artist against mediocrity in Lloyd has degenerated into a state of rage without any enthusiasm or hope or the power to praise or love anything. He works, and his work is beautiful. But in daily life he is filled with poison. Even his sudden laughter and humor I don't understand. He is too obsessed with the absence of power and effectiveness. He has lived protected by Helen. The entire family lives in a childish absence of control or awareness, and say "spontaneous" and "honest" things to each other, by which I mean disagreeable and harsh. At first I was shocked. Lloyd calls Helen "stupid," and Helen calls him other derogatory adjectives. While playing music, Lloyd will rise suddenly, lay down his bow and refuse to play.

Rupert calls it honesty.

After a while I learned to detach myself. I never let myself be drawn into arguments. At first we used to get into hellish confusions. Poor Rupert. He is caught between Reginald, who always arrives in a "dying" state, and Lloyd, who is delirious, eager to destroy the world that has hurt him, and pours into his family life the aggressions he should be practicing to assert his work.

Rupert fights back, but I can see how this has prevented him from expanding. A bourgeois, narrow outlook (this in reaction against FLW, who lived freely and caused scandals), a neurotic suspicion of artists and bohemians (and I was both).

Their worst predictions did not come true. I did not "take Rupert away from forestry." When Rupert and I talk, I say, "But it is a work you love and that you feel you do well without effort or anxiety." I did not lead him into a sophisticated or bohemian life. But at what a cost to myself.

While I work the phone rings: "Can you give me some information as to how to get rid of horseflies?" "Are there fish in Santa Anita Lake?" Or there is the arrival of those who must use the phone to call their parents to fetch them as they are tired from hiking in the canyon.

We sit at the Beach Club, the original one in Hollywood, with the old families of Los Angeles, who hold out against the movie stars, vulgarity and the influx of newcomers. Umbrellas, salons, a dining room with the finest chef, pretty young girls in the locker room discussing, at the age of sixteen, what their wedding gowns will be like, whether they will be covered with seed pearls and cost $2,000. One little girl exclaimed: "Think of spending all that money on a dress you only wear once!" No talk of the young men.

But I am free of anxiety, detached. *I am free of fear.* It is so wonderful to lie in the sun, to look at these young girls and not feel stabbed and destroyed by their beauty, and just when I can lie back, self-contained, indestructible, without fluttering from an anxious heart, without feeling less beautiful, less young, less strong, less lovable, then Rupert chooses that moment to look at these girls with mere detachment and say, "They are pretty, but in such an exterior way; they are hard and standardized. And as for figures, you know, you look just as good as they do on the beach."

How good to have an inner balance, to be able to lie back whole and quiet, to read, to turn the right side to the sun artfully to suntan evenly, to enjoy the Martini later. In the locker rooms, I actually approve of the image of myself in a chartreuse yellow skirt of coarse hand-woven linen from Cuernavaca, a black linen blouse, bamboo bracelet and earrings, straw bag and Yucatan fiber shoes, trim and smart, and later enjoy an exquisite dinner.

As we leave the dining room, Rupert meets old friends, and the mother of the girl he once escorted to dancing school examines me and asks, "Are you a Los Angeles girl?" after Rupert presented me as his wife. I chose New York, far enough away to not prompt an investigation of my family!

Then to a movie, this time *The Sea Around Me*, which stirred and fascinated me, with a sense of vastness, horror, terror and beauty. In a way, America is at the pre-man stage of evolution. It can grasp the spectacle of nature, examine it under a microscope, see the relationship between tidal waves, icebergs, volcanoes, the birth of fish, all that happened *before man was born*, but about man it knows nothing. The nature of man they cannot perceive. It is the scientist's old failure and indifference to the human being. For that reason they cannot write novels.

They are not afraid of cataclysms, prize fights, fires, tornadoes, atom bombs, but they are timorous and cowardly before investigations of the unconscious!

Rupert plays the guitar and sings. It is the moment of his greatest charm. It is difficult to believe that the same man, at breakfast, will say, "Couldn't you just *once* remember the price you paid for the hashed beef?"

Sierra Madre, Saturday, July 4, 1953

Rupert went off on a fire.

I had a dream: Several of us were in a high-ceilinged room of white tile, large, wide, an arched ceiling, and a very small aperture, like a bathtub drain, at the top. I said, "We will die of suffocation here." The others agreed, but seemed to consider the inevitable. I felt that I would die before Rupert returned. Just then the aperture was completely closed, and I felt dizzy and began to perspire. It felt like a steam bath. I realized it was not as acutely painful as I had feared, that I would probably faint before the end. *I was losing my sense of gravity.*

The realism of the dream was so strong that I awakened, realized it was a dream, fell asleep, and continued where I left off!

The dream has stayed with me. It is my life with Rupert.

I have lost the freedom, brilliance and fire I had attained in New York.

I have not solved my problem—the diary and the novels are as irreconcilable as my lives with Hugo and Rupert. I seem unable to write in the abstract manner I wrote in the novels. The diary alone continues.

One night I saw Gonzalo in the Village walking alone and thought: I have loved a madman. Nothing can render the abysmal emptiness of this, the devastating sense of waste. It is like discovering your life's entire current of your possessions, acquisitions, exchanges, nobilities, memories, treasures of words, caresses, has been treacherously flowing into a sewer, creating nothing, for at the very least a man needs to believe that his life is an edifice he constructs, of greater or lesser grandeur, *but that it exists.* To have loved a madman is the supreme waste and loss of love. In madmen nothing is created, engraved, retained; the relationship is distorted, caricatured, is worse than death. Not left alone to die, but to be killed with grotesqueness.

To me, intent upon human unity, oneness, the idea of the wasteful death of the other half is as terrifying as the loss of a continent, the disappearance of a twin. It is similar to the horror of a man spilling his seed upon a dry earth, wasted, destroyed, something less pure than death, for it lives only to betray itself. It proves and exposes the capacity of a human being not to love, not to understand, not to see, or to seize, or give to another human being, and it denies and mocks the illusion of fusion. It is the deepest betrayal.

That was his bond with Helba. He was closer to her than to me. My doubts were right. I refused to look at the nature of the bond, for then this love of Gonzalo would have been threatened at the base. In his moments of lucidity, he loved me. In his moments of darkness, he was bound to the one who echoed his malice, his doubts, his distortions.

I struggled to answer his elliptical phrases, even though I was wary of men's mental alchemies and believed, like a primitive, that in their laboratories they had achieved nothing more than a transmutation of living forces into fakery. My knowledge of man's achievement was summarized in a fanatical prejudice against alchemy.

The day that the blood and flesh had been turned into a wafer was the day the flavor of life became endangered. As a child, when given a communion wafer, I had struggled to transmute it back into flesh and blood. Reflecting the symbol, I proceeded to transmute the wafer into a man of flesh and blood who had now descended into my heart. I pictured my heart as a room, feeling even the housewife's preoccupation as to whether I had time to prepare the room for a visitor, disliking to be late and to miss the moment. While speeding down, I closed my eyes and prepared my heart's room for a celestial visitor who possessed a certain and definitely alluring physical reality. The descent of Christ into my little girl's heart became a most equivocal lover's meeting, and later I could not draw a demarcation between sacrilege and sensuality. For me, all communions were relationships, and all relationships were communions. What I had learned from religion was, in essence, that religion was not intended to be taken literally, and that love, all love, contained the ritual of possession, devouring and intermingling.

A Spy in the House of Love finally achieved what I have been struggling to achieve, the level of deep analysis, the subterranean richness, but linked to a narrative, and the design of this narrative I have been faithful to, so that it has both a surface and a labyrinth, and anyone can get hold of it.

Sierra Madre, July 5, 1953

Some people have minds like spaceships or jet planes, and nothing can keep them from soaring into unexplored regions. I was doing that with my novels until people began tugging at me, asking me to descend, to be clearer, to be human, which threw me off my scent.

Today, after a swim in the pool, a 4th of July party that made me write a savage story, after a Martini and solitude and music, I realized I must go higher, gain altitude, go as far as I can go, but *up*. I have been paralyzed for days, unable to work, trying to fly low and crash-landing every time.

I was equipped for heights, and I would be betraying my gifts to become a reptile and crawl along my much-despised earth. I belong with the men who invented spaceships—and I must not betray this.

Altitude. Immediately I feel free.

Whereas when I try to land, I can only write bitter and rebellious things.

Oh, Anaïs, how you have almost succumbed to the weight of the earth.

I go out in the garden. There is news of a fire that Rupert is fighting. I no longer feel the agony of protective anxiety. Instead, I feel the ultimate independence of each human being. Rupert has to live out his atonements for whatever crimes he believes he has committed. I cannot help him because he does not understand; I can only wait for him, be here when he returns, black with soot, tired. I can only hope, like a primitive woman, that watering the lawn and feeding Tavi will exorcise the danger he is in. I went out after a light dinner to lower the flag from its pole, taking care that it should not touch the ground. How careful we are that the flag should not be desecrated by touching the lowly ground. We have even made laws. It cannot be dropped, torn or burnt. But there is no law against human beings being forced to be grounded. I pick up a dead branch to be thrown away behind the garage. I see if any bit of lawn has escaped the water. I pick up a discarded drinking cup, an empty cigarette package left by people on horseback who stopped for a drink of water at the fountain. I am cooled by the wet lawn, but not proud of having spent an hour on such a task. A precious hour. I prepare my monologues, solitude, my constant meditation on writing for Kay's and John's visit. The death of her father has freed her of economic anxieties, so her concern is with television sets, vacuum cleaners, dishwashers, a new dress.

Twilight. There is no one I want to see. It is too painful a change of gears. It is like someone who carries an orchestra inside his head being asked to play the tune of an auto horn, a trolley bell, a telephone ringer. I can't do it.

Back into the house, too warm, I think of Rupert longingly and also realize he would at this time be listening to Chet Huntley or choosing a movie to go to at full speed.

Everything is wise and rigid. I went through my emotional, spiritual, metaphysical, psychological infernos. Rupert is going through his physical ones. He was not one for symbolic infernos. He understands this: physical hell—fire, smoke, hard pick work, gigantic breakfasts. It is his idea of a Man. A man who does not wish to destroy, but to conserve, preserve, protect nature. It is not my kind of hell. I cannot deprive him of his. To each one his own element. He has chosen Earth. I, space. The kind of space he talks about, admiringly, of the Texas plains, the Utah valleys, Californian terrains, I find empty. A desert for me is a land parched with the absence of music, of painting, of theatre. For Rupert, it is the desert of Palm Springs where he played as a child. So he is sweating, his beautiful face all dirty from the work he chose, was attracted by. Nature. Nature, sweet and peaceful, singing birds, cool grass and crickets—and demonic nature, fire, cruelty, danger.

You cannot interfere with such designs, or rescue anyone from them. They must be lived out, liquidated, transcended.

I cannot suffer with Rupert anymore because I am not in sympathy with his devotions, the object of his sacrifices.

The only truth is what one feels, sees, hears at the moment. Later, the truth is not able to be captured. I wish I had now, possessed now, what I saw and felt when I first met Rupert.

Sierra Madre, July 7, 1953

Rupert is still fighting the fire. Now I cannot sustain my detachment. I feel the strain on his body, his tiredness, his perspiration. I feel all that happens to his body. Compassion. Tavi and I now share the waiting. But just when he was coming home today, another fire started nearby, one I could see. And I began to suffer. I could not sleep. I took sleeping pills and too many Martinis, and I was sick. So last night I took nothing. Read Proust. I had a dream that in New York, I discovered Rupert had another woman, old, as old as his mother, one he would not surrender, because she was *good*. This may have come out of my writing about our first fantasy of his marrying someone else and my being the mistress.

Then I awakened this morning and wrote eighteen pages, almost without pause, in the book I call temporarily *Change*, the final novel of change in all the characters. It is Djuna's analysis of Lillian.

My solution to the problem of the psychological novel is that "psychoanalysis" must be done by the writer.

I was happy. I have not been able to work for almost a year, not on the novels.

So I went out and watered the garden carefully for Rupert, bathed Tavi carefully and went down to the Campions' pool. Pam is twenty-nine, sweet, humorous. Paul is thirty, humorous and kind. *C'est tout.* We lie around the pool and play games. Swim a little. The water is so cold.

It was when I was returning from the pool I saw the new fire and felt sorrowful. The little conflicts were consumed by the fire Rupert has fought Friday, Saturday, Sunday, Monday, Tuesday.

Here, against the brown walls, I could do nothing. Rupert said it was forbidden to paint them. So I made the bed cover of a rough off-white rug and I added the off-white rug I made in France. Gil Henderson gave us a white painting (a chalice, a spider web, a drop of blood), and that, with the Japanese dolls from San Francisco, colorful Mexican clay figures, and open shelves on which I pile colored scarves and a jewel box, makes the room joyous.

In the other room, the books, four paintings (one is Varda's) and the chartreuse couches and curtains also seek to assert life against the oppressive walls.

Rupert built the couches. He built the shelves and the tables. He is an intense and hard-working craftsman. He wants to build his own house.

What does he think at night when he is about to sleep in the mountains? I don't know. With all my intuition I cannot enter Rupert's mind. How strange it is. You ask questions. Or you wait for signs, revelations. The passionate, the lyrical, the prosaic Rupert are at variance. In adolescence everything is contrary, conflicted, his sweetness and irritability, his longing for home and for travel, his excessive kindness to strangers in distress and disregard of my important wishes.

And on our last trip, because it took place six weeks after my major operation, I still felt weak and wanted to go first of all to Acapulco, and we didn't.

Rupert's love for me is not protective, and that is why I am always driven back to Hugo.

Then yesterday Rupert returned, blowing his siren, sooty, and bearded, dazed. I took him into my arms. I filled the bathtub; I dried him; he was so weary. While he shaved I prepared food, I opened the bed. I was delirious with joy to have him back and stirred by his fatigue. He slept. I kept watch to intercept the people coming to the door, asking if we wanted volunteers to fight the fire, or asking news of the fire, or asking if they could disregard the sign forbidding entrance to the canyon.

At night he awakened, to eat again. His eyes were red and blurred. He talked about the fire. "I had fifty Mexican nationals to direct. They couldn't speak English. On the Sulphur Spring fire, the backfires were lit with bombs containing sulphur, which made me vomit. For two days, desperately thirsty, I could not keep water down. My sleeping hours were from ten in the morning to two in the afternoon, in full daylight, so I couldn't sleep well. The rest of the time I was on duty. I was finally able to keep milk down. I was on watch at night. The men loved me because when there was no danger, I let them sleep on the line while I patrolled. I saw the dawn every morning. We were high up, 8,000 feet. It was lonely. I felt sorry for myself. I thought if I didn't have you, if I didn't have our relationship to return to, I couldn't take the physical torture."

A night of sleep. This morning a seismographic upheaval, passion like a series of shocks, tremors, delight, and then as his back hurt him, I used the vibrator on him for a long time, on his beautiful back, brown to the waist, and the buttocks so white, round, firm, and the skin so tender at the end of the spine, the blue veins show. He could be a beautiful statue to be served and loved and spoiled, but he chooses to be a man (according to his ideal), a husband, a lover. He is inarticulate about all he felt up on that mountain, alone, while the fire lay low, threatening, smoldering, at any moment ready to flare up, while the worn-out men slept, and once Rupert himself, in the cold night, lay down on the warm ashes and fell asleep.

So the day glows with the fecund, illuminating fire of love, and courage. And I read Rupert the short story I wrote on the 4th of July spent next door, and he laughed at its humor and was amazed at its terrible veracity.

He has gone to buy new boots, having worn out his old ones completely, right through.

Letter from Jim Herlihy to Anaïs Nin:

Black Mountain College, July 10, 1953

Dear Anaïs; I can't understand why I have so much trouble writing this letter to you. It is about the fifth try and I'm beginning to wonder what's wrong with me. I find now that the only way I can handle the telling of this past strange month, at least for the moment, is in abbreviation. For example, Hugo! How can I tell you, even if I were to take time and pains, what he has done for me? It is perhaps because I myself am none too stable that he seems to be a pillar of strength, but being objective as I possibly can, I do feel that he is to be so greatly admired for the growth that is taking place, almost visibly, like a plant; he is kind and gentle and protective in a way that seems to spring from a genuine internal strength. I'm very grateful to him; there's more to be said about this, but it wouldn't be abbreviation, which is what I've set out to do. But anyway, I have grown to like Hugo in a way that I like very few people: deeply.

As for Dick, we are separated and will remain so until I feel certain that we are both strong enough to build something good.

Anaïs, I have seldom approached writing a letter to you with a greater feeling of inadequacy than the present one. In a way I have the confusion of an orphan, an unwanted child who has been sent to camp here at Black Mountain, but who, when the summer ends, doesn't know what will become of himself. If only René would work a miracle, or MCA, or I!

René told me *New Story* was doing *Spy* this year, having unraveled their $ troubles, and I am very happy about that. Are you? Or are you maintaining your detachment, even when the moment is a successful one? To be consistent, you should of course maintain the detachment. I have a hunch you will be consistent. But anyway we'll celebrate whether you like it or not; it's good business.

Hope you have a fine summer, and are having one; the news that you are working is the most welcome of all. I want to see what comes of it as soon as you can possibly send it.

Jim

Sierra Madre, July 11, 1953

Wrote beautiful, profound pages on Antigua.

Pursuing two spheres. Rereading diaries 63 and 64 and am fully aware of their value. I am continuing my distillation, to end the novels, for there are two truths, one near and immediate, in the direct feelings, another as seen from altitude and distance, the abstraction. What art gives us, and the near and individual document does not, is the vision of all that lies beyond the personal, which makes the personal, the human, bearable. Otherwise it is not. *La condition humaine* is not bearable. We get ill, we suffer wars, we lose those we love, we torture human beings, we have famines, revolutions, horrible diseases, concentration camps, enough to lose our minds! Art then comes to give us altitude.

Rupert returned from another night watch at a fire this morning. He goes through the same process I do, of sifting through the irritants of his own flaws, and returns more tolerant of my idiosyncrasies. His "lectures" are mellower. I had the car filled with oil but I can't remember if it was one quart or how much I paid!

And then he says, "In this week I earned $100 besides my salary, as much as you earn when you go to New York, and we were only separated for one week, so next time you go you can come back one week sooner."

The diary serves as a safety valve for the rebellions. Actually, I have said very little to Rupert about his profession. I felt he had to live it out. He had to prove he could assume the responsibilities of a profession, as a husband, which he fulfills very beautifully. He has done exceedingly well in his job; he is respected, admired and relied on, he never spares himself, he is courageous, tenacious, thorough. He is liked by the men, which was difficult because he does not look like them or live as they do, and they were at first wary of his appearance, his youth.

But now it is Rupert himself, who, after refusing several "advances" and raises because they meant living in a shack in some lonely place, says, "In New York, to live and work outdoors seemed a wonderful thing to me, but now I realize it is not enough. I had a romantic idea of forestry. I hope someday we can get free. You are right when you say I need to prove certain truths to myself. My mother always said I was like Reginald, shiftless, could not stick to anything."

I did not pull Rupert away. I rebelled mostly in the diary.

But when I began to work and to live only for Rupert and writing, I was at peace. I suffered because I tried to continue my vast life of New York here in Sierra Madre.

Tonight Rupert is patrolling a dead fire (in case of sudden treacherous flare-ups) and instead of seeing Kay and John, or Gil and Olympia Henderson, I went to bed as soon as it got dark, with Proust, the diary, a new magazine, Lila's manuscript. And I will write letters to Jim and Hugo.

Quartet: Rupert is intense, as he is in all his activities, playing imperfectly but with brilliance and warmth, sitting on the very edge of his chair.

At dinner Helen told the story of Rupert's birth. "Reginald left me at the hospital, completely overwhelmed and upset by all these happenings. He shocked everybody by leaving me, disappearing for three or four hours while I was in labor. Then Rupert came, and later I fell asleep. When I awakened I was told Reginald wanted to see me. Now, Reginald had one trait that intrigued me at the time: he had a very foreign moustache and an imperial beard. It made him look rather dashing. And now he appeared before me, *all shaved*, a terrible disillusion, and carrying a small bouquet of flowers picked from someone's garden!

"Now, when I was expecting Rupert, he stayed by my side reading poetry and Shakespeare to me all the time. He wanted Rupert to be influenced by the best literature."

"Oh," I said, "now I see why Rupert dislikes reading!"

"No," said Lloyd, "it didn't make him love to read, but it did achieve the making of a troubadour. He is a troubadour, with his guitar and ballads, and you are just the woman from the Middle Ages who would appreciate a troubadour!"

And then Lloyd proceeded to evaluate Eyvind Earle as I did (in the diary), as a mediocre painter, whose mediocrity is what is causing his success at Disney—the kind of evaluation Rupert has heard all his life and at which he may have rebelled, for I have never heard him evaluate anyone from the same high, intransigent, pure artistic level as Lloyd's or FLW's. His taste may have become entangled with his rebellions against Reginald's Cambridge pedantry, Lloyd's intolerance, the secondary effects of FLW's *rightness* in matters of art.

But how strange it is that having breathed the air of taste in art first emitted by FLW, he was never again able to breathe mediocrity, and yet he was neurotically set against all contemporary art when I met him. In the case of Earle, of course, I understand. Earle is his friend. He would hang his painting even if it were the worst. But in other cases, he is set against modern experimental music, prefers the Mexican school of painting to the French, and the documentary to reading.

Letter from Anaïs Nin to Jim Herlihy:

Sierra Madre, July 14, 1953

Dear Jim: I understand about not being able to write, but the key to the difficulty really lies in your words about feeling like an orphan. Sure, it is rationally true that neither Hugo nor I, nor anyone, has deserted you, that you moved away of your own volition and impetus. However, in the world of the personal myth in which we live, you *felt* deserted, so that is real to you, and I should have guessed how you felt and written you sooner and more often. *The feeling is the reality.* I did have to go away, too, just when you were in trouble, and that, you know, is emotionally unforgivable, even if you knew it was inevitable. So forgive us our sins against your feelings, and let us see what we can reconstruct on this irrational treachery human beings are forever committing against one another.

I understand how you feel in Black Mountain. It is too bad the heat drove you away from New York. I am sure Hugo was grateful and enjoyed your companionship, and you could have stayed on. Too bad you could not go to the Cape. I know how you feel about adolescents, and the psychological past effect of returning to a place from the past, if not a past state of being. You have leaped far ahead of wherever you were at Black Mountain, you know. I am sorry you have to be in a place that does not match your mood or yourself of today. That is always painful. If the solution is material, let me help you get away and you can go to the Cape instead. If you find you can dig in and work, it will be good to be farther away from Dick and not tempted to return too soon, before he is cured. I was very happy to hear of his going through analysis. It would be a beautiful miracle if he faced his illness, and the source of the trouble turned out to be altogether neurotic.

If you forgive me for that desertion, I know you will be able to write me freely. You see, I consider the art of relationship so evolved and intricate and subtle and profound that I felt very badly about leaving at such a critical moment for you. And let me confess, we are all equally hurt by desertion. I felt deserted when you went to the Cape while I was still weak after the hospital, just to show you how I know how you feel. Only remember, you were not sent away, and we all want you back at any time, and I miss you more than I could ever say.

I had a good month, though, doing what I call consolidating my positions. Taking stock of what I have, what was not done, and what had to be done.

I wrote a skeleton play out of *The Four-Chambered Heart*. I wrote fifty new pages of the synthesis book to tie up the novels, and reorganized the novels themselves so as to clarify the sequence, with scissors, tore up the books so that next time they will be printed all in one volume like Proust, and the design will come out more forcibly. And then this will please you: I will then devote myself entirely to writing the diary, my real work. Your reading it started an awareness of its being my major work, and how I should put all I have into it. So I have done that. I wrote of the Tree (Rupert) and the Pillar (Hugo). You refer to him as a pillar too. I feel that the way you see Hugo now is the way I have always seen him, barring that terrible period of his illness, which I call the awkward age of his ego and from which you had to suffer too. I am glad that he helped you. At the time he was unable to see all you did for him. I feel, from far off now, that what blocked him from entirely appreciating or responding openly to you was an underlying jealousy of our relationship—yours and mine—that I can see now, looking back on it, and that made it hard for him to receive so much from you.

Love, and believe me, far from deserting you, I consider ours the most permanent, inextricable, unbreakable relationship.

Anaïs

Sierra Madre, July 15, 1953

The novel's place in the study of character.

America has tabooed introspection. There is no understanding of character possible without introspection, awareness, analysis. It cultivated external action, and this, reported by skillful newsmen, reveals nothing. When the character gets sick and neurosis becomes widespread, then the doctor is called. America would study character only as a scientist in a laboratory studies a disease or even, as is often the case, a dead psyche. They considered psychology like medicine, concerned with illness, but never was the study of character encouraged in the novel or in the play. Too many taboos. When a character appears as a neurotic, there are outcries.

Americans consider it healthy when relationship problems are solved by divorce, or humorously disposed of, when no effort is made for knowledge or understanding of human psyche while it is not yet acutely ailing.

The novel is dying from lack of interest in character. We think of other planets in place of accepting within ourselves strangeness and uniqueness. Any manifestation of individuality or originality is mercilessly persecuted. Standardization is the supreme ideal.

Letter from Jim Herlihy to Anaïs Nin:

Black Mountain College, July 17, 1953

Dear Anaïs,

About your work: I have the strong feeling that it is a good thing you have come to regard the diary as the truly important, major work of your career thus far. And even though it's a goddamn shame that you will reap very little of the superficial harvest from it, it seems wise to be realistic about the fact that, secret or no, it is one of the major literary works of all time, not just of your own output. And I can well imagine that you might one day hit upon a way of converting some of its powers for contemporary consumption—as far as that goes, we have to just wait and see what happens—but it seems to me that whatever energies are put into it are well spent.

I haven't much more that is organized well enough in my mind to put down now, and I have to get ready for dinner soon, but I do know clearly and can say very easily that you're the most beautiful woman who ever lived, even when thought of one facet at a time.

And let's make a pact: when I don't hear from you for any considerable period, I promise not to make fantasies to explain why; you promise me likewise. Because I feel just as you do about our relationship: if it's not indestructible, then neither is the sun. (And if this is one fragment of our neuroses, let's cling to it anyway, because, at least for me, it's the part that makes all the rest seem less hopeless!)

Love,

Jim

New York, July 31, 1953

American Airline flight 11 PM to New York

Saturday:	Party
Sunday:	Filming with Hugo on ferry ride with Jim
Monday:	Filming with Hugo and Jim
Tuesday:	Lunch for Ruth Witt-Diamant
Wednesday:	6:00 Thomas Gainsberg of *Paris Review*
Thursday:	Ruth, Tia Antolina; 6:00 Thomas Gainsberg
Friday:	Work on diaries; 6:00 Herbert Alexander
Saturday:	Shooting with Hugo 12:00 to 2:00; 5:00 Dr. Rosen, nephew of Jakob Wasserman wants to translate diaries into German; 11:00 PM shooting with Hugo on 42nd Street

New York, August 1953

A different Hugo met me at La Guardia. He has lost weight, and looks more as he did when I first knew him, except for the thinning grey hair and lined face. His genuine sweetness is back, except now he is free, independent, natural. He does not have to assert himself. He is himself. Also, the mask has fallen from his face. Life shines through, pleasure at the filmmaking, at the "shots" he finds, at his successes (*Ai-Ye* was given a prize in Paris, and his Mexican Zoo film will be shown during the Omnibus Child Program at the Ford Foundation). I am amazed to see his body come out of the heavy, clogging flesh like lobsters who periodically shed their entire carapace and emerge tender-skinned, new. The shedding of the mask reveals pleasure, enthusiasm, aliveness too.

I said, "It is amazing, the change. You were closed before and so buried that I used to say you were blind. Now, as you go around with your camera, you see more than I do."

"I always had a periscope," said Hugo.

We walk the streets, filming, and sometimes I act for him, appearing reflected in shop windows. We stop to reload the camera and have a Martini.

At home I cook lunch for him and for Jim, who is staying with us until he finds a home.

I wash dishes because I gave Millicent her much-needed vacation, and the girls who come just do cleaning.

I see Herbert Alexander, from Pocket Books, who sent me a message from the Koran about my work: "It is written."

No more writing, but I give myself to Hugo's film.

And all the rebellions and restlessness I felt in Sierra Madre, which for a moment

I took merely as a destructive mood, become clear when I arrive here: here, I do not rebel or feel restless. I like my life. So my rebellions were not merely destructive, they were caused by the too-narrow life.

I like the place as I decorated it.

I like Hugo's thoughtfulness: as soon as he sees me doing Millicent's work (for Millicent's sake), he tells me to get another maid.

I like Hugo's free-flowing improvisations with the camera. He says, "You are a wonderful wife for an artist," because I inspire him and understand what he is doing.

I can come and go without explanation or control, or justification.

On Broadway, we see a dress I like and Hugo says, "Get it."

I see Tia Antolina.

I see the Barrons, and I hear their new composition, which is like a Miró painting.

In the dress shop, I sat waiting for the dress to be packaged. A woman was startled when I moved, and drew back, saying, "Oh my. I'm sorry, I took you for one of the mannequins; you looked so perfect!"

Hugo heard her and laughed.

William Inge came, author of *Come Back, Little Sheba*. Half brute, half woman, physically, in appearance.

I saw Thomas Gainsberg of *Paris Review*. Maxwell Geismar was the strongest supporter of William Styron, who is one of the editors at *Paris Review*, but when Geismar asked to be an associate editor, they turned him down because he was not young. And because of their attitude, the magazine is a colorless piece of driftwood without any character at all.

The real point, I said to Jim, referring to Geismar's book of criticism *Rebels and Ancestors*, is not to praise its *contents*, but to ask: is it *written*? Dreiser's content suits Geismar, but Dreiser was anything but a *writer*. A social document can be a card index, a statistical file, a text book, a catalogue. Annotations, marginal notes, synopses, scenarios... None of them are *writing*.

A dream of a quarrel with Rupert.

I telephone him, but I have no longing to be there. I have lived with him long enough to know that Rupert the husband is impossible for me. I feel free without him. I wonder how he feels without me. His life and character drive me away, and the passion is not enough.

It is raining. Hugo is asleep. The cat sleeps on his stomach.

I have just phoned Rupert without feeling.

Letter from Rupert Pole to Anaïs Nin:

Sierra Madre, August 1953

Love,

Somehow engulfed by so many things since your wonderful call Sunday, and here it is Tuesday and no letter yet.

So now is the time—quick—before the concert.

Everything happens at once. The Forest Service told me to take down all my signs Sunday and report for a special forestry project Monday. Worked till dark Sunday trying to get all the signs down, got stuck in the mud, had to get under the truck in pouring rain to get the chains on, got out, but I had developed severe pain all through my leg. It is still painful today but better from heat treatment from your lamp. As if this wasn't enough, I discovered a big tick biting me on the chest. I could not get his head out (the body just broke off with tweezers), and Monday it was very sore and festering so off to my FS doctor who had to dig ten minutes with a scalpel to get the head out. And if *this* wasn't enough, Tavi chose this moment to be sick too. He woke up and couldn't get out (very cold so the door was closed) and had diarrhea all over the white rug. Tried to clean it up but no good so ended up washing the rug in the bath tub, looks fine now. Tavi is well again, also on a diet of toast, and he is forbidden, under threat of deportation, to eat lizards. Playing viola solo with Monrovia orchestra anniversary concert in *three* minutes.

Your voice sounded fine.

Got to get this off now, will try to write again tomorrow.

Our love is ever *deeper*. You are *nearer* to me than ever before.

R

New York, Sunday, August 9, 1953

Miranda d'Arcona, Audrey Hilliard to talk about play for Theatre de Lys. Gave them Jim's play.

9:00 Chez Nims

New York, Monday, August 10, 1953

Took 500 pages of diary to Herbert Alexander

11:00 With Tia Antolina to see *Rome*

8:00 Lila tells me about life in Cherry Orchard, Fire Island decadence, AA discipline

New York, August 11, 1953

Filming in the streets with Hugo. His eyes open mine to the unexpected beauty of shop windows, a window of chandeliers, mannequins, masks, magic tricks, souvenirs of New York, jokes, etc. A world of street cripples.

I suggested he shoot 42nd Street lights on a *slant* that voids reading the ads' words and produces a ballet of lights. I suggested beginning with a pinpoint of light (cars coming off the ferry) and ending in a frenzy of lights.

I have a genuine enthusiasm for Hugo's film work, and I can help him well. We walk the streets. I carry the tripod. I am dressed to act too, if necessary. I also make discoveries. It is summer. A happy month of expansion and activity.

I only have *one* moment of anxiety, just before going to sleep, because that is the moment when I feel the absence of Rupert.

I prepare more diaries for Max Geismar and Alexander. That is all I can do now as the writing stopped when I gave myself to running a house without Millicent and collaborating on the film.

Jim flits in and out, visits Dick, and has black, withdrawn moods during which I can't reach him.

Lila explains why on one side of himself Jim writes like the sons of Hemingway, and in his diary and in his talks with me he manifests a more subtle, poetic self (his feminine self identified with me), his use of symbolism, his tenderness. But this side he will not give to the world.

Anaïs Nin in a still from the "42nd Street film"

Letter from Rupert Pole to Anaïs Nin:

Sierra Madre, August 1953

TO: My Love (without whom there is no life)

FROM: Her Man (tonight the musical man)

SUBJECT: Her

Strange, I connect you so intimately with my music now. You are in it and behind it and woven through it, and the theme and all the variations are...YOU!!!

Wonderful evening tonight. Went to poor old Scott's orchestra, but played very good music, and being the only violist there played a big solo the regular violist is to play at the concert Tuesday. I just read it and played it so well, but I thought of YOU while I played, and after, when everyone came up and said I played so beautifully, YOU were in my fingers, dancing, and in my viola, making love.

YOU are always with me in so many ways, but most of all in music, the true language of love, when love expresses itself in sound.

And the fascinating thing about our love is that it expresses itself in so many ways, in all ways, in SOUNDS, and in SILENCES.

The most wonderful SILENCES ever created.

R

NEW YORK, WEDNESDAY, AUGUST 12, 1953

Shooting with Hugo.

Evening: Mr. and Mrs. Rollo Williams and Barrons for dinner.

Letter from Anaïs Nin to Rupert Pole:

New York, August 12, 1953

My darling Chiquito, Sunday is always blue because I'm less busy, because I hear your voice and I want to be there! I *knew* it would be longer. But I was happy (oh, the cruelty of women!) that you were lonely because I was afraid I'd been so bad about the radio and about escaping all our duties and going off by ourselves that perhaps you weren't missing me at all and were enjoying your radio in peace without your Spanish wife.

My imagination is freer, because I believe when the artist "plays" with ideas, he is really creating, and specifically you and I always manage to carry out our ideas. I think you are still afraid of fantasy-making because Reginald's led nowhere, just uprooted him, made him restless and not truly creative in his life. I mean, he could have created more if he had not dispersed his energy wastefully.

Darling Chiquito, it's always useful, my being here, for us. And you should sleep well, deeply, and think only of our next love affair. The returns are so exciting; the separations teach one to disregard the small troubles that one makes too much of when one takes the other for granted. But I do ask you, please, to get earphones, only when you have something more than commentators, and I promise to rebel against nothing else. Earphones enable me to read or work, which I find more profitable than radio.

Te quiero. Sleep soundly, for your wife in NY is being notoriously faithful, having the best, already, so far away, and goes to sleep every night thinking of you, but with sleeping pills as I always get low at that hour, missing you.

Tu mujer

Letter from Rupert Pole to Anaïs Nin:

Sierra Madre, August 1953

Light of My Present Darkness!

Hope you didn't think I was negative about Rosen's idea of a German edition of your diary, and know you'll work out what's best with help of de Chochor and Geismar, etc., but I do feel (as you do) it's not only a great and monumental work, but also your greatest financial asset, and part of its economic value is that it is completely unique and virgin and has never been published, even in fragments. Therefore, a German publication *might* diminish its value here either for publication now under a pseudonym, or later. I'm not really sure of this, so get the best advice you can there and then act on your instinct. I don't think you'd get royalties out of Germany, so consider that too.

You must help me with my negativism and fear of seizing the tiger by the tail; there is a side of me that is too damn rational and always sees all the pitfalls, which eventually persuades me to do nothing at all.

But let's seize the tiger soon—just for fun—and we'll swing round and round on his tail, and as long as we're together, nothing can harm us!!!

Love ever more,

R

NEW YORK, MONDAY, AUGUST 17, 1953

Rain. Went with Jim to Beauford Delaney's studio to see it since Jim is renting it.

At six gave cocktail party for Charlie de Cárdenas' wife and two sons.

Letter from Rupert Pole to Anaïs Nin:

Sierra Madre, August 1953

My Love,

Back from fire alive and healthy and tired and wealthy—gad, the money we're making this month!!

Damn it—*merde alors*—wrote you funny little notes on the fire and put them in *stamped* envelope, had it all ready, and then realized I didn't remember Lila's address. I'm now back and of course can't find the letter.

So a new one.

Tavi is looking very old. He's developed bad arthritis in the shoulder (from swimming too much and sitting on the wet lawn). I took him to the vet and got lots of pills to give him for two weeks, three twice a day, one every other day, real fancy, and that afternoon they called me for a fire. I called Mother to get Tavi; no one was home, so over to Pam's with full instructions—how to feed, give pills, etc., and if I wasn't back by the next day she was to call my family.

Well, first little Molly pulls Tavi's sore shoulder and he nips her hand, and the hand swells up, so Paul and Pam take her to the Dr. and he says it is infected, but not badly, but the dog must be put in quarantine and observed for rabies. Meanwhile Tavi, knowing he's done something wrong, refused to go near the Campions even to get his food. Pam was all ready to call my family as per instructions when she talked to Mrs. M., who said, "I'll take care of Tavi," and so she did for two days. Tavi lived high on steak and pills and slept under Mrs. M's bed and was (she says) completely devoted to her. I got home at one in the morning and Mr. and Mrs. M. appeared in their nightclothes (and what nightclothes) to bring Tavi back!

Then the next day the villain, the county health officer, came when we were gone and pinned a big sign saying QUARANTINE in red letters. I tore up the sign (Tavi has been vaccinated for rabies) and today he came again when we were here. "It's state law," he kept saying, "The dog must stay in the house for fifteen days." I got mad and he got mad, and just as we were about to come to blows—Tavi growling all the time—it suddenly struck my sense of humor and I laughed, and then he laughed, and he came in and had a beer. I said Tavi would be quarantined in the house when I was there and in the car when I was out, and at my family's if I went on a fire, and he said he supposed that would be all right—and we had another beer. Everyone is happy now except Tavi who still has lots of pain in that shoulder. I'll have it X-rayed if doesn't get better. So tired. Must get to bed now, where the only attraction now is that I can devote my entire energy to dreaming that you're close, tight beneath me, and I can spear my pez vela again and again, far under the surface of consciousness.

R

New York, Tuesday, August 18, 1953

Cocktail party for Bill and Letha Nims.

Herbert Alexander telephoned (he has 500 pages of the diary): "I don't know what to say. It is *immense*. I haven't read it all, but I have the intuition you're the most important writer of your generation."

He is a principal editor of Pocket Books. Irony that he, and not Signet, recognizes the vision of my work. He can't do anything for me. He may find other ways—a way.

Meanwhile *A Spy in the House of Love* languishes in the dishonest hands of Eric Protter of *New Story*.

I took a taxi the other day. A very slender, youthful but grey-haired driver said, "I am very thankful to have a passenger who adorns my new cab."

Surprised by his language, I made him talk. He was a captain of a ship during the war, brought up in comfort in a home of twenty-eight rooms (always these American statistics), but his career meant separation from his wife, and he preferred happiness. He intended to own a fleet of taxis and to write a book at the age of sixty. By the time we reached 9th Street I had persuaded him to write his book now.

In my dreams I quarrel with Rupert. Last night we were to meet at a hotel. There was confusion. He could not find it.

In another dream I went to a party and the host's mother was ill. I went to say good evening to her, but finding her in pain and in need of care (she was suffering from spasms of the breasts caught in Mexico), I stayed with her. When I came out of her room the party was over. I was aware I did not like the young man whose mother I had been devoted to.

Another dream: Rupert was driving a jeep. There was a man lying on the roadside. I asked Rupert to slow down, but Rupert was sure he could continue to speed, that he would not harm the man. But he caught the man's head in the wheel and I had to free him. Fortunately the heavy mud and rain had slowed down the car so I could save the man.

Sunday when I telephoned, Rupert said, "I am lonely. I can't sleep." Then his physical presence became vivid once more, as if he were standing before me, his eyes, mouth, and hands, the oblique slant of his cheeks, the ears…and I missed him, but with the full knowledge that he is bad for me, as any drug or alcohol would be.

With Hugo I share looking at all things, people, plays, films, events, with a psychological insight, through the eyes of the artist, or through the eyes of Proust, or his camera eye, or mine. Rupert's beautiful eyes are blind.

Family Portraits

Tia Antolina: "The family must keep together, must be loyal to each other. They must not be dispersed."

Ti Coco: "There is peace in my heart, peace and harmony."

Tia Antolina: "Ti Coco will be all right now, she has Uncle Gilbert's pension."

Ti Coco: "Money is not everything."

Tia Antolina: "Did you know Graciella's husband was operated on? They took half of his stomach out and he had bleeding ulcers. Poor Graciella. He's such a good husband."

Anaïs: "But he didn't die!"

Ti Coco's expression is that of a Christian martyr who will not be disturbed by the lions while Tia Antolina continues her gory conversation, on eye operations, nervousness, Charlie's testament he made before leaving on a big trip to enter an annual yacht race, etc.

Ti Coco: "I have harmony in my heart."

Terrible to see the same kind of eyes as my mother's in another human being—ferret eyes.

New York, Wednesday, August 19, 1953

Experience with Dr. Rosen who wanted to translate the diary for a German publisher. Nephew of Jakob Wasserman. My intuition told me he is the wrong person.

After two talks I realized he was a second-rate Dr. Kinsey, could not write well in either German or English, was curious but unaware of my value as an artist and was seeking only the sexual revelations. I sent him away and told him why.

New York, August 20, 1953

We went to Rockaway Beach with Jim and Dick. Dick is flushed, expansive. Jim at the moment is in the Dark Ages of neurosis. He looks like the hypnotized young man in *Dr. Caligari*, a German decadent. At five I met my publisher from *New Story*, and I was with René trying to salvage *Spy*.

Letter from Anaïs Nin to Rupert Pole:

New York, August 1953

Darling Chiquito,

Swamped in every way. Mother still here because her leg is numb and Jacobson is trying to clear that up. Two aunts and countless cousins. Because of my mother, I could not escape. Work, lots of it. Mr. Alexander of Pocket Books called me up after dipping into 500 pages of the diary.

De Chochor only returned from France a few days ago. He's swamped, so we can't talk until Tuesday. Everything takes time. The *New Story* publisher is here for six months, as he is a Czechoslovakian naturalized U.S. citizen and has lived in France five years and as a naturalized citizen returns every five years for at least a six-month stay. He says I will have the unbound copies for reviewers in three weeks, so I have to prepare a list of where they must be mailed and given. I will do all this and Jim will follow it up.

You *were* right about a German translation of the diary. I have to wait until I sell it as an original in the U.S. Sometimes your sense of the practical is dampening, but you are *very often* right and I do not act without consulting you. I would not have acted without de Chochor's business consent.

I feel tired, and I miss you, even though we were very close last night in a dream that would not get by the censors!

Did you ever try to find my good sunglasses at the little Italian pizza place by the beach were we had such a merry dinner?

New Story magazine and press floundering because their backer withdrew, so I am lucky to get my book out at all!

I may call you up tonight instead of waiting till Sunday, darling.

Tu mujer

New York, August 21, 1953

Saw work done on a mannequin in a window with Hugo.

3:00 Tia Antolina, Ti Coco

6:00 Lee Travis, costume designer, half-Broadway, half-artist, eccentric. Uses the word "weird" constantly, even about his own writing, or songs, or costumes

New York, August 24, 1953

2:00 Posing for film at studio as a mannequin

6:15 Lila for dinner. Shooting on Broadway

New York, August 25, 1953

Beach with Hugo, Jim and Dick

Lunch with René de Chochor

7:15 Dinner chez Lillian Libman

New York, August 26, 1953

12:00 Antolina, errands

New York, August 27, 1953

Errands with Hugo

Saw Jim's apartment

5:30 Chez Rollo Williams and his family at Great Neck

Hugo has a way of finding beauty in Broadway lights using the camera at a slant, oblique, upside down, filming even the back of signs like the Budweiser sign whose beauty I discovered from behind. A good symbol for how to find beauty by destroying the familiar face of it, the trite, the common, and find the aspects that lie hidden. I made a humorous takeoff of Hugo, holding my head upside down, or waving it (as by a distortion lens). Finally it was I who discovered the jazz in the lights. Superimposition was the inception of Hugo's work as a poet, and it came from me. Now he reads Proust all the time, as I do, and we work in the same direction so that we have a great deal of pleasure working on the film.

Yes, I still suffer still from his rhythm, which is slower than that of anyone I know, his bad memory, and the appalling, incredible disorganization of his mind, but as an artist in film he is showing real creative and inventive genius. I think he is the first real poet in film, better than the artifices of Cocteau. He fills that very space between realism and abstraction. He uses human material to fabricate poetry with, just as I do. We are in perfect accord with our method of free association of images, finding the themes later, and working as if with mosaics from the unconscious. I can no longer see the lights of Broadway as I saw them; Hugo opened my eyes to the streets, but not in the same way that Henry did, just as décor, as objects without meaning. Hugo gathers it together and animates it with his own meaning.

Now, at last, we give each other true freedom.

New York, August 28, 1953

Errands, work on the house, copper plates and mural of Hugo's engravings, a big task.

The same nightmares I used to have about Hugo, I now have about Rupert. The theory that they issue from guilt is doubtful, because I had them all through the first six years of my marriage when I had no cause for guilt. Last night I dreamed that Rupert was going out with a girl, and he showed me her photograph in the newspaper. She was, of course, a beauty queen at the Pomona Fair, and a wealthy girl. Meanwhile I had to go to a family reunion, a duty, and I knew that the evening would be torture. If I had been going out with a young man I could flirt with, it would not have been so unbearable. I could have forgotten Rupert, but a family reunion would accentuate the contrast and heighten my suffering. I tried to make Rupert admit he loved the girl, tried to incite him to tell me the truth. But he was indifferent, callous, inaccessible. I wept and pleaded. After a while he said soothingly: "You are like a bad Rembrandt." I awakened unhappy.

Wednesday: Stanley Haggart, Jim for cocktails

Friday: 5:00 cocktail party, Haggart, Sue Fuller (string composition)

Saturday: Permanent

Letter from Rupert Pole to Anaïs Nin:
Sierra Madre, September 1953

Love,

Had to laugh at you with your mixed quarters and dimes, but I've never heard such an ill-tempered operator—she needs a man, or something. The next time, put quarters in first, and then dimes, and all slowly, and count 25, 50, 75, 1.00, 1.10, 1.20, etc. so the poor things can keep track (I can hear coin tones perfectly here on this end).

No real news here; hot and smoggy, lots of paper work, got to beach once. Less than two weeks now till you leave your sophisticated life again for your simple life and your simple husband who loves you more and more each time you return.

R

New York, September 8, 1953

One evening Jim, Hugo and I went to the Theatre de Lys to shoot captions for the 42nd Street film on the marquee. It was very hot. Jim stood on a tall ladder and changed the letters fifteen times; I fetched and carried letters. We worked four and a half hours. Went to sleep dead tired. Jim has become thin, wan, nervous, irritable, and difficult. His neurosis is blooming in the tension of New York. I am so tired of difficult people that I no longer try to sustain relationships with them. When the deforming mirrors start operating, I do not have the energy or desire to work at resuscitating a true image every day, so I withdraw. Jim and Hugo quarreled; Hugo was generous. Hugo has changed so enormously. I like him and understand him and feel with him. We have a sense of unity, now that the misunderstandings are clear. We work very well together.

Spent three days locked in the house, working on the film, and on two large panels of Hugo's engravings for which I made mattings, a huge job yielding beautiful results. One whole wall in the bedroom is covered with colored engravings, another with grey on white, another with white lines on a black background. Hugo was pleased.

But now I'm tired out by the work and two weeks of temperatures of 100 degrees, film work, and Jim's erratic behavior. Now I sit at Jacobson's office, seeking energy.

Rupert seems far away, unreal, and our life together seems unreal. He spends three minutes of our long distance phone call telling me about Tavi's illness. Sometimes he makes me think of a wife's petty interests, and I am the husband bored with household *details*.

It is strange that while traveling by almost opposite routes, Hugo and I reached the same attitude towards work, art, living. Hugo proceeded more slowly, more confusedly, but now we see things the same way, a film, a play, his work, or mine.

There is a mutual accord that has improved the temperamental dissonances. I can be more patient, because I agree with his ultimate intensions; I respect his goal. He is amazed because I am urging him to spend all he needs on his films *because I believe in them*. This is a construction I understand and I'm willing to be devoted to (as I was to Henry's writing).

René de Chochor tells me: "The France you loved is dead. Too much suffering, too much tyranny and tensions between Russia and America. The youth spends its time jazzing, and they read Mickey Spillane. The people who grew up with me, who were students with me, before the war, have changed."

He was, for the first time, sad. I had tears in my eyes. Usually he is light and witty. He is dark and handsome, with soft eyes, a shy smile, but with poise, and we have a charming "business" hour. He treats me like a queen of writing, but nevertheless, he cannot help me. "A publisher accepted a beautiful book the other day, was wildly enthusiastic, but when he discovered the author was forty years old he cancelled the contract."

The very day of my lunch with René, at Lillian Libman's party I met Cyrille d'Arnavon, a most sensitive and cultivated French man of letters, who translates from English to French. His father was a close friend of Giraudoux. He was amazed that I knew Giraudoux so well and said wistfully, "No one reads him anymore in France. We are all in reaction against fantasy."

I said, "And you don't think Mickey Spillane is a fantasy, and Sartre's *Nausea* as well? To choose one element of our life and to call it reality because it is grotesque, ferocious, animal, as Henry Miller did, or Sartre, is as much a fantasy as to deliberately choose only the poetry. The total vision is lacking in both."

M. d'Arnavon did not hear all of my words, but registered the radiance and wrote me a letter the next day on this particular aspect of my personality. I sent him my books.

New York over-stimulates me. My head is surcharged, and there are "congestions of lights." I am overly full of ideas for the house, for clothes (I started the fashion of the small fur collar around the neck of a dress), for Jim's writing (I found two girls who will produce his play), for Hugo's film.

Wearing my hair *à la Grêque* now, high up in the back, pony tail, and curls on the front.

James Merrill, poet, finds *The Four-Chambered Heart* not good at all, a fairytale, mere meandering, a picaresque tale, too naked. He plays the harpsichord and delivers these cat-pawings very sweetly as if he were handling flowers, and I know his name will only live here in the diary—he will be buried with all his Stocks and Bonds in an urn from Lalique, but no masterpieces will lie beside him.

Beauty and poetry are selections we make from the chaos offered to us.

I am not blind to the horrors of the concentration camp. I only believe that what I am doing is the creation of a world in which such cruelties could not take place.

Party for Maxwell Geismar's *Rebels and Ancestors*.

New York, September 13, 1953

Seven-thirty. Hugo is working at his film in his room. I hear the sound of the splicer, of the wheels, of the film passing through the viewer. He is reaching the end of the cutting.

The first autumn wind.

The first cold knowledge that my life with Rupert is impossible, an illusion, that our passion is incongruous and doomed. I must rebel or hurt him.

But I must leave him.

He is the last of the passions that reality destroyed. I see him in the light of a trite and purely physical California, and the background suits him. I spun my own poetry around him, but he dissolved it. I do not belong in his life. It was a role. I belong here.

It is strange that it is my disappointment in Jim that accelerated my detachment from Rupert because the closeness to Jim was an illusion too, and it dissolved. You cannot marry the Son.

The son's love is like trapeze work—every now and then the net is gone, the abyss is revealed, and he is too small to save you. You fall.

Mature love is infinite.

Immature love is finite.

Jim was revealed as a child in contrast to Hugo.

Even though Hugo has childish traits, his love is not childish, but immense. In some way I cannot define, I have moved away from Rupert.

New York, September 15, 1953

Hugo said, "You have helped me tremendously with my film. You helped me to clarify my ideas, to develop them, to reach them. I was going off on tangents, and you kept me close to my own intuition. I owe you a great deal. You taught me to select the essential, to sift, to go to the core. You are wonderful."

I said, "I am only good for one thing, to be an artist, or the wife of an artist. I am glad that my life-long obsession with art is what enabled me to help you. What I give you is the sum of all I acquired during the years I refused to be a banker's wife or the property of the bank. I recognize that *your* obsession with an economic basis to our life has enabled me to fulfill this creativity. But I am glad also that I can give to your films because you deserve to be given back all that you gave to my writing."

I act like a psychoanalyst of the work of art. Hugo tells me what he intends to do. I understand the image he was to capture, the strangeness and beauty and ugliness of 42nd Street, its essence.

I finally helped him to eliminate his obsession with the instruments for seeing: the camera eye, telescopes. His guilt about looking with his own eyes, for which he was punished as a child, made him a timid peeper, and the camera was the excuse for looking into life-scenes. He had an obstructed, cluttered beginning to the looking, and I suggested eliminating all preparatory mechanics to what we were going to see and plunging into the scene itself. So the film begins as immediate experience.

I note this because this journal has also been my spiritual balance book. For all the guilt I suffered at rebelling against spending time being with bank people, or living a banker's wife's life, I felt delivered from by enriching Hugo's artist life.

So yesterday we reached a wonderful understanding, a mutually grateful acknowledgement of a partnership that needed not to have been so painful but for our neuroses, Hugo demanding that I enter fully into his plan, which is to attend to the economic realm and *then* to be an artist. If I had accepted this, I would have spent twenty years working for it, and instead I rebelled and started to live as an artist, creating the second world that Hugo could never have reached without me.

So we are at peace.

I see poor Rupert at the beginning of this pattern. When I suggested we begin modestly to take a little footage of film of him (thinking of the poetic use I could put it to, his poetic beauty and radiance), which involved $20 (he spent twice as much in Mexico taking shots of fires and eroded hills for the foresters), he says, "We don't have money to make films. It takes money to make films."

First it was money, then a house, and then living and creation as the luxury, later, later, when I won't even be alive!

Hugo feels guilty about the money he is spending on his films, yet he worked for twenty-five years and felt no guilt for all he spent on my books, for my writing was a luxury. He paid for the publication of *House of Incest*, for the Press to do *This Hunger*, *Under a Glass Bell*, *Winter of Artifice*, and now he pays for *A Spy in the House of Love*.

Last night, with Bebe and Louis, we looked at the first version of the 42nd Street film, *Jazz of Lights* (title suggested by Jim Herlihy). Bebe commented beautifully on Hugo's use of me as the elusive figure in a crowd, unattainable, haunting, fleeting. She said that no matter how human or how real, I was always idealized, glamorized, like poetry, never destroying the illusion, never real in the sense that when we grasp someone usually the illusion is destroyed.

Max Geismar is struggling too with the concept of my "artificiality," which is *natural* to me, which comes out of the American confusion between *art and artifice*. To accept my artifices as natural phenomena may help Max to extend his knowledge of art.

Bebe tells me that Jim's love for me is so powerful that it is not good or natural for him and may explain his deep disturbance and withdrawal from our intimacy because, as he said, "I don't want to be a member of the wedding."

His name is on the billboard of the Theatre de Lys. Audrey Hilliard and Miranda d'Arcona suggest I continue work on *The Four-Chambered Heart* as a play.

Our party for Max was warm and brilliant. He did not get drunk, and was his most charming and appealing self. Anne was humorous and natural.

The light, manna, or substance I give off so intensely has again drained me. I sit at Jacobson's office to receive artificial energy, to replace the lost strength.

Part of the strain is timing, for my trapeze life. I have to undertake each time certain definite tasks and complete them. Hugo worked in an intermittent way on the 42nd Street film for two years. He wanted to finish it in time for the Museum of Modern Art premiere of *Bells of Atlantis* at the end of October. My share had to be done by the middle of September (my sixth week away from Rupert). I had to forestall delays, defeat obstacles, solve Hugo's procrastination, the loss of Jim's help in the middle of the activity due to his rebellion against Hugo. I had to guide this film towards completion through Hugo's tangents and circuitousness, his errors and camera accidents.

I also had to celebrate the Nims' move to New York with a cocktail party that lasted from five to eleven o'clock. I had to beautify the house for Max's party.

I have no life of my own here. Hugo calls me ten or twenty times when I'm dressing, talks incessantly, recalling the humor of Molière's play on the mute wife who is cured and then chatters so much the husband wishes her mute again. Hugo, the silent man of Conrad novels, who talked only in conventional phrases, who always hesitated when asked a direct question, who baffled all my investigations, now talks all the time. The tiring element is that he thinks aloud, makes no selection, no excerpts, and has no awareness of what interests the other. It is now an uncontrolled flow of talk. And now, at times, I want to run away from the monotony of his all-inclusive talks. He sometimes talks like Rupert's father, about the trivial weighing of details, whether he will drive to the film studio first or second, about *everything*.

It is an ironic joke on me. He never gives you the essential. That was also why I became deaf to his talk about the bank. I was willing to discuss general facts and problems, but not to live with constant details; I was willing to help him with problems, but I never could bear long discussions about a trivial matter.

Today I am more apt to see my own defects, and one of them is my inability to accept others' defects. I am intolerant and impatient. I admire fervently, wildly, and then as I uncover the reality that does not conform to my desire, I grow critical. I have always done that. I never accepted Hugo's flaws, or Rupert's. Part of my intense creativeness is this drive to transform, to alter, to recreate and enhance, but the negative aspect of it is my rejection of the flaws.

Poetization and idealization are crimes against the human. I have been, as well as a creator, a *rebel.*

Letter from Anaïs Nin to Rupert Pole:

New York, September 16, 1953

Oh, my poor darling, I felt so badly to think of you on fires; you must be tired. It's too much to ask of a man. My feelings are with you. When I sent you the telegram giving the flight number and hour of my arrival, Pam answered that you were gone for at least a week, and that you had suggested I stay here rather than wait for you, and so I'm working intensely not to think so much about you and how hot or sleepy you might be. It's like having one's man at war. Today I should be on my way to you, but instead here I am writing you. As soon as you return, telegraph me and I will leave. What a conflict this is, the summer when you are away so much. I'd rather be working, yet you need me too and I'd like to be there when you return from your war on fires. My sweet love… I stopped writing too, too worn out by the care of Mother, job, heat, efforts for the new book.

I got the jacket of *Spy*—quite simple and good by a modern Dutch artist—very striking. But *New Story* has lost its backer, so René de Chochor is looking for a good distributor. The book is all ready except for the need to find a distributor, which will hold it up. I was keeping all the news to tell you, but all I can think of now is the wish to embrace you and kiss away all the grime, dust and heat from your face, the scratches and cuts, and I told Pam I would phone Sunday for news. These fires are never reported in New York papers so I never know what is going on.

Well, I got my mother all well and cheered up. And I have pushed everything along as far as I could. I will keep all the news for our talks. Will work on until I hear from you, darling.

Jim's play *Moon in Capricorn* will be done in a Village theatre Oct. 27, and he will get about $600 out of it, so he is very happy, but otherwise he has changed for the worse. New York is such a challenge to the ego that it makes everyone anxious, desperate, touchy. You get rebuffs, and Jim has felt them sharply. It's a tough city, and everyone gets hurt. He is nervous and irritable and difficult. Everybody lives on sleeping pills and Benzedrine, and all the rhythms of nature are upset. But everybody is creative and full of sparkle. I hear Tavi is with your family and I'm glad for his sake.

Te quiero, my courageous darling, but I hate to think of you at the fires. I only like the fires in the hearth.

Tu mujer

Letter from Anaïs Nin to Jim Herlihy:

En route to Los Angeles, September 20, 1953

Dear Jim: I am truly concerned now about the neurosis because it is getting too powerful and beyond the help of the insight of those who love you. I hope you will seek analysis in some form or other. I even felt the shadow falling between us, all through my last visit. No amount of talks can help one when the irrational pattern really takes hold and acts itself out. I felt as I never did before, that you were caught in a distorting mirror and acting out compulsions.

At the moment I don't know what more to say. I could seek to interpret, but it does not help now, because I also am now part of this inner drama, not as *myself any longer*, and you need complete objectivity now.

To free you of guilt, I told you accidents happen, forget about it (your misplacing a diary), but you and I know that everything we do has a meaning.

I don't need to say more. But I can't write you about less important things when this seems so urgent, and I hope you will act. *Neurosis is curable*, and you must know that better than anyone, after reading the diary.

Love,
Anaïs

Letter from Jim Herlihy to Anaïs Nin:

New York, September 28, 1953

Dear Anaïs: Your letter frightened me, and I have to make time now to answer it. My schedule is an eighteen hour one now, even though I had to withdraw the play because of a conflict in casting.

Please tell what you mean when you refer to a shadow falling between us. I don't care about my billfold and my salary and all those things, but I care about you. You've represented to me for so long now a truly solid, endurable force, and my love for you is deeper than any I have ever felt for a woman, and more beautiful. I must tell you that I have never felt this, Anaïs, I mean the shadow; I didn't know it existed. I believed that this would never be, and I still don't believe it is there. But you mentioned it twice before you left (in the last two weeks, I think), and now when you write it, it takes on a different meaning, and it frightens me. I don't want anything to happen between you and me. It's never occurred to me that anything would. Apparently I have done something that you've not mentioned. Being terribly busy may have caused me to be insensitive in some way, and I know that you're vulnerable; both of us are.

You said that I was caught in a distorting mirror and acting out compulsions. Please tell me what you mean. What compulsions? I have a dreadful fear I have hurt you in some way very deeply, and it bothers me and troubles me constantly.

Dr. Bogner advised me against staying with Hugo while you were in New York. She said that it would cause tension between the two of you, and though I didn't feel free to tell you this when you first returned, I must tell you now in the hope that it might shed some light on what seemed to you my withdrawal during the earlier part of your visit. Along with this advice, I got the impression I had come up in Hugo's analysis or in yours in such a way that Dr. Bogner felt that the three of us together would be dangerous. Of course, I didn't know what she meant or how she arrived at this feeling and was not able to question her further.

But it seemed to me terribly important to leave you and Hugo alone. Many times I wanted to tell you about this, but everything seemed so tenuous that I thought it better not to.

As for my neurosis, I'm going to act against it as soon as possible because, of course, it is urgent. But I don't want you to worry unnecessarily; I've perhaps led you to believe that it is more urgent than it actually is. In some ways I was living the lives of two people, I mean in the sense of work and time spent in activity, forty-five hours a week in a bastard landlord's office, and then the moving, etc., etc. It was a gigantic period for me, Anaïs, and I want you to understand that and not worry disproportionately. My psyche is in critical shape, but I'm sure it's not worse than it was six months ago.

The important thing to me now is to understand what you mean when you mention the shadow. What in the world do you mean when you say you are a part of my inner dream, but "not as myself any longer"? You are the one person in my life whom I do not confuse with others. You have never been mother, wife, daughter or sister to me, but always Anaïs, my twin—if any of the former, my sister. I love you purely and marvelously, and in all of my dreams you always appear as yourself, beautiful and understanding and sympathetic. You've never so much as made an appearance in my summer nightmares. I must say that I do consciously and in every way resist the idea that there is a shadow. If there is, I am forced to believe it is one of your own creation. And I beg you to investigate this possibility and tell me if you can come up with any reasons for it.

And if I have hurt you *in any way*, please tell me exactly what it is, and I promise you with all my heart I'll make it up to you.

Love,

Jim

P.S.: What do you mean when you say, "I don't need to say any more"? I must say, Anaïs, that I don't want this letter. If you feel that I'm resisting it because it contains a hurtful truth, please explain to me what you mean. Because the most alarming thing that has happened to me in many months is the letter itself. If you meant it to be helpful, it has thrown me into a panic that I may have lost you or failed you in some way.

Letter from Jim Herlihy to Anaïs Nin:

New York, October 10, 1953

Dear Anaïs: Your letter was beautiful, and generous. I'm glad you understood that the greatest part of my anxiety was brought about by the fear that a shadow actually had fallen, but a darker one than you intended to indicate. In a relationship as important to me as this one, I really am not strong enough to bear that possibility. So now, after your truly magnificent letter, I feel that what has happened can be forgotten, and when even the shadow of it is gone, our relationship may be the stronger for it. I wasn't sure that your first comments in the other letters were motivated by love and concern, and that's what frightened me. You're entirely right that my strong reaction against this possibility is strongly integrated with the nature of my neurosis itself.

Hugo said you'd had bronchitis and I hope you're over it. Was the visit with your mother difficult?

Love,
Jim

Sierra Madre, October 20, 1953

A month here in Sierra Madre. A few days after I arrived, Rupert got very ill with bronchitis. I took care of him, but being so worn out by all the work on Hugo's film, I got ill too, the day he got up. Barely recovered, I went to San Francisco to stay with my mother while Joaquín took a three day trip for the university.

My mother sits in the house with the shades down, shutting out the sun (a Cuban habit), rushes out to confront dogs and children who are noisy, works on knitting, reads detective stories, and waits. The horror of aging, the deafness, the false teeth, the restricted areas of life. The only moment of closeness was when she told me Father used to humiliate her when he discovered my Danish grandfather was Jewish, and I tried to console her and make her feel proud of this; and then I felt such compassion and tenderness, while realizing at the same time the irony of this situation. For as I condemned my father once more for being vain and proud of qualities that are not humanly valuable, why be proud of being a Spanish aristocrat? At the same time I am still more identified with my father; that is, with the admiration of him as a character (an inhuman monster) and not of my mother's human qualities, which makes my acceptance of the human in my mother, in the Jews, in my Jewish friends, more and more difficult. For every day I am riled by the human condition, chores, nursing the sick, marketing, motherhood, and I have a religion (art), a class, a race, outside of the human, all of which allows me to bear the human, which I hate. It happens that my father fits in this image of the artist. It is not the aristocrat (cold), the eloquent man, but the aesthete, the artist who enhanced and transformed reality. "Your father," said my plain, prosaic mother once, "had such a power for illusion."

I returned from taking care of my mother chastened, clearer as to *la condition humaine*, which I hate. Sickness, old age, babies, houses, stagnation, family, war, patriotism, nationalism.

I returned to my great and diabolical punishment: Reginald at the hospital undergoing an operation. And now he is here at home, recuperating. Upon his arrival, he handed me a blood-stained, urine-drenched pajama to wash. I turned away. For hours, he talked about his digestion, his colon, food, medicines, the hospital... The worst of all agonies for me is the petty fussing about details: "Do you know, the carrots gave me indigestion. I must find bread without salt. Where is the health shop?" We spent three hours on errands, fussing, searching. He filled the closet with medicines and special foods (as did my father, as did Helba). He described his operation in detail until I felt nauseated. He never stops talking, follows me with talk even to the bathroom—a monotonous monologue—always reverting to himself. He is a parasite, never does anything, just lies and talks. A useless being, a burden to everyone, and yet he did not die when he should have.

After a week of this, we went Wednesday night for music at the Wrights'. Another dismal evening. Even though Helen and Lloyd have grown fond of me, for me it is an act because we have nothing in common.

The next night Rupert returned there. Then I rebelled, but it is useless. I have always rebelled at two nights there a week. The selfishness of Rupert appalled me.

Then I realize the need and the vital necessity of art. Human life—you nurse your father even though he is the most selfish, self-centered neurotic of all. You nurse him although he is worth nothing, although it is all to flow down the drain. But a whole day, a year, a lifetime spent making breakfast, housecleaning, tending parents, marketing, would drive me to madness. So today, while Reginald discussed egg yolks, melba toast, his operation, debating whether he would take two eggs or some Wheatena, telling me how many times he had awakened during the night, wetting his bed, I started to copy a diary, preferring to relive the end of my relationship with Gonzalo, the collapse of the Press, the multiple affairs with Albert, William Howell, Chinchilito, rather than deal with the present.

Rupert was very understanding and took my side. He loses patience with his father (like Helba did with Gonzalo, he takes Rupert's socks, underwear, and then leaves them scattered in hotels where he never returns, he never gives anything, not even consideration for Rupert). He sacrifices everyone to futile errands, invents things for them to do rather than minimize his demands. The only relationship he knows, is capable of, is of an infantile helplessness and demandingness. This morass of petty obsession is punctuated by inflated and trite remarks on Beethoven and Shakespeare. Embarking on politics, he will talk about Adlai Stevenson's qualities and then say, "Stevenson would be interested in my Lincoln play."

My deepest sorrow, however, is my rebellion against Rupert. It is accomplished with guilt. I have *tried*. Once I remember the analyst saying, "Did you try hard enough with Hugo? Or did you find that his inadequacies were good alibis for your unfaithfulness?" I tried for six years to love Hugo alone. I have tried for six years to live Rupert's life as he wants it.

Rupert will not allow the others to be free, or themselves. All he wants is an appendage of himself, an extension. He demands complete control.

I was shocked when he brought me paper for typewriting from the Forest Service office. I found it was two inches smaller than standard and of such poor quality that it didn't take the third carbon at all. And from experience, I know that the giant task of copying the diary must be done on good paper. I used cheap paper ten years ago and it is already disintegrating. So I bought good paper after *explaining* this to Rupert. Yet when he came home and saw the boxes, he frowned and scolded me for extravagance.

The only explanation I can find is that this petty and constant faultfinding is an expression of his greater dissatisfaction. He too feels trapped by passion perhaps, to live with a woman who is not right for him. I am not an outdoor woman, I am not domestic, I am not young in my tastes (I don't care for silly movies or silly people).

I have to work with Bogner, for perhaps I too am a faultfinder. I do rebel against Rupert's ways.

SIERRA MADRE, OCTOBER 1953

When we were invited to a masquerade party by Paul Mathieson and Renate Druks, in which we must come dressed as our "madness," Rupert confessed that his could not be expressed in a costume. "Before I met you, I used to hear noises, big clumping noises, and I couldn't sleep."

When I suggested painting eyes all over him, he agreed enthusiastically. "That's very good, because I always feel eyes watching me. I always think people are looking at me. It makes me self-conscious."

SIERRA MADRE, NOVEMBER 4, 1953

Sometimes I feel I'm losing my mind. Is it Rupert's neurosis harming me, or is it something in me?

I got up today feeling, for the first time in weeks, energy and clarity. I went for my mail and I was happy because *The Four-Chambered Heart* was sold in Sweden. Then I called up Hugo (intuition) and found he wanted me back the 10th or 12th to redo the soundtrack of *Bells of Atlantis* for a showing at the Museum of Modern Art. I did my errands. I exchanged four bottles of the wrong water for the kind Rupert wanted (delivered by mistake by the liquor shop). I cooked a good lunch. I gave Rupert the good news (not the news of my leaving) about the book. He was in a good mood because he had taken good photographs of fire areas from a helicopter. I admired the photos. We sat down to lunch. I mentioned I had exchanged the four bottles. He looked annoyed, and he said, "Why didn't you take all twelve bottles?"

I had to explain: "Because I can't park near the liquor shop—it's too crowded. I thought four would supply our drinking for tonight."

"I would have taken them back."

His overflow of guilt, if it is that, causes him to seem annoyed with me. He says, "I feel badly I can't provide you with a maid. I don't want you turned into a hausfrau."

But meanwhile his attitude makes me feel I do nothing right. He is overly critical. He will nag or make a scene. And a deep depression sets in.

I have tried explaining quietly, quietly. He doesn't understand. This time at lunch I blew up about the bottles, saying over and over again, "I can't take it. I can't take this constant control and criticalness."

He protested that I only noticed the negative, that he praised me as much as criticized. But still, I can't understand such an irrational comment. In exchanging enough bottles for the evening there was nothing to criticize.

Guilt makes one angry at the person who makes you feel guilty. But if everything makes Rupert feel guilty, our relationship is doomed.

I feel lost and confused. He does such stupid things. I have often told him I don't care about his flirtations if only he carried them out when I am not there. I have often said he was free, could do as he pleased, but that I wanted him clever at dissimulation, subtle, and since I took so many trips, for him to fulfill his flirtations when I'm away. But no, he is as crude and obvious as he can be.

At the beach a girl with a dog came and seated herself near us. Rupert began to talk to her, about the dogs.

At the "come as your madness" party at Renate's, all the pleasure was killed. Rupert became nervous, concerned over the costumes, unhappy because he would have to miss the quartet, because on Halloween night he should be available in case of fires. He spoiled his pleasure.

Then, in a room full of pretty women, he withdrew, did not dance, became effaced and negative. Why? Shyness? He criticized the party. It was not well organized. There wasn't enough to drink. The music wasn't good. It was too dark.

He was jealous but will never admit it. He referred several times to my dancing so continuously he could not dance with me (actually I stopped several times to ask him to dance).

The party became painful for me too. I invented a costume for him that was very much admired. Black ballet tights on which we sewed "eyes" of all kinds, in rubber and plastic, one pair staring from his sex, his torso painted by Gil, strikingly. Hair ornamented by Rupert himself, a wire crown of staring eyes painted on ping-pong balls. I wore skin-colored net stockings up to my waist, leopard fur earrings glued to the tip of my naked breasts, a leopard belt on my waist, the rest painted by Gil, and my head inside a bird cage. My hair was dusted with gold and I wore eyelashes two inches long. Around my waist were strips of paper on which I had copied lines from my writing, out of context, and I unwound these and tore off a phrase for each person at the party. Curtis Harrington called it the ticker-tape of the unconscious. I was quite a success, the most striking of all, the most photographed. People were shocked; the men reacted pleasantly. One rearranged my writing, kissed me on the cheek and said, "You are the greatest!" Another wanted to bite my breast.

I, who had been frightened of coming to the party and thought I would lose Rupert, became suddenly assured and even danced with Paul Mathieson and Kenneth Anger, an African dance to someone's drumming. My assurance was defiance.

Rupert had said, "Yes, I have met artists like these, but I have never let myself fall into their clutches."

"Why their clutches? Don't you like their way of life?"

"No, it's too unstable."

"But don't you see, all they are doing is trying to live out their fantasies, the same fantasies you have only you don't try to live them out."

He is afraid, and it is because he is afraid that he flirts when *I am there*. Faced with his Don Juan fantasies, he is frightened.

Anaïs Nin and Rupert Pole at the "come as your madness" party

For him, as for all Americans, fantasy is an inanimate object, unrelated to vital living, a separate activity like dreaming, which has nothing to do with reality.

I don't know why I let Rupert affect me, or hurt me, really. Why can't I detach myself from his confusions and not care? I get sucked into his confusions, bewildered. All I can wish is to get away from him.

After a quarrel the air was cleared. There was a better understanding. Rupert is merely living out his need of domination, his need of nourishing a weak ego, without knowledge of the consequences on others. I explained to him the "reservoir" of guilt, but if guilt is making him turn his anger against me, soon he will have the same relationship with me that I had with Hugo. At his first realized flirtation, he will feel enormous guilt and treat me badly, which also brings on "punishment and retaliation" such as I expected from Hugo.

Peace last night, and peace offerings. Rupert brings me vermouth for a Martini. I turn on the radio for him so that he will catch the five o'clock commentator. He was upset that I should be leaving. But even though I cling to the delectation of his body against mine, I feel tired inside, of this life we lead, which I now see is Rupert's way of avoiding all disturbances. Living, people, relationships, travel, all this he finds difficult, and they become ordeals. This is what binds us too, what binds me to adolescence. I have not yet reached casual living. The party was also for me a challenge. The difficulties were greater in proportion to the pleasure. At my own parties in New York I did just what Rupert did: to avoid the difficulties of talking, of relating to people, I took refuge in serving drinks and food, in introducing people. He took care of Gil (who got ill). He kept the fire going. He danced only with Olympia because she was left alone. He was diffident and quiet.

Neurosis is the killer of pleasure.

I was frightened too. I was surprised at the sensation I caused. There were more beautiful women there, but they seemed effaced by me. But to see Rupert's personality clouded surprised me. Confidence is necessary to beauty; it is its illumination.

Kenneth Anger, filmmaker of Fireworks, protégé of Cocteau, was dressed like the Madness of Venice, confounding man and woman, face hidden by a gold lace, feathers and black cloth.

Renate danced with Ken, then stopped, all out of breath, and said, "It is so tiring to dance with one's madness!"

Rupert, of course, could not keep it a secret that he was "intrigued by the girl in the short black costume with her hair painted silver," but that she had gone away before he was able to dance with her.

One night, in the car, returning home from the usual movie, he talked gravely and sincerely about our relationship: "I can't imagine anything bigger or deeper than what we have. Ours is a good relationship; it has everything. I am only intrigued by little things, curious. I know you think I would be better off with an 'outdoor girl,' or a 'domestic girl,' but the domestic one would bore me, and the outdoor one might be fun now and then, but I would hate it all the time. No. I like what we have."

His simple, naïve faith touched me. At these moments his own sureness, his conviction, his unshakeable attachment seem solid, and I forget that even if he clung to me through and beyond his passions as I clung to Hugo, it would not be the same, because his passion is all I want; the "relationship" he is satisfied with is one that does not nourish me.

But it was a moment of sweetness and faith. And because I was leaving, I could bear the gardening for his parents, the dinner at their home where they reveal their sweetness, their helplessness and neurosis. Because I was leaving, I could mend fifteen pairs of socks with tenderness. Because I was leaving, Rupert did not drive to the airport at 80 miles an hour, his usual speed. Because I was leaving, he did not rant because we got there too early. Because I was leaving, I could encourage him to fulfill one of his dreams, a house on a hill near the sea. We have saved $2,500. We drank a Martini in the car (to save money). I always dream of taking the separation lightly...humorously. I know my trip is the only thing that prevents our relationship from catastrophe. Back to Hugo, a bigger life, and the care I need: Bogner and Jacobson.

And Malraux says what I have been saying: "Art is our rebellion against man's fate."

La condition humaine is what I have never accepted. That is why I tried to create my own world.

New York, November 9, 1953

Near breakdown again, and I never know if it is due to a feeling of physical depletion. Bodily, I feel my chest is "caved in," my energy low, and simultaneously there is a feeling of failure, of weakness, of certain catastrophe, a feeling life is too difficult, that too much is expected of me.

At both ends there is a man who takes my whole life.

This time, after suffering bronchitis, nursing Rupert and Reginald, and wasting my time on the house, I arrived very low, with hardly enough energy to do the reading for the new sound track of *Bells of Atlantis*. I found Hugo belligerent and tense. The relaxed Hugo of the summer changed into a grim, willful, egocentric maniac determined not only to make a success of his films (which I had offered to help distribute), but a financial success (impossible in America—only Hollywood films will do that). Even an interesting film like *The Tell-Tale Heart* by Poe (an abstraction) can't make money. Because Hugo says we have to make $5,000 a year to maintain our way of living, I suggest instead we lower our standard and then we could continue to be artists without trying to commercialize our work. "Movies are a mass medium," says Hugo, like any Hollywood salesman, and at this point I do not respect him, because like most Americans he ceases to draw an important distinction between being an artist and a commercial filmmaker. Hugo the artist is now gone. This is Hugo the businessman. When he talks about refusing to go back to the bank, I understand. "Now I feel as you do—I want to be an artist. I feel it's a waste of time to be in the bank."

At this point I would give my life to be able to make enough money to prevent Hugo from going back to the bank and enable him to work on his films.

Yesterday I arrived at six in the morning. Poor Hugo was there to meet me. I had asked him not to come. But his sweetness does not last long. He has been quarrelling and boasts of it; he threw the upholsterers out of the house, has a legal battle with our apartment landlord. Despite years of analysis, he is still a somber and willful man, a heavy man. Now, his work is beautiful, and I love it, but his ego is bigger than his work, inflated, bloated. I am embarrassed by it. I want to collaborate, but I hate high-pressure salesmanship, publicity. He has allied himself with publicity agents Lillian Libman and Constance Hope. America is monstrous, a burlesque, a circus. Now my pleasure in introducing the film at the YWHA is spoiled by anxiety and the fear of ridicule.

I realize I'm in a bad state. I dreamed that Bogner looked like Rupert's mother! There is something wrong with me, or else I would not get into difficulties with both men, both lives.

Depression is enormous, suffocating. My mind is foggy. I can't write. As if I had settled permanently in a climate without the sun, all fog and frost.

One talk with Bogner. Just to see her sitting there, neat, dainty, collected, smiling, creates a moment of peace.

At first I felt a constriction of the throat, which I have on such occasions.

I said, "I can't explain how or what happened, but I know what I feel. I feel suffocated at both ends now, overwhelmed by the demands put on me by both men. I feel pushed and imposed upon." I described my six weeks with Rupert.

"And then," said Bogner, "you expected to escape his demands, his selfishness, the constricted life, and what did you find?"

Shocks. First the shock of Hugo saying, "We either have to make $5,000 a year out of our films and books or else I have to return to the bank and give up my creative work."

And the shock of Hugo saying I could no longer take trips to California.

Added to the shock is Rupert's growing interest in other women and the knowledge that he is not evolving inwardly in any way, not creating a life in which I can evolve. The potential Don Juan in him, which I have always recognized, is the only fantasy my presence is helping him to fulfill. He can play without being hurt. His heart and soul are mine. He has me for a refuge. He can enter the periphery of the roles he likes in the movies: the humorous, carnal, playful lover.

This time I had the feeling that I should not return.

I have to face the fact that Rupert is an adolescent, mentally undeveloped, a purely physical and emotional person, that he belongs to the life he was born in, that his inner mediocrity has been revealed.

"You see, Dr. Bogner, I could never submit to Hugo's obsession: the American dream that first of all we make enough money and then we begin to live and travel, or be an artist. I can't submit to Rupert's dream of first we build a home, and then we begin to live and travel."

Bogner thought I was seeing everything clearly.

"There must be a third way of life I can create myself," I said.

"But," she explained, "you must understand that these obsessions come from insecurity. Actually, success would give neither one of them the feeling of security they seek." (Hugo attained sufficient security seven years ago, $100,000 capital, but then instead of choosing to live within this income, as I wished, he became obsessed with making more, carelessly speculating and launching into high living, which seriously reduced the capital.)

Bogner's statement, which explains their fantasies, also explains why I could not devote myself to either dream (because that is not what I believe—I believe in having just enough money for necessities and living the artist life). I couldn't devote myself to money-making, or house-building. I know that in a house with Rupert I could not find the comfort or security I need, the emotional kind, because Rupert can't give me that. He can't make a home for me, for my real home is art and the creation that the artist life provides: my security is in spiritual values, not physical ones.

Rebellion makes me feel guilty. Rupert is blind when he says we want the same things; he is blind in placing his sincerity and trust in me.

Now, enough of seeking to create a life through neurotic men. I must create my own. A third life. My obsession, my dream, my fantasy has been a love I can believe in, deep and strong, and creating, writing.

Bogner also worked on making me objective about criticism, publicity, and Hugo's and Rupert's neuroses. She pointed out how my life with Rupert is not what it appears to be—idyllic, simple, peaceful, healthy—because of Rupert's erratic behavior, anxieties, obsessions, and selfishness. The day before Renate's party he insisted on going to the beach to get a suntan (it was cold and foggy), and I said we might both get a cold out of it instead. But we went to the beach just the same, and I had to sit for three hours in a cold wind, when all Rupert needed to do was use makeup (at night, a light suntan is not important). If we go to the Coronet once every six months to see experimental films, for the next six months I have to listen to his criticisms. If we do what I like, I never hear the end of it, or else I am made to regret it because he fusses and frets over it.

Equally, my life with Hugo is not what it seems to be, expansive, comfortable, big, because of Hugo's lack of lightness, ease, and power of relaxation.

So the only reality is feeling. How one feels and sees.

"Rupert does not look like a person who should be a forester," said Bogner, studying his photograph.

A forester is one of his negative efforts to not be his father. His image of the artist consists of three impossible human beings: Frank Lloyd Wright, Lloyd Wright, and Reginald Pole.

"They are unstable," said Rupert.

"But I'm an artist, and I'm not unstable as a human being."

"Yes, that's true."

The strangest thing he said to me the night we were driving home was: "With you, I feel I can give myself. With Janie, I don't know why, I felt frustrated; I couldn't give myself, all of myself."

Last night, Hugo and I laughed at *The Captain's Paradise*, a light, amusing film of a man with two wives. He sails between his two homes, but they are neatly divided: one domestic, the other sensual and gay. He loses both wives because he wants to keep them static in each role, and both women experience a change. The nightclub dancer, after many late nights, champagne, eating out, wants to settle down, to cook, to be a wife, and the domestic one, after raising her children, wants to enjoy her life, to dance, to stay up late!

We laughed. It was so pat, wise, and light.

But my situation is deeper, subtler, more intricate.

And it changes every day. No matter how I arrange the lives, values shift, the men change, and I do too.

Let me see, now, if I can create my own life.

The kind of life I liked best of all was my bohemian life in Paris on the houseboat. The boat cost $10 a month. We could live the kind of life I like, the two of us, for $200 a month. Only the artists know the secret of living a rich life with little means.

I won't live for more than ten years. For ten years I need $200 a month. That is $24,000 for the life I want.

So I will aim for that.

Paris.

Houseboat.

It may mean alone, without Hugo's ambition, his extravagant, willful living (when he wants something, nothing will stop him from buying it), and without Rupert.

So there is my choice.

Naturally I will continue to share and suffer Hugo's and Rupert's nightmares.

When I left Rupert this time, and seeing his frustration at not having his own home, I suggested he could start one, as did the man in *House Beautiful* who had land but no money.

The entire life in California is based on *House Beautiful*. Nobody reads. Nobody is informed, and nobody works at anything interesting. The film colony is exclusive, and even there few are interesting as personalities.

I should leave him there.

My adventurous life was entirely interior, created from the inside. His, like most of America, is external. Why he was drawn to me, I don't know.

Bogner did say Hugo was "difficult." Obtaining objectivity from her, care from Jacobson, giving up my two daily Martinis, I finally regained color and strength. Hugo is still, as he has always been, a tyrannical, egocentric man, a man who awakens without a smile, whom Millicent describes as "crotchety." Millicent said, "I would work for you till eternity; you're considerate and you don't make one's task harder. But I pay him no mind. I just let him rave. You spend a tenth of what he does. You're careful. I know you save on clothes to cover your trips. He is wasteful. He is cross and difficult. He nags."

In the kitchen we have coffee together. We both try to save each other work. Millicent tells me how Hugo sends her out on errands *several* times a morning when all of them, with a little care and forethought, could be done at one time. I never go to the post office without asking if Millicent or Hugo needs stamps, or if there are letters to mail.

Today I awakened calm. Hugo was awake at five. At last he realizes that he wanted me dependent, because as a dependent I never had any power to decide how the capital should be handled or spent.

He is ambivalent. He wants dependence, wants me to have no life of my own (except when I'm away), but he wants me practical and able to discuss shares, stock markets, the details of business. I am terribly tired of the enormous price one pays for protection. I should have started to build up my independence long ago. I revolted against my mother turning me into a kitchen maid and went to work. When I married, I should have worked so that Hugo would not try to enslave me to the bank. The status of wife is worth nothing. If I had worked, I would be free and not afraid to stand alone, as I am today, for Hugo's attitude towards money is medieval. I still get a month's allowance at a time. I have to ask Rupert every day for money, after depositing all I have into his account when I arrive.

They wanted this. That is why they both carefully avoided the American female.

If it comes from insecurity, then there is no hope of change. After six years of analysis Hugo is more domineering than ever. Before it was negative domination, by sulking, by the pretense of passivity, by all the indirect methods used by women. Now it is rage, vehemence, violence.

I'm just tired of the entire relationship with men.

Will I ever be free?

After another talk with Bogner, and two or three storms with Hugo, we finally reached peace again.

I went to the Columbia University lecture bureau, where hard-boiled Mr. Boomer has the manners of a prize fighter agent, and left my material.

I want $50,000 for the diary originals, so I will never again be tormented by Hugo's dramas with money.

Today, Saturday, serenity.

But my heart is jittery. I awakened with palpitations and full of anxieties. The loss of Rupert is becoming a reality; I feared it constantly, expected it, and hastened it. Rupert is trying to maneuver me into the role of the Big Deep Love and the center of his life while he fulfills his adolescent curiosities, and I cannot play this part. Our days together are now numbered.

Dream: A costume ball. A sumptuous, open place, Scheherazade à la Hollywood. Columns, pools. The sultan is fat, he gives away presents. I am carrying on a forbidden love affair. An atmosphere of pleasure.

It took a week to repair myself. Dr. Bogner's words. (I have looked upon all my wishes, desires, as a criminal does—my loves and passions were stolen goods. My self-assertions were "rebellions.") Dr. Jacobson's injections. A realization that Hugo is impossible because he now has applied his drive for power to his art and therefore has killed the pleasure. I must help him. It is an illness. I have lunch with Lillian (our publicity agent) and tell her to give Hugo the entire spotlight because he needs it. He is a new, adolescent artist. She answers me: "That makes my job more difficult because people are more interested in you than they are in Hugo; you already have a name."

She also had reacted to Hugo's commandingness and noticed how he is only interested in himself.

"It is a phase," says Bogner.

Like the Captain in *The Captain's Paradise*, I had tried to divide my life in a way to suit me. If Rupert was childish, petulant and difficult, then I could escape to Hugo who was more intelligent, more aware, more mature. Not true. I forgot the theory of relativity.

Rupert, at times, is more mature than Hugo, more adequate, more masculine as a lover and firefighter.

The shock I received when I returned to New York this time has to do with the old pattern of Hugo's, living versus power and money-making, at the beginning of our marriage.

Now, this drive is to be applied to our art work—same tactics, same big schemes, same *myths*. Only now I know it is a myth necessary to his ego, a game that he likes and I don't, a compulsive effort, and I know that when we restore our capital, or earn $5,000 a year, it won't stop. It is his illness...the great American illness. So, I have to become independent of Hugo's economic life; I have to build my own life, in my way, and live it.

I will go along with Hugo's scheme, but I want my share of whatever we make to be separate.

I must build up my independence.

We will make $5,000 possibly, but all the pleasure and freedom of filmmaking is gone. We see people we have to see. We seek contracts with museums, foundations, or wealthy corporations.

Letter from Anaïs Nin to Rupert Pole:

New York, November 1953

Today I was so lonely without you, missed you so much, and felt anxious about such a long separation, that out of loneliness I might lose you. I felt depressed, because everything here will develop but it is all so slow, and I wish you had a job nearer. I wish you had a job in Miami, where we could swim together and be warm and go to the islands on our vacation, to Haiti...

At least I wish we had this until I made enough money out of my books to be free. The diary will free us one day because it is more down-to-earth, but it is all so slow; we are so far apart, and days and nights pass. I felt I couldn't go on, couldn't bear it—it's too hard, too far, too long. What can we do, darling? What else? Think about it, will you? Think hard about it.

Te quiero,

A

New York, November 1953

Dream: People are entering a lecture hall to hear Martha Graham speak. In order to be allowed in one has to have a drop of negro blood. I try to lie about it, but it is not effectual. I end up by saying the truth: "I am a writer, an artist," and I am allowed in. The next theme is that somehow I found a way to break down barriers, distinctions, classes, races. Martha Graham is friendly to me. She is at work, and I am helpful to her. There is an understanding between us. I cannot remember the details.

Nov. 12 10:00 Bogner; 11:30 Jacobson; 5:15 XIV Restaurant Herbert Alexander

Nov. 15 Jim and Dick

Nov. 17 Jacobson, Bogner; 4:00 Museum of Modern Art—*Bells of Atlantis*

Nov. 18 11:00 AM Martha Graham; 12:30 took film to Brandon;
Lunch Lillian Libman

Nov. 19 Bogner; cocktail party at Pen Club; 8:15 guitar concert 70 East 12th

Nov. 20 Dollie Chareau; in bed with bronchitis

Nov. 21 Bronchitis; read Simenon in French

Nov. 22 Bronchitis

NEW YORK, NOVEMBER 23, 1953

Returning to an origin.

At ten and eleven years of age I started out as a dime novelist, writing adventure stories. While reading Simenon I remembered that he is the true storyteller. He has a good story to tell, and then he works subtly at characterization. His characters are beautifully wrought, his details are significant. Each detail counts because it is related to the drama. He kept the design of the adventure story (suspense, violence), and with care and skill embroidered upon this the psychological drama.

The last one, *Le Passager Clandestin*, is wonderful. It made me forget bronchitis and my foggy head. I am alarmed at the way I live, by ups and downs, by depression or elation. And my head is the same: clarity and luminosity or dense fog and inertia. I can't think at the moment.

Hugo has a destructive effect on me. I don't know why. I always considered him a healer, a refuge, my guardian angel. He is no longer that. He is all self-assertion, and I must help him as I have helped young artists. I must also escape his domination.

We have both hardened towards each other, toughened.

I am not sure that I love *this* Hugo. Bogner repeats it is a phase.

NEW YORK, NOVEMBER 24, 1953

11:10 Bogner; 3:45 Museum of Modern Art *Bells of Atlantis*

7:30 Dinner de Chochor

NEW YORK, NOVEMBER 25, 1953

An end to the story of Gonzalo. At a party at René de Chochor's, I met Dr. Manrique, one of Gonzalo's closest friends. Dr. Manrique is a small man, like many men from the North of Spain, a descendant of the Duke of Alba, an aristocrat, an intellectual, and a doctor, who gave all he had to the Republican war and lost an eye, a leg, his home, wealth, and was exiled. He is fluent in his talk, mixing psychoanalysis, surrealism, Spanish anarchy, irony, and emotional fireworks. I had expected to dislike him, because Gonzalo had often talked of him as a disintegrated, diabolical figure, had described his sexual habit of little girls suckling his genitals, and although the "hero" and the brilliant mind were there, to me at the time he seemed more like the companion of Gonzalo's drunks, dissipated by time at cafés and a part of the life he carefully kept me out of, his man's night life. But when I saw Dr. Manrique, I liked him. He approached me with a feeling of intimacy.

"Anaïs, I feel I know you so well. For years Gonzalo talked about you. You were the great love of his life, perhaps the only one. He never loved anyone as he loved you. He regretted losing you. He often raved about you. And I know how he lost you. I was called in to take care of Helba. I told Gonzalo the truth. She was utterly and hopelessly mad, even dangerously so. I urged him to put her in an institution. But he would not do that. You see, what you did not realize is that Helba was an alibi for his failures. He could always say it was Helba who destroyed him. If he had put Helba away and lived for you, he would have had to become somebody, politically, and he couldn't. I didn't understand this at first. She was at once his bad mother, his father (because she possessed the creative faculty he so much admired and lacked in himself), and she was also his child, which made him feel strong and noble. You, my poor Anaïs, were good to Gonzalo, and you were his pleasure and his happiness, and that he could never accept, reach for, keep. He let Helba destroy him, and you. He has never loved again, not as he loved you. You had a great love, I know. I was with Gonzalo the night before he left for Paris, two months ago. He was deported by the FBI; his papers were not in order. He was happy to escape the girl he was sleeping with, the most stupid girl in the world; she was pretty and in love with him, but he was always running away, telling me: 'Oh, she's so stupid, so stupid,' and talking about you, Anaïs… 'Anaïs had everything.'"

We sat on a bench in the entrance, and I felt sad. I compared the wildness, the inferno, the magnificence, the frenzy of my life with Gonzalo and realized how after a great tempest one recedes into smaller loves. The core of my passion for Rupert, the physical core, was just as intense, but it is like living on a small island instead of the vast, limitless jungle Gonzalo's character was.

Soft, gentle regrets…

Dinner with Cornelia Runyon. Cornelia, as a sculptor, is a poet of stone. She uses semi-precious desert stones, but carves like a primitive. It is half formed of the earth but it remains of the earth. It has weight and density. The luminosities come from within the stone. She lives in a beautiful house on a hill by the sea. The stone pieces are set against sky and sea. She looks as Queen Elizabeth should have looked, talks as the Sitwells should have talked; she is the *Folle de Chaillot* on certain days and on other days very wise and acute. The fire in her was partly destroyed in the early half of her life by a fanatical Christian Science training. She became suddenly free of it when the woman who instructed her stood at the bedside of Cornelia's mother who lay devastated by the sudden death of her son in an avalanche. "The death of your son means you allowed evil, animal thoughts to live in you; your thoughts contained evil or else your son would not have died." The cruelty of this freed Cornelia.

New York, November 29, 1953

Hugo and I carried all our equipment to Ann Rennel's apartment, mainly to show *Bells of Atlantis*. Good response from the people there. Hugo stood by the projector against a plain, dark, heavy curtain and looked pale, drawn, as if he would suddenly burst into tears, or at least tremble. Who did he remind me of? The long, well-molded head, sensitive, reflecting a little of the beauty of Bill Pinckard at seventeen. Our quarrels have ended. I understand them. I fought against his pretenses, façades, his roles and lies: I am strong and powerful in the practical world. I always loved people who admitted their weaknesses and errors. Hugo's authoritarian manners annoyed me too, and the leadership and domination, which were a cover. And all the time I knew this I was helpless. He kept me out of the "business" of our life, while he bungled it (three times seriously). All that was left to me was rebellion.

Now he knows I can help.

New York, November 30, 1953

I took the train to the Geismars' to talk over the problem of the diary. Herbert Alexander is disappointed that I can't use my name, which he likes. He says, "Let Hugo go away." What nobody knows is that without Hugo there might never have been Anaïs Nin. I tried to say, "Hugo, go away." Anyway, aside from the personal, human reason, there is a better one still. The diary is not finished. The condition for its continuation is secrecy. Exposure will kill the diary itself, just as the exposure of a spy will put an end to his activity. My identity cannot be exposed, or the diary ends. The public eye and the spotlight will kill it.

Tuesday I discussed with Bogner the increase of courage to be myself rather than disguise myself.

Eduardo says, "You have changed so much that for years I felt I did not know you, felt I was not related to you."

The Museum of Modern Art tells Hugo that the hall will not be filled, so Hugo has to take to the telephone, and at the four o'clock premier, the hall is filled. But before this, I carry curtains to sew on the bus on my way to Bogner. Having ten minutes to spare, I call up the film council so they will register the film showing on their bulletin. I have lunch with Eduardo and he tells me about a Spaniard and a passion of three days that he found exhausting and that he walked away from to avoid trouble or pain.

After lunch I have my hair done, and while it dries I sew the curtains as the entire room had to be done over, the old felt having faded, and we can't afford an upholsterer. Then at the museum, I talk with Irina Aleksander and Cornelia Runyon. We have tea after the film showing and go uptown for a crowded cocktail party at Elsa de Brun's, where everyone talks so loudly that by seven-thirty I have no voice left and Hugo and I go home, cook dinner, and go to bed with a Martini and Simenon.

At nine in the morning I am sewing the last two pillow slips, telephoning Cornelia because tomorrow we give a cocktail party in her honor. I met her through Rupert, and when she walked into the film showing by accident, I merely dropped my head on her shoulder and whispered in her ear: "Keep my secret. I am here with my husband."

Everyone always accepts it all as natural and enters into my life's complications with a smile, willing to help and to share in the games.

Max Jacobson gives me the pin-cushion treatment and a tender pat. To Max I confess: for seven years, I have suffered from hot flashes (relieved only one year by

Jacobson's "crystal graft," which other people say caused the tumor). I have stiff, aching limbs, night cramps in my legs (rheumatic fever as a child), and an enlarged heart and heart murmur, chronic nasal passage irritation with bleeding. When one malady is relieved, a new one appears. This, with intermittent anemia, is enough to wear down anyone's patience. I also possess no body heat, am defenseless against colds and subject to several bouts of bronchitis a year.

At ten I am in Jacobson's hands. From there I go to pick up a book by Faubion Bowers on the dance in India as he is coming tomorrow to our cocktail party for Cornelia. Then a film for Hugo to be called for, another to be delivered, blue felt for the last two curtains to be bought. I sew on the bus and in Jacobson's office, stop at the Spanish store on 14th Street to buy Mother pasta de guayaba for her birthday, have an interview with Agnes de Lima seeking to show Hugo's films at the New School, and then the whole evening is spent sewing felt and hanging up the last two curtains…then Simenon, a Martini, a sleeping pill, and this dream:

I am with Stewart Granger in some relaxed, pleasurable place, and we enjoy an easy companionship. We understand each other well, and it is pleasant. I'm proud that he likes to be with me because he was once married to Jean Simmons. But then I feel a wave of desire, which I express to him, and he is surprised. He just had not thought of it; we were such perfect companions. He would, of course, make love to me, to please me, but this took all the pleasure out of it for me. I wished the impulse had come from him. He made love but stayed outside of me. I felt it was better this way as I was too old for him anyway; it was better to remain just comrades.

In reality, of course, I do not like Granger. I hear of his impending divorce. Rupert adores Jean Simmons and swoons at her performances, and I have taunted him and asked him why he does not try to meet her.

My relationship with Jim came to the same standstill as with other homosexuals. You strike the bottom, the limitations. He did not absorb enough, go deeper; he was facile, adaptable, gave the illusion of receptivity but behaved childishly. His plays I never liked—banal—but the reviews pleased him and gave him a feeling of success. The dialogue we had ended. Perhaps my deep relationship with adolescence ended with Jim and Rupert. I found his rebellions against Hugo absurd and his relationships with other people childish and without value. In fact, the childishness, instead of attracting me as it undeniably did before, now repulses me. His refusal of analysis and the illusion of success after a week's running of the play began to expose the distortion. He has distorting mirrors in himself, and he misunderstands me. I no longer feel like making a great effort to translate all I said. I guess now I have really emptied the nest for good. Jim feels I launched him, gave him a start, and now he can do the rest himself. I no longer feel close to him and have no sympathy with his behavior.

Party for Cornelia: As she is sixty-eight and invited her contemporaries, people who appeared to have walked out of Henry James novels, I saw for the first time the Village's earliest inhabitants, those who built the graceful, solid houses, who sat under crystal chandeliers and possessed civility and wit, a good vintage, a mellow wood, a mostly vanished civilization of a vein that is disappearing in the hands of the fake bohemians.

The atmosphere was elegant but warm. I am so tired of the chills and fevers of adolescence, and to suddenly find myself in the world of the old was not sad, but rather gentle.

Hugo laughs to see me at the restaurant later, seated between two bankers, my once-hated enemies. Now I don't see any bankers. I see a man who might have been anything else, one of Simenon's characters, a man seeking a little life wherever he is put, the size that fears allow him to move within.

Stanley Haggart took me to lunch without any preparation, told me in detail how Hugo met a woman called Faith Dane (one of the Lester Horton dancers), "the very opposite of you, a down-to-earth, rather common girl, who speaks with a 14th Street accent," and he made love to her so violently that she asked Stanley if Hugo were "insane." He frightened her.

The news affected me, but did not hurt me in any way. Strangely, I felt angry at the girl for being so stupid as to be afraid of vehemence. I felt compassion for Hugo awakening so late to sudden desires. I wondered why it had not happened before. I was relieved to think that now he would not desire me anymore. I felt uneasy, wondering why Hugo made me come back (I was delaying my return after the bronchitis).

If the affair were ended by the girl's childish terrors—she is over thirty—then was Hugo hurt? How could I let him be free of guilt? In contrast to my feelings about Rupert, I wanted Hugo to confess, and I would have consoled him. Of course, all this is easy when you do not love a man with desire. I was detached. Yet it affected me in another way. It matured me. I had always *needed* Hugo's faithfulness desperately. I do not need it anymore. I felt sorry for him, as if he were my son, and curious, and detached, and critical of the woman. "She is very destructive," said Stanley. It also puzzled me: why had Stanley told me this? Was it because he himself has been humiliated by Woody, one of Horton's dancers, and his ex-wife whom he wanted to remarry and who ultimately returned to her present husband? Was it the usual homosexual sadism and treachery? He should not have told me.

It would be difficult to keep my secret. And finally I had to say to Hugo: "Why not? You have been a good husband long enough. You have a right to whatever pleasure you can find. It is good for you to discover you are desirable. I don't mind at all. It has nothing to do with us. The only thing I ask is that if you do fall in love, and find someone you can live with better than me, then I want to know."

When Hugo made love to me after this revelation, all I felt was a satisfaction of my ego, an ironic and vain satisfaction that I could still arouse his passion.

If only I could behave this way toward Rupert, to not care.

Hugo was amazed. I did not let him admit, confess or explain. I wanted him to feel as I wish he could have made me feel all these years—guilt-free.

Dream: I am with Gonzalo again. But when Gonzalo rages and rants about politics, I know it is insanity. His ex-mistress, a model, is there. Also, some women are eager to show me they are on my side. We go to a swimming pool. I don't have the right suit. I am wondering how Gonzalo will feel when I leave for California. He seems tamed and subdued, as if he were trying to control his great rages. Then I meet Bill Pinckard again. He has been to Egypt. He has the same aloof and mocking manner. So lightly dressed. We are walking along the Seine. It is bitter cold. There is a traffic jam on the river. I leave my unicycle on the road. Then Bill gets drunk. He begins to drop all his belongings. I pick them up and follow him. He professes a great disdain for details, but I think that someone must be there to watch over such people. He gets into bed at the top floor of the Ritz. By the time I go down again for the rest of his belongings, his pen has been soaked by rain and is hopelessly bloated. I see Rupert. He says he saw me creaming my face, looking almost ugly. I tell him I always try to spare him that sight. I wonder if he still loves me.

Letter from Rupert Pole to Anaïs Nin:

Sierra Madre, December 1953

SUBJECT: Extreme Negligence in Writing His Wife!!!!

How could it have been so long? I must have written sometime in between; my sense of time is all loused up. Darling, darling, I won't even ask forgiveness—no excuse—just know that I love you deeply and that I'll make it up to you somehow when we're together.

Darling, we'll live in Florida or anywhere you want; we'll work out something better together next week. Meanwhile I'll try to write *every* day as punishment for my sins.

But one sin I have not committed, and will never commit as long as we live—the sin of not loving.

And the pain of suddenly realizing the pain I've caused you by not writing is punishment enough.

R

PS Just realized as I addressed this: I've been writing to 141 W 73rd Street, Jim's old address. Perhaps the letters were not forwarded. I didn't know the 85th Street address till you sent your cards!! You haven't put return addresses on your letters.

Card from Rupert Pole to Anaïs Nin:

Sierra Madre, December 1953

Love,

Another day, another letter!!

Sitting here high on mountain eating my favorite tuna sandwich washed down with good red wine from the thermos. So beautiful here now, warm (in the sun), and very clear with very soft wind in the pines making the music we heard on top of Grand Canyon. The grass is soft and dry and the color of the sunlight, so each enhances the other, giving a warm shimmering effect just over the top of the grass. Tavi is sitting, head high, looking very alert and very wise and strong and protective.

Glad you saw and helped Cornelia. She deserves recognition more than a lot of artists who are getting it.

Wish you were here right now, close to the sun and the grass and me.

R

EN ROUTE TO LOS ANGELES, DECEMBER 10, 1953

In the air. A new kind of plane that makes the trip to LA in eight hours instead of eleven. Flight 1, American Airlines. And looking back at the figure of Hugo undergoing unbelievable changes. This month the major theme was an understanding of Hugo. It is he who has been exploding and living with such intensity and conflicts that he "stole the show."

One morning he awakened and began to talk: "This is almost too much to bear, this pushing out. I feel caught in it, trapped. It's a destructive drive. It leads me on and on. I feel the strain, but I can't do anything about it."

I never knew *he* was a victim of the inhuman drives and efforts I rebelled against! Immediately my rebellion ceased. I felt immense compassion. But it was even more complicated: it was not only that he tackled big tasks, moved towards difficult aims, but it was also that at the moment of success, of leadership, he used as much strength to defeat himself. He gave up the bank just before he became vice president. He works intensely to form a filmmaker group and then relinquishes leadership. (Probably with me too, as soon as he won me, he proceeded to lose me.) His troubles, now that he knows them (before Bogner, it was not that he did not want to tell me what he felt, or what was happening to him, he just didn't know), causes me to respond as I always have responded to people with troubles, with maturity and understanding.

I could not help Hugo when *he did not know anything* about himself. Now I can. I knew and sensed a drama in Hugo that was destroying us both, but I did not know its nature. To call it a power drive, or a drive for security, is not enough.

Just before Hugo made his drama clear, I was saying to Bogner that I like people who are open, who admit, confess, expose their troubles. Then I can act at my best and help. But I feel anger when a role is played (my father), a pretense is sustained (my father), or I feel left out of the inner life. My mother leaned on me, and so I gave my best. My father shut me out. Hugo was absent. The first years of my marriage I sought to explore him, and found what Freud had discovered: life, like an iceberg, shows such a small fraction of itself in proportion to its huge, hidden base. That's Hugo. Of course, his troubles—among them his difficulty finding his true self, his oscillations between vulnerability, dependence and arrogance—were difficult to bear. He shows his last film everywhere. He lectures to everyone. He has no integrity as an artist. He wavers. He seeks an audience with complete egotism. Just as before he opened his eyes and started to worry about the bank, now he opens his eyes and begins: "You know, about *Jazz of Lights*, if Cinema Sixteen wants to show it later..." Last night, our last evening together, he was still cutting the film, and he almost made a disastrous change because Irene

Wilson (who is not an artist) suggested it. The obsessional quality is what frightens me. I love the films, filmmaking, but at eight in the morning Hugo is already talking vehemently, and there is no respite—there never was—no rest, no letup, no break. He can't relax, he can't play. He resisted Acapulco, disliked the utter languor, which I found good as a respite. And so we struggle not to destroy ourselves or others.

Hugo, who was so sexually and emotionally submerged, now has volcanic eruptions, always in a direction I do not want.

There is the hole in the middle. He speaks of his absent "core." I understand. But what kind of life is this, where Hugo lags twenty years behind me?

I don't know. I didn't know.

Yes, he has energy, an abundance of it, but it is sapped by anxiety and ambivalence.

I never knew how serious Hugo's problems are: breakdowns when he has to speak in public, insomnia, nervousness at social occasions. With women, he does what he first did to me: teases, and then treats them like children. Now I see a Hugo who is alarming, rough, more willful than ever, violent, and farther from mellowness than ever.

"What you failed to understand," said Bogner, "was that Hugo's inability to be truthful or natural or open or to share his troubles was his problem. This angered you because you felt left out. He wanted to talk endlessly about the bank, and for you to listen, but he never consulted you on big decisions. Thus you felt pushed, pulled, swept into Hugo's patterns."

For the first time I left New York without guilt, to live my own life, to pursue my own inclinations.

One reason why I failed to understand Hugo (aside from the fact that he did not understand himself) is, of course, that the patterns of our relationship endowed him with too much power over my life, and therefore his aims, errors, blunders and obsessions were constant threats to me and my own development.

Unable to cope with him, I yielded to a negative escape and merely created "another" life.

I have a tendency to give the man the reins, and then to feel utterly trapped in his patterns. I did the same with Rupert.

But, for example, if Hugo's own undisciplined, disorganized nature makes a jumble out of his room a half hour after I have completely sorted it for him, I can't justify spending my life on this activity. That is *his* problem. And mine is to have not one, but two men who act this way!

What should I do? Inevitably, I have learned to always carry money, to have my own keys, and I pick up their clothes.

Then, after weeks of quarrels (Anaïs pleading for a simpler life, fewer expenses, less strain), when I had understood that all this unbalance was Hugo's *illness* from which he suffered, I went to see the Barrons to call for a film and found Bebe crying: "I can't do it, I can't keep this up, it's too much. Louis thinks only of his machines. We have no human life. We don't even have time to make love!"

On the last day, I rushed to Bogner and Jacobson, the photographer, errands for Hugo, a cocktail party for Cornelia at the Lewins', met Agnes de Mille and did not like her cold blue eyes, shrewd nose, and did not like the old, wealthy Lewins who made films I do not like: *The Moon and Sixpence, The Flying Dutchman.*

Their collection of paintings and statues is amazing, but in this room filled with successful and powerful people, charming, gracious, I did not feel and never will feel at home, for I belong with those who made the objects, the paintings, the statues. It is no longer an artist rebelling against anything. It is I, Anaïs, who knows what life she wants but can't reach it.

I must, at this late date, build my own life upon my own strength. Let us hope the diary will free me.

Max Geismar is even more impressed with volumes 40 to 50 (the Otto Rank era): "Better than the ones on Miller, and different. I thought there would be a continuation, did not expect such changes of theme. They are good, so very good. I was going to read just a little, but I could not stop. I went on all night. I made notes."

And then comes that strange effect of writing upon life and Max says, "Last night we saw a famous Jewish actress, a character right out of the diary."

Anne is almost speechless, but filled with admiration. They have given me the sanction I needed to seek a way of publishing the diaries. "They must be done," Herbert Alexander said.

Sierra Madre, December 12, 1953

Rupert appears slenderer, younger, lighter, in contrast to Hugo. The sensuous contact is instantly elating. Tavi is wild with joy. In the car Rupert serves a Martini from a thermos bottle. We have dinner at our French restaurant, but I can't eat. I was shaken by the trip, tense still from the ordeal of New York. Rupert has tidied the house and painted the cupboards of the kitchen as a surprise. He is full of politeness and thoughtfulness, expressing his joy at my return. "Do you want the radio turned off?" I am grateful for the peace. When the light is out the physical hunger mounts like a fever and we staked claims on the whole body with our mouths. The nerves are keen. The sensations sharp and new and wild. The climax is potent and long-lasting. Rupert's passion is total, and I forget all the reasons I had accumulated to withdraw.

I am awake at dawn. The tension is gone. What I must do now is not rebel against the mediocrity of the life, to preserve the passion from being corroded. "I got out of music tonight, but we'll see my family tomorrow for dinner. Eyvind and Alice invited us for Christmas. I would like to see a bullfight, but I dread the crowds, and we may not find rooms." Later Kay telephones: "May we spend New Year's together?" It was Rupert who suggested a trip, and I had agreed enthusiastically, anything to escape his friends and family. But then he thinks of all the obstacles. "Las Vegas will be crowded. I hate crowds."

Relativity: here, it is I who probably repressed effort, intensity, restlessness, and searched for better forms of living. Rupert said, "I told Lloyd if he buys that land on the hill, we would buy our share with our savings."

This had been my own suggestion before leaving, in a desire to help Rupert fulfill his dream, not mine.

We could not sleep late because he had to work, but the silkiness of the tangled bodies is like the warm waves of Acapulco, the sun, the palm leaves like fans in the breeze. He takes his own tea and toast, having developed his "system" like a bachelor. I stayed in bed. The tightness around my heart was lessening. I thought myself gravely ill, recently, due to the way my heart felt.

I hung up my clothes, thinking I will have four happy weeks. I will accept his life.

Last night, a movie. There was not good movie playing, but we had to go out.

Tonight his family.

But our second night together in the dark makes him break the silence he usually maintains—too great a joy!

Sierra Madre, December 18, 1953

I got Hugo's letter, which shows that he can work out quietly, with Bogner, what I have to struggle and battle for. If only we could achieve these clarifications without crises and storms!

We could not talk to each other last month, only shout, quarrel, weep. With Bogner we each reached quietness, but Hugo's willful, aggressive attitudes brought on, in me, what felt like a heart attack, an emotion of strangulation. I almost died. I could literally no longer breathe in his presence. Bogner's emphasis on Hugo's illness helped me.

When Kenneth Anger makes up a film born of the masquerade party and asks us to act in it, Rupert, instead of considering it an adventure, deliberates solemnly on the obstacles: he is afraid it will be too "arty," he does not want to be recognized in it, he does not want them to use our names.

When Lloyd designed a "fireplace" for our house, Rupert enumerated all the problems: the bookcase would have to be moved, we may be moved out of the house, etc.

Now, I have learned my lesson. I do not fight. I say patiently: "There are obstacles to everything. You have *first* to want something badly and then work at removing the obstacles." Lloyd was so irritated by Rupert's petty concerns that he threw the drawing on the floor and stalked out. Rupert frustrates others and himself.

When you study these matters objectively (as I do with Bogner) then you can look upon them coolly like a scientist.

Rupert was troubled about the film, yet Thursday night when they sent him on a fire, he was frustrated and unhappy to miss the filming. One word to our supervisor next door and he is getting freed tonight (the fire is contained anyway and today should be his day off), and so I managed to have him included instead of left out, and I am waiting for him now.

Kenneth Anger said to me, "You are a magical person." He was to capture in his film that luminosity that made my entrance into the party so startling. It is an inner light, and so difficult to capture. Last night in Samson de Brier's studio, from seven to one in the morning, in floodlights, with Paul Mathieson, Renate Druks, Kenneth Anger, Curtis Harrington, Rupert, three photographers, chaos of rage, makeup, valises, Kenneth's nightmare, the common error of the contemporary artist was made: the chaotic material of the unconscious was reproduced without its pattern of meaning, like the worlds before birth, unformed, shedding no light on our true nightmares.

Sierra Madre, December 23, 1953

Last night I awakened from the following nightmare: I had been bitten on my arms, and they were swollen terribly, four times their size. Then I saw what had bitten me, and they were insects about six inches long, with wings and the head and the darting tongues of rattlesnakes. I caught them in a box to show the doctor so that he would know how to help me. I asked Millicent to take care of them, but she let them escape. I was afraid now I would die because the doctor would not know what counter-poison to use.

Rupert was in bed with bronchitis. Hugo disturbed my peace by suddenly deciding he wanted to rest and asking me to join him in Haiti or Acapulco, disregarding completely my "lecture tour" with which I had said I was engaged, disregarding the fact that the money had not come in, that he sent me all the bills to take care of. I resented the caprice and the willfulness once more, and, above all, these *delayed* fulfillments! I finally said quietly I could not leave until my work was done, but I felt guilty, disturbed, to be where I want to be.

Sierra Madre, December 27, 1953

I am at peace with Rupert, accepting his way of life.

My efforts to "transform" our life are defeated anyway by California, distances, obstacles, intermittence of friendships, and Rupert's bondage to his family and his friends.

The themes of our disagreements have not changed.

When we spend one long evening a week with Helen and Lloyd, I have asked that we do not go there the following evening. But after spending all of Christmas Day there, we went there again the next day.

Every time the maid comes, Rupert expresses his fundamental opposition by some peripheral criticism: she comes too early, or she comes on the very day he decides to stay and work on his Forest Service film, etc.

But he gets the benefit of my emotional dramas with Hugo. I am able to speak quietly with Rupert. At the same time he tells me just how to close the door of the car or how to prepare the Spanish rice, he relinquishes with regret his total control of the house, his little habits. The first morning he gave me breakfast in bed (because he knows I like it) on the black dishes he gave me for Christmas.

Our life is on a key so much lower than the key of our passion.

I want to hold on to the illuminated moments, and once more realize the necessity of poetry. That is what poetry does, to select the illuminated moments.

I reread my new book, *Cities of the Interior*—the part I wrote three or four months ago—and liked it.

I feel like writing, but my energy is low.

So I write letters, spend a day on business for Hugo (paying his bills, which he asked me to do). I deposit in Rupert's bank account the $400 I am supposed to have earned in New York.

WITH HUGO THERE IS NO RELIEF

1954

Sierra Madre, January 1954

On a Sunday around five in the afternoon while Rupert was recovering from bronchitis and splicing his first film for the Forest Service, a man came in to announce he had seen smoke on Monrovia Peak. Rupert rushed off in his truck. As soon as it darkened, Reginald arrived, and we looked out of the window and saw the two mountains facing us on fire, the entire rim, burning wildly in the night. The flames were as tall as the tallest trees, the sky already coral. The fire raced along, sometimes descending behind the mountains where we could only see the glow, sometimes descending towards us. Reginald admired the spectacle. I was anxious about Rupert, seeing him battling the flames, feeling his body just barely recovered from his cold. At six the fire was on our left side and rushing towards Mount Wilson. Evacuees from the cabins began to arrive in front of our station. The street was blockaded by policemen, and cars were turned away. Some were sightseers, some relatives of the cabin owners, the park station family, or foresters' families (some live in trailers in the canyon). The policemen lit flares. The red lights on police cars twinkled. Fire engines arrived. Hours passed. Rupert rushed in once and said, "This is it, this is the fire to end all fires."

William Mendenhall, Forest Supervisor and our neighbor, came to the back door and told me to be ready to abandon the house, to pack the car. Rupert dashed in again (after seeing that everybody was out of the canyon) to help with packing. We put in the car the viola, the violin, his music and clothes, the radio and typewriter, my clothes, the diaries and manuscripts, films and slides. We parked the car in the open field below. As soon as I was notified I called up the Campions, who were out for the evening. I told the babysitter that if the parents did not return in time she was to bring the children warmly dressed to my car. Meanwhile, I made coffee for whoever needed it. I answered the frantic telephone calls. I was cool, playing my role, but was appalled by the danger to the firefighters, the hopeless size of the fire, the immensity of the ravage. The fire did not descend towards our house until dawn. The "cats" had dug wide open trails through the bushes and trees, but the fire could jump over them, depending on the wind. At two in the morning Reginald left. I did not go to sleep. Rupert came back at about five, and I gave him breakfast. He was on duty for 24 hours. At noon, the danger to the houses was over, but 33 cabins burned and 4,000 acres of forest were still burning. Rupert was away all day. He returned looking like a man who had gone to war. I brought him his favorite bourbon, cooked dinner, drew a bath, and he ate and fell asleep. He has so much courage, so much endurance, and such a sense of responsibility.

At five in the morning the next day he was called out again. I could see the fire burning to the back of us now, and a rain of ashes had fallen over everything. The

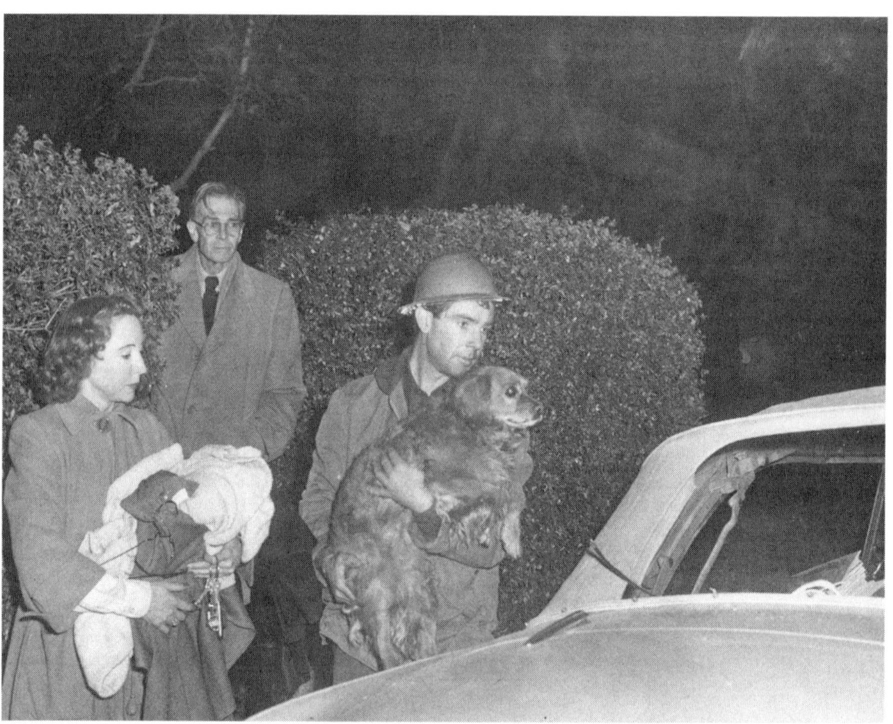

Preparing for evacuation: Anaïs Nin, Reginald Pole, Rupert Pole, Tavi

smell of burn was in the air, acidic and pungent and tenacious. A grey day for all. The acute danger was over the second night, though there were outbreaks, but the third day the Mount Wilson Observatory was almost burned down. But the men were on hand, running from one front to another, from one spot fire to another. Rupert stood nearby backfiring up the mountain, so that the ascending flames would counteract the descending ones. Every evening he came home exhausted, ate, drank, and went to sleep. Thus we slept through New Year's Eve, and awakened every morning at five or five-thirty. Now there lurked the danger of flood.

A week later, the danger is gone, but everyone is on the job. I spent days answering telephone calls and inquiries at the door, buying the papers for Rupert to read at night, washing his jeans and mending them, washing and mending his thick socks. I was thankful that he did not have to sleep out in the cold. I stood by. I did not go out. I felt this way I could help sustain his strength.

Dream: A group of us—Rupert among them—were gaily getting ready to go out when we discovered that Rupert had blue streaks on his shoulders, like accentuated veins. We all wondered what kind of illness it was but decided to make light of it and go out in spite of it. However, when I looked at myself in the mirror for a last touching up, I found I had a red stain on me, extending from the chin down over the neck and left shoulder. This alarmed me and I wondered whether I should go to Jacobson and submit to his quick magical cures (not knowing what he did or what the illness was or whether his cure had "consequences") or whether I should go to Dr. Bogner's doctor who would be "slower" but more careful, cautious, and proceed with checkups and tell me what was going on.

Dream: A big old man was pursuing me. One of his hands was bigger than the other, as big as a giant's. A young man came to see me as well as several young girls. Rupert was there. The young man fell in love with me. We were alone, and I asked him what the girls thought of me. He said they thought I was too old, and a "cheap character" for Rupert.

Dream: We were at a party, drinking from a bottle of whiskey. The bottle was left half-finished and open. Lightning struck it, like a welder's spark, and started a fire. The image of fire was framed like Rupert's slides of fireworks in Mexico. Wild. After the fire, everybody was searching for loved ones half-buried in sand. One by one they emerged unhurt; a horse had been covered completely, even his eyes, to prevent his panicking. Blinded by sand, he kept edging towards me, and his legs were seeking mine as I edged away. Then Marlene Dietrich appeared. She looked very old but still glamorous. Rupert was fascinated with her. I left the party so as not to witness his long talk with her and her interest in him. When I returned, however, he was talking with some young girls and taking down their telephone numbers. I asked him: "Why must you do things like that?"

Dream of the Giant Screws: I had to fetch some screws for the car. It was a garage of gigantic proportions with a floor like a sand desert, great spaces. The screws were as big as I, made of lead and iron and too heavy. I was alone, in a desert, and felt anguished and helpless. Far off there was a blonde woman, but she was sitting down and weeping, with her hair over her face. I was tempted to ask her to help me, but realized she could not, that she was in distress.

After that I had a dream of Helba's suicide. It took place at night. The setting was somber. A tall house in charcoal tones. From the roof of this house Helba shouted at me; "Stay there, Anaïs, I'm going to jump!" I rushed to help her, but before I could act the entire house collapsed from within and Helba was hurled, screaming as she fell. I realized I could not have saved her because the house itself had collapsed due to a fire inside.

New York, February 10, 1954

When I arrived a month ago, the plane landed in a snowstorm. It was six in the morning. I wore no rubbers. Several passengers shared a cold taxi that had difficulty getting through the snow. All night I had felt such a pain in the chest that I thought I would die of heart trouble in the plane. I was surprised to awaken alive.

In the cold taxi I felt so weak I thought this was truly the end. Hugo had arrived only a few hours before from Haiti. I got into a hot bath, to warm myself. In the bath my sense of illness and weakness overwhelmed me. I wept. I went to bed. I got up later to see Dr. Bogner. We arranged for a medical checkup the next morning. No heart trouble, no tuberculosis, no cancer, but low functioning of the thyroid and a lack of estrogen. I was given pills. The pain continued for a few days, but the anxiety disappeared. Once more I was repaired by doctors. And then I faced a gigantic task.

Hugo's project to launch the three films at the YMHA that I had rebelled against as "too big"—too pretentious—*was* too big for *all* of us. From Jan. 10th to Feb. 1st, the night of the show, the Barrons, Hugo and I tackled an inhuman amount of work. Thousands of programs were mailed from the house. We contacted everyone. There were millions of errands, fetching and carrying programs from the printer, the mimeograph company, the post office. The second week I had to get help. I posted and stamped programs until I had obsessional nightmares. Hugo strained for publicity. I was panicked by the idea of publicity, had nightmares of more slapstick farces by *Time* magazine.

The announcement of the film showing:

THE ART DEPARTMENT OF THE YM-YWHA PRESENTS:
3 FILMS BY IAN HUGO and ANAÏS NIN IN PERSON
JAZZ OF LIGHTS
(What Hugo saw by night and by day in Times Square)
Electronic Jazz by Louis and Bebe Barron
New Multi-Dimensional Sound Projection

New Color Screen Projection System
For the First Time in the USA
With
ANAÏS NIN AND MOONDOG

BELLS OF ATLANTIS
with Anaïs Nin
Electronic Music by Louis and Bebe Barron

AI-YE (MANKIND)
with chant and drum music by Osborne Smith
(Critics Prize, 1953, Paris, France)

CONCURRENTLY in the Gallery of the YM-YWHA:
Exhibition of prints, copper plates and illustrations by Ian Hugo, and first edition books by Anaïs Nin and her new book "*A Spy in the House of Love*"
The Exhibition of Ian Hugo's art is arranged for the purpose of showing how his interest in filmmaking arose from his interest in rhythms and sequences.

RESERVATIONS: BOX OFFICE, KAUFMAN AUDITORIUM, YM-YWHA, Lexington at 92nd Street
Prices: $1.50 and $2.00 Tel. Trafalgar 6-2366

Hugo made these notes during the turbulent preparations for the film showing:

> Anaïs says she finds me under great strain because of the changed financial situation, that I am obviously preoccupied with security, that this is a repetition of the same kind of strain she has endured for years; she says that her own values are different, that she can stand it no longer.
>
> She says I am putting the knife to her throat because: (a) she thinks it is not practical to expect that films and lectures can yield as much as the $5,000 I say is a minimum required and (b) it is unfair of me to threaten that if this cannot be done, I will go back to the bank.
>
> I do not believe in all this; if I have been preoccupied with security I would have accepted already, or at least explored more actively, a bank job. On the contrary, for perhaps the first time, I have been weighing carefully the demands of my own recently found creativity along with the practical ways and means of satisfying it. I believe that Anaïs is not looking at the facts and is refusing to treat this as a joint problem to be resolved by joint efforts, that she is drawing a line between them and saying that on my side are facts and on hers, feelings.
>
> I am no good practically and never have been, just as my father told me. I am no good at handling facts. I am a failure. I have made Anaïs unhappy. My father said I would never be able to support a wife as he did.

Hugh Guiler in a film lab

But I also want to be like my father, or rather to reconcile his values with Anaïs's, but I fought him through Anaïs. I want so much to unite what has been separated in me.

But now I have failed both in my father's values as well as in Anaïs's, and they are both my values. So I am at zero.

Anaïs's drawing a line between her world and mine happens just at a moment when I am engaged in an effort to remove the wall between these two parts of myself. I see her hand superimposed on the very hand that has been removing the barrier, erecting it again.

I am shocked and angered that Anaïs, who has successfully lectured and who has wished for propagation and distribution of her books as well as the films, should now turn down what seems to me a carefully thought out and reasonable plan to accomplish those very ends. I am convinced that in the case of the films, Anaïs is arguing without knowledge of what is, even for 16mm, a mass medium. In general, Anaïs is refusing to look at the situation realistically.

Hugo became the villain, because he was pushing so exaggeratedly, disregarding fatigue and sensibilities, and then came the equipment problems, the dimmer board machine of Rollo Williams (my idea), the special projectors, electricians, the Barrons' problems with sound, Hugo solving "crises" well, but also working chaotically and increasing work and tension (losing papers, lists, phone numbers, etc.). I collapsed two or three times. Wept. Finally, a week before the preview, twenty silent, anonymous people who don't clap, a caterer serving cocktails. My fears of publicity were unfounded. The dailies passed the show over. But on Feb. 1st and 2nd we had the largest turnout of friends, bringing four, six, eight other friends. The Y was filled to capacity twice at the nine o'clock shows and half full at seven. I stood from four to midnight during first show (at four I was still inserting additions to the program that had not been properly planned). People came; the films were a success. *Jazz of Lights* was received humorously as it was intended. *Bells of Atlantis* still makes the deepest impression.

I talked concisely and very clearly. People bought books, saw the engravings. It was overall a success, as prestige, as extending the boundaries of 16mm film attendance. I managed, by a dint of massages and facials, to conceal the fatigue and to look beautiful. Theatrically we gave people a quality spectacle. In money, we lost several hundred dollars.

Then the four of us collapsed. Hugo was still calling up the critics. I bought my ticket for Sierra Madre.

While all these big events took place, my dreams revealed a state of feeling utterly removed from external developments. In my dreams my fur coat was all worn and disintegrating at the edges and was linked to Mitou's fur. By contrast *she* sat and slept, aloof, graceful, idle, relaxed. Her fur was glossy and beautiful. Hugo admired her. She represented what I desired and envied: relaxation, beauty. I felt strained and worn. True, I had repaid Hugo for his protection of my work. True, I had helped to get his films known.

But once more, as always with Hugo, love, pleasure and human life were sacrificed to ambition.

The first morning he wept over my physical debacle, as he deposited on my bed two voodoo figure charms against illness.

The second time he wept over "the pain of breaking through, pushing out." And I consoled him.

The human being Hugo suffers from Hugo the neurotic. Hugo the artist suffers at the hands of Hugo the businessman. He is in hell. He is in the hell of the ego asserting itself, of a young artist being born.

He cannot do anything alone. Ralph Schoolcraft and I have to file his papers with him. He misses important appointments. He was relieved that I talked about his film on the stage. He was sentimental over Rollo Williams (a 99% businessman) who almost ruined my presentation by insisting I mention his "associated with Century Lighting" in a lecture on poetry in the film!

The show itself was a success, but the Barrons were exhausted and rebellious: "Hugo calls us up several times a day. He doesn't let us work. He asks our advice for hours and goes off and not only does not follow it but takes the advice of a new friend he met casually at a cocktail party."

He pushes beyond everyone's strength. He needs a staff of people at attention. At moments I hated him. Then suddenly he weeps, or he says, "I know how much you had to do with the making of the films. Nobody knows, but I do. I'm aware of it and of the superhuman efforts you made on the program." When I leave he becomes tender. He suddenly looks soft instead of grim and willful.

Whatever Bogner has unleashed or freed, it is at the moment like a cyclone, almost unbearable. It is a mixture of ambition, aggression and helplessness, of daring and confusion, of hesitation and willfulness. It is frightening. Does he enjoy the morning light on the church steeple or the modern building top that looks Grecian, the idea of breakfast, the luxurious beds, the sleeping cat? No. He is already talking, and it is like a presidential campaign. "I have to have a print made for the film critic of the *Times*."

He lost the United Press man's story he wanted to show Bogner. This morning he was not well. Bogner advised him yesterday against antihistamines for his cold, and nevertheless he took one last night and it upset his stomach. The house is not a home any longer. It is an office.

During the shows we met Ralph Schoolcraft through an agency. He was a quiet, able, intelligent boy who soon became indispensable and who shared the work with incredible initiative. We became friends. He hung up the engravings with Hugo, he sold my books, he sent programs. He substituted for Jim's agility and efficiency in work.

In Hugo's analysis Bogner caught the phrase "like a prima donna" that he used about someone who did not like "details" and turned it to expose his own dislike of details. He only wants to play with grandiose schemes.

The telephone starts ringing—friends who are giving exhibits want to know how we handled ours, want our lists of names.

"I am Hugo's spiritual investment," I said to the Geismars, "and now I too must yield something."

Irina Aleksander thought the films were marvelous, Hugo was a "*grand artiste*," that he was *en beauté*, that he looked forty years old instead of fifty-five, but that there was still something "heavy" about him.

Everyone was talking about Hugo's films. At the party, Anne Geismar told me a dream she had that explains her remarkable lack of jealousy of me while Max without any subtlety exposes his desire; Anne dreamed that I made love to her, that she enjoyed it. Max told me that Herbert Alexander is avidly reading the abridged diary as a result of my saying, "Go ahead, do whatever is necessary to make it ready for public consumption." I too have dreams of freedom, to have enough money to escape from the irrational attitudes towards money of both Hugo and Rupert, to be no longer the victim of Hugo's expansion, speculations, and new goals, of Rupert's "savings" and bourgeois aims to own a home.

I arrived in New York in a black coat and dress. I left in my white coat and white dress with leopard accessories, towards a holiday and my dream of passion and human life, but I know Rupert will fulfill the passion but not the "living" unless we escape to Acapulco.

We only communicate by telephone. His letters are too rare and forced, and I lost my desire to write him. He cannot answer me.

At night, before the show, I was so tired that I only read a few pages of Simenon, drank one Martini, took one sleeping pill and went to sleep at nine or ten o'clock.

At the show, I saw everyone I knew in New York. Edward Graeffe towered over everyone, but he is so coarsened by weight, all his beauty lost—only the Valkyrian height, teeth and voice remain.

Friends, friends.

At the preview, among the silent critics was Carter Harman, now of the *Time* music department. Being a composer who has not composed for several years, he was critical of the Barrons' music, but he liked the films. He was negative, but I knew why. Only a few weeks ago he had finally separated from Nancy.

Mysteries of desire. Some die (as mine did for Chinchilito), some continue. As soon as Carter and I saw each other the sparks of desire were reanimated. In the car, driving to dinner, he invited me to sit on his knees. And his arms crushed me. It was astonishing for me, one of the rare intoxications I have felt since I have been with Rupert. Once or twice I was tempted to call him, knowing that he would not make love, but knowing he wanted it.

This moment of desire saved me, probably, from a satire in *Time* magazine.

Who else? Dollie Chareau. Jimmy Spicer. Peggy Glanville-Hicks. Stanley Haggart. Woody Parrish-Martin. Millicent and all her friends and relatives. The engravers from Atelier 17. My readers. "I have all your books, and I wanted to meet you." Shy, mysterious young men. Thurema and Jimmy. The Nims: Bill softer every day, and Letha harsher. The bond with the Barrons strengthened.

Letters of praise. Hugo embarrasses me when he compares himself to Martha Graham. Bebe also dreams of peaceful living, children, and no tensions.

To forestall a catastrophe, I told Rupert I was launching Hugo's films to lure him to New York and to obtain, in exchange, a divorce (which Rupert still begs me for).

Hugo talked at first about his Christmas vacation in Haiti. He brought back a film in which I saw Albert and his French mistress, and a sample of his architecture. What would have happened to me if I had married Albert at the time? He is unhappy, frustrated; I let him marry his childhood fiancée because she seemed right for him, but she was bourgeois, rigid, and did not make him happy. Now she won't divorce him.

Hugo said, "I was lonely." The human and the inhuman Hugo are both there.

"He was more charming before," said Irina, "when he loved and protected you, than now when he uses you to establish himself as an artist."

"But Irina, I never would have become the writer I am if Hugo had not protected me, so now I am helping him to be born as an artist."

None of these people knew the selfless Hugo, the sacrificed Hugo of our life in Paris.

To balance is imponderable.

"How moral you are," said Max ironically. And the statement he made about the program was the most encompassing of all. The first film, he said, was the life of nature, the primitive, the origins of life (*Ai-Ye*—Acapulco). The last one was the life of the city (Times Square—*Jazz of Lights*), and *Bells of Atlantis* was the story of the soul caught between both.

In four lines he described the drama and the theme of my last seven years—my flight to Acapulco, the only place where I have wanted a home, my flight towards the nature Rupert represented, my flights to New York, and Anaïs caught between them, in the silences, the hammock dreams, the storms and crucifixions. The murders accomplished in silence are the crimes couples commit against each other—Hugo denying me a simple artist life, Rupert and his lack of adventurousness.

In *Touriste de Bananes*, Simenon describes such a desire for nature, its horrors, dangers, failure. It made me feel like writing about Acapulco, the grand hotel life and the drugging beauty. The little house and the horrors I never wrote about, the dangers, fears, the irresponsibility of the Mexicans. The rats, the impossibility of getting ice, food, light. The dangers of living alone. The failed promises, cheating, immorality. The noises. The old man dying of asthma. The crowing cocks. The sea elephants at play. The incredible sunrises and sunsets. The cistern overflowing. The thieves. The illnesses. Leprosy and elephantiasis and fevers. The doctors' inadequacies. The art products in the market. The bullfights and anxiety, the heat and feelings of the people, the loneliness and loss of music, the *agua mala*, the dangerous motorboats, the dances on the rocks, the storms, the polluted drinks, the Mexican who read a book on "how to make friends" and the one who wanted me not to go out with anyone else…the sensuality and disintegrations, the non-caring, the pull downward, the willingness to do anything for pleasure, to commit any crime to possess the voluptuous life, the inability to work, the dissolution of the mind, the full life of the body and contempt for work, for mental exertion, for the city, for clothes, for effort.

As soon as I leave the atmosphere of Hugo's tension, I relax. Then the pity for Hugo blossoms, but his will discourages its expression. I find his face in the morning forbidding. The moments of tenderness or emotion in between are like fissures in a wall. He is like a man possessed by various spirits, not just one. Once it was the bank. Now, fortunately, I can love and serve the films.

Sierra Madre, March 2, 1954

This month with Rupert has gone by too fast. A week of honeymoon. A week of recovery. Slow renewal of habits: music at the Wrights', a movie with the Wrights, a concert with Eric and his girl, evenings of quartets with Caltech students, movies, good and bad. Bad when we are too tired to drive to Hollywood.

A weekend working on Kenneth Anger's film (*Inauguration of the Pleasure Dome*). An empty shell, simulation of fantasy, all external rococo effect of strangeness, but no meaning. The interesting story actually took place in the relationship between Ken, the cameramen, and the entire cast. Ken oscillates between tyranny, tension, impatience, and exaggerated demands, to a cloying sweetness towards me, as if I were a prima donna.

Once, when beads fell off one of the dresses and we were cutting our bare feet, I picked up a broom to sweep them and he would not let me. Everything was arranged to suit my plans, the others had to follow, and I never knew this until later.

At first as Astarte, goddess of moonlight, I was illuminating the film. Later Marjorie Cameron, as evil, won out, and the elements of decadence and destruction took over. Renate Druks with her Austrian Jewish beauty, very much like Luise Rainer, only more voluptuous, represented the human and physical; I, the dream. Paul Mathieson struggled out of orgies to reach for the luminous erotic figure of Anaïs. Cameron was startling, in dead white makeup, a vulture face, enormous mouth, and slitted eyes. She is insane. Paul is attracted to the atmosphere she creates, finding it exciting because he only deals and understands and communicates in symbols. Renate suffers from his relationship with Cameron. Renate is more human. Cameron's morbid predictions terrorize her. Cameron's husband was a scientist delving in the occult who was killed by an explosion during an experiment in his garage. Cameron's paintings come from the sulphurous regions. Renate said, "She even wanted to take my motherhood away from me. She tried to win over Peter" (Renate's son, who is eleven and also acting in the film).

They all walk a tightrope. We all talk the language of symbols, but there must be knowledge of its meaning, and this Ken does not share. Cameron wanted Peter to suckle her breast in the film, and Renate became hysterical.

Paul was the boy I called the fairytale boy, whom I first met in New York when he was seventeen and wrote childish letters like a boy of seven. He loaned me a painting of a faun, which was a self-portrait. He looks like a Danish or German prince, so blond and so mythical that he does not awaken any human warmth. Once, at a Maya Deren party, I had a sense of warm contact with him, but it vanished when he came for a masquerade party and slept in my bed but could not take me although he wanted to. Gonzalo destroyed his painting in a fit of jealousy. Later I saw Paul in Acapulco; I was surrounded by Gore and others, and we were in a frivolous mood. Paul was mute and remote, like a reproach, and I hated him. He danced badly. Once I sat on a raft sunning myself, and he swam out to me. He stuck his head out of the sea and said plaintively, "Anaïs, I love you." But it was a bodiless love, which I was in revolt against, as I was seeking full sensual flowering. I missed Rupert and did not know if I ever would see him again. Paul's unreality was distasteful to me, a walking mystic from the North, the enemy of earth and joy.

But he has changed. He now dances sensuously, laughs, draws and paints with imagination. The adolescent dissonances have all disappeared.

In the film he dressed me. Mute again. But the other night at Renate's house, he talked. He explained the film. "Samson is the false man, the man of many faces, which is why he changes makeup and costumes all the time. The various women, Renate as the sensuous romantic lover, Cameron as the satanic woman, Joan Whitney as the virgin beauty, all offer him gifts that he rejects. Curtis brings the wine of ecstasy from the caves of the subconscious. They all drink and are transformed. Anaïs refuses the drink. She has no need of it. She is Astarte, the moon. I, the romantic lover, want the unreachable moon."

All of this is very decadent. They are all young, in their twenties and thirties, but they still use outworn symbols, as Tennessee Williams used in *Camino Real.* This fixation on the past seems to be a homosexual trait and may be connected with the fixation on the mother (or grandmother). In this I have been the very opposite of them, seeking to escape from it, liking unfamiliar countries, new settings, liking to change my décor, the changes of fashion, frequent metamorphoses. After a time, I discard a dress not because it is worn (I cannot wear out my dresses—I barely tear or fray them at all) but because the self that enjoyed that particular dress is outworn. I need a new set of feathers to match my new feelings. For example, two trends are now uppermost: one towards a more human reality in writing; the other is humor, and both of these eliminate the wearing of certain dresses, the vivid Mexican orange cotton dress that looked like the orange jacaranda flowers in Mexico because the tropical bursts of color have become more modulated, more suffused, less representational. A splash of color a few years ago gave me the satisfaction of matching nature until I absorbed this color intravenously and it became distilled into humor. Now the dress reminds of me of the summers when I was a failed chameleon, donning the joyous orange jacaranda flowers without being able to match the joyous recklessness of nature, indifferent to jealousy, fear, or the taints of the past. For another reason I discarded the black cotton dress with turquoise ruffles, a dress Rupert loved, but that I wore in Acapulco when the mourning clothes of neurosis were thinly disguised by the turquoise ruffles intended to charm, entice and flirt, but it was neurosis that danced, smiled, fluttered its feminine flounces, mourning still the father never possessed, the wounds made by lovers. Not today. The mourning is over. I can live with the Wrights for an evening without trembling at their quarrels and offensive words. I am less victimized by earthquakes of the soul, by tidal waves of anguish.

Quarrels once were prophets of separation and loss (my parents' quarrels led to the loss of my father, the loss of Europe). Jealousy was the messenger of divorce. Today I can live months without the strangulation of anxiety.

This month, for example, I had only very minor attacks of nervousness or panic, no nightmares, no guilt, and very little of the excruciating fatigue that tightens my neck in a vice until I can no longer think. I sleep easily and deeply. Tavi's barking, the telephone, cannot awaken me fully.

I believe in the depth of Rupert's love, and his superficial enthusiasms do not annihilate me.

I sit writing while Rupert plays in a quartet. The music of Beethoven does not correspond with the lives or the feelings of the people playing it. The little American room, barren, the innocuous books, the absence of taste, no paintings—the functional home, the scattered, literal tack. Rupert alone, with sparkle in his gestures, brings an element of richness.

Rupert.

When we first got home, he turned the music on. I was undressing, combing my hair. He could not wait for bed but came up to me, naked, his desire erect, and I turned towards him. He embraced me, lifted me from the floor. He was vital, tense with desire. Firm. He carried me to bed. Such a powerful passion he poured into me. A strange mixture of strength, fire, emotion and eroticism. Then he lifted his head and shoulders up by resting on his elbows and said vehemently: "Would you ever have thought such a relationship possible, one that gets deeper and stronger all the time?" It was a torrent. He could not sleep until he possessed me a second time. It was like wine and the sun together. "This is our private Acapulco," I said, feeling his resuscitation of the body, this awareness of it, this dilation of the flesh.

In the morning, desire again. His body burns with it. The wonder of it is so great that the night before, while the pleasure and the music were confounded and liquefied me in pure delight, I felt that this moment was the highest of all...this mixture of communion of the senses and of feeling.

A joyous morning. It is only slowly that the daily life imprisons us again. The telephone: "What shall I do if a storm comes? I have only two rows of sandbags put up." And the heavy rain. At four o'clock the streets are covered with mud. It is Rupert's job to take photographs and make movies of the disaster. The naked mountains cannot hold down rocks and mud. Rupert dresses me in a raincoat and hip boots and we drive a little way up the road. At the third curve it is impossible. A river is rushing across the road. Rupert takes pictures while I hold the umbrella over the camera. It is terrifying to see the muddied water and rocks, the mountain disintegrating. When we are ready to return, the road behind us is covered by large rocks, but Rupert pushes on as if the truck were a jeep, forcing it through. The edge of the road is being carried away. We returned and continued our "patrolling." I was laughing and scared too; Rupert is at ease in nature, and without fear. It was a wild moment of danger.

Passion again kept him awake. The next evening, his family and a movie. Another evening a bad concert, but the Debussy harp quintet moved me painfully.

In the car Rupert kissed my hand as if I were a princess.

March 1954

Return to New York

Letter from Rupert Pole to Anaïs Nin:

Sierra Madre, March 1954

Love,

Felt like Tavi looked after seeing you disappear into the gloom of the fog. The hardest times are when you first leave and the last week before you come back, to say nothing of the nights. There's nothing you can say that isn't too sad. Tavi was so downcast at the airport, finally couldn't make it back to car and had to be picked up and carried; he crept along lower and lower and finally just lay there and refused to go any farther, as though he just wanted to stay there and wait till the plane brought you back again. It's the way I really felt too but didn't admit it to him; I told him we'd just have to be strong and have some guts, and anyway there was a lot waiting at home for us to do!!!

No fires yet. I was alerted twice but each time they caught it before we were needed. Working on maps here each night now till my eyes get too tired and then to bed to read the Bowles book on India furiously so I won't be able to remember you're not there—but it never works.

Must go to bed—big day tomorrow—have to keep moving fast, fast enough to keep from noticing that my life has moved to NY. But at night inevitably things slow down, and I'm caught by the bare facts—but they're not all painful, for then I think of what my life would be if you were never coming back, and four short weeks seems a tiny price to pay for the beauty of our life together.

Te quiero siempre más

R

New York, March 1954

Post office. Letters about film showings. Talks on a campaign for *Spy* with Miss Parker of British Book Centre, who is distributing the book. They always begin by saying they will do everything, and then they ask me to call up Harvey Breit because he has not answered the invitation to a press party. I get unhappy, humiliated, buffeted, hurt and poisoned. The inconsistencies. Mrs. Murray tells me Mondadori's reactions to *Spy* were wonderful, yet they did not publish it. So I see Bogner, after a nightmare of the meeting with the press. I see Jim. I visit bookshops. I pick up the crumbs of praise from Jim and Eduardo to be balanced against the hostility of James Laughlin, of my exclusion from the Poets Readings at the YMHA.

As you accept your own irrationality, you see the whole irrationality of the world, its absurdities, contradictions, and utter subjectivism.

To Dr. Bogner with more nightmares. Rehearsal at Columbia University. I buy my ticket for Mexico to meet my life and love Rupert. At the Nims' party I look around and people seem dust-laden and petrified as if they had been lying on shelves for years.

Letter from Rupert Pole to Anaïs Nin:

Sierra Madre, March 26, 1954

TO: *La Mujer de mi Vida*

FROM: *Su Hombre*

SUBJECT: Our Anniversary or My Seven Years with Spanish Fire

March 26, 1947, New York. Fateful night, fatal woman. The beginning of a little weekend—364 weekends—with a Danish Spaniard too. No one believes it, but I should be thin and haggard, and I'm not. Something went wrong somewhere, but I love you. I loved you so much the first year and now I love you seven times that much. Again, no one will believe it but us.

The premiere of Anaïs Nin the actress (on the screen that is) this Monday. Special showing Monday through Friday. Awful Coronet man hasn't sent out announcements yet, and I'd not have known if I hadn't called Renate today. Ken stayed up seven nights without sleep cutting film, Paul three and had just collapsed when I called. There are two shows Monday—seven and nine. I'll go to the late one and then to the party afterward.

Don't get too tired. We'll have a big night first night in Mexico City. We'll get to the nightclubs this time. I'll leave here Sat. or Sun., April 2nd or 3rd, and will be in Mexico 8th or 9th. Will meet you at airport. Don't want you there first unless it can't be avoided. Wire me at Hotel Geneva your arrival time, Mexico City time.

My major occupation so far it seems has been bringing you down to earth again, but soon we will be flying together and only come down when the air gets too rarified to breathe. I love you always.

R

Letter from Rupert Pole to Anaïs Nin:

Sierra Madre, March 30, 1954

Darling,

So tired and so much to do yet before I get off but do want to get a note off before I leave.

Well, last night was the great premiere (*Inauguration of the Pleasure Dome*)—saw it twice—it was pretty much all that we've said before. The color is really beautiful and striking, and Ken did fine job of cutting. No more meaning or integrity than before, but good acting and beautiful effects. Cameron all death white with bright flaming hair, Renate all flesh-colored with red tine, Paul very golden, lots of sun. And you, my love, were really beautiful; your entrance in the cage was superb. You looked so happy and literally shone with radiance. I'm going to photograph you a lot this trip—you're very photogenic with soft light and the right angles and when you're in motion, not frozen in one position. Hope you see it in NY. Ken is going out there about 4th or 5th (with film) and has your address.

So soon now we'll be dancing close again. Our first night in Mexico, (remembering what the city does to us anyway) is going to be a real Pleasure Dome, not an artificial one dressed up in a costume.

Till then

R

New York, April 9, 1954

On Tuesday I telephoned Rupert. (I always tell him I am staying at Eduardo's bachelor apartment where there is no phone as it is only a pied-à-terre between his long trips.) He was preparing to leave for Mexico City, driving to meet me there tomorrow evening. The excitement began then, a pleasurable excitement, such a contrast to the painful experience of meeting the press. This was a party planned by Miss Parker of British Book Centre, to which twenty critics were invited and none came except William Rogers of the Associated Press and Maxwell Geismar. The others had more important things to do, one of them receiving a free copy of an encyclopedia with his name embossed in gold. The night before I got ill, vomiting, and saying to Hugo at two, "Don't give me medicine. It won't help. This is a spiritual nausea against commercialism. I do such beautiful writing, and I have to face such humiliations as this."

The party, on a genuine basis, was a success, and covered up the failure, the indifference of Harvey Breit, of Charles Rollo, of *Harper's*, *Vogue*, of *Saturday Review of Literature*, etc. Because William Rogers was the most important of all the critics, my publisher Felix Morrow (British Book Centre) said, "I am pleased." But I did not delude myself on my failure. Max, loyal of course, a loyalty born of friendship and desire, said, "*Spy* is your best book." But every one of my "public" presentations has pointed out my failure as an artist, my failure to receive my due, the respect my work should command.

I hated to be exposed to this. I had to work it out in analysis, realizing once again the small, intimate and genuine loyalties and the proved indifference outside of this small group.

Rogers called up a few days later. He does courageous work for the good artists, in ballet, music and literature, giving the Associated Press news of an art world they are not interested in.

New York, April 1954

One night at a nightclub Rupert and I were given a table right beside the bandstand, and we were drenched in the jazz that exploded from the trombone, the clarinet, trumpet, piano and drums. The subtle, the incredibly developed variations of these accomplished dexterous players. The increasingly accelerated rhythms of the blood, the mounting ecstasy. I felt that next to the wild moments of passion with Rupert, I loved this jazz, and then the beach at Acapulco and then more music, and I turned towards

Rupert and asked him: "Tell me what your greatest pleasures are, in order of their importance," and Rupert answered unhesitatingly: "First when we are together, in bed, then music, then the beach, and then our talking together, when we enjoy our intellectual life together, your writing—they all form a whole that I enjoy, and then jazz, like this jazz, and music of both kinds.

Jazz is the music of the body. I wish I could give back to the jazz musicians the joys they have given me. I feel jazz in my blood, in my nerves, in my flesh. I receive the drumming in my body. I didn't say all this well enough in *A Spy in the House of Love.* I have so much more to say—I can't catch up with all I know. I hope I will be given the time. Sometimes when I think of death I think merely that it would be too bad, for I have not yet yielded up all the treasures I have collected. The chemistry I am producing of turning experience into awareness is not yet finished.

What a contrast of this evening to that of sitting in a large hall at Caltech listening to a Brahms quartet—the spiritual continuity, the eternal quality, the deeper layers of soul and feeling. The jazz musicians are Dionysian people, seeking fire and impulse and ecstasy from drugs.

There is such a subtle way of metamorphosing one's life. If forestry proved too earthy, too prosaic, too close to farming, I never opposed it or expressed my dislike of it to Rupert. But I expressed such response to Rupert's musicianship, his interest in the quartets, and even said what I loved best after Rupert the lover was Rupert the musician, so that Rupert was inspired to play often, to rehearse even. And now this element is pervading our advice to picnickers, cleaning of campgrounds, re-seeding, and photographing flood damage, giving to our life the color and depth that Rupert, to my great surprise, felt that my writing gave him, for I always thought he could have dispensed with my art, since he does not particularly care for reading and has not even read me too carefully!

He asked, "Would you rather I were a jazz musician?"

"Oh no, darling, we are not in the mood for jazz every day; that is only an intermittent mood whereas your other music is deeper and more continuously a match to your temperament."

In every book I have written I was faced with a painful conflict of protecting someone. Now I would like to write about my trips in America and Mexico with Rupert and Acapulco alone. I can't. That is what drove me into poetry. Max Geismar is right: it is fear, not of material, but of human consequences.

How, how, how can I tell all without damage, betrayal, murder even?

In jazz there are all the volcanic explosions of the drums, the wails, the moans, the sensual vibrations. And above all, in bebop, the curious mystery of the withheld theme known to the negro musician but kept a secret, and then he gives us only the variations, free associations, the peripheral explorations. This is so close to my own destiny; I too withheld the theme (diary) and played all the music permitted me to play.

Lillian, the heroine of the new book, will be caught between nature and the city, between life of the body and the synthetic life, between nature and the distillations of art. Was the swamp, the lagoon, the jungle, less than Max Ernst's swamps, lagoons and jungles? Was the desert less than Tanguy's deserts and the ruins less beautiful than Chirico's roofless columns?

So much to tell. Lillian deserted her husband, returned to find him younger, relived the beginning of her marriage and discovered the errors. So many stories… The American prisoner in Tehuantepec, the guide who invited tourists to visit him and then asked for money to free him. Lillian's sympathy and intuitive doubts. The discovery that as soon as the tourists left, the prisoner and jailer shared the haul, went to the café together and to the whorehouse, until the American was poor again and jailed himself once more. Lillian was more combative, sought out the American ambassador to report the case of the jailed American. The jailed sailors in Acapulco were tenderly rescued by an Irish anthropologist. Then there was the zoo owner whose helper stole the animals and returned the next day to sell them to him again. The ex-President's mansion with rooms occupied by tropical birds, and snakes asleep in the bathtub. Every scene in ochre yellow pierced with dazzling light, altering the tone of cruelty. The stabbed Mexican staggering across the beach in the floodlights of the nightclub, his shirt all bloody. Violence and innocence. The dirt floors in the huts, the cribs hanging down from the ceiling, and as in oriental homes, minimal possessions—one trunk of goods, one set of clothes, one shawl perhaps. This reduction appealed to Lillian, this great simplification forced by poverty.

Her friendship with Pablo at the post office, who wanted only stamps from foreign countries and postcards from America. Through him the discovery of the pueblo's night life. The leap over a trench to enter cafés that were antechambers to the whorehouse. A young man absolutely without hair, singing. The whores modest and submissive. Discovery of Lillian's inability to be alone; first of all, the feeling of desertion when people did not invite her out, even when they were people she did not want to be with; worse, evenings when she forced herself to go out with the slaughterhouse man from Chicago. Mr. Pam, she called him. Or the Mexican doctor. The lonely hitchhiker. The virgin who felt his first lovemaking was like a Christmas tree and was grateful. The widower who rented a motorboat to see the dawn at a far-off beach. The pool at midnight. Will you float me home? The pool locked. New Year's fireworks in contrast to a family Fourth of July.

Paul's appearance and how he seems to destroy Lillian's joyousness. He is a pale dreamer, ill at ease in frivolity. Annette dressed like an African.

The guitarists, the two girls in love with the guitar-playing doctor. One left weeping on the stairs. Cockfights. American girl frightened by her lover's intensity and asking what he meant by repeating during lovemaking: "*Eres mi vida, mi vida!*"

I remember standing backstage at the YMHA waiting to deliver my speech at the end of Hugo's films, the Barrons' strange music from the age of anxiety and the age of nerves so well described by Lippold's wire mobiles and structures, and feeling: I can't talk now. It is wrong I should talk now, yield to the American need for explanations, footnotes, indexes, interpretations. It kills the magic, dissolves the mood. Hugo wants me to speak. He now knows why. He himself is the person who needs the explanation.

Now that my relationship with Rupert has deepened and I have gained in balance, why can't I break with Hugo? I keep saying he will be the husband of my maturity, but his own is so delayed, and Rupert is maturing so fast that soon he will catch up. Perhaps the difference is that in this game of life with Rupert I am aware of all the traps, frustrations and dangers that inevitably issue from two human beings trying to live in union with different dreams and temperaments.

Hugo would never have answered as Rupert did at the nightclub...the same answers as mine to the basic importance of passion, music and Acapulco. The negative Hugo (kind, paternal, selfless, non-excited, non-present, giving me the father I needed and no more, not the companion to my youthfulness) was bad for me. But the positive Hugo (self-assertive, possessive, ambitious, egocentric, needing a staff and luxury, cumbered with possessions and needs, coarse and obvious in his joyous moments, but never light) is not good for me either. I do not know what ties me to him. I once thought it was fear of Rupert's inevitable desertion. But when I think of Hugo, I think of nothing that attracts me. I think of a complicated, cumbersome and labored life. The best month we had together was creating *Jazz of Lights*.

Strangely, his letters touch me; they contain none of that aggression or combativeness that he expresses with body and face. They contain only the great sincerity and humility and a courageous search for the truth, not the aggressions. I think of him as ill-humored, worried, always anxious or tense over something. Yet I know objectively that is not all true. Perhaps the joyous Hugo is there when I am gone. I have seen him joyously dancing at Harlem, but there is still in him something that alienates me.

I think we have been bad for each other.

Back on my treadmill of unsolved problems.

I feel I can live now with an acceptance of Rupert's superficial infidelities, that I have more confidence and strength.

The three of us are changing, evolving. I think of the happy ending, Rupert strengthened, able to love a woman his age, free of fears and no longer in need of emotional protection, Hugo free of anxieties about money, able to take the $60,000 he has and stop investing it, and make out of this a simple artist life without a car or penthouse—as I would, in Paris—with plenty of the rich nourishment provided by the artist life. Yet when I asked this of Hugo seven years ago, he refused.

Dream: I am in a foreign city that seemed at first to be Paris. It looked like the very fine pen point structures of Ynez Johnston, all greys and whites and soft colors. I was happy. I was shopping for a black and turquoise sweater for Rupert while he was doing other errands. The shopkeeper asked me for coupons. I said I did not have coupons, but money. He said he would prefer that when I returned to America I send him a sausage. I went back to the car and waited for Rupert. There was a river, like the Seine, only exceedingly colorful and filled with little sailboats with orange sails and fantastically shaped boats of all kinds. One boat was standing still in the middle; it reminded me of a train signal house. Another was like a gigantic caterpillar. It lifted its huge machine to give a gentle push to keep the boats from bumping against the shore, kept them floating in the middle channel. I was amazed at the simplicity of the device. As long as they were kept away from the shore, they floated. Then I found myself amidst a group of people who were preparing to act in a play. They told me what was expected of me. A man would enter and I was to enact a lover's meeting scene. Only then did I realize I was in Italy and I could not speak Italian. But the directress said she would coach me. My net stockings had long threads at the toes that I had to cut off. I felt they should have asked Rupert who was the actor and knew Italian.

April 1954
Mexico trip with Rupert

Letter from Hugh Guiler to Anaïs Nin:
New York, April 1954

I have been going through a psychological crisis. Superficially I was taking the bank's negative attitude about my possible return well, but apparently it has affected me unconsciously. At the same time I got a negative answer from Roy Archibald, and the two together depressed me. Apparently I want, while having rebelled, to be taken back and taken care of, so I had built up going back as a necessity. And today I got a fifty dollar fine for not having my auto use stamps on the car. Also, more frustrations with the films. As a result, I have nightmares of being condemned to death, and I have been going through a kind of suicidal period in my unconscious, which is plain destructive. Fortunately I got on to it by myself, as soon as I had the dreams, and Bogner helped me today to elucidate them further.

It is all very exaggerated, much like your reactions to some of your setbacks, partly real, but also partly self-made, and I am now getting myself straightened out. It has been just as exaggerated as my reaction to the loss of my stock in 1930. The big difference is that in this crisis, I have been able to correctly interpret my own dreams instead of having to have someone slap me to bring me to my senses (as you slapped me when I became hysterical and threatened to commit suicide) and to make a beginning of waking up by myself, followed by help from Bogner. But she had to point out some disagreeable things, my utter lack of sense of reality where my emotions are involved. I juggle my budget to suit these emotions and like or dislike people according to whether they are my kind or not. All a lack of objectivity. What a struggle. But at least I have made a beginning of awareness, and I am actually acting in life better than my unconscious tends to prompt me to do.

My relationship with my father is characterized by fear and hostility. This had the effect of creating a self-image of a person removed from the practical world but thinking that in so doing he was entering a greater reality.

The removal was not entirely the act of the convinced mystic, and I was always too physical to be anyone but the special kind of mystic (and I discovered that this kind did not exist) who had his feet on the ground and his head in the stars. The removal of myself from the actual scene was made with a glance over my shoulder to see if anyone was looking. It was I who was looking for confirmation and approval of my withdrawal, and when I did not get it I went back and argued with words in an effort to persuade and convince. It was not enough for me to have my private world. I must bring others into it because eventually I had goods—I discovered goods—the competent banker, solid achievements in engraving and then in motion pictures.

Theoretically I do believe in my work in the movies, and I take joy in its creation and believe it is certainly a very real part of me. But I may not believe this unconsciously because of the pressure of that person who is looking over my shoulder, another father, another me sometimes represented by the "man in the street" (my father again, probably) whom I must drag in and get his approval. Whether he is ready to give it or not, he must give it now so that I can go on. And it is not evidenced that *I believe in my work*, have confidence in my own judgment. If I can now gradually grow confidence in myself, then I will no longer demand so aggressively that other eyes turn my way, nor be so afraid when they do.

I could gain a reputation as the best filmmaker of my time and it would give me no satisfaction, because my real objective is to win the debate with a dead man (my father). Bogner finally focused me on the heart of the problem, and added that this is why I constantly sabotage the successes I work for.

Bogner says we have only begun clarifying this and we have much more work to do, as she says it is a very interesting and complex problem to unravel.

Got your letter today and am so glad you understand that working all this out with Bogner does not mean that I cannot accept it from you, just that the only place I can work it out is in my own unconscious and that is something that has to be opened up by objective surgical hands, just like any hidden place in the body.

I also often see, perhaps more clearly than you are able to at a particular moment, some of the answers to your problems, the problems of others being relatively easy to see, but I know that I am not the one who can help you to get at them and that all I can do is avoid feeling personally hurt when they seem to work themselves out on me, and try on the contrary to be sympathetic. I know neither of us can be objective enough all the time, but I know we are both trying.

Love,

Hugo

New York, May 1954

I spent twenty days in Acapulco with Rupert. Never has a period of my life seemed more like a dream, a dream in which I wept with joy.

It seemed, at the time, to be the only reality of my life. Everything contributed to it a dreamlike atmosphere. I was spared the hardship of driving with Rupert from Los Angeles. I climbed on a plane, dressed all in white, with a leopard skin beret, bag, earrings. I arrived late. Rupert was already in the hotel room. He had time to bathe, dress, clean, and eat dinner. He leaped towards me. We intended to go out, but could not until we had repossessed each other. In Mexico City, in the altitude, we never feel well, but mysteriously we have always been most sensual. Nights to remember, always. And then a nightclub, Rio Rosa, dancing and drinking. But we were still awake in the spring night, irritable due to the pressure of altitude, tense. We drove out the next morning to Cuernavaca. It was a Sunday. It was overflowing, the cafés were crowded. A heavy rainfall spoiled the afternoon, drenched us.

That night Rupert was ill, as he always is once in Mexico. Fever, vomiting. I took him into my arms, wanting to make him well.

But the next morning he wanted to drive to Acapulco. We did. He had a fever still. The drive was harsh, difficult. The new road is not yet ready, the old torn up. We drove over rocks, dust, over riverbeds, new tar, gravel.

In spite of this, the sight of Acapulco Bay was like a mirage long desired for years. In all the world, the maximum beauty. No need of painters. No need of anything but eyes to see.

Habit led us to the same Hotel Las Anclas where we always stay. At what moment did the drug of Acapulco enter our veins? When we first saw the bay? The sunset with its interior of shell rose, so much like the flesh of Venus? The palms that create a landscape distinct from all others, which make other trees seem fussy, like a woman with her hair too curly, too many ribbons, jewelry, other trees with their gossipy, chattering small leaves, their thin and crowded twigs? The palm has a naked elegance. Its stylized body lean and pliant, nude, throwing all of its adornment into a woman's nakedness and luxuriant hair (*chevelure*), the plunging plumes and feathers of Mistinguett.

The palm has a graceful beauty. It is languid. A child or an abstract painter can draw it easily, a sensuous feather duster ever sweeping the tropical skies of clouds and mists, keeping it brilliant even into the night.

At what point did the drug begin to act upon us?

First we had to chase out of the bureau drawers a mouse well-fed on flower petals, who scarcely managed to escape, so fat she had grown unmolested by tourists. Then we asked for ice for our Martinis and remembered that impatience is a major faux pas in Mexico, a breach of taste, a futile gesture too, one that is inevitably frustrated by the Mexicans, just as tyranny might be resisted by some other nation. It awakens the most solid resistance. A smile, a joke, any other way will be effective, but not impatience. It is the sin against timelessness.

Rupert not being well, we did not rush into swimming.

But from then on, even after we moved to a bungalow and were free to eat anywhere, our days were spent at the beach and our evenings dancing, and as I remember it all seemed like *La Ronde* except that we played out all the various love affairs between just the two of us.

Wild, high waves, wind, suntanning. The water warm, elating. The swimming, then the ride back to lunch in our own bungalow, a siesta, another swim in the afternoon at Hornos, shower and dressing, Martinis, dinner out, driving in the open car, the soft night, and music. The gentleness of the Mexican voices dissolved me, then by the songs I was carried by a musical aerial notation, Lippold's scaffold in sound, to a harp being played while we ate dinner on the square, to the marimbas, to the jukeboxes filled with Cuban mambos, a street singer, a nightclub singer, and always the sea, rhythms, a sound of being washed, of being lulled, drugged yet never more alive, alive with the body only, warmth, sea, sun, lovemaking all interwoven, and the musical notations in the air, waves of sounds linking sea, dancers, swimmers in a rotation so sweet, so complete that I sat and wept with joy. At Bum-Bum, an African bamboo hut, the sea's washing of the sand and shells was like a strange anarchistic theme upon which the mambos and American jazz played their accelerations of the pulse in the same quickness of desire and languor of completion that love practiced upon our bodies.

Another night, in another African hut, this one high on a mountain above the bay, when a spotlight from the nightclub lit up a leafless jacaranda, looming like a giant Japanese design against the purple mountains, the lights of Acapulco, and a bay that had the texture of silk, I wept with joy again, not only at the still, serene beauty, but at the soft, tender breath of the tropical night so rich in tone, perfumes and textures that it seems to touch you physically; this night, so voluptuous, whispers to the cells of the body, and one can reach across a table to the rough-hewn hands of Rupert, who embodies the night, an essence of all lovers, always present, alert sensually, always responsive to the currents of the music, the rhythms, colors, perfumes. His body within reach, to dance with, to hold. He photographs the night, as I did with my senses. The way the waters lie, for the waters of the bay are like capricious bolts of silk that have a sinuous way of lying to offer different exposures to light, sometimes reflecting and other times elusive, ruffled, and contradictory green opposing the mountains' heavy violets, asserting turquoise obstinately against a crudely orange sunset—or like that sleeping night, having enfolded into itself all the colors of the day and night, creating the ineffable colors of sleep no painter has been able to name or reproduce.

The body photographs the night, wants to take into itself its touch and its voice. Its voice is languid, like the hammock.

The first time I wept; I thought only the Latins and the negroes were right, that happiness is in the physical life. At least I can say I had it. But it is late now, a little late to devote myself to the life of the body.

In Acapulco I could not think or remember, but the serpent that lay coiled awaiting the moment to inject its passion was patient. I know its name. It is Art. The need of art, the need to be an artist, the curse of it, the unrequited gift to the world. I knew what awaited me. The enormous, the stark, harsh defeat. Nothing can cover it up. The party for *Spy* at the British Book Centre, the words or letters of friends, the reviews, they are all like flowers for the dead.

As an artist, America has killed me, killed me with insults, blindness, deafness, indifference. I can name all the offenders; that is the reality. They could not kill the life and beauty of my writing, but they could slowly strangle the books; even Maxwell Geismar uses inadequate words: "surrealist novel." And there is the irony of adding the vivid, warm personal note, by contrast.

Acapulco had anaesthetized me against this poison, I believed. But the anesthetic wore off as soon as I landed in New York.

One radio interview with George Hamilton Combs, sensitive and intelligent and gentle.

One with a slapstick, horseplaying comedian, Barry Gray.

One stupid review by Jerome Stone in *Saturday Review of Literature.*

And nobody, nobody lifts a finger to fight for me, to defend me, neither Edmund Wilson, nor Geismar, nor Wallace Fowlie, nor Charles Rollo…

La Ronde passed quickly, too quickly. I seek to evoke it, to recapture the pleasures.

Letter from Anaïs Nin to Rupert Pole:

New York, May 8, 1954

Darling: I kept thinking of you driving home, and it was hard to concentrate on the present. It's a good thing I didn't postpone my return. The day after I arrived I had a half hour radio interview by George Hamilton Combs on "Spotlight" at WABC. Combs, although he had not read the book, was extremely gentle, intelligent and sympathetic. I was unprepared, yet I managed to be humorous, and not too shy. BBC's only criticism was that I "not aggressive enough," but the reaction of the public was good.

Next day an autograph party at Gotham. Very successful, full, from three-thirty to seven, a stream of people. Last night at midnight Barry Gray's program at WMCA (of the *Post*). He was as vulgar and cheap as Combs was subtle. Jim Herlihy heard me and said I made him appear a cheap fool and kept a gentle poise, humorous again, and silent when his questions were too silly. Jim said you would have been proud.

But I came home alone at one-thirty (talk was at one in the morning) blue and thinking I had handled him well. He said at the beginning that he'd fallen asleep at the first page, and I answered very sweetly: "You seem awfully young to fall asleep while reading a love story."

But I'm *not* a career woman—I hate it all.

Then I have a whole evening discussion with the Writing Class at New School, a reading at a ballet school, etc. What a month!

I'm going to be on TV in Los Angeles June 4. "Cavalcade of Books"—very important. They usually only take successful books. So I will arrive June 3rd at night. I have to prepare for the show the next day. This will stimulate sales, I know.

Sometimes I close my eyes and all of our moments in Acapulco pass before me incredibly dreamlike and perfect.

Te quiero

A

Letter from Anaïs Nin to Jerome Stone:

New York, May 1954

The ambivalence of your review of *A Spy in the House of Love* interested me.

In your last paragraph you indicate that my new book is "neither as psychologically profound nor as poetically imaginative" as my earlier works, which might be taken to mean that my earlier works *were* poetically imaginative and psychologically profound. However, your first statement was that my former books were "dream-haunted, phantasmagoric and defeatingly esoteric." Isn't that contradictory?

The poetic novel, may I say, is not esoteric. I share this common literary form with Isabel Bolton, Jean Giraudoux, Georges Bernanos, Isak Dinesen, Anna Kavan, George Barker, Virginia Woolf. Perhaps you never read Truman Capote or Tennessee Williams either.

Then you also state, rather disparagingly, that here is a most explicit description of "five sexual encounters." If I have been so explicit, how is it you did not notice that only three of the "encounters" were purely sexual, one was a marriage, the other a non-sexual relationship?

I am very curious to know by what qualifications you happened to be given such a book to review. We are all aware today that there are very few serious, professional, educated literary critics, and a great preponderance of untrained, unskilled, immature reviewers. Yet it is a work of great responsibility: *you* are the interpreter, the guide, the clarifier for the public. You are the middleman, in part responsible for what people read.

If you are a young writer (which I would assume for the immaturity and arrogance of the review), all I can wish is that your life's sincere work may not fall into hands like yours.

I hope my letter may cause you to hesitate when you review your next book.

I am certain that you only read one of the earlier books, probably *Under a Glass Bell*. In that very book there was a story called "Birth" that was as direct, simple and realistic as Hemingway. You would not remember it. The novels were related to each other, the characters continued from novel to novel. As they appeared, the meaning of their lives grew clearer. When a writer gives his entire life to his work, I think he has a right to expect a more thoughtful, more objective, more responsible study. I would like to know who you are to feel you can pass judgment, evaluate a work you have not even been able to read accurately and to pass judgment on poetry, imagination or psychological depth. Your own lack of psychological depth is revealed in your observing only the most superficial aspects of the book. Evidently the presence of sex in the book prevented you from studying the multiple other aspects of Sabina's character, the much wider implications of her behavior.

Anaïs Nin

New York, May 1954

I wrote to Wallace Fowlie, asking him why he had deserted me. He did not write to me for five years or more, never tried to see me in New York, and finally devoted a chapter to Henry Miller in his book on surrealism while ignoring me. His response was that he "was overcome" by my letter's "injustice." "In what way have I abandoned you as a friend and a writer?" he asks. He said his book on surrealism was on the movement in France, and that he "never expected to receive such a letter, especially from one I continue to respect and esteem."

Max Geismar sent me his review of *Spy* and says that he wants the book to appeal to the ordinary reader. He added, "The first drafts of this review were so ecstatic I toned them down in the interest of not having it seem like a blurb."

Letter from Anaïs Nin to Max Geismar:

New York, May 1954

You're right, of course, that friendship does not break down because one does not understand the other's work. There is a lot in your work that I may have failed to get too. But now that time has passed and we are both more objective, I do want to explain what bothered me in spite of the fact that I know you meant well. It was not what is called a rave review I wanted from you. But I felt you did not understand the novel. Faced with a theme in which the problem was to go deeper into the motivations of Don Juanism, to go beyond the usual story, to go deep into its meaning, dissociation of the personality, the break in the wholeness of love, to re-write, in our terms, *Madame Bovary*. You, I felt, were embarrassed by open sexual scenes and, as a result, flippant in the use of "amorous exploits," taking away the gravity of the neurotic conflict. That was one point. Another is that Sabina sought man's liberation in separating the pleasures of sensuality from the pains of love, but failed to do so. To win your heart and your respect one has to write a bad book against Senator McCarthy, and that is what made me sad for good, and divorced from America, that literature as an art has nothing to do with themes, time, and the so-called mainstream of life, which we quarreled about before, but that is your sociological point of view, irreconcilable with the point of view that builds for eternity, not the small circle of family, country, etc. This is why I no longer want to talk this over, because they are opposite points of view. I am continuing the work of Freud, which I believe more valuable than the work of Marx. If we had gone deeper into Freud, we might have emerged wiser and nobler, politically, than we are. Freud knew what lay behind all these wars and camps and cruelties, and until we face that we can't progress. That is what I believe. Our failure (wars) proves the error of Marxism; but anyhow, you have to go on with your work and I with mine. Mine is psychological deep sea diving and America's literature is just the opposite. The time will come to balance the true psychological realism with the external one. Meanwhile you, *who are the best and sincerest of them all*, still represent what I have to deny in favor of psychological research and experimentation. Of course, you win, you know. I am the loser, the failure in this present scene. My next book will not be read here, for American writing is committed to false realism. And until neurosis is recognized as symptomatic of the negative presence of a negative unconscious, we will continue to refuse the inward voyage I believe essential to wholeness, the whole vision you talked about. I am sure of my faith, but lonely. You are lucky; you need not be lonely. Your point of view is shared. I am working hard now on the finale of the novels, a long book, which I will publish in France, where I hope to return one day. I don't believe that social awareness is what will destroy McCarthy, but psychological awareness. I'm working from the other end, and it's a damn lonely one, with everyone feeling virtuous when they write about pertinent themes, or about the Cinerama events, which are merely bigger projections of a million, individual, personal hostilities. It is like waiting for the world to realize that instead of more jails, they should provide psychological help for children before they become delinquents. I have a long wait. But I will inherit the world of Freud one day.

Anaïs

New York, May 1954

Peggy Glanville-Hicks restored my courage. By a gesture towards the book, a phrase, a tilt of her head, she gives to *Spy* an absolute, total valuation: "It is the only new writing. It is what writing will be. It's a perfect work of the intuitive intellect."

She believes it is the intellectuals who block the way by their subjection to tradition. People who are not highly cultured receive intuition with less difficulty.

She feels I cannot return to what I believe is the European source of my work, because I have gone beyond it. Does that mean that those who were loyal to Joyce, Woolf, Giraudoux, Barnes, will not be to me? In a strange way, I am quite aware of the stature of my work. I reread *Spy* today with utter delight. It is a beautiful piece of music, and it is full of awareness. I am proud of it.

For me, people with intuition are like wall-less houses, ballets, abstract painting, music. They are transparent, and you are never in danger of breaking your head against a brick wall. With all of Henry Miller's genius, and Max's brilliance of mind, they are non-intuitive (Henry because he was too earthy, Max because he is earthy and intellectual). There was always an interference with the penetrative or absorbent activities. It is not the physical youth of Jim and Rupert, but the swiftness and directness of intuition, the vibratory, the sensitized awareness (neither one of them has *intellect*, or learning).

Jim's lyrical improvisations about my writing came closer to what I want to hear: it is the response on equal terms, it has to do with the freedom that lies in jazz, in the unconscious, in the poet, in children, in Jim and Rupert, so that without the impediment of maturity, they seize upon the convolutions of sensations better than the Edmund Wilsons and the Geismars. I will never forget Henry Miller saying when he first read *The House of Incest*: "Is it any more than brocade?"

A letter that pleased me keenly was Joaquín's, for the first time saying something about my work! He was, until now, silent, evasive.

Mary Green, of the *New Leader*, who was employed by BBC to get me on the radio, is sincere and intelligent. She said, "I have felt uneasy, unhappy even, about getting you in the hands of such people as Barry Gray, wondering if it was a kind of crime to expose you to that, whether it was not best to leave you in your literary world."

But in the first place, my literary world has not treated me so very well. The intellectual critics have not even studied me. Wilson started me off, but because of a small personal quarrel did not continue to review me. So what I feel is this: naturally I do not expect to be a popular writer, but there is an in-between world of people I want to make a bridge with, who are not intellectual snobs, who have intuition and can accept intuitive emotional works directly. I know they exist because I am in touch with them. They write me the simple, emotional letters. I'm willing to work at making this bridge.

I had also in mind my deepest disappointment, Geismar's review, although objectively I realize his true love is the sociological novel, not literature, and that he is weakest in his estimates of books as literature, and that his knowledge of poetry and style is not even comparable to a minor intellectual such as Wallace Fowlie, who nevertheless interprets the poets perfectly in spite of his religious bias.

Mary Green's radical political life has not interfered with her enjoyment of my work or her estimate of Miller.

While reading Malraux's *Voices of Silence*, Hugo wept over the theme of loneliness. I showed great compassion and yet I said what I believe: "Loneliness is self-made."

He discouraged all my attempts at drawing him out, until analysis finally achieved this. But his loneliness is also due to the fact that he lacks to such a great degree a sense of aliveness, which makes me want to escape his company.

Annette and her green gate

I met Annette Nancarrow when I was alone in Acapulco, at the Hotel Mirador. I sat in the dining room, and when I saw her come down the stairs, my eyes were caught by the brilliance of her dress. She used the entire palette of Mexican colors and textures from many places, but artistically. She wore barbaric jewelry. We became friends.

We talked on the terrace at night after dinner while waiting to see what the evening would bring. In spite of her children, two boys of seven and nine, the men treated her like a young woman. Her laughter was inviting, and as she lay on the chaise longue, she offered herself. Her body was explicit. All its erotic and brilliant covering was a plumage she was uncomfortable with because her natural state was nudity.

She was without discrimination about men, so I found it difficult to go out with her. I couldn't flirt and provoke men I did not like as she did, like a nightclub singer. She never conserved her charm or refused anyone the full spectacle of her tropical displays.

Acapulco was a beautiful background for her. Her skin was naturally swarthy, and the suntan suited her. She seemed like a native, in harmony with Acapulco, except for a head designed by Toulouse-Lautrec. She was natural, talkative, fluent, and always effervescent.

Her arrival in New York, to begin her life with Stan Smith, a newspaper man, was a regression to what I sensed had been her life before Mexico, before her life as a rich oil man's wife, before her incrustations of travel, international friendships, exotic colors. My intuition was justified when I met her sister, a simple New York Jewish girl, commonplace, and Annette had returned, in her life with Stan, to some familiar early atmosphere.

But when she took her apartment on 3rd Avenue, she brought into it her acquired atmosphere, her Orozco paintings, her jewelry made of fragments unburied from the old Aztec and Mayan and Zapotec grounds. And when Hugo and I went to visit her she did not meet us behind an ordinary dark door, but behind a gay, latticed green garden gate, hung with Mexican bells, with a bird cage overhanging, and some of Mexico's sun and music had been transplanted there, with Annette in a violent orange dress and a piece of heavy jewelry, tinkling like a bell, moving as if she were either emerging from or re-entering her sheath dress. On the windows, on the bed, on the floor were the woven and embroidered textures of Oaxaca, clay figurines and stone pieces.

To see Annette walking down Broadway or eating a sandwich in a delicatessen, after having completely identified her with Acapulco, was difficult because we shared a passion for Acapulco and we shared the same dream; only she, being economically independent, fulfilled it. She built herself a house in Acapulco.

But the house was barely finished when Stan appeared, representing the "Fish and Fowl" column of the *Post*, and everything she had escaped for twenty years. Annette, bravely and gaily, and with Mexican panache, came home again to a smaller, shabbier life. These circles no one escapes.

The Hugo of this month was a Hugo depressed because he had offered his services to the bank and the bank did not respond immediately. This morning, the last "scene" may be the key to the depression he gives me.

During the week, while he was taking still pictures for publicity about his film, I spied an iridescent horse in a display window, stylized and magical, and we decided to investigate. We found out that the shop belonged to a man called the King of Feathers who had dressed Mae West and fan dancers, feather-covered dancers. In the store workshop a woman (who was absent that morning) designed the horse and other extraordinary figures for the window displays, abstract and imaginative enough to be used in a film. For a moment, the pleasure of discovering an artist, new materials, the use of plastics, beads, textures, and talking with the Feather King was pure. Hugo was enthusiastic. But soon his mind turned the encounter into a business concern and the entire situation clouded. He committed various inconsistencies: trying to interest the old Feather King in his films (not realizing the abyss between this man's taste and Hugo's work), trying to present the possibility of making a film that would "sell" the figures to window displayers (a film vastly different from Hugo's way of making films), getting interested in the Feather King's talk about the need of a salesman, Hugo saying he was "broke" and needed a job, seeking to reconcile two impossible, irreconcilable worlds, muddling them, confusing his need of a job with his filmmaking.

The result was that my interest ceased. I knew the film we would make would not please the Feather King.

If I had to face the economic problem, I would separate it from my work.

This aborted creative pleasure this morning depressed me.

In my dream of the night before, Rupert and I were about to fly in a diminutive plane, too small for a takeoff in a wooded mountainous place, so we decided to hike instead through jungle and snow, mud and rain, but laughing.

Now, in reality Rupert is not always light and free, but rarely depressed, and usually alive and responsive to adventure and enjoyment. During the recent flood he was smiling at the dangers. He asked me: "Are you enjoying this, or are you frightened?" I found myself answering truthfully: "I enjoy the adventure."

Jim and Dick are elated, feverishly working at painting, plastering, remaking an old apartment. Joyousness.

Years ago in Paris, Kay Bryant, the wife of one of Hugo's co-workers, was ill, and Hugo asked me to visit her in the hospital. It was a friendship not of my own making, but my answering a distress call. Years and years later I hear an old, broken woman's voice over the telephone: "Anaïs, darling. I tried so hard to get a hold of you."

She has spent two years in hospitals. Her husband died. She lives in a small, drab hotel room on a pension for the disabled. She is my age but looks seventy, shrunken, toothless, bent, a skeleton. So she reaches out for me, to pull herself out of this living death. I outfit her with clothes, add a little to her allowance, visit her, give her my books. This helps her. But the relationship is her fabrication and I cannot deprive her of it. At this moment it is the luminous point in the tunnel.

But I revolt against the recurrent demands people make on me: always it is me they want; they want to see *me alone*. Every time I appear in public someone wants to see me alone. A young man wanted to commit suicide, and his friend said, "Wait until you see Anaïs first." So he waits seven years and tries to meet me. Finally he comes to my autograph party.

Perhaps it is the price I must pay (a terrible drain on my strength) for my gift for seeing and contacting the core of others.

Yet why, why, why can't I have this for Hugo? For all the others' weaknesses I have compassion. For Hugo's, anger.

What a turmoil to always be fertile and constantly unable to impose my ideas. I lack the aggression. Somewhere my Spanish fierceness was castrated. Whatever obstacles I encountered in publication (500 pages of the diary in Herbert Alexander's hands for a year and nothing has happened), I felt neutralized by the work on the movies. And now Hugo stops the movies because he cannot be a complete artist and live simply on a small income.

Sierra Madre, July 1954

It is only today, twenty years later, that Hugo discusses the cause of his absence and fogginess (smokescreen to the arts he disapproved of) so that what seemed to be a part of his character from which I suffered (a wintry climate) was not truly his character, but a neurotic excrescence.

This is the personal myth that is then projected onto the exterior and presented as a person's definite character, when it is, on the contrary, an inadequate and negative accretion to the character. To dissipate this is what should occupy us, to find the organic self and free it of its parasites, microbes, tumors and abscesses, fevers and cancers of the soul.

Love occasionally has clairvoyance, as when I reached for the serious and sincere Henry beyond the surrealist clown, or when I reached for the serious, sincere and deep Rupert beyond the compulsive Don Juan. I never saw Rupert's neurotic Don Juanism as clearly enacted as with Joan. Joan is Rupert's friend's girl, a violinist, writer and painter, with a sickly prettiness and cockney accent, rather big, sad eyes I thought attractive. Rupert turned upon her the entire concentration of an act. He was acting charm, thoughtfulness, attentiveness, intimacy. He was creating an artificial bond (bringing out their mutual hobbies), working upon his effects (for example, he never dramatizes the dangers or his heroism in firefighting because he knows I believe in his courage and suffer from the dangers) by engaging her in a detailed dramatization of the time he burnt his hands.

I felt he was not genuinely interested in the girl; as a neurotic, artistic girl she was but a minor, ineffectual Anaïs, and what he does like is what I do not possess, the purely external *jeune fille*, pretty and natural, a delight for the eyes alone. Yet I also felt how he set about (unconsciously) to establish a friendship.

When I brought it up later as a part of what I reproach him with, flirting in my presence, he was truly unaware he had done so. I could see all the compulsions. Elmer, Joan's boyfriend, represents the intellectual, sensitive, non-physical young man. He was puny, delicate and is today filled with obsessions with his health.

Only a few nights before, Rupert and I had slept at his family's, in the little bed he occupied as a boy. After we had made love fiercely, I asked him what he used to think

Anaïs Nin being interviewed in Los Angeles, June 1954

about while lying in bed at the age of sixteen or seventeen. He answered, "I worried about three things: about doing well in school and what I was going to be, my career, etc. Then about my health not being so good and whether I would grow up strong and muscular and manly—I looked *too* sensitive and felt uneasy about this. My third worry was girls. I did not like them; they seemed stupid to me, and I was not interested in them as the other boys were, and that worried me."

These three fears had a great effect on forming what Rupert became: his conflict about a career continued until he found one in which he felt adequate and that strengthened the "manly" rather than the artistic side—the forest ranger. To this he added a love of the outdoors and exceptional courage as a firefighter, succeeding even in strengthening his body so that he looks vigorous and muscular. And about girls, he has an obsession and a fantasy, yet when he met me he was worried about the ephemeral unfulfilling relationship he was then in, and was worried (due to his incapacity to form a deep attachment) about his masculinity. All these worries should have disappeared with his success. But his rapport with girls, his effectiveness as a man, his fear of the artist continue. When I express my jealousies, he admits how he worries about the fact that he does not give me what another man might—the power to make money or to create a bigger life. The rapport with young girls reaffirms his sense of power as a man.

The evening with Joan caused me pain. I no longer create scenes. I asked him quietly about it. He answered with great sincerity. The sincerity of his attitude towards me, and the falseness, the poseur quality, the studied effects of his other relationships, are apparent to me. I get confused because I'm vulnerable. I overestimate his interest, and my own neurosis takes over, in that I visualize women lovelier than I and having more to give Rupert. That night, because I talked quietly in the dark, Rupert and I felt close. He took me with passion. He expresses his own doubts and jealousies when I go to New York or when we see in a movie the wealthy man who gave his wife a household of servants and fairytale luxury.

To separate Rupert's flimsy mirages from our love should be easy, and I have gained much ability in this, but I am still, because of the neurotic tendencies, more vulnerable than I should be. Because I know, too, how many insincere relationships I have engaged in when my true feelings did not direct me, but a thousand other compulsions, neither love nor desire, but a hundred complex myths to be enacted and by which I was enslaved. I should understand when this self takes possession of Rupert.

That night we spent in his boyhood bed, I felt as if I had been given a Rupert of fifteen or sixteen to watch over.

I have, I believe, made it clear that it is not his freedom to live or have other relationships that I tamper with, but his inclination to play these games in my presence. Is it because he feels more confidence in my presence, more power? I do not believe he wants to hurt me, since my "hurt" is a merely neurotic panic that he seems to understand.

He has jealous panics, too, but is equally unaware of them as he is of his flirtations. When Elmer (who is extremely enthusiastic about me and my work) goes into ecstatic gyrations for me, monopolizes me, Rupert is always there to bring us back into general conversations.

This was the only painful moment in two happy, fervent, playful, passionate months. I have finally appreciated the benefits of the physical life in an experience of physical wellbeing, so rare with me. I have appreciated a day of intense writing and the pleasure of the pool, the three "adopted" children, the beach, the cocktails, the music by Rupert, so my "solitude" and longing for the artist life have not been as acute. I had a few crash landings after working, days of *doubts* about the work when I needed help and did not get it, except from Paul and Renate who live in my world entirely and therefore make it stronger for me.

The difference between the genuine Rupert and the pretender showed itself not only in how he behaved when we were alone—a piece of music without dissonances—as compared to the way he behaved socially—an actor on a stage—but also at the moment when he wished to placate me, or felt guilt, or wanted to gain an end, and then acted in a way he did not feel, like a timid young man fearful of my anger. When he was acting he acted like a strangled actor, over-acted.

Rupert Pole, 1954

August 1954
Return to New York by way of San Francisco

New York, August 1954
The last day I spent with my mother I tried to persuade her to dictate the story of her life. I wrote these words: "I was born"...and waited. But she made fun of the idea and I desisted.

She died Wednesday, August 3, 1954 at approximately five in the afternoon.

New York, Thursday, August 12, 1954
Every time I went to visit my mother at Oakland I felt it might be for the last time. She was over eighty, and although not ill, she had had one light stroke some years ago. I was always preparing myself for the separations. I would have liked to be able to sense when I should be there, but then it might have been more terrible. I would have liked to know so that I could express my love, which something in her prevented me from doing fully. I would have liked her to die when we felt the closest (during her last illness, or the time she told me about her father being Jewish).

But it did not happen like this. I had no intuition. It was an ordinary visit.

After dinner, Joaquín and I went to a movie. I wish I had stayed with her, but as she always went to bed at eight or nine, I did not feel it mattered. But before dinner Joaquín, to please me, made Martinis. We became gay and clowned for Mother. I always tell Marius and Olive stories, in the true south of France accent. Mother would smile, but she disapproved of the cocktail. Mother's expression of anger, like my father's expression of severity, was mostly reserved for our acts. The laughter and exuberance were given to strangers. I missed the in-between moods of tenderness, gentleness.

Then at seven-thirty I left. Mother kissed me and said, "Next time you come, stay for more than two days."

At the airport I did not let Joaquín stay until I left. Noise and crowds make intimate talk impossible and the "separation" really begins as soon as one arrives at an airport, so it is better not to delay it, to hang on, to talk like deaf-mutes in the deafening roar of propellers.

"Go home," I said, and Joaquín agreed.

In the plane, I took a Martini and sleeping pill. I did not know that when Joaquín returned home mother was ill with what she thought was stomach trouble. She had vomited and felt pain. When I landed in New York, Hugo told me: "Last night your mother had a heart attack. Joaquín called me at six this morning."

"Last night...why last night? I didn't guess. I could have stayed."

I called Joaquín. Mother was rallying under oxygen and drugs and had talked and joked with him. But the next afternoon she was semi-conscious and did not recognize Joaquín, answered feebly when she was called. That evening she died unconscious, painlessly. Joaquín called me at midnight.

The pain of irrevocable loss. A greater, deeper loss because there was no sense of unity, of fusion, of closeness, which I had struggled for all my life. The cake she baked not yet finished. Her game of solitaire unfinished. That ordinary family last day, nothing to lift it from its ordinariness, the usual family disharmonies. The pain not to have been there, to see her, to help her and Joaquín. Joaquín having to live alone through all the horrors, the loss itself, the finality, and all the details of attending death. Once I called him. He had been fixing her room. I heard him weep. "Joaquín, remember, you made Mother's life very happy for many, many years. She had a happy life. You were a good son."

I rebelled against death. I wept quietly. Every now and then, the sorrow pierced me, in the street, in a movie, at dawn, anytime. The guilt for my rebellions against her. The anguishing compassion for her life... She started at fifteen to be a mother to her six brothers and sisters (because my grandmother Culmell ran off with a lover, to a life with many lovers) and to give them the same fierce protectiveness and courage she gave us. Her brothers and sisters speak of her as her children do: an impossible temper (*un caractère impossible*) and a heart of gold.

I am awaiting Joaquín who had to take her to Cuba where she wanted to be buried beside her beloved father.

We are still like animals. We think we understand intuitively. We do not. My mother closed the door on me the day I sought an independent life from her in my marriage. After that I spent endless efforts on returning to her, being a good daughter. The night she told me about her father being a Jew, she was standing by her closet, looking small and shrunken with age, but looking humiliated by this revelation. Later I consoled her. I praised her and said I was proud of her human virtues.

What a burden of guilt when a mother serves you, does all the menial tasks, feeds you, works for you, but then condemns *what you are*.

Do we all withhold our thoughts and feelings because of this fear of condemnation?

It was only after Father died that Joaquín hung up his photograph as well as Mother's in his bedroom, as if he felt she could no longer fight him after his death. A few years before his death, Father asked if he could come home again, which Mother refused.

The loveliest image of my mother I want to keep is when she stayed here once while an Irish carpenter was building bookcases; he sang Irish songs and my mother sang with him.

Joaquín came to New York on the way back from Cuba, so pale, so dead. And his pain, deeper, more terrible, was added to mine. To see him weep, to see him lost, alone. I tried to give him all the love I could.

Today he is better. He feels the exhaustion caused by the sorrow.

Yesterday at Thorvald's he played the piano for the first time since she died, and after that he wept. This caused in me such a violent re-awakening of my past role towards Joaquín as a substitute mother that I had to control my terrifying impulse to enclose, hold him, protect him, but I had to keep from acting like my mother, had to make myself be tender but not possessive, remind myself he is forty-five years of age and mature, to let him make his own decisions. He is today a remarkable person, not by any means childish as people may expect from his long relationship with my mother. He successfully reversed the roles as my mother grew older and dependent. He imposed his will in the house, took care of Mother, handled great responsibilities as Chairman of the Music Department at Berkeley. He is objective, witty and well-balanced. His sorrow was naturally deep, not neurotic. He handled her death, the problems of her funeral, his relationship with the whole family, his trip to Cuba, well. He respected the taboos, the family customs, the religious rituals. He is charitable and controls his emotions. He decided I should not go to the funeral, first to spare me extra suffering, then because my presence would have made it harder for him (my own emotionalism would have communicated itself to him). He was sustained by his responsibilities. Also, my going would have meant that Thorvald would have to go, and Thorvald is very ill (pernicious anemia).

I, who refused to wash or iron, washed and ironed Joaquín's shirts and felt myself becoming my mother. I took on her maternal virtues, but I also carry within me her defeat: her anger.

Joaquín has no anger. He has become a saint, but human, tolerant. I would have run away from the pain. He has faced it. He is returning to the house two weeks after Mother's death. I did ask him quietly to delay the return. It will be painful. The death of a loved one is like a horrible mutilation; a part of your body is torn from you brutally; you die a little. Then the spirit of the dead one enters into you.

Joaquín inherited Mother's wholeness, I my father's dualities. Joaquín became the respectful and devoted son, religious, who never loved anyone more than his mother, while I forfeited closeness to her by my rebellions and growth. There was a time, at the age of sixteen, twenty years, even until twenty-six when I was more like Joaquín. I was close to my mother then, but I lost her, first by my rebellion against Catholicism, next by my marriage to Hugo and departure from her home, and then by my not having children.

I tried to continue to work when I returned to New York after two very happy months with Rupert when I was truly able to enjoy the scope of my life there, writing all day, an hour at the pool with the little girls I love so much, the movies with Rupert, the beach, to tolerate the evenings with his family and his friends, to have the rare evening with Renate and Paul, and to balance the trivialities and banalities against the emotional and physical fusions with Rupert.

When I returned, Hugo was in a more normal, more neutral phase of analysis, not violently self-assertive, not unstable, but for me, in relation to me, a man only half alive, too moderate, too slow in his rhythm, and with whom I have no contact but friendship. The divorce as man and wife is accomplished. We live fraternally. He received me with fraternal kindness, helped me fraternally through my grief at the loss of my mother, but did not make love to me. He is truly the quiet one. Reading, resting too much when not electrified and vitalized by business, the same monotone voice (I have difficulty hearing him and no one else). "Don't talk like a priest," I said finally, after asking him many times to raise his voice.

The development of his analysis, which has clarified his thinking and calmed his anxieties, has not freed his life, which is like a stagnant subterranean lake. I know he loved my mother, but he did not react when she died. He consoled me; he was full of sympathy. That he was disturbed showed up only in his health. His stomach bothered him, he did not sleep well.

I helped him get interested in a film he wanted to make that requires no money; he has all the material here. He thanked me for the idea. I said I had only helped him as an analyst does, to bring out what he had intended to do.

We live a subdued life.

We drive to the beach, alone, or with Jim. He has taken several people to the beach, but most of his comments on them are negative. He has no fervors, no enthusiasms, no great hatreds. Usually he is negative, cool. This is interesting because I am at work on Lillian's return to her home and children. In musical terms, Lillian is struggling with the muted tones she had not been able to hear.

Felix Morrow says over the telephone: "I have the statements for your book. I am disappointed." But he does not say it bitterly or reproachfully (as Charles Duell did). It is what René expected, no more. René is a realist and spoke quietly: "All I expected was to enlarge your circle of readers. I do not delude myself. You are a tough case, but your recognition will come."

I said to René, "In view of this, in view of the possibility Morrow may not want the next book, why do you make me work, why do you make me write? After all, I could go to the beach and save you from a poor financial venture." I said this playfully. We always talk playfully. He answered me quietly, seriously, saying, "Anaïs, you are one of the great writers of the world. We have plenty of writers who sell, and that is very nice, but I would not be happy just to be handling them. They take care of my living expenses. You are my pleasure. I am proud of you. I think we have accomplished what I wanted to accomplish. More readers. You are alive. People have seen you. Now the expectation is that your next book must sell better. It may be wise to give up trying to finish your Proustian work that requires the reading of four books that are out of print and to write an independent novel. You may have to do that."

He speaks so quietly and reassuringly and tactfully that I always listen. I write him a humorous letter: "Thank you for always making me feel that I am not a dead end kid!"

I expressed gratitude so fully that he telephoned Hugo and said how he would treasure the letter (for it is true I am reaching a dead end in my communication with the world).

Herbert Alexander did not fulfill any of his promises, not out of dishonesty but out of his own self-deception as to the extent of his power: I can, I will. But he could not. He does not rule the System. The System is an army of robots obeying orders from the God of Commerce.

Letter from Rupert Pole to Anaïs Nin:

Sierra Madre, August 1954

Love,

You did sound wistful on phone, but guess I did too. The days have not passed as quickly this time, and I find in spite of all the work I am doing and more I should be doing that I miss you more than ever. The separations make us realize how much the relationship means, but they certainly haven't prepared me to live without you any more than at the beginning. Ah well, stop your moaning, Pole, only two more weeks... you'll live...somehow.

Love, didn't mean to push about the lawyer. I know what you've been through this trip. I only mentioned Hugo because I hope we could avoid a long separation somehow.

So tired tonight, and still have to write a rough draft of the report for an engineer coming tomorrow. So what happens? My father phones a minute ago. He's pleased with himself that he's driven straight down from SF and now of course is determined to stay here.

Here he comes now.

Te quiero más y más—hasta muy pronto—quedamos juntos

R

Sierra Madre, September 1954

My first quarrel with Hugo came after I had talked to René and felt that my two months' writing was being rejected. This caused me such distress that I asked Hugo to read what I had done, over a hundred pages. Lillian (patterned after Thurema—aggression and primitiveness) returns home after "the change" (analysis) and begins to understand her inarticulate husband. I took only *one* aspect of Hugo, the inarticulateness, wrote about it with a new, terrific compassion and dramatized Lillian's new power to decode it. Hugo read in absolute silence. His silence affected me as it always has: like a wall, a kind of destruction. I realized I was in a dangerous moment of desperation regarding the fate of my writing, that I could not endure once more the ordeal of Hugo's silence. Meanwhile he was reacting neurotically and destructively. He said, "This is me."

It took us a week to repair this, for I took the manuscript away from him. I said, "At this moment I can't bear your silence. Silence is what I get from the world, silence and more silence. If it hurts you, you are wrong, for not only is it but one aspect of you, but that *is* the drama of the book, and I am writing with *sympathy* for it." This started a chain-reaction of quarrels. I rebelled against his depression, his psychotic rages. He was depressed and frustrated because he had not heard from the bank, because he cannot make more films. But above all, he was reacting destructively to Dr. Bogner's being away.

I lost patience. But I began to realize that Hugo was ill, that he had always been more ill than I had realized, that his "absence" was a grave illness. We talked about it. How bad we are for each other!

With Hugo there is no relief; he is a manic-depressive. What he wanted, I believe, was the mother, yet he was very careful to treat me as his child. When my mother died, I became acutely aware of my split vision of Hugo: the Hugo who held me was the kind, protective one, but this was really a cover for a destructive Hugo, one who wanted closeness but feared it, who admitted no contact except with the one over whom he had control (my dependency gave him a feeling of control).

What I was unable to do, because I did not understand it, was to be in full sympathy with his anxiety over money, no matter what the cause, but it was so oppressive, unrelenting. My nature seeks escape, I know it now. I have only been able to bear the cruelties and abominations of human life by transfigurations: art, poetry, fantasy. Hugo was diabolical in his way of cutting off all escapes. Now he says he left the bank because of my values, that I *undermined his own*. He regrets having left. Analysis demonstrates your responsibility for your character. Why didn't Hugo choose a wife who would have identified with his economic drive? Because he himself was split between economics and the arts. As a young man he read poetry and played the guitar. And why did I choose Hugo? Because I did not want to cope with economic problems. I had other jobs to do.

I am faced with this at a time when I have less energy. My art has brought me not one penny.

The quarrels, or rather explosions, were distorted, obsessional and terrifying. We have failed to give what we each wanted, but we won't face this. It is a marriage irreparably damaged.

Returning to Rupert seems to restore my sanity. I returned weak, physically, after the ordeal of my mother's death, which brought on a desire to return to religion, to become a saint, a mother.

Everywhere I turn there is failure. I can't suddenly abandon my novels and write an independent novel.

To be able to make Rupert happy helped me. And I returned just in time to help him through a crisis. The very afternoon I was traveling towards him, he was taken by two sheriffs and brutally questioned after a little girl of eleven complained he had "molested" her. Rupert, of all people, protective, chivalrous, romantic and shy, with four years of this life when he has had every opportunity of being alone with young girls. This one (he told me the story, and in the dark as I listened I knew he was telling the truth) was a homely little girl whom he helped to climb up to look at signs and posters she wanted, with her brother three feet away. I not only divined the fantasy of the child and helped Rupert by my faith, by reminding him of his behavior all these years, and I was able to track down even the motivation of the fantasy. An older and prettier girl had come with her once, and I am sure Rupert was gallant and charming to her and the little girl was jealous. Anyway, I helped him. He was shocked, anguished, fearful of consequences in the community, the destruction of his work. He, so sensitive, was suddenly treated like a criminal for the one act he would never do. He was traumatized, could not make love to me. He felt guilty (the severity of the police), and I helped him dissolve that. There was the natural anxiety, added to the fear of scandal, that people might discover we are not married (adultery is a crime in California). I gave him strength. I analyzed the situation. Our first night together we slept badly, but the next day we went to the beach. No other incident followed. The sheriff had talked brutally with the crude psychology that this would bring about a confession. He was frightening. "If the mother presses charges, we'll put you in jail." Rupert must have made a good impression. He is the very image of an idealistic, innocent young man. The second day, no sheriff. We went to the beach again, movies. We slept better. Slowly the anguish diminished.

I had analyzed the child, the sheriff. We began to breathe. Only on the fourth night did Rupert take me, relaxed and free.

I called up Joaquín. He had been to "a retreat" for three days and felt better. He sent me a photo of Mother, the Catholic cards announcing her death. He does not escape from pain. He went back to the house.

Sierra Madre, September 1954

I would like to know why Malraux called his history of art *Voices of Silence*.

I thought tonight of the mystics hearing voices…

Hearing voices…

Hearing voices…

The repetitions have exceeded the voices of sympathy and understanding. Jim alone hears every word I write. Once he called me up at night after reading the new book (now titled *Solar Bark*) and said, "Oh, Anaïs; this time I wept. The passages in which you break away… At first, the first few pages, I felt you were earth-bound…but after that you took off…the ancient city—that was the work of a mystic. You know, when you write like a mystic, it silences one…the death of the doctor, the outbreaks."

I will never forget that talk, but I cannot recapture it. It was strange. Hugo and I had fallen asleep. It was near midnight. I had taken a sleeping pill and a Martini as I always do to sleep in New York (whereas I fall asleep easily with Rupert). So I cannot recapture Jim's talk, although it was very long. It was not so much like praise but like one musician saying to another: I hear, I hear, I hear. It was such a complete experience of closeness that I almost wept. Although Jim is very articulate, he identified with the drama of inarticulateness because he is not as articulate in his writing as I am, as he wishes to be, or as he is with me.

I am returning to the diary, my solitary refuge from the world. I feel wounded in a million places. I need this to reconstruct myself.

I had talked eloquently to Hugo, tried to help him. My faith in analysis is shaken. It has brought monsters up from the deep. I am strongly tempted to stop here. I see a distorted Hugo, one I do not recognize.

On this side of my nightmare, there is sweetness because Rupert openly admits his dependence and does not fear it.

The self-destructiveness and destructiveness in both Hugo and me have been exposed. And it's unbearable.

The second quarrel came out of my realization that his kind acts—making breakfast, or a Martini, being kind to Joaquín, driving to the airport, his help, sacrifices, buying a dress for me—are all annihilated by his possessiveness, and, like my mother, when this possessiveness is not satisfied, he becomes destructive.

The truth is that Hugo, while pretending to do so, has never forgiven, tolerated, or truly understood any of my departures from the role of a totally dedicated wife occupied only with him.

I believe it is true that some people *feel* more acutely than others. It is impossible to measure this. I am convinced that I feel more than the average person, that I lived through the death of my mother as if I had been there. Once, when I went into my closet and saw the bathing suit she had sewn for me, I felt a stab of pain so acute, it was like that of a physical knife. I have not been able to wear this bathing suit since. In crises, I have reacted almost to the point of madness. Only a few months ago in Acapulco, I re-experienced my father's death. When one has this terrifying faculty, one has to seek palliatives. Everyone does. Americans go to the movies, get drunk, or speed in their cars. I choose art, fantasy and delirious passion. I love jazz because its voice, its living voice, is so loud that it stills the voice of death.

Escape. Not all escape is an act of cowardice.

Letter from Anaïs Nin to Hugh Guiler:

Sierra Madre, September 1954

To Hugo: May I remind you gently, unreproachfully, purely mathematically and objectively, that I have not been away every other month but often stayed home two months, and when you were ill, three or four months. However, your mention of it again convinced me that our quarrels are due to our unacceptance of each other *as we are*. You have tried (I grant you that, tried with all your might) to accept my unconventional behavior, but deep down have not been able to any more than you were able to have a good summer after Bogner left; so let's face it rather than delude ourselves about it. And I have to face the consequent guilt for my behavior, and that's that. Of course, my absence (in travel) and your absences (absent-mindedness when I am there, at home) are to me the same thing. They are different forms of withdrawals. You resent my absences, and I resent your absences for the same reason. I have said to myself: he is not there. He does not respond immediately. He is not present. So in a way, we are stalemated, and I don't know when one is going to accept the other...or...if.

Anaïs

In all my books the end is a return to the dream, the source of the mystery, where the character seeks the key of meaning.

Winter of Artifice ends with a return to the dream.

Projects I have to do:

Short stories, some of which are half-sketched in.

Rearranging of separate novels into one with inserts and connections.

Final volume tying them all together.

Preparing of diary to sell to publishers in the future, or a college library.

A full time job.

I need a maid.

Letter from Jim Herlihy to Anaïs Nin:
New York, September 1954

Dear Anaïs,

Early in the morning, a few quiet moments before the day begins.

The most important item in your letter, your idea of making your life there in Sierra Madre; it is a complex question and I wish I could help you with it. I have always seen excellent reasons for both lives, the trapeze, even though I realized that in one way or another it would inevitably resolve itself; perhaps now you are really nearing that resolution. It's an unusual situation on the surface, but in a deeper way it is the classic one: a long, emotional bond vs. passion. The choice between the father and the lover. And just as you realized in my own problem, that the decision would have to be a careful one since it is so dependent on one's own preparedness to make it, there is nothing I can say, except to utter the old and futile question: why can't life be simple?

Please let me know if you want paper plates. I can get them at my new job.

Love,

Jim

En route to New York, September 1954

After being with Rupert, I stopped at San Francisco to see Joaquín. He had been at the opera and stood far away at the end of the gleaming airport hall, small, black and white, and, even at that distance, had the tragic way of standing of those pierced by an arrow. I felt I was right to have come. It is strange, but when my mother died, the current between Joaquín and me was re-established. It had been interrupted. When, I do not remember. Perhaps in Paris when Mother felt that I might be a bad influence on him. As children we were very close. Now this contact was open again.

It was when I entered Mother's bedroom that I broke down. I slipped to the floor and sobbed. Joaquín wept. I kept saying, "I am sorry, I am sorry" to Joaquín because I had come to cheer him, and to lighten his sorrow.

I awakened the next day resigned to the ordeal of helping Joaquín to dispose of her belongings. A box of holy medals, *chapelets* for the Sisters of St. Vincent de Paul. A box of lace remnants, a box of sewing threads, needles, which I wanted as if inheriting Mother's maternity.

I asked for the sewing machine, the knitting needles, the gold thimble, Mother's jewelry (most of it gifts from me, earrings from Mexico, which I will wear). Joaquín gave me her lighter. I wanted her unfinished lace, but Joaquín wanted someone to finish it, a nun who made bobbin lace. Now the sharing of photographs, a pile for Joaquín, one for Thorvald, one for me. Joaquín gave me all my letters to Mother that she had kept—three enormous boxes—I had expressed my devotion.

She took nothing, possessed nothing but what was given to her. But she kept all the mementoes, our childhood teeth, my first embroidery (petit point), hair, our first notes.

A very sad day. Joaquín cooking and discovering *how much a woman has to do*, the endless repetitious tasks. He talked. He wanted me to read Lorca because he wants to write an opera based on *Blood Wedding*. He talked about the girl who has loved him for four years, a girl fifteen years younger, a pianist, but "bossy." She would convert to Catholicism for him. But neither one dares altogether. "She talks about it like a lawyer."

He looks wounded, mortally so. It causes me anxiety. I control my own distress. I hide myself to throw away Mother's toothbrush because I know the sight of it will hurt him, yet he wouldn't be able to throw it away. I do it for him, hurting myself. The final casting of one object that belongs to the dead is full of taboos and full of the pain of the ritual of separation.

Finally, I found out, with delicate probing, that on Saturday evenings, before concerts, Joaquín and Mother went to the San Francisco church for confession. I suggested we go before the airport, and we did. "I won't take long," said Joaquín with one of his half-smiles, alluding to his "sins" not being very many. I waited for him in the church. I was watching the little blue candles wavering in their glasses, some freshly lit by the penitents, some already burning out. I watched one that was burning out, and I could not bear it; it was my mother's life burning out, so I went and lit a new one and thought of her with the most purified love, the deepest sense of sacredness.

Joaquín's sadness, the austerity of his life, which I have spent a lifetime running away from, rebelling against, and my mother's life—humble, simple, primitive—was the unbroken thread that took me to Rupert. And I can see the continuity. I inherited from my mother not only a gold thimble, but the maternal passion, and what made my love for Rupert the strongest is my love for Joaquín.

New York, September 1954

Hugo smiling and tender. A fraternal kiss on the cheek. Immediately a larger universe. He has seen Arthur Miller and other people interested in making a film in Haiti. He has a possible film job. He has read three novels from Haiti. He has met several people who want to meet me, including Montgomery Clift's brother. He bought caviar to celebrate my homecoming.

Already my hair is recurled, nails repolished, the grooming and chicness necessary to New York. I wrote Joaquín. I wrote Rupert. I cut material for my rag rug. I telephoned Max Geismar: "Are you mad at me?" "No," he answered. "We had a dull and wholesome summer waiting for you to bring us to life." I called Jim: "What's the altitude today?" I paste Hugo's small engravings on cards for Hugo's Christmas cards, to save money when I cannot earn any. Felix Morrow says, "We are not selling enough books," but it does not hurt anymore. He is interested in my translating Giraudoux's *Choix des élus*.

Lecture at the City College Faculty Room. *Ladders to Fire* is on a required reading list.

I told Bogner that after the lecture I suffered depression, a malaise. I finally realized that I was distressed because my fear of being hurt, mocked or rejected by the world was such that it blocked my human contact with the students. I kept the contact at an intellectual level. All of the time, as in life, I am fully aware of a human sympathy that is imprisoned by my greater fear of my vulnerability to derision, irony or hostility.

Some of this sympathy must come through, or people would not, as they invariably do, confess their intimate lives to me. But in public, I am tense. It is an ordeal, a tournament, not a pleasure. I fear attack.

I say people in America do not have contact with each other, but Bogner insists that because of fear it is I who do not have it and project this lack onto others.

For example, I liked Mary Green of *New Leader* when I worked with her for my publicity. She was intelligent and sensitive, aside from her political fanaticism. But she accepted one of the worst reviews I ever had, from Frances Keene, which characterized individual growth as "egocentric." Mary assigned *Spy* to Keene, but were I in Mary's place I would not have published the review since she said she liked me and my work.

Work, work, work. Retyping the *Spy* manuscript because Northwestern University paid me for it and Burford in Paris either lost it or kept it. Spray-painting the stained grey rug into royal blue, sewing six covers on pillows for the couch. Finding a rare Lorca play for Joaquín, after calling Spanish bookshops and tramping in the rain. Mailing packages of cast-off faded felt for my rag rug to Sierra Madre.

I went out in the rain to bring Kay Bryant a much-needed $10 because she is the one in the greatest trouble, a wreck, but I cannot spend time with her because her mind is puerile, senile, petty.

Her son Paul ran away. He could not bear her. It is the "Way of the Cross" all the time, like Reginald. I can no longer make such sacrifices to those I do not believe in. *Le Suicide Perpétuel* of minor Helbas. I lived through that hell too completely. I see everything, as Henry did. People think I don't. But one has a right to turn away, to dwell on other people, those who fought against self-destruction as Hugo has, step by step. Last night he said (during the waking hour at dawn) we should not be impatient with those who refuse to enter the inner world. It is very painful to seek to completely alter one's self. Hugo's self-destruction was terrifying, as was mine.

After talking with Bogner about contact, I had a dream. I was bitten by the largest snake ever known, with a head as big as a man, and some smaller animals like bats. Last night I was covered by animals shaped like flat toads, with octopus tentacles that fastened like leeches around my throat.

Claude Fredericks is surprised that after James Merrill's irrational attack of *The Four-Chambered Heart*, I banished Merrill and his books. I explained how I had more than my share of such attacks and I needed warmth and understanding to go on working.

If my work were entirely me as Frances Keene said, would *everyone* feel they could confide their life history to me, their most intimate feelings, the rough woman hairdresser in Sierra Madre, the old hobo who lived in a cabin, taxi drivers (always and immediately), Edna King, who never talked to anyone? Would I get confessional letters, calls from those in trouble such as Kay Bryant? If I were self-centered, would I know every detail of Millicent's life, her feelings, her children's lives and her grandchildren's? Would Pam's three little girls like me to play with, and to tell secrets to?

Bogner's attitude fluctuates from a soft, steady sympathy to sudden, sharp severities. She has no patience with the ignorance of general medical knowledge, but she has patience and skills in teaching one to "expose" one's projection of the *personal drama* onto an external situation. Today, for example, I understood why the "social criticism" constantly accusing artists of egoism made me suffer. When I was a child my mother constantly spoke of my father's "selfishness," and I dreaded any resemblance to my father. I dreaded to be selfish and was happiest when I acted *unselfishly*.

Later, I realized how many of the acts I had considered "altruistic" were not truly so, and I became more sincere. But I have remained vulnerable to this particular accusation, so prevalent in criticism today.

Bogner says what I said to the students: there is no objective novel. In fact, there is no objectivity at all.

I am confused about selfishness and individuality because my father, who was selfish, deserted us, and my mother, who was "unselfish," clutched at us and possessed Joaquín and kept him. My father did not love us. My mother did. On such a primitive basis we face our image of the universe. For years I believed Hugo's possessiveness to be a sign of love.

Letter from Carol Sharpe to Anaïs Nin:

September 1954

Dear Anaïs,

I've written several letters to you lately but haven't had the courage to mail any of them. Perhaps this will get off to you under its own power.

I wish we might sit down and talk about your book, for then I would understand by your immediate reactions just how much to say, or could be delicate in a situation that calls for delicacy. I just don't know if I can manage by letter.

A Spy in the House of Love is uneven, disjointed. The rhythm is broken, disturbed by, I suspect, your own occasional doubts about the book and about Sabina. Certain words and sentences jar; it's like someone running and then limping. Even the lyrical passages seem mechanical. Anaïs, did you really want to write this book? Is it from your heart?

It seems to me that you disguise when you most want to reveal, and so Sabina is obscured at times by language that is ambiguous. There are many words about her, but she does not emerge from them as a being. The terror of her disintegration is vivid, but she is never a real person. Why is this?

The opening passage about Alan is fine, accurate, perceptive and tender, but he grows monotonous because only one facet of his personality is revealed. I know that this is the Alan Sabina recognizes, but in order to heighten this illusion it might have been wise to explore some of the other facets of a complex personality that is hinted at but never fully explored. Alan is a tremendously sympathetic personality, but he is revealed as all good, and, because of this, he is not real in any sense.

The impression you leave is that all the men in the book simply materialize when Sabina has need of them, and this is not true. Shadow figures depending upon Sabina for their existence. Isn't the emphasis wrong here? You don't fulfill our expectations for any of those people—there is no thrill of discovery, and readers like to share in that.

Some of the unevenness in the book stems from the lack of balance between the selection of incidents. Do you feel we have little control over our lives? Or just that Sabina does not over hers?

Daily living can be greater than the firebirds or gilded cages or brilliant colors of the life you write about...it's just that there's a lot more of it, and, to be truthful, I think a writer should let us be aware of it as a background. You almost did when Sabina walked past the trucks along—is it 18th Street?—I could taste the air there. I felt I was in contact with Sabina, and I recognized her then. Again, I'm not advocating trucks and dirty streets, but just that through some magic I was there.

But I've come to feel that every person is Everyman (Ma'am, could I use your pen, could I borrow your paper? Mama, could I have this old checkbook? I have some checks to write this morning. Mama, isn't it too cold for Julia out on the porch, and does she have her bonnet on and hates her bonnet? Is she hungry?)

Well, perhaps I'd better give up entirely. It's difficult to go on anyway since I don't know how you feel. I would like to know what you are working on now. A long time ago we talked briefly about Sabina and where she fit in the scheme of your planned books on women. I think you said then that she would be the last, the ultimate in disintegration that you must write before you could go on to explore the possibility of integration. Do you feel that way now?

About balance, form, emphasis. Let me tell you of my waking experience after Julie was born. When I awoke from the ether dream in the cold gray light of the hospital dawn, with fog obscuring all but the moon in my view from the window, my first conscious thought was the first line of a poem by Wallace Stevens, "God is good, it is a beautiful night." My second was the voiced question "Is it OK to smoke here?" I remember both things, one with a feeling of serenity and calm and gratitude, the feeling I had when I recognized that I was returning to the life I love...and a second with a sense of humor of the question with which I immediately took up the routine business of living, the mundane after the poetic flight, and both after the dreadful and wonderful experience of the delivery of the child.

I've seen this experience repeated since then when I have watched the people in our neighborhood clear away the debris after two hurricanes and have appreciated their good humor, their orderliness and even, on occasion, their heroism. Our neighbor was out nailing new shingles on his roof before the whiplash of the first hurricane had passed beyond us. He is a squat, emotional, shy, antagonistic man, but he was a wonderful sight perched on the roof with the wind whipping his sparse white hair into a halo around his head, his nose red from the cold, his mouth full of rusting nails, and his grief over the fallen trees that he had planted when he first came to this country, and this neighborhood was very real indeed. Most of the people I watched with pride and understanding during that time are generally unattractive and rarely heroic, and if one were to write about them, all these things would have to be taken into account. What is there, secret, deep down in the little person that allows him to soar and even to conquer when the occasion demands it? Well, don't you suppose St. Francis had a runny nose once in a while? Or stomach trouble? Or sore feet? He didn't spend all his time chatting happily with the birds.

Are you angry with me? If so, don't let anything I say, or anyone says, discourage you. As far as I'm concerned, I'd rather you were angry with me than that you felt I had written lies to you about how I felt about the book. And I'd rather you'd be angry than hurt. I repeat, I wish we might have talked about this, for under the circumstances a letter is rather cowardly. Meanwhile, if you feel I am all wrong, please write and tell me so.

Love to you and to Hugo. And, if ever you wish to come here, we would welcome you both as guests.

Carol

Letter from Anaïs Nin to Carol Sharpe:

New York, September 1954

Dear Carol: You letter did not make me angry. Why should it? You gave me your *personal* reaction to the book. However, I am not going to explain what I intended to do, except in your own terms. If instead of saying "the rhythm is disjointed, uneven," you might have come closer to the meaning if you had said, "Sabina is disjointed, uneven," for in the poetic subjective novel you are *inside* the consciousness of the character, and you are Sabina. For the same reason the men are painted as she sees them, and I do not interfere as an author and paint them as I see them. This is stated in the novel. If you are reading a novel about a criminal, the crime is the theme, and you are not there to pass judgment on the crime or the character. You are inside Sabina's world in order to understand a character you have not known before. If you do not wish to be inside Sabina, that is another matter. I felt the same way about Paul Bowles' characters. I do not like sadism, and I do not like a hero who feels related to no one. But I am aware that this is a personal reaction, not a literary evaluation of his books. But you must be certain not to confuse the element I have chosen to portray in Sabina with such dangerous generalities as: *did you really want to write this book*, for that is a doubt implying you do not have faith in my artistic integrity. It is also a personal, most un-objective statement to deduce from a characterization that the author is saying: I do not believe we exert control over our lives. Your only error throughout is that it stems from a purely personal feeling to which you have every right provided you had worded it in terms of what you like, need, want, seek, or admire. To pass judgment on a book through such a subjective eye of what you,

Carol, think a novel should say and do and depict is the only grave error. I wish you had said: I feel… I dislike… I prefer… For example, you speak of lack of balance of the book when the lack of balance of Sabina is precisely what I am dramatizing. To make me responsible for Sabina's dramatizations when that is the theme of the book obliges me to say what I did not think I needed to say and was implicit throughout the book: I am describing a neurotic character. I have known many Sabinas. You have not. I have underlined neurosis in all my characters because I believe this is the Age of Anxiety, and I am trying to cope with a problem, and I believe, furthermore, that there are milder forms of such neurosis in all of us. I blame you only for passing judgment. If the experience or characters I study are uninteresting to you, unfamiliar, and you have no desire to explore them, leave them alone. In your letter you proceed from a rejection of Sabina to a description of the characters, situations, and form of novel that appeal to you. Dear Carol, have you considered that perhaps what attracted you to my work in the first place may possibly be no longer there for you, that you may have changed? That you never seriously contemplate experimentalism in writing from the unconscious, or search for new language, new dimensions? Your taste is for naturalism, folk novels; perhaps you should read Styron. Nevertheless, the characters I have chosen to study have as much right to exist. But please do not confuse your personal evaluation with literary evaluation and accuse me of being mechanical or not having my heart in what I am writing because your heart is not answering. I think we should choose the writing that suits our temperament, our taste, our individual world without necessarily being destructive towards what lies outside of it. Read the writers who describe your world, your neighbors, as you see them. But leave the Sabinas alone, and do not confuse the author with the character, and do not doubt the integrity of the author who has chosen to describe what she knows. I am sorry that you have lost an adventurous, explorative feeling for reading of unfamiliar worlds, or uncommon characters not directly related to you. The only important thing, in the end, is not to pass judgment.

Anaïs

New York, September 1954

Jim's party. A tenement apartment transformed by tremendous tasks of papering, painting, plastering walls, making the fireplace, making the closet, making the place into one of beauty.

John Kierman, a little man, his face smudged, not sculptured but like mastic worked by thick fingers, *Monsieur Tout le Monde*, occupied in translating Genet, condemned in the homosexual world to be unloved, as he looks like a little French shoe salesman, and when drunk he became a lyrical Irishman: "I don't mean to be maudlin, believe me, Anaïs, I hate women. But you, you are the essence of femininity. I love you. And I will love you all my life, and right now, when I see how you listen to me, never paying attention to anyone else or anything else happening at the party, well…I feel like weeping. Give me your hand." He closed his eyes, he was about to weep. I smiled. I let him spill his drink on my dress. I did not dare desert him because I feel sympathy for the unloved. I knew the world he moved in where beauty is a requisite, the ever-adolescent, ever-romantic life. So I let him remain adhesive and trying to tell me that Harrison, the boy on my left, was the most clever and intuitive one of all, a genius. Harrison said he had lived with Fowlie in Chicago, and that Fowlie was full of cruelty and wickedness. Harrison felt Kierman was boring me with his overflowing sentimentality, hand-kissing and extravagant praise, but his eyes were murderous eyes, cold and sharp, as were his remarks, and I could read sadism on his face so clearly as he talked to Kierman in true voyou underworld language—*décolle toi* (he didn't say it in French but I know more French slang than I do English). He wanted to separate us because Kierman wanted to talk about his protégé, and Harrison wanted to tell me about how Jimmy Baldwin, the negro homosexual writer, fell in love with him. As Harrison went on insulting everyone in slum language, Jimmy Spicer, puerile and pretty like the young women in *Harper's Bazaar*, was immediately attracted to Harrison's sadism (which he did not practice on me in words, but the sadists have a way of fluttering their nostrils, a certain carnivorous facial grimace one can catch). Spicer said drunkenly to Jim Herlihy: "I must get rid of Claude. I must get into bed with Harrison." Jim said, "How do you know that because Harrison is a verbal sadist he will be one in bed?" While Jimmy Spicer pursued his masochistic impulse, I eluded Kierman, who reproached me: "Why is it that as soon as you tell a person that you will love them for life they run away?" As soon as he made his most passionate declarations, I did feel enmeshed and sought escape. I was surrounded, closely, by five young men while others hovered waiting for an empty chair, and escape was difficult. Harrison helped me. I did not like the way he talked to Kierman: "She is way ahead of you. You bore her." I wandered to the kitchen where Jim said, "You're a sensation. They all come to tell me how much they love you, even though they hate women."

Pepe Zayas, whose paintings hang on the walls, just back from Italy, embraces me.

What happened that night? There were only five women there and fifteen young men. Is it that I am one of the few forgiven for being a woman, or what is it that arouses their passionate tenderness? It was almost collective...the actor back from Italy, Pepe's former lover, dark-eyed and a young architect. I was told that after I left Stanley Haggart read from *Children of the Albatross*.

Dick speaks the language of Broadway. He has a glittering impulse, uses endearing terms profusely, and all he says is permeated by a neon-lighted smile. He is capable of a sincere feeling for Jim and for me, but it is dressed in such spurious quality of language, and so similar to his delivery on the nightclub floor, before TV or the public, that it loses its depth and evaporates. His facile charm disappears when he is alone and relaxed, and the true face of an affectionate expansive nature appears. He distorts his emotions by borrowing ideas and mixing them up like a pack of cards, deceiving no one. Jim's ideas about writing or mine on character and relationship, his manager's ideas on how to make a success, his public's ideas, his admirers' ideas, all shuffled together, make him seem like a *pacotille* (trashy) product of the Broadway bazaar. His compulsive chattering is like the "noise" made on New Year's Eve, made to give the illusion of joy and life, but his voice seems to come from a jukebox instead of himself.

Jim was a grave host. His finely drawn features and his stylized body give him an elegance contradicted by his natural, strict language. The boy born poor in a tough neighborhood has stylized his ordinary lingo by a speed and smoothness resembling not the crude speech of common people, but that of those who by their own agility and quick wits are opportunists of language and have great facility, great accuracy, perfect aim. It is the fast-moving rhythm that gives it its character and a vitality of style that has no relation to cultured or affected speech.

In Jim there is no slurring, no limpness, no drawl. It comes from the same nimbleness that permits him to enter any world and handle it. Tension is part of his style. It becomes an attribute. He is tense as a magician would be. He always looks pale. He has no pleading in his eyes as Rupert has. I have a feeling of twinship with Jim's prestidigitations. Their anxieties (Rupert's too) compel them to do all things more deftly than anyone, to erase all possible traces of doubt, ignorance, fear of failure, bewilderment.

You live in a world for a little while, you dramatize your adventures, and this world continues an existence of its own and is never completely detached; it returns as your past returns, even if your illusion of it, your passion for it, no longer exists. My relationship with the homosexuals is no longer active, dynamic or essential. I feel related only to Jim, and not to his homosexuality. Yet I felt today that if I had described Sabina's behavior as that of a homosexual, it might have been more plausible, acceptable. I do want to write the definitive, deep novel on the homosexual. They are not doing it, none of them. Genet's is not a love story; it is a story of passion.

Henry Miller's watercolor exhibit at Brooklyn Public Library sparkled with delight, delicacy, fantasy. The librarians were somber, the keepers, the guardians, the cataloguers. *No one* entered into the playfulness, the lightness of the watercolors. No one had humor or osmosis. No one had empathy or delirium. I tried to counter this by reading from Miller's *The Angel Is My Watermark* on his watercolors, in which he juggled words as colorfully as he juggled colors. Later, because the discussion was going into whether or not government should subsidize the artist, I tried to return to the essential theme of Miller's contribution to the flow of life by reading my preface to *Tropic of Cancer*. Marino Ruffier, the librarian, had wanted to avoid this theme, but the people insisted on it, returned to it.

One man insisted, "I get no insight into life by reading Miller." I said, "We can find insight in other writers, but not life, the living flow. Most of our writing today is dead."

It was disturbing to see all that I knew as wild living and creation, wild faith, desire and life as if they were museum pieces in glazed windows. The original intent had been to help Miller because he is poor.

I cannot assume leadership, because of fear of my anger, an uncontrollable anger that might explode. This anger is inextricably woven into my active and positive impulses. It forces me into a passivity I do not enjoy. Every active manifestation is followed by depression. So when I saw James Laughlin come in, I said to myself: "Be careful of your hostility, Anaïs."

He is not only the most repulsive character in literary history, but the most commercial, neurotic, sadistic figure who assumes power over writers because he himself is such a bad one. Laughlin created the false legend that he publishes writers no one else will, posing as an idealist, but doing so at the expense of the writers—that is, giving them paltry advances of $50 and hardly ever any royalties. He gained prestige while the writers gained no money. He refused Miller money when Miller wanted to come to the USA because of the war. But he is very shrewd, and he will make money on Dylan Thomas, Miller, etc., by outliving them.

I went up to him and said, "You made me so happy writing a letter in which you said my writing was deteriorating, because for years I have felt your taste was deteriorating." He was startled but said, "Oh, you must not take this personally."

I asked him during the meeting why he had not fought for Miller's banned books in court. He answered that his lawyers told him he could not win. But that is not a reason for not fighting, as we know from political battles.

Holding the runaway horses of my anger.

Sierra Madre, October 6, 1954

When the time comes to return to New York (I managed to stay here by inventing lectures and seminars), the conflict starts again. I get so exhausted by my "decision" that I get ill. When I decide to give my life to Rupert, to break with Hugo, first it all seems right. I am obeying a more sincere, deeper impulse, my love for Rupert, and the Hugo I see is the Hugo I do not love. This Hugo I can break with. But as soon as I have arranged in my mind a Hugo I cannot live with, another image comes up to haunt me: a Hugo in distress, a Hugo semi-impotent, helpless, confused, insecure, anxious, bewildered…and then my heart breaks, for this Hugo is far removed and unattainable. The Hugo I seek to reach is in Rupert, and with him I can make contact because the Hugo I cannot accept is not in Rupert. Rupert is alive, immediately responsive, emotionally present, and cheerful, active, passionate. So the other aspect, the one that arouses my compassion, is linked to qualities I enjoy that Hugo does not possess: a love of living, a capacity for enjoyment, a lightness and swiftness. Then Hugo's letter comes, depicting his sincerity, his struggles, his wiser and deeper mind (and I hear Rupert saying, "I am mentally lazy"). As soon as I make the decision, Rupert says something like: "Don't give up your job in New York until you have something as good here," which means that our life is still dependent on Hugo's material protection.

Strange irony—humorous?—to appease Hugo's economic anguish I leave him so I can sell books, give lectures. These efforts were interpreted by Hugo as a way to help him (by supporting myself) and by Rupert as a way to earn a living in Sierra Madre so I will not have to go to New York so often. Both are true, but it is also true that I failed. I earned exactly $100 this month.

Pressure from all sides, from Hugo to return, from Helen to marry Rupert, from Rupert to get a divorce, from myself the need for peace.

Then, when I can't bear it anymore, I begin to put my belongings in order. I get satisfaction from perfect order in my papers, my clothes, the house. I carry this to excess, as if I am unable to organize and control my life and seek to exert it on the world of objects. There is a mania for discarding the useless, uncluttering the house, beautifying, a kind of super efficiency.

I spend hours on this. It gives me peace. With Rupert I have moments of peace. Yesterday in the garden he was re-photographing an aerial photograph of the mountains that he had colored (the burnt area). The sun was gentle. I held the measuring tape, helped him to measure and to keep his shadow off the photo. Tavi was lying nearby, content.

Moments of peace when Rupert turns towards me in the morning, in his sleep, and we embrace.

When Rupert observes the failing energy of Tavi, who is less eager every day to follow Rupert on long hikes or long journeys in the hot truck, I identify with Tavi aging. Yet, the depth of Rupert's love is inescapable. Everyone can see it. Helen said, "While you were away he was irritable and quarreled with Lloyd. Tonight he is radiant."

A day of lively pleasure with Renate and Paul. Their house, on top of a hill overlooking the sea, is full of paintings. Paul talks. But one does not remember what he says. One remembers an elfin, mysterious smile; he does not open his mouth to smile.

Thursday. Rupert does not work. He sleeps late. I slipped out of bed, tense, thinking of Hugo, of the break, and try to calm my anguish. I have tea and an English muffin, watch the garden, the children next door playing, the birds, rabbits looking for food and am calm again.

Can I live in Rupert's doll house? I believe I can.

Deep down Helen does not want me to marry Rupert, but, succumbing to Rupert's choice, she then proceeds to force me into it because of convention. She suffers from the unconventional situation. People ask her, "Is Rupert married to Anaïs?"

I do believe she has grown fond of me. I am thoughtful, I take her side, and I help her all I can.

But I hate my evenings there. We always drink. Helen becomes sentimental. She weeps as she tells the story of the movie *Tea and Sympathy*. Lloyd arrives and begins either to bark, to bicker, or to go off on a psychotic rage. The dinner is exquisitely cooked by Helen, and Rupert enjoys the food, but to me it is completely poisonous because there is no conversation possible, no genuine gayety.

Rupert has the sentimentality of his mother and the quarrelsomeness of Lloyd.

I leave, tired and depressed. Now I have to be truly clever not to spend our second free day the same way. Helen asks Rupert to trim the oleanders on one of her properties, so yesterday we went there and gardened for about an hour. Then we spent an hour looking for a dump to unload our branches. The gardening in the sun I didn't mind at all. But then Rupert had to clean up at Helen's, and then there was a cousin of Lloyd's coming, a Helen Enwright who writes children's stories. So we were to be there for cocktails. Lloyd starts by giving me a compliment on my appearance, but two minutes later he and Rupert are arguing about whether bartenders measure their drinks.

I have never met anyone of any interest or value at their house.

Dream: Rupert and I are on a ship. There is a fire on board. We wait until it is uncontrollable and then jump into the sea. A powerful current carries me away from Rupert, but finally we meet again.

Dream last night: I arrive in New York. There is a party going on. It is to celebrate Hugo's engagement to a girl. All the family was there, quite shocked that Hugo should celebrate his engagement before obtaining a divorce. Tia Antolina is there. I speak to the girl very kindly and say, "Don't you think it would make everything better if I asked for a divorce?" Her attitude was independent and beyond convention. Hugo was withdrawn and indifferent. Then to salvage my pride, I began to introduce Rupert to everyone. Tia Antolina was impressed with him. The girl Hugo was going to marry was young, fresh-skinned, but she had small, childish, spoilt teeth.

Last night I decided to live in the present. Rupert and I were tired from Sunday's trip to Tijuana to see a bullfight. We went to bed early. I was whimsical, humorous, playful. I teased him (because he loves to conserve, preserve, accumulate rags, etc.) about cutting up his best shirt for the rag rug I am making. I pretended to cut all I could into ribbons, also pretended to be Tavi (whom we left at Helen's) so he would not miss him, which means butting my head against his tummy. We laughed. Rupert always enters into the spirit of a game.

I have a terrible resistance to leaving Rupert. At the same time, when I imagine the break with Hugo, it is as if Hugo were dead and I were never to see him again, and then I feel as much pain as at the death of my parents.

So once more, I tear myself away.

New York, October 20, 1954

An old man in the street picking out his daily newspapers from a scrap basket.

Over the telephone a voice: "Are you a Protestant?"

"No."

"What are you?"

"Nothing, but I am not interested."

"Wait a minute. You don't know what I'm going to say. We are approaching families about a marvelous place called Beautiful. It's a burial place."

I hang up the phone.

Near Jim's apartment I look for "workers" to make long distance calls to Rupert. I go to the United Nations to breathe the air of internationalism, my favorite country. I buy Christmas cards for Rupert and me.

I know now that I do not love Hugo, but I can't leave him. Bogner was quick to seize upon the dream of Hugo's engagement to a girl while not yet divorced. "You want to put the responsibility of the break on Hugo. You cannot yet reach for what you want. You have too much guilt."

"I know what I want. I want to live with Rupert."

She thinks (as I know) that my mother's death pushed me closer to Joaquín and Rupert, that my asking for the sewing machine and gold thimble was identification with my mother.

But at night, before going to sleep, I have anxiety at not being with Rupert. And with Hugo I am lonely because I do not feel close to him.

Last night, a party for Hugo's films. The Haitian contingent was there. A wealthy couple who own many Haitian paintings. Stanley Haggart playing the role of producer, seeking to unite a patron with an artist to make a film on Haiti. The wealthy couple was interesting, the man uncommonly intelligent, discussing themes of cosmetics and chemistry. The Seeleys, who lived in Haiti, are friends of Albert Mangones; he is a sculptor and she works at Scribner's. Brooks Clift, brother of Montgomery Clift. All of them were extremely enthusiastic about Hugo's films, eloquent even in their silences.

I played the devoted wife and hostess, serving drinks and foods, allowing Hugo to shine. Such an evening should have made him blossom. I would have blossomed fully after that. Yet Hugo's first remark after such a party was: "You see, when I was asked how much it would cost to make a film on Haiti, I was able to answer immediately on the basis of the budget I spent three weeks making. From now on no one is going to tell me what to do. I was right."

This outburst was directed at both Bogner and me. He constantly asks for advice and when he is given it, he rebels. Bogner thought that before making a budget he should have found out what he would be paid for his work, which would, in turn, affect the scope of the budget. I had suggested a more modest "pilot" film, at a small cost, all done by him, controlled by him as an artist, because I know he will get into difficulties in a more ambitious project (employing a cameraman, expensive equipment, and he cannot effectively direct or command because of his lack of technological knowledge).

Anyway, this summation of a human, warm, generous evening killed my own pleasure and threw me into a depression. Very often the neurotic acts like the criminal—*no matter how much love or devotion he gets, it is never enough.*

Lately I have been thinking not of the harm I might do Hugo by breaking with him, but of the possible good. It is quite possible that while I am here he will make no effort to have another relationship. It is quite possible that the fact that he does everything wrong, the self-destruction, may have been due to not being *sufficiently loved in the way he wanted to be.*

Bogner was ironic about the gravity with which I treated *not* loving Hugo: "It is not the first time someone fell out of love with one's husband and fell in love with someone else."

Hugo has not touched me physically since I arrived, and I know he feels as I do, disconnected. Just recently he compared me to the woman who was a fantasy in Hudson's *Green Mansions*, just as before he compared me with Ondine.

Bogner: "The want—what you want—is the strong drive that makes you either provoke Hugo's worst traits or keep an account book of them so that you may be able to say he *drove* you away. But this is only a maneuver to save yourself from guilt. You can't bear the guilt, and you are right, for if you break with the feeling of committing a crime, this feeling will follow you everywhere and ruin your life."

I wept. We went back to all my inabilities to break. I could never break a relationship, only run away or shift the responsibility to another.

The want is the key.

It is possible that Hugo is aware of this estrangement and acts destructively, revengefully.

New York, October 26, 1954

Josephine Premice arrives. Her hair is cut boyishly, with bangs on the forehead. Her black eyes look bigger as she is very thin, and she has had her nose made smaller. Her laughter is continuous, like a breeze. She has a long story to tell, about Jacques Blum, a wealthy Jewish French count, not handsome, but tall and blond. "We have broken up, after three and a half years, but he is here now and we are good friends. He thinks I have no brains. We talk a spiral language together."

(I heard them later talking over the telephone, a mixture of baby talk and chatter.)

"He has a sadistic sense of humor. Once we sat in a café and for an hour insulted each other: *Ma sale petite négresse! Mon sale petit juif!* People were so shocked they tried to interfere.

"Another time he told me to wear my best evening dress, that we were going to Maxim's. We were three couples. When we had settled around our table, Jacques and his friends went back to the *vestiaire* and took off their evening trousers. Underneath they were in leotards, and in this costume, half evening dress and half leotard, they insisted on dancing.

"Another time I went into a tantrum at the Ritz bar and I began to break glasses. Jacques called the headwaiter and said coolly: 'Bring a tray with a dozen of your best glasses. If Madame feels like breaking glasses she must have the best.' This embarrassed me and I left the place in a fit of anger. He always had the upper hand, he always won and I liked that.

"I had a neurotic fear of automobiles and he made me go about in a horse and carriage. Another time he got me a Rolls Royce with the whitest, blondest chauffeurs he could find and I went about in it dressed in dungarees. Entering a café in this costume, a man stopped me and said, 'You must be Josephine. I am Cocteau.'"

Now Josephine is rehearsing for Truman Capote's *House of Flowers*, which takes place in a house of prostitutes in Haiti. She likes Capote.

When she left Jacques for five months while on tour, he found another woman he loved more sensually. "With us, it was not so much the physical as a mental fascination. We were both crazy." This was in February, and for the first time she experienced despair and decided she needed an analyst. She said, "Dr. Graham asked me what I missed most about Jacques and I said, 'He made me laugh for three and a half years.' Dr. Graham said I didn't need analysis, that I was a well-adjusted neurotic. I thought I was just well-adjusted."

Everyone treats Josephine as a highly delightful playmate.

"Here in New York I don't feel the same way as in Paris. The life isn't the same."

Jim says, with his speedy jazz rhythm, "Let's talk about the Third Man," meaning himself as the one who will be there when I leave both Hugo and Rupert, because he feels he has with me the best relationship he has ever had, and I feel with him a freedom and elation I would like to have with Rupert and Hugo and don't have.

While talking to Bogner of my conviction that Hugo and I are permanently disconnected, I wept. Everything with Hugo becomes corrupted into pain and worry. The possible pleasure is destroyed by the commercial drive. I must stop expecting Hugo to create a life I like. I must do it all myself. I have to let Hugo live in his own self-made world of errors, delusions, failures, and self-destruction. I am not in sympathy with his needs, desires, aims. He wants "security" on a large scale; he wants a capital of $100,000, the apartment, the car, and more money to make movies with.

When I set about to build my own life, I realized I didn't know how.

Once, in Paris, encouraged by Thomas Woolf's publisher, I prepared 600 pages from the diaries (Hugo was in London and I was living in a small hotel room, working at this all day). However, it was a fake version, arranged for Henry. I felt sure that by using another name I could keep Hugo from reading it, but I knew Henry would. This fake version is what I have shown now and then (recently to Herbert Alexander). It was, naturally, considerably expurgated. Today I burnt it in the fireplace. If the novels are symbolic, at least the diary must be intact; I must have no corruption of the truth in connection with the diary. I feel better now.

I also have taken a step further in maturity. For example, I realize my *passivity*. Hugo's moods determined my day as much as the climate did. *I have no independent life* or moods. I succeeded in separating myself from many of Rupert's moods, his fretting and fussing and fuming in place of depression. What has become unbearable has been the conjugation of Hugo's depressions and mine. I have the power to combat mine, but not to resist his.

New York, October 30, 1954

Talk with Bogner yesterday about my hatred of America: "It is cold, hard, and has treated me badly, indifferently."

The remembrance of life in Spain after my father left brought a flood of tears. It seems all warmth, affection, from the singing maid, the nuns, my grandmother, and cousins.

Bogner says this is only a projection, that Spain was a continuance of my relationship with my father. We were near him, staying with his parents, and seeing his sister and his nephews, so I may not have believed in the loss. But coming to America was the real break, and the fatherless child looked for an exterior warmth here that did not exist.

I do not believe this. I believe my hatred of America is objective. I dislike its atmosphere, its aims, its literature, its characters, its way of life, everything, I hate it all. I feel Americans are without contact with each other, with other countries, or with themselves, their secret inner selves. I feel they cannot relate or have relationships.

New York, November 2, 1954

I succeeded in reacting against Hugo's depressions instead of succumbing to them. I turned the atmosphere into comedy. I expressed to Hugo the excessive indulgence of these moods and the fact that I added my depressions to his. I made a game of them, laughed at the both of us, played at having our depressions in six hour shifts, made it all appear ridiculous, and triumphed. Got Hugo laughing. Realized *why* I had admired Caresse Crosby and Josephine Premice for their spirited gayety during adversity. I found this quality of gallantry in rereading Caresse's autobiography. People may say she was shallow, but emotionally she lived fully and took blows well. Just as the professors at City College of New York yesterday commented on Henry's immaturity, I said, "It depends on what realm. Ideologically he was immature, but in the flow and vigor of his actual living force, he was more mature than any of the pusillanimous writers of today."

Yesterday I talked to the students at City College. Professor Henry Leffert was pleased that I roused them to a discussion that three or four students would have continued for hours, and I had to be pulled away to lunch. Good or bad, it was lively. I had arrived incensed by Malcolm Cowley's fanatical narrow-mindedness, his allegation that the novel should treat only the big political or historical themes of the day and not the themes unrelated to the essential *function* of American life. The Age of Mediocrity. The Age of How to Do It Yourself Books. The Age of Functional Books. Anyway, changing the atmosphere of my life with Hugo is the beginning of a new active chemical that may help me create the life I like, separately from Rupert or Hugo.

This month I have earned $100 and did the upholstery and house repairs as a dutiful wife, for which no estimate was made.

The inner resistance to outside obstacles, like the macabre weather, all rain and wind.

Morrow over the telephone: "I can't understand it. Only 1,300 books sold. And what mystifies me is the lack of response from your passionate list. We worked hard on that (thousands of names). My hunch is now you must write a *big book*, no more sections of novels."

René de Chochor at lunch: "Americans, let's face it, are bourgeois. They want novels about a man who works, marries, raises children... But don't forget what is happening to you happens frequently to good writers."

He was humorous and even imaginative in depicting Morrow's future business, disposing of the carcasses of unsalable books. "He will do it in a black suit, black tie, a new kind of funeral home."

"But I thought drugstores performed this function."

"He has a new method, one that, like the remainder, manages to leave the writer out (when a book is remaindered at 49¢ the writer gets nothing).

Then I see Lila always either in hell or walking out of hell, but unable to enter any other realm. She had an ulcer, another broken relationship, cannot write but has been investigating the fascinating paradox: why do homosexuals always caricature their own lives, their own worlds, a question I have often asked of them. Why do they not ever present it romantically, with sincere depth of feeling, as when Lila told me of her relationship? So far she only knows that they wish to be identified with those who pass judgment on them (as some Jews are always passing judgment on other Jews to appear separate from them), as Sabina judged herself, and I had hoped this would prevent others from judging her, but it didn't. Lila confesses she does not want to write about homosexual experiences, that she was never completely at home in the homosexual world.

"But you don't have to write about the homosexual world; can't you isolate and study a relationship as I do?"

Dream: I am going to give a lecture and reading. I have worked very hard on my lecture. It is written exquisitely in French. Then just as I am about to face my audience, I realize they do not know French. I ask Hugo to get me copies of my books in English while I try to translate the lecture as well as I can.

I left out the introduction to this dream. A huge tarantula, hairy, hanging on a thread from the ceiling was moving towards my face. I killed it. It fell on the floor, burst into flames, and then it shed black seeds like those of a watermelon.

The monsters I have created in my dreams recently—giant snakes, leeches, tarantulas—are my fears of human beings, the dangers I think I am incurring when I expose myself to their criticism and opinions.

A return to France is impossible because it is a return to the artist life separated from the rest of the world, and that was only possible because of Hugo's work at the time.

The concentration upon creation, which was my paradise, writing with Henry and breathing the artist life, is not possible here.

"Why?" asked Bogner.

"I am not sure."

I reconstructed for her the efforts I made to live with the artists here. I knew them all. But it was not the same. I remember when we tried to meet at a café on East 13th Street, and one of the painters turned on a loud radio to listen to a prize fight. It is intermittent, not continuous. And the fraternity is destroyed by competiveness. The pressure from the outer world is greater, the pressure of economics, the problems of living.

I don't know what the artist life in Paris is like today.

Gay morning chopping and tying up wood for Jim, and on our terrace Hugo is using his electric saw. Jim carries the bundles. Hugo reports his news: there is war between him and Maya Deren (she set up a rival film society). There is also a war between Jim and Dick, a war between Anaïs and the world.

When I told Jim the dream of the burnt tarantula, I said "watermelon seeds." Hugo corrected me: "First time you said pomegranate seeds." "I was just trying to be folksy," I said.

I bought my ticket for Sierra Madre. It is Saturday afternoon. After the "keep Herlihy warm" week, as Jim put it, the chopping of rotted flower boxes, we had lunch and Hugo slept.

So much takes place within me that by comparison I find a paucity, a stinginess, a silence in people that drives me to excess. I would, at times, be less of a rebel if people did not seem so inert, cautious.

Am I creating my own isolation? It seems to me that most of my acts are acts of integrity. It is true I do not belong to the cults of T. S. Eliot or Dylan Thomas, that I broke with the Living Theatre after seeing plays by Rexroth and Gertrude Stein. Sincerely, I do not care for the Sitwells. I do care about Tennessee Williams and Capote.

Do I still really deserve this solitary cell treatment?

Those I call my relatives: Giraudoux, Proust, Djuna Barnes, Isak Dinesen, Anna Kavan, Pierre Jean Jouve, Genet...did they feel as I do?

Imaginary talk to the students of Claremont:

We must protect the minority writers because they are the research workers of literature. They keep it alive. It has been fashionable of late to seek and force such writers into wider channels, to the detriment of both writers and an unprepared public. Educators do all in their power to prepare you to enjoy reading after college. It is right that you should read according to your temperament, occupation, hobbies and vocation. But it is a sign of great inner insecurity to sneer, wise-crack, to be hostile to the unfamiliar, the book for which we have no frame of reference, which has not been blessed by the majority. This closed door trend is manifested in such absurd titles as *The Last of the Romantics* and *The Last of the Bohemians*, when we know that in ourselves the romantic, the bohemian, the adventurer never truly dies. It is suppressed. This suppression of our inner life in favor of the pattern created by our society may be the reason why any manifestation of artistic revolt or experiment is met with hostility. It is merely because it disturbs an established order or an artificial conventionality. You see, I don't believe in people's conventionality. It is merely a façade. If you take time and have patience you will find beneath the most standardized behavior an individual, a human being with original thoughts or innovative fantasy, a being that he does not dare expose for fear of ridicule. Now, the artist is the only one who is a guide, a map-maker, who holds the blueprint to a greater sincerity. He is useful to the community. He keeps the variations that make human beings so interesting. A great deal of our delinquents are young people who have a perverted sense of adventure. The men who built America were the genuine adventurers in a physical world. Once this world is built, there is left for us adventures in the realms of art and science.

It is too bad that we have created such a standardized life, that some young people feel they can only break through the monotony, the uniformity, by acts of violence.

It does not matter *who* started the fight.

I spent a great deal of time trying to find the culprit, the origin (original sin), the one responsible for my anger. This, says Bogner, is not what matters, because I cannot bear to see myself as a person capable of anger, as one possessing a quick temper.

Repression of anger caused the *intensification* of it.

Hugo doesn't like his image of a man of anger. Whether Maya attacked first, or he, does not matter now.

Bogner says, "You pick up the waves you want to pick up, is that what you mean? There is hostility in the air. But like radio waves, you pick up what you wish.

"In your family each one was very preoccupied with shifting the blame. Your mother in a violent way, your father in a simulacrum of rationality and logic."

This is probably the major occupation of most people, this fixing of the blame on others, and *projection* of personal drama onto people, countries, arts, sciences, philosophy...

Letter from Anaïs Nin to Rupert Pole:

New York, November 4, 1954

Darling Chiquito:

Last night I had the blues for you.

Half of life in New York is composed of mirages. Several telephone calls to find out about the rights to Giraudoux (French consulate, French agent, a letter of French publishers, talks with Morrow) and nothing definite yet, no contract and here it is November 4th.

Now, darling, I did not want to look at the calendar, but I will have to work through the week of the 18th and arrive Saturday evening the 20th. How does that work for days off? Can you take Sunday off? Is it inconvenient? I am buying my ticket for that day and can change it if necessary. So tell me on Sunday. Study the dates. I do want to finish that week of work, and I must get a contract for the Giraudoux translation and a statement on the sale of *Spy*. People are so busy you have to ask them everything five or six times. The original manuscript of *Spy* was lost by the Dutch publisher, and as Northwestern University sent me a check for sixty dollars, I have to retype the whole book and make them believe it is the manuscript with corrections. That's what I do in the evenings as I don't want to return the check.

Te quiero, y te beso,

Anaïs

New York, November 17, 1954

When Hugo has a filmmakers club evening, I choose to spend it with Jim. His beautiful face (I love his face, and I am happy that I am immunized against desire by my passion for Rupert) and the rapid ta, ta, ta, ta of machine gun talk. Directness like a thousand arrows, and utter freedom. We can say anything. There are no pauses, no examinations of what we are going to say, no effort at sequence. It is elating and invigorating. And afterwards, there is no hangover, no backbreaking, no censorship, no malaise. That is why I have felt I could let him read the entire diary, as I can read his.

Whereas Max Geismar, with whom I wanted a literary relationship and who is forty-five or forty-six, is a spiritual crab. He had the diary and stopped reading it because it disturbed him (caused a conflict? The diary is a blueprint for living, for freedom), so I took it away and gave it to Jim who nourishes himself on it and locks the "black children" like opium in his desk drawer.

Max was right to be jealous of Jim, because my affection for Max is deadened by his intermittences.

The diary is like life itself, *une œuvre inachevée*, incomplete. Sometimes I would like to live long enough to terminate it in every detail, make of it a Proustian work. But to follow the life-line is always of greater concern to me than the perfection of detail. I put enough perfection in the novels.

American Airlines Flight 5 non-stop to Los Angeles, November 1954

I summed up the month's analysis with Dr. Bogner: "I feel so much better, so much less angry, so much lighter, and full of energy and buoyancy. I have had anger but no depression. I feel better towards Hugo and more understanding of his very serious problems. I feel closer to *seeing* my fears of the world's cruelty and understand how the fear made me hostile. I accomplished a lot this month—tracked down a translation, repaired my friendship with Geismar, was asked to speak for Henry (no longer hampered by the personal sense of pain that made me avoid reading him or speaking of him). A good relationship with Jim, enjoyment of the café. Less guilt. Less oppression. Less fear. As I discover the personal drama behind *all* I did, I also discovered the personal reasons why people attack me (Carol's letter) or exclude me."

"Are you saying," asked Dr. Bogner, "that you need no more analysis?"

"Oh no, I do know that I will not be finished with analysis until I have reached a resolution of my dual life, an economic independence, and a better relation with the world. I am fully aware of that. Analysis is one of the powerful elements that draw me back to New York, and the loss of it counted heavily in my choice of life with Rupert, for I know life entirely with Rupert would mean the end of analysis."

One night, when I sat with Jim at the White Horse, he told me: "The other day, after I walked you to René de Chochor, I saw standing on the street an extraordinarily handsome man, well-dressed. He looked at me, his eyes followed me. So I came back and we both shook hands and greeted each other pleasantly as if we knew each other. Both of us had appointments. But he telephoned me and I went to see him one evening. It was a great disappointment. Everything was all right, mind you, he behaved beautifully, and so did I, there was no failure, but something was lacking in him, I felt."

"Electricity, a spark?"

"Yes. There was no charge."

"It might have short-circuited through a lack of tensions, too direct, too easy. The direct sexual approach, which is intended to dispense with the complication of relationship, sometimes misfires."

"Has it for you?"

"When I met Edward Graeffe years ago in Provincetown at the beach, it misfired for me, but later, when I knew him better, it didn't."

"But Rupert..."

"Yes, it's true. With Rupert it was instantaneous and complete, from the first visit, the first time we were alone."

When Jim talks about these casual encounters (he is not too promiscuous, not like Gore, and there is no cynicism or coldness in him), he speaks of them with a directness that gives them a sense of virility that he does not express when he speaks of Dick. It is as if, in the homosexual, all intimate relationships had a weakening effect upon the sexual life. Only in the casual, direct encounter do they seem able to manifest a male aggression. Whenever they talk of this they look rigid, tense, like the hunter. Does a woman have that expression when describing adventure?

Hugo's gravest trouble this month was that the bank kept him in suspense about returning to his old job.

Maya Deren, behind Hugo's back, jumped ahead of him by starting a society for fellowship grants for filmmakers, smartly and efficiently cutting through the most basic needs of filmmakers, while Hugo was creating a large, unwieldy artist equity.

I had to be sympathetic (he was kept awake by his hatred of Maya) while aware that she had performed a *coup d'état*, and a masterful one at that, which gave her a right to reclaim her old title of Queen of Experimental Films. So now there are two rival societies, and many members (like the Barrons) are caught between them.

What has complicated my relationship with Hugo has been compassion mixed with an awareness of his errors, which I can see. I would have acted like Maya in the same situation. Her mind is clearer, and she is capable of direct action.

Maya harmed him deeply, exposed his ineffectualness. And I have to support, console, help him. Because she is so *male*, everybody obeys her. Hugo rebels, but can't win.

He is honest and courageous. I no longer add up the traits that drive me away.

But I am grateful to be flying towards lesser difficulties.

I told Hugo: "I wish I could give *you* money and the freedom to make your films as you gave me money and the freedom to write."

Analysis has made us "rough" with each other.

The relativity of character and truth has not been emphasized enough.

The "ideal" Hugo has disappeared completely. I have trouble seeing him. The defect is in my own vision.

The most difficult revelation I have had to face is I have not been able to give Hugo my *allegiance*, nor could he win it. I ought to believe in him and I cannot, because the neurosis has so corroded his banking, his art, his relationships that I no longer *believe*.

The certitude that he does everything wrong and succeeds only in righting himself by analysis (retrieving losses, etc.) makes me feel I need to stand on my own two feet.

What is the most important thing to tell a student of literature and writing?

The human being is always better than the artist. That is why, while loving human beings (Pam Campion, her children, even Paul Campion, Millicent), I do not care to write about them, because unlike the artists, they never go into the territories I am interested in exploring. The artist submits himself to adventures into the irrational. He is merely another type of adventurer. He does not climb Annapurna, but he risks both his human life and loss of reason or health as did the mystic who withdrew from the world to pursue a vision. The hell traversed by the artist most human beings are unwilling to traverse. When Jim accepts the journey, then he becomes, to me, more interesting to write about than Pam, just as if you went to a party you might wish to talk to the men who went to Annapurna in preference to Pam who went nowhere, and who lives a quietly protected life in which the only dangers are poverty, illness, raising children badly...

So it goes...wounds (even when involuntary) and retaliation.

Dr. Neumann cannot understand why, after seven years, I still have "hot flashes"—that is, I become extremely hot to the point of perspiring. I am trying to analyze what I was thinking when they occur. I caught *one* today. I was remembering that in the past months Hugo has shown less desire, less physical interest, and that he has expressed this by not coming to the bathroom anymore to watch me bathe. The interest was necessary to me, and I am humiliated by the loss of it. At the same time I realize that I lost mine in Hugo only a few years after our marriage, and I therefore do nothing to arouse or sustain him; in fact, I have always unconsciously discouraged it.

I now understand Rupert's attraction to what he described as my talk on writing as one of the essential things in our life, when I didn't think it was important to him. He is almost totally an irrational being who finds pleasure and relief at my ability to articulate what he cannot.

I had imagined that when Hugo would *come to life* as a result of analysis he would come to life in the form of Rupert or Jim, which is one of the dreams that drew me back to him. But he needs baggage, possessions. He allows objects to collect and stagnate. I see something of his father in him, the man who was an engineer with a jutting chin and a tightly compressed mouth.

Love embellishes, so I cannot understand what holds me to Hugo—it is not love.

Now I have had a Martini and have re-powdered my face.

I have felt I must love Hugo for his courage, his efforts, and I allow myself now to travel towards Rupert's full mouth, towards his warmth, even towards his sentimentality.

The truth is this: I do not love Hugo, but I feel I *should*. I feel I should love him in return for all he has given me. I feel that not loving him is like pushing away a drowning man.

I remember when I was in Provincetown with Gonzalo and Robert Duncan. Robert was a friend of Tennessee Williams, and he talked about Williams' short stories and wanted me to read them. Tennessee came and was shy and quiet. I was not attracted to his passivity and negativity. No friendship ensued. Today I admire his writing, but when I see him he is still colorless, flabby, absent. When he read at Circle in the Square he never once looked at his audience. He read like a priest saying mass, with his eyes lowered, face closed. He once dismissed my writing as "*avant garde*" and never admitted to reading it. There is among the homosexuals a greater prejudice towards women than society's prejudice towards them. I was not aware of it because I had a sort of passport, but I was aware of it in their writing. Tennessee is more deceptive because woman is not caricatured in his work. He is identified with her. He is Blanche DuBois, and the girl in *The Glass Menagerie*.

Sierra Madre, November 23, 1954

On the plane I became aware that in my effort to store away the diaries, I left behind an envelope containing several duplicates that I intended to bring back with me and left the key hanging on the closet door and brought Hugo's attention to it. Both men were always unhappy about the locked closets. Rupert was always looking for a pretext to open it while I was away: "There is a mouse in the closet, eating away at the manuscript—send me the key." Hugo always said, whenever anything "got lost" in the house, "It's in the locked closet!" Anxiety started. Would Hugo open the closet? Would he read the first editions? An accident! The anxiety spoilt my return to Rupert. I could not enjoy his sensuality. I had a nightmare that Hugo was reading the diaries. I telephoned Jim on Sunday. I did not know until Monday that all was well. I called Hugo. Then today Jim's letter:

New York, November 1954

Dear Anaïs,

Everything is fine. I have the black children, and I am enclosing the key. I took the five volumes in the gray envelope, so in case you feel like mailing the key to Hugo, you will know it is okay to do so. And I'm putting the children in my cabinet at home. Millicent was there alone, knows I have the key, and that if the subject should come up (it probably won't) she doesn't know anything about it.

At work; must stop. Just wanted you to know your children are safe.

Love,

Jim

As soon as I had talked to Hugo and knew he was not hurt, my passion for Rupert was set free, and last night for the second time in all our life together, I invited him to make love (the other time was during our first trip while we crossed the desert and I wanted to make love on the sand, at night). And the joy and life of it!

Sunday we went to the beach. Summer-like weather. We dined with Helen and Lloyd at the Beach Club, drank and were merry, saw a movie.

My élan in my writing has been broken: I was working well on Lillian's "return home" when de Chochor and Felix Morrow both said I must abandon my *roman fleuve* and write a Big Book if I am to continue publishing. My temptation in answer to that is to give them 500 pages of the diary.

In bed Rupert reads books on politics.

And I a book on Joyce.

Rupert awakened humming and we laughed about last night.

Dream: Henry Miller is now very old, and very gentle. He has come to visit me. We are spending several days together. His wife is in the background. We have not met yet. She has accepted this reunion. The atmosphere is gentle. Henry tells me he has cancer of the stomach. I put both my hands on his shoulders and say, "It is a real pity that now, at this moment, I have become 'tough' enough, and if I had been *then* as I am now I could have stayed with you." We take long walks, talking, but he gets very exhausted.

I awakened not feeling well, and still angry at Frances Keene for her personal and vulgar attack on *Spy*, purely a defamation of character. Stupidity is not an excuse for hostility. I should have answered her review by exposing its lack of objectivity.

This anger I diverted into a creative effort to organize my notes on "writing."

Letter from Jim Herlihy to Anaïs Nin:

New York City, November 26, 1954

Dear Anaïs, To begin with, in case you have not received my special delivery letter, everything is well. I arrived during H's absence, absconded with the black children in the grey envelope and the key in my pocket. The key was in the special letter, so I hope you have rec'd it by now.

I, too, wanted to call Hugo to see if I could find out from his voice whether or not he had detected the missing key. So I did. He hadn't. I invited him to the theatre, a dress rehearsal of a farce called *One Eye Closed*. And of course there is a deadly irony here.

But the truth, dear Anaïs, is that Hugo does have one eye closed. We enjoyed the show, mildly funny, never dull, competently acted, though not brilliantly.

At the risk of everything I must say again that *Solar Bark* is inside me as no other book has been. I know that I have personalized the experience by now; but I have not exalted it. It exalts itself. It has that power. And I talk and think about it, and am able to convey it to others. Not the power itself, but a sense of what you did. There are sentences I am able to quote, and would like to, even now, but I won't because they are not a total but a partial view; and the book's great virtue is its perfect balance of life and death, the sensual beauty of the earth combined with the beauty of the flight. Death, as it is used in this book (and in life, I believe), charges life with meaning and significance and force. The senses of man, the most beautiful animal of them all, require this urgency; they stalk him into life. I think that if you said nothing else in your life, this alone qualifies you as a great woman and a great artist. And it has a stunning effect on a reader, an awakening, empowering effect.

Now, goddam you, listen to me! You give it to a reader with *one eye closed* (de Chochor), and listen more to him than to me! We will crank the book off the press by hand, if necessary. (And it won't be necessary, is my guess.) But if so, I hereby vow that I will work with you at publishing this one word at a time if it takes a year. And I am *not* badgering you into writing the rest of it. I know that it can take from six weeks to six years. I don't really care when. I only want to be reassured. I want to know that when the time comes, you will listen only to people with *both eyes open*. Assure me of this, and I will leave you the hell alone, as they say. Okay? I repeat, this is not pressure about now; it is a feeble attempt at exorcism. You have no room inside you for their demons, only for your own. And if you accept the world's demons they will copulate with your own and you will be besieged from a nation of monsters and never be rid of them.

"Now get with it, honey, get with it!"

Jim

Letter from Anaïs Nin to Jim Herlihy:

Sierra Madre, December 1954

Dear Jim: First let me tell you that your letter was perfectly beautiful, and wise. Every word was true. I am fully aware that Anaïs the human being and Anaïs the artist are two separate people and that Anaïs the human being should be scolded now and then. But let me reassure you; even when the human being gets tired and seems about to give in, the artist has never given in one inch or one word. Nevertheless, your letter was a marvelous antidote to all the gentle poisons of the one-eyed people, as you so aptly called them, and on days of depression I will reread it. I should have written you as soon as I received your special delivery that all was well. I was so immensely relieved and grateful. You were, as usual, a magician in underworld matters. The prestidigitator of the underground life. Thank you. I will continue to write *Solar Bark* and have put your letter at the head of it, as a MEMO. I am also trying to earn money and be free of guilt. I have two writing students, and two lectures to give.

Paul and Renate are giving a Roman supper party. I am also working on the booklet *On Writing*, weaving all my notes together.

Could I please have some more paper dishes, only the large dinner size? I have plenty of the small and the medium, and plenty of soup bowls.

Thank you.

Anaïs

Sierra Madre, December 1954

Our Lady of the Portable Roots

Kay Dart, growing immense like the fat women of the circus, dressed like a gypsy, and John, looking more and more like a Protestant priest, were saying, "We need roots. We want a home, a garden, a job, all that our American culture has developed in us, and neither Kay nor I have had it."

I flipped my eyes, my billowy Italian dress and said, "My roots are portable."

Later in bed, reading Bernanos' *La Joie*, I tried to convey to Rupert (who does not believe it) a France so metaphysical and so poetic, a combination unequalled in the rest of the world.

Rupert was still high and kissed me as he does occasionally, with a romantic gallantry, not with his usual hungry passion, but with a fervent tribute expressed in kissing the hands, the eyelids, the shoulders, a courtship, a bouquet. And he reminded me: the lady of the portable roots.

The next day I was not in Sierra Madre, but in Paris with my old friend Conrad Moricand—Henry Miller had sent me a newspaper notice of his death.

TO HELL WITH THE LAWS

1955

New York, January 11, 1955

My first day back in New York: At nine I walk to pay an overdue hospital bill, to pay for the telephone, garage, grocer, stationery, drugstore, to get a typewriter ribbon for Hugo, labels, string, to open an account for Film Matters, to call for films at the Lexington Hotel.

I talked with Bogner and Jim over the phone the second day, mailed films, filed bills, bought a present for Millicent's daughter and new baby, wrote Rupert, fought a cold, got overhauled at Arden's and restored at Jacobson's (blood count 65%).

The theme of December was anxiety and jealousy. Soon after I returned to Sierra Madre, Paul and Renate invited us to a Roman party. We had to read the *Satyricon* (a book for a butcher's delight), devise a skit for entertainment, and bring a dish.

We worked several days to produce all this. First I made Rupert a fantasy helmet out of silver cellophane that was winged and gorgeous. Then I sewed a silver mesh short gladiator skirt. He wore our Mexican sandals of purple velvet with silver stripes, the anklets on his arms. His belt was a wide band of purple felt held by a narrower belt matching the sandals. He carried a trident and a net—as a gladiator. I wore a Grecian-shaped nylon nightgown, pleated, graceful, over which I threw an orange chiffon draped cape from the shoulders, much jewelry, hair à la Grêque, sandals.

Rupert devised a Latin skit: I held a tiny flower on which he, with an eyedropper, delicately dropped a drop of water, and the flower responded with a jet, all done very

Anaïs Nin and Rupert Pole at one of many costume parties

stylized and presented as Trimalchio's dream after the banquet. Part II: the masculine voice of the drum and the feminine tinkle of a music box, but suddenly out of the music box pops a virile-shaped devil. III: Rupert gives me a snake that I domesticate with a gold ribbon tied around its neck. Not subtle but amusing to all. Then we brought a potent punch that we pretended was an aphrodisiac.

Paul was dressed in a luxuriant salmon-orange cape of Surah silk, Renate in a more authentic Roman dress of pale blue. Peter was a slave boy. Around Tavi's head we sewed a fiery orange mane, and called him our lion. Paul had painted one wall with columns. The table, all white, was covered with exotic-looking food; each of us had devised a dish that bore no resemblance to familiar food. There were about a dozen people. Rupert served the punch. There was a fire in the fireplace, and a brasero on which incense burned. Renate's meatloaf was shaped like a phallus.

There was a couple at the back of the room who remained effaced all evening. But Johanna, a boyish girl with short hair, a humorous nose, and humorous behavior was already "attracting" Curtis Harrington. Katie (who was in the film with us) was there, a petite, plump and pretty Viennese, and Samson, a homosexual maiden aunt who survives his homeliness by the illusion that he initiates the young.

Another couple was expected, and I felt the fate of the evening depended on them, as those who were there were not apt to cause me the indescribable tortures of jealousy. I was both intuitive and not mistaken. It was the missing couple who would be the cause of my anguish.

When Raymunda Orselli entered, my heart missed a beat. It was not that she was beautiful, but she was arresting, a personality. She came dressed in black, as Hecate, swinging a long pony tail of black hair. She had a Jewish face but one drawn with a very fine pen, with hard, intense, willful, small eyes, a delicately aquiline nose, a thin mouth, imperfect teeth, but the ensemble, because of the grace of her dancer's movements (she had just finished dancing in the movie version of *Oklahoma*), the fixity of her glance, her swift darts, created an illusion of beauty. After Rupert sang a few songs on his guitar, she took up her guitar and sang with a beautiful voice and an actress's expressiveness. Before the singing, her escort, Douglas Brian, had walked straight towards me when he entered. I wondered why, but I felt his interest. He was very tall, handsome, manly, but not in any conventional way. We exchanged a few words on the *Satyricon*, playfully. He and Raymunda acted like lovers, but Raymunda watched Rupert. The guitar duets being engaged, singing to each other, or together, they did not cease for the last half of the evening. Seeking consolation, I sat near Douglas, Raymunda beside him, and Rupert in front. Douglas caressed my neck and repeatedly said to Raymunda: "What beautiful shoulders."

My anguish was increasing so much that I could not enjoy Douglas's admiration, even his kiss at the end. At two-thirty in the morning I reached the limit of my endurance. Raymunda had a thousand songs in her repertoire. She had her legs wrapped around Rupert's feet.

Yet in between, she said to me: "I read *Under a Glass Bell*, in Italy, in Italian. I loved every word."

As we were getting ready to leave, I felt I was in a nightmare. Rupert, drunk, and packing our props, wanted to kiss me, but I refused violently. By this time Johanna had realized Curtis was running away from her (with me) and wanted us to stay, particularly Rupert. Having Curtis and Samson in the car, I was silent. I asked questions about Douglas (to anger Rupert), but as soon as we were alone, I exploded. To convince me he had not been attracted physically to Raymunda, he spoke of Johanna throwing her body around. We quarreled bitterly on the same theme as always: his obviousness, his lack of control. Why, always, when I am there, why not wait till I'm not there? We quarreled all the way home. I fell asleep at last, lonely, frightened, and he, being drunk, fell asleep being unable to help me.

Two days after the quarrel, we went to visit Cornelia, and there was Raymunda, and the guitar duets began again. She wanted to learn one of Rupert's songs right then and there. Then I saw, while she was intensely aggressive and Rupert merely passive, that she was not beautiful, but interesting, willful, and in full control of her feelings. I behaved as I would like to behave, but with a cold heart.

Then later, Renate, to help me, told me the truth: it all started with Douglas's fervor for my books. He and Raymunda were in love. But he came to Renate and Paul and talked obsessively about me. At the party he had said to me: "I never expected you to be as beautiful as your writing!" To Renate he asked: "Why didn't you tell me she was so beautiful?" I could have drawn close to him, instead of suffering from the guitar duets and feeling as Renate once felt about Paul. Raymunda suffered. She arrived at the party afraid of me! Then, of course, she found Rupert fascinating. The result was a quarrel between them, and Douglas later went to Mexico and Raymunda back to New York.

From November 20th to January 10th, two outbursts of jealousy. Afterwards I feel ashamed. Rupert will not change his interest and pleasure at interplay with women, his naïve enthusiasm rarely followed up, his flirtations so superficial. He is unaware and compulsive. He is so unsubtle that when I said, "All I ask you is not to concentrate on one girl. Be friendly, move about, get her address and see her when I'm gone, but don't flirt," at the New Year's Eve party he was so self-consciously passive that it was absurd and only increased my guilt.

I arrived in New York determined to cure myself. I talked with Bogner, adding other facts: "This is the one time I made the *greatest effort* to consider my life with Rupert permanent, to settle down in it, to take his family as mine (while we were trimming the Christmas tree, I tried to feel: this is my family now). I felt detached from Hugo and I wanted to be whole."

Immediately Bogner realized that it was *because I had tried to settle down permanently with Rupert that the anxiety grew worse.* It was provoked by the fact that I wanted to give Rupert all of myself.

And then panic, terror, helplessness, pain, a feeling of being trapped in a sadistic situation.

And the desperation to escape.

What would happen if I could not run away? To peace?

This time I find a Hugo stabilized because he has found a good job, hopes to make money. As an artistic filmmaker he felt helpless; he admits art cannot be sold, "merchandized." He turns over to me not only the management of his three films, but suggests I make films myself. I accepted all the responsibilities. I took over a load of work, mailed films, wrote letters, picked up films, kept accounts, cleaned films, repaired splices, paid bills. Last night we entertained his business associates M. and Mme. de Saint Phalles...lightly and smoothly...assumed the duties of partnership.

But Rupert and I planned a trip to Acapulco February 15.

I had also told Bogner about the problem with the diary. I have to make a will. If I died today the diary would cause a catastrophe. The vaults and storages would ultimately open and they would be sent to the nearest of kin: Hugo. I have no one else I can trust. Jim Herlihy wants to take charge. He is devoted to me and to the diary, and he is my spiritual son, but he is too young and not objective, and he does not love Hugo.

I cannot go on living with Rupert with such an illness. He cannot change because he is not analyzed; I have to change. And I don't know how much I can change.

For a neurosis such as mine to take root means to be rooted in a situation of pain. So even if I would like to have a beautiful home, a fireplace to sit by, a view, these things are dangerous because they conceal the bars of a cage. To take root means cutting off all avenues of communication with the rest of the world. Against the wish for repose is an impulse to remain mobile, fluid, to change surroundings.

When Hugo ceased to be my "refuge," I felt like an escargot who had lost his shell, and then I learned to live without it. I felt I could stand alone; but then, if you have claustrophobia of the soul, you have to maintain a vast switchboard with an expanded universe—the international life, Paris, Mexico, New York, the United Nations, the artist world. The African jungle seems far less dangerous than that little, mediocre Forest Service house in Sierra Madre.

Adapting myself to Rupert's life by force (I do not belong in it) would not be difficult, but because it is done by force I have the feeling of being a fraud, a pretender. It is not sincere. I love Rupert, but not the life he makes.

Over-reaction takes place when *too much pressure* is put upon an individual, such as my overreaction to spending our last free evening drinking with the family at four in the afternoon after having been there the night before.

New York, January 17, 1955

Dream: I am in a locked room. Gonzalo breaks the door down. I am in my slip and it is not very clean. He wants me to walk with him, as I am. At first I resist. Then he wins me over and we walk like lovers. He kisses me, not passionately, but gently. He looks like the good Gonzalo, the one of the mellow moods, not the dark and violent one.

In spite of Jacobson, I got bronchitis. In two days I made a swift descent into weakness, insomnia and suffocation. The heated apartment is airless. If I open the windows, I'm cold.

I called up Rupert and he had a sore throat. He too lives in terror of bronchitis because when he gets it, it is a major illness. We have the same weakness. One day we look vital, radiant, well, and the next we are utterly sick, weak.

I got out of bed to see Bogner because I wanted to face the last (I hope) of that downward spiral. I became aware last night of the anxiety grafted onto the bronchitis, which increased the illness; the weight of it oppressed and sank me. I wanted to catch myself in the *act,* and once again I did.

I did have a congested chest, throat, nose. It hampered my breathing. But upon this was grafted a multitude of old anxieties. I am helpless, weak, suffocated. I could not sleep (would I die?). I looked for oxygen. Then I had the dream of the room I locked myself in (like Proust). Someone else breaks the door down. All this dramatization of the initial illness, the fatalism, the sinking…

Bogner and I talked. I always get a sore throat on the plane, either way. "Because you are shut in, more shut in in a plane than anywhere else."

I was uneasy, fearful of being deserted, not loved, particularly when ill. My father left when I was at my lowest ebb.

I felt less congested while I talked with Bogner. Then, on the way out, this phrase came to me very clearly: my mother was very nice to me when I was ill.

So is Hugo; it is only when I am ill that he expresses tenderness.

But when I'm ill, I'm locked in, dependent. And I hate this. It stifles me. A conflict sets in. Reading about Proust's illness last night disturbed me.

Illness makes me depend on Hugo, and I dread this. When I returned I wanted to separate from him.

But…my mother was very nice to me when I was ill.

No voice left after Bogner's, but I'm determined to exorcise this downward pull. At the slightest incline, I shove myself all the way down. I make exaggerated associations: this is like the night at the hospital. No difference between bronchitis and post-surgery insomnia. I do remember the overwhelming gratitude for the silent night nurse watching over me. Midnight, two o'clock, four o'clock. Dawn at last. When I went to the bathroom I could look out the window and see people beginning their day. It seemed as if having lived through the night all would be well, as if one couldn't die in the morning or at noon as well. No, the night, the solitary night creates ghosts and voodoo.

I have *feared* Hugo's hardness. It is there. It was never turned towards me, but it is there. It's the other face of his weakness.

I came home from Bogner, face red with fever, swollen, and yet shivering with cold. I got into bed, took Jacobson's pills, and three hours later the fever was down. The next day I was up, cleaning Hugo's films, filing them away, cleaning his room—eight hours of work. A talk with Jim by phone.

Early to bed. Hugo down with flu also. Another day of working.

So at least I am earning my living and feeling less guilt.

I was given enough time to write, god knows, more than anyone else, and yet I failed at it. *Spy* has sold barely 1,500 copies, and the British Book Centre is making it hard for me to be paid what I am owed. Felix Morrow is disappointed to have believed it could sell.

I think what I should do is devote the rest of my time to preparing the diaries for publication. No more novels. Earn my living like everybody else around me.

I must find out why I cannot feel the compassion for Hugo I feel for other people. Is it something in him that does not inspire it? His manner? His demands, commands, the naked ugliness of the "business" attitude? In my full maturity I make the same judgment I made at twenty: money is not worth the price you pay for it. It is Faust's exchange. To have money or make money you have to kill the artist, the spiritual, emotional self.

Hugo has made his choice...again.

In the life of the artist he could not wield *power*.

So once more, breakfast over stocks and bonds, the big portfolio of investment charts, talks in figures of millions, big talk, big schemes; perhaps this time he will succeed and become strong.

Meanwhile, Rupert will never understand that if only he had not made me jealous last month—I had come closer to marrying him than I ever did.

Hugo is struggling with *his* problems: his unacceptance of *any* point of view but his own. Why can't I be patient? Why do I find all his personal habits irritating?

Why? I write about it as if to exorcise it.

Dream: I return to Rupert. He lives in a hay barn. I lie on the hay and wait for him. The three little Campion girls rush over to say hello. Rupert leaps off the truck. It is a sunny, rustic, innocent scene.

Woke up with an acute ache at the base of the neck.

Max Jacobson was called on an emergency by Cecil DeMille, on location in Egypt making *The Ten Commandments*. Max and Nina lived in one of the set "tents." His photographs are less of Egypt than Mr. DeMille, the fake sphinx head of papier mâché, the actors, Max himself in an Egyptian costume—Hollywood's Egypt.

"Didn't you see Cheops' ship?" I asked, as all my fantasies have been absorbed with this discovery.

"No. There were too many difficulties, permits."

Hollywood's invasion of Egypt, of Yucatan, of Peru, is one of the most monstrous of all invasions, far more terrible than war.

I wonder if I could not leave Hugo and build my own life. I wonder whether it is the *dependency* that makes his peculiar ambivalence and paradox so painful. But I must put an end to the irritation, one born of thirty years; I must stop caring.

All these pages could be collected under one title: Rebellion against Hugo.

Or truer still, "Rebellion."

Because I cannot reach a mature control of my own life.

Letter from Anaïs Nin to Rupert Pole:

New York, Tuesday, January 11, 1955

Darling: I want to explain to you a change that has happened to me. I have finally been won over completely to your dream of the house. The last small volcanic eruptions were very small indeed, and right after them I realized they were the last sputterings. I have been finally rid of the restless, romantic, adventurous, homeless nomadic state; I felt this strongly when I got in the plane. I realized that I saw in your father an extreme, negative, destructive form of the flight anxiety. Mine was positive, creative, and bohemian, but still might lead to that non-creation of roots. Now I am quite sure of this, and I was beginning to accept staying in one place, having a family.

So, I am quite willing not to go to Acapulco, quite willing to take a small vacation when I return, a few days, Las Vegas perhaps, or just to play in LA, hear jazz or dance and save the money for the house.

Decided to call you up…glad we talked, darling, and I'm glad you're well. Now I will concentrate on work.

Te quiero mucho…A

Letter from Rupert Pole to Anaïs Nin:

Sierra Madre, January 1955

SUBJECT: Shall We??

Love,

Your voice so good and strong, and happy, considering. But you're terrible—just as I get my mind all made up for Acapulco in Feb., which is just what we need and should do more than anything else in the world, you call and announce you think as I do?? And you really want to stay here and work toward the house??? Women!!!! Such a difficult species to please—you better have your swims—Acapulco will have to be our heated swim pool for the present.

Let's plan to go anyway and then see about accommodations. Didn't you say Feb. was fiesta in Acapulco? We'll see what La Roca and Annette say. We might write Billy Clyde if La Roca is full. Tell him we haven't much money but are coming anyway (our top for apt. is about 500 pesos a week).

All sorts of wonderful love-things to write you but it's so cold here I can't write them now (how's that for an excuse). I'm saving money by turning the heat off in the afternoon, and now it's so cold I can't get the house warm again, or perhaps it's just that you're gone and took the warmth with you. So I'm doomed to shiver and chatter until you suddenly fly out of a bright red Mexican cloud and return to me the fire of my life.

R

Letter from Anaïs Nin to Rupert Pole:

New York, January 21, 1955

Darling: That was a sweet letter. But, my love, woman is not so capricious or whimsical or contrary as you may believe. It's her desire to please her man. The truth is all my "changes" came out of my initial impulse: to go to Acapulco (as a consoling thought after our separation) was not being answered by you with the *same* impulse, but by your statement: "We should save money." Then I tried to move towards your wish, to adapt myself—I can't enjoy wanting something you don't. By the time I rallied to your mood, you had changed! Then again, after seeing your father, you again wanted to save money! So you see, men are just as changeable as women. We are up to our old tricks again, trying to *please* each other, and ready to give up our own wishes. The truth is that I don't deeply want anything you don't also want—it spoils my pleasure. I think the fantasy about Acapulco helped me to leave for NY this time. As you know, I don't find leaving easy. But as to a *real* need, now, well, I told you, what I need is to be sure Acapulco is what *you* want now. I can wait for it. I couldn't enjoy it unless we both want it equally. So if we both don't want it, let's postpone it. It means the moment is not right. As soon as you measure the cost, it means your desire is not strong, and if it is not strong it is not worth doing.

Jim wants to know if you need paper plates.

Te quiero

A

New York, January 28, 1955

Jacobson, Bogner and Arden, and once more I escape illness, old age and tragedy and neurosis. Each time a new battle won.

Last night Willard Maas, poet and filmmaker, arrived at our cocktail for James Broughton very drunk, blubbering and slubbering, praising Broughton's and his own films as the only poetry in cinema, falling asleep between speeches. His second speech was: "My God, Anaïs! I can't believe it. You look absolutely beautiful! You look younger than you did fifteen years ago. And I know your age more or less. You must be about forty and you look thirty." Then he fell asleep again, grey hair disheveled, face crumpled, eyes so deep set you wonder how he can see. When he awakened, he began again: "I can't get over how you look!" Blessed be Jacobson, Bogner and Arden. The racehorse is running again!

Broughton's description of his four years in Paris made me jealous and envious. He said, "There, you have a right to love life above all else!"

Not here. First of all you love security, work, comfort, wealth, possessions, power, never other people, yourself, or life.

Lawrence Maxwell without his beard would have looked like a small boy who had been inflated with a bicycle pump. When I first met him he had a small bookshop at 45 Christopher Street. He handled my books. He gave me autograph parties. He was fond of little girls, either the pretty ones or the gamines. His wife was actually a handsome man. Brusque. Forbiddingly short of speech. She was as hostile as Larry was friendly. Because he loved to talk, people dropped in and listened. He sold very few books. He gave books to the pretty girls. The only time he appeared as a human being capable of inarticulate suffering was when his wife left him (because of his promiscuous interest in other women), and his bookshop was bankrupt. In money matters he was irresponsible and ruthless. He took over our edition of *House of Incest*, never paid me, and I had all the trouble in the world getting the remaining 300 copies back (700 are unaccounted for). The only time I felt sympathy was when he destroyed his bohemian life, reached a trap; he was surrounded by lesbians, fell in love with lesbians, was frustrated by lesbians. They treated him like a eunuch, stayed with him when they had nowhere to go. He never uttered a word of understanding of the books. But from the beginning I was, to him, a celebrity. Certain speeches, similar to official reception speeches, were reserved for me when I went to the shop. It took me a year to break the barrier down. My own kiss on the cheek and casual attitude finally brought out a spark of affection.

But under stress he was a loyal friend. When Rupert appeared in New York and Hugo was lying on a hospital bed in traction, Larry was one of the members of my active underground who helped me. He played the role allotted him. He played his own role, and that may have been what gave all he did a performance air. He was of the race of heads of salons. And even if his love of literature or writers was not profound (his heart was in politics), he liked to be Ambassador.

It is amusing that eight years ago Rupert went to Larry's bookshop by chance to sell him his Henry Miller books (bought in France) so that he might buy new tires for Cleo, and Larry offered so little it made Rupert angry. And Rupert bought my preface to *Tropic of Cancer*, which caused the first scene between us (we had only been together three times). He was so shocked, and I had to soothe him.

New York, February 1, 1955

I'm working with Bogner on my hatred of America, prodding its origins. My earliest memory of France is of sociability. I invited everyone on the street for tea. In Germany, I hated our governess, but nothing else. In Belgium, I don't remember any rebellion. In Spain, I was happy.

America first appeared in my eyes as my father saw it: "*Un pays de commerçants. Barbare, sans culture.*" He never accepted a concert tour in America. He said the greatest two catastrophes in the world were the birth of Christ and the discovery of America.

"He had a prejudice," said Bogner.

"He did, since he did not know America, or know English. How much his caricature of America stemmed from his antagonisms towards my mother, I don't know. My mother was brought up here in a convent. She spoke English. I don't remember whether she liked it or not. She may have. It may have been a subject of discussion. She had the money. She decided to come here instead of continuing to live in Spain (nearer my father). Interesting contradiction: I inherited completely my father's prejudice. I arrived with a fear of 'losing my soul' in a materialistic civilization. My diary was at once a refuge, a home, a shelter and a jungle adventure."

Bogner said, "When you have a prejudice, you proceed to pick up proofs, to strengthen your original premise. You proceeded to accumulate proofs of America's hatefulness. But the anger was already there."

"Since I persist in generalities, persist in accusing America, I want to look at what I hate, which was, as you say, a projection of my own feeling. Today I added systematically what I hate: America is cold, undemonstrative, inhuman, and incapable of relationship. It is rough, uncouth, and full of hostilities."

One by one, I am willing to question: "You mean *I* am unable to make a relationship with Americans? You mean *I* am the one who is angry, so I tune in on American anger?"

"Yes."

The paradox is that the one who is *truly to blame* for my having come to America is my father. Instead of being angry at *him*, I got angry at America. I identified with the real cause of all my troubles. I took on his prejudice. I identified with my tormentor. No doubt I also shifted a lot of anger towards Hugo who brought me back to America a second time and who has the American obsession with money. Yesterday he expressed real joy at making money, as keen a joy as when he made a good film. But making films did not give him as strong a sensation of virility as making money.

About relationships: "Well, in France I could not make relationships with French writers."

"Why?"

"I was writing in English."

"So your idea of your life in France was not of a life with the French. You were living with Miller and with Gonzalo."

"I tried. I remember trying to make friends with Breton, and he classified me as a bourgeois and *une femme d'un banquier*. I was offended and withdrew."

Rebellion is an important part of my personality now. I am angry. No matter what America is, even if it is *all* I say it is, there is still no reason for hating it.

Arthur Miller was saying he was tired of Western movies. I agreed and then added, "We should not have the Indians in the center of a shooting gallery at the fair and the white men and picking them off as they ride in a circle."

The hatred has increased in violence as I get older because I feel I have only a few years to live and I am still here. I could fall in love now with the man who would take me to France, as I fell in love with the captain of the Spanish ship sailing towards America, because he was the last fragment of Spain and I was losing it.

Activities: Cleaning and filing miles of film

Getting dresses repaired

Mailed films for showing

Changed Hugo's typewriter ribbon

Bought two bathing suits for Acapulco

Wrote Anne Metzger, my French translator

Gave *Under a Glass Bell* to Val Telberg

Saw Irina and her husband (who has an important position in the UN; atmosphere of international politics)

Bought stamps

Got two hundred copies of *Spy* from British Book Centre because they won't pay Hugo what they owe him; I daringly walked into the bookshop and took the books

Paid electric bill, rent

Changed and bought cases for film reels

Bought two bathing caps

Ordered Lektrosol to clean films

Saw Frances Thomas, a writer

Secretarial work for Hugo, errands, telephone

Paid bills

Wrote letters

Sent corsage to Joaquín's friend; she sailed to Europe, no marriage

Talks with Jim over telephone

Hair tinted

Letters to Ruth and Rupert

Read Jim's diary

Read Frances Thomas's poems and sketches

Read three Simenons
Histoire de la Littérature Française by René Lalou

René Lalou raises the question of whether "individualism" is obsolete. But no one except the psychologists realize the interior, subjective, irrational life *must be dealt with first*, cannot be ignored, covered or inhibited. In America, because the masses are not made up of individuals, but of blind, ignorant, irrational subnormals, the total sum of the country is a dangerous, brutal, hysterical ego.

The world will always remember that I went out in the evenings with Henry, Gonzalo, Albert, Bill, etc., but not that Hugo was asleep as soon as he had dinner, that "business" always meant Hugo asleep. He is asleep at eight and I am sitting in the front room to escape his snoring. I wish I had Rupert here.

I am, though, so grateful to Hugo for his determination to "recreate" himself, to lead a *new* life. I see his effort.

I have lost a great deal of my guilt for not giving Hugo any advantages of success in my own work, because he now admits that indirectly I am responsible for all his important contacts, resulting in his capital, beginning with my relatives to René de Chochor today. So I have, in a way, returned some of Hugo's giving to me. I have such a desire to return what is given to me. I would like to be useful to the development of psychoanalysis as an experiment, to the development of medical knowledge by giving my body, my eyes, to be useful to the development of art (America *could* have been taught the art of literature, but those who destroyed this possibility are the "critics" like Max who have no knowledge of art whatsoever).

My desire to place the diary in Bogner's hands comes out of *my respect for her objectivity.*

Just as I *displaced* anger, deflected it from my father, Hugo and Rupert to America, I wonder if one could not deflect depression away from the present. Then to Jacobson where one always waits two hours, yet when I rebelled against this slavery, I got anemia. I bring my diary and correspondence, the "writings" I'm given to read by young writers, which are utterly and hopelessly bad. You cannot teach taste, ear, rhythm.

But Hugo the businessman is succeeding (with Bogner's guidance), and Jim sold a play. Immediately Jim says, "Will you come to Paris?" "Of course!"

From Felix Pollak at Northwestern University, who has purchased my manuscripts: "I got word from the Film Society that they have decided to pay your and your husband's transportation—any transportation, plane or Pullman—to Chicago and back, that they are delighted at the prospect of having you come and present your program."

Dream: I am in a carriage, dressed in a fantasy costume, a veil around my head similar to the *Gates of Hell* veil. The men in the carriage are intrigued, and want to unveil me. I get angry, get off the carriage, and take another. I am on my way to a festival at which I am to play a part. On the way I stop at a village. My mother and Joaquín are there. Joaquín is weeping quietly at being imprisoned in this out-of-the-way place.

Dream: I look down at my legs and they are covered with vaginal bleeding, brilliant, healthy, abundant blood, but more like a hemorrhage than a period. I examine some records I have been carrying, take them out of the envelope and find I have broken them; all of them are "*émietté*" (crumbled). They are my father's music.

I have a feeling of sympathy for Hugo, but I am reacting violently to his abnormal disorganization, his self-defeatism, and self-frustration.

I have to solve this, as I have solved problems of jealousy. Thinking of this, I had this dream: A big man is playing with several little girls. Suddenly he becomes lustful. He carries one of the little girls off and I know he is going to rape her. I am sexually excited. I follow them to a closet. I want to get inside the closet with them. Meanwhile, people are worried about the rape and want to call the police, but I try to stop them, to protect the big man from the law!

The flaw in Geismar's virtuous preoccupation with politics is that he is frustrated in his personal life (too routine and domestic), so he drinks, is temperamental and moralizes about writers who live freely (such as Hemingway). It would be more honest if he did his political work directly, not under the cover of literary criticism. But when he was asked to join the Civil Liberties Union, he refused.

As soon as I leave the house, I breathe freely and get calmer. I go about my full day harmoniously, swiftly, efficiently. Last night during a film showing I went out to buy more beer (ostensibly) and telephoned Rupert.

"I will be on Air France in Mexico City at eight in the evening."

"Do you know where the black cover for the camera lens is? I can't find my yellow bathing suit."

This obsession with the frustration both men give me and the way they *waste* my energy has become as obsessional as my hatred of Helba, who stifled and destroyed my life with Gonzalo.

Is part of my habit to deflect angers, or frustration, and then to project the sense of frustration onto the men a deflection of my own personal sense of frustration? Is it that I can't face my inability for self-fulfillment (except in passion, I have not fulfilled any of my wishes)? But then a woman's life is secondary in the sense that the man's profession creates the initial place, frame, atmosphere, design of the life.

Meanwhile Hugo has become aware that he has become the "businessman" completely, in an abnormal way. He has changed his entire personality, his way of dress, his mannerisms. He has closed the door on art. He is hard, tense. I was appalled by the change when I arrived. This was accompanied not by efficiency, but by disorganization and obsessional tension.

But he knows it now.

Our talk in the kitchen, while cooking dinner:

Hugo: "I became aware today of the abnormal tension. I had a diffuse, vague, unsatisfactory talk with Bogner and a terrible sense of inadequacy. My father always said I was not practical, and I was determined to overcome this weakness."

Anaïs: "But if the practical world is such a torment to you, why don't you give it up, live simply, like Telberg or Varda, on little money?"

Hugo: "I can't do that. That for me is failure, and helplessness. I would feel castrated."

I was able to talk about the effect of this on me, my revolt against being dedicated to a practical life, my suffering from his disorganized mind. He should be, by nature, a sloppy bohemian like Gonzalo and Helba, living in perpetual chaos. But he dreads this.

For the first time we were able to contemplate the frightful deformation brought on by neurosis and my reaction to it. The *human* Hugo emerged, not the *possessed* one, tender, honest, seeking, courageous, and aware.

He made me sit on his knees and said, "I am sorry. I have not even had time to love you."

A completely honest talk. At the same time that he could see the driving anxiety and obsession with which he took up his new business. Hugo could see that I felt the same sense of inadequacy for the enormous tasks he has placed on me, how I would not be able to accomplish them with a more limited physical endurance than his. I became equally obsessed with organization. Hugo's procedure—errors, loss of memory, changefulness, a hysterical inability to plan or coordinate—destroyed this and increased my work twofold, if not three- or fourfold.

For the first time I was able to feel the sympathy I had not yet felt for Hugo. I realized that the three people I had most rebelled against and felt the least compassion for were my father, my mother and Hugo. This struck me as perhaps originating in their *power* over my life, my being involved in all their irrationalities by fibers not of my own choice, involved, victimized, but *lucid* enough to rebel. And so it is with Hugo, only what remained in me was an image of Hugo when he was at the beginning of his illness, just as I might have remembered how Hugo looked in the early stages of tuberculosis—not deteriorated, still roseate, emotional, tender, human. This became buried in distortions, in the ugly personae Hugo built around this, the defenses growing uglier as the "possession" by the neurosis grew stronger.

And this occurred in me too, naturally. Lately I have contemplated honestly the ravages of *my* "possession": bitterness and hostility (as, for example, my jealousy is now expressed in wild furies against Rupert rather than secretly as before).

The rebellions against Rupert's neurotic way of life were less violent because I never believed truly I would submit to it. His way, unlike Hugo's, was to shrink into a small life that would not disturb him, but I remember how disturbed he was by his TV show for the Forest Service, by our filmmaking with Kenneth Anger, by our masquerade parties (challenges).

My tendency, I said, was to avoid the big life, to avoid strain, but when I lived with someone who has no courage (while Rupert has courage in firefighting, in a speeding car, in cross-country trips, he has none for adventures of a deeper kind), then I realized I could not live in his small, dull, narrow life.

It may be that I control my jealousy by understanding Rupert's "possession" the same way I control my rebellions against Hugo's inefficiencies and disturbances.

And my own!

My blaming Hugo is born out of his absolute control of all I do except when I *leave*—where we live, the car, accounts, our way of life, who we see...

Rebellion is a negative expression of independence.

Farewell to René de Chochor, who is leaving for a year-long sabbatical in France.

Lunch at Irina's with ten women of distinction, wives of UN delegates, a countess, Luise Rainer.

Letter from Joan of James Brown Associates to Anaïs Nin:

New York, March 8, 1955

Dear Anaïs: Herewith our check in the amount of $186.62, which represents:

Royalties from The British Book Centre on *A SPY IN THE HOUSE OF LOVE* as per attached statement, through 12/31/54 $207.35 less: 10% commission $20.73.

I know you will be appalled at the size of this payment, but as far as we can tell the statement is correct, unless you have some different information. I hope that you will not decide to give up writing as a bad job.

Sincerely,

Joan

February-March 1955

Mexico

En route to New York, March 27, 1955

After five weeks of intense work in New York (for Hugo) I left for Mexico to meet Rupert. I myself could not believe that the ecstasy of the past trips could be repeated. Such high moments could only happen once, and Jim feared it too. But the miracle was repeated. And Jim's comment was: "I should have known that you are capable of repeat performances."

But I had worked for it as the Tibetans worked to achieve their religious ecstasies. I had subjected myself to discipline, analysis, Dr. Jacobson and Arden, to emerge one morning at the icy airport all in ivory white wool, leopard belt and bag, festive, calm, strong for life with Rupert.

Once more I waited at the Hotel Genève, and once more he arrived tense and strained by five days of feverish driving (always as if it were the last time). Once more my young lover, our moment of delight and euphoria. The drive to Acapulco is faster now. Can I keep this peace and strength?

Have I overcome my fears, my jealousies, my panics? I was grateful to all those who had healed me. I passed on to Rupert radiations of deep happiness. Once more the modern apartment at La Roca, where it is like a home. This time it was the "season," and we plunged into social life, not as when we came last April and met no one we knew. I was ready to live more courageously. We swam. We met Annette Nancarrow and her boy satellites, Albert Lewin, Alice and Ed Fitzgerald, their friends, the Miss American Airline queen of 1954. We went to a masquerade ball, to La Perla, to all the nightclubs. We took mambo lessons from two Cuban dancers. We danced every night. We had two days of graceful, beautiful and wild living, and the passion was full and rich. I had only one attack of violent despair: when Rupert felt compelled to tell me he had been coerced into sleeping with a whore in Juarez (because she cried, she was on the spot, and the patronne was bullying her) and could not complete the act, and I rebelled and made a violent scene. "Why do you tell me? Why? Why? You will destroy all the confidence I try so hard to build! I don't want to know!"

Rupert was aware he had blundered. But I punished him for his blunder by telling him about Bill's visit before returning to Korea. "At the height of our relationship, I slept with Bill. Do you want to know all the details?" He didn't want to hear. He was upset. Then I took two sleeping pills and fell asleep and he lay awake all night.

But since all gentleness fails, now I will use violence. I didn't feel guilt for this.

Then on the way home he began to talk about marriage. It has been an obsession for seven years—first divorce (which he now believes I got) and then marriage. I exhausted all the defenses I could invent—that I was neurotic, that I did not want marriage, that I wanted to stay as we were, that I wanted to protect him from a feeling of responsibility. I know the persistence of his obsession. I also felt tired of resisting, feared the effect of my frustrating him, felt also an ironic mockery of the laws, a feeling that if this was going to be a source of irritation and insecurity, oh well, to hell with the laws, I would gamble once more, one more gamble, I would grant Rupert his wish someday, and gamble on the consequences. It would relieve all the strain at this end.

But then Rupert stopped at Quartzsite, Arizona, before a Justice of the Peace, to inquire, and I let him, thinking there would be some obstacle or other (I don't have divorce papers). But he came out of the place radiant, his eyes blazing, laughing, his lips humid, his smile incandescent: "Let's get married!" He was at that moment irresistibly beautiful, so gentle, so happy. I felt like a murderer to kill his joy, yet I did it that time, but that did not discourage him.

One week later we were driving to the same place, and this time we went through with the ceremony. I was moved. Rupert was so sincere. The place could not be more isolated—a remote village, just a few houses, in the middle of the desert. A grey wooden house. Two witnesses—Mr. and Mrs. Truitt. An enormous, fat German man, joyous, talkative. He had a beer-barrel stomach, a thick butcher's neck. He could not be uglier, nor the place. Its ugliness was so extreme it became humorous. He had a joyous beer sincerity too. He read the words with dignity and simplicity. His name was George Hagely. He wore, for us, a new, freshly starched white shirt without a tie. He had on a small telephone table a huge book of criminal records. I smiled, thinking the world will put my name down, but I knew that I was making one person happy in the present, and that is a great and rare achievement. Rupert was happy, fulfilled, calm and grateful. He had been humiliated, harassed and worried by the situation. He pretended it was only legal protection, but it was security, making peace with conventions.

I was elated by the danger, the adventure, the challenge once more, the overcoming of difficulties, the chess games with the world's literalness, and although my intelligence saw all the absurdities and dangers of the marriage, emotionally I had lived it with the utmost purity and wholeness, its deeper ritual, having felt deeply married to Rupert so many times—this was one more time.

We were very close then...and now, to New York, and the difficulty of leaving.

BIOGRAPHICAL NOTES

Kenneth Anger, born Kenneth Wilbur Anglemeyer in 1927, is an American avant-garde filmmaker whose work has gained underground notoriety over the past several decades, beginning with the homoerotic *Fireworks* (1947), for which he was charged with, but later acquitted of, obscenity.

Louis and Bebe Barron (1920-1989 and 1925-2008 respectively) are best known for their innovations in early electronic music. Early on, in order to make a living, they began "Sound Portraits," recordings of authors reading their work, among them Anaïs Nin, whom they met in 1949. The book *Cybernetics* inspired Louis to build electronic devices capable of producing sounds never heard before, which he and Bebe were able to incorporate into musical scores for experimental and, eventually, Hollywood films.

Inge Bogner (1910-1987) was a New York psychiatrist whom Hugh Guiler began seeing in 1946, followed by Nin in the early 1950s.

Rosa Culmell de Nin (1871-1954), a classically trained singer born in Cuba and of Danish and French descent, married pianist/composer Joaquín Nin y Castellanos in 1902 and gave birth to three children: Anaïs (1903), Thorvald (1905), and Joaquín (1908). After her husband abandoned the family in France in 1913, she and her children first went to Barcelona to live with her husband's parents, and the following year they came to New York where she took in boarders and did mail-orders for her wealthy Cuban relatives in order to make a living. She lived with Anaïs and her husband Hugh Guiler in France for a time and then came to America once again with her son, Joaquín, living with him in Williamsburg, Massachusetts, and then in Oakland, California.

Kay Dart, a failed actress and bonne vivante, was a neighbor and friend of Rupert Pole in Sierra Madre.

René de Chochor, who worked for James Brown Associates, was Anaïs Nin's literary agent from 1952 until 1955, when he left New York for France. Under his care, Nin was able to get *A Spy in the House of Love* published.

Maya Deren (1917-1961) was an avant-garde filmmaker who befriended Anaïs Nin in 1945. Nin and several of her friends, including Gore Vidal, acted in one of Deren's most acclaimed films, *Ritual in Transfigured Time* (1946). Deren gained the respect of many young filmmakers, including Kenneth Anger, who cites her as one of his inspirations.

Ruth Witt Diamant was a professor at San Francisco State University and played the role of hostess to prominent writers such as Dylan Thomas, W. H. Auden, James Broughton, and Stephen Spender. She invited Anaïs Nin to read at San Francisco State in 1948, and they became friends. Diamant allowed Nin to store several of her original diary volumes at her home.

Renate Druks (1921-2007) was born in Vienna and studied at the Vienna Art Academy for Women. She eventually came to New York, then Mexico, and finally to Malibu, California, where she built a house and studio overlooking the ocean. She lived there with her son Peter (from a previous marriage) and was a prolific painter, all the while supporting herself by working day jobs. Her home became a salon of sorts, attracting the likes of Colleen Dewhurst, John Houseman, and Christopher Isherwood.

Millicent Fredericks, Anaïs Nin's faithful maid, was born in Antigua to African and Portuguese parents. When she came to America with hopes of teaching, she could not get a job and settled into housekeeping. She played a key role in keeping Nin's love affair with Rupert Pole a secret.

Maxwell Geismar (1909-1979) was an American critic, author, and editor who wrote the introduction to Eldridge Cleaver's *Soul on Ice*. He and his wife Anne befriended Anaïs Nin and her husband Hugh Guiler in 1951, and he was one of Nin's few ardent supporters during that period.

Edward Graeffe (Chinchilito) was a Viennese tenor who met Anaïs Nin in Provincetown in 1941. The two had a sporadic but long and fiery physical relationship, and Nin felt he was the first man with whom she could have whimsical sexual encounters. Graeffe was the longtime companion of millionaire Alice Tully until his death in 1969.

Hugh Guiler (Hugo) (1898-1985) married Anaïs Nin, a Catholic, in 1923, which estranged him from his wealthy Protestant family. Having studied both literature and economics at Columbia University, he became employed at National City Bank in New York City. He took a position at the Paris branch of the bank and moved there with his wife, her mother, and two brothers in late 1924. After the crash of 1929, they moved to the Paris suburb of Louveciennes. It was through an associate of his that he met the rogue American writer Henry Miller and introduced him to his wife, setting the stage for one of literature's most famous love affairs. When war broke out in 1939, he and Nin fled to New York, where he undertook another bank position. During this time he became interested in engraving and produced artworks that adorn Nin's self-published novels—preferring to keep his artist life separate from the bank life, he used the nom d'artiste Ian Hugo. Much of this era is recorded in *Mirages: The Unexpurgated Diary of Anaïs Nin*, 1939-1947.

Carter Harman (1918-2007), a composer, met Anaïs Nin and Hugh Guiler in New York in 1947. Almost immediately he began to collaborate with Nin on an opera inspired by *House of Incest*, which never came to fruition.

James Leo Herlihy (1927-1993), born in Detroit to a working-class family, was a novelist, playwright, and actor who would achieve fame with his novel *Midnight Cowboy*, which would be filmed and win a Best Picture Oscar. Herlihy was introduced to Anaïs Nin when she came to visit Black Mountain College in 1947, and the two of them struck up a close friendship, each supporting the other's work.

Helba Huara (1900-1986) was a Peruvian dancer who married at the age of fourteen and bore a daughter. She met Gonzalo Moré in Lima, where he had come to interview her after a performance. The two fell in love and fled to Paris, where she was known as "the dancing Inca," performing sensuous and savage dances in native attire. Failing health ended her dancing career, and she became a near-invalid totally dependent on Moré, who had become Anaïs Nin's lover in 1936. While the Nin-Moré relationship lasted for ten years, Huara's jealous rages slowly helped destroy it.

Max Jacobson (1900-1979) was a German-born physician who was aided in fleeing Europe at the beginning of World War II by Hugh Guiler and Anaïs Nin. As a way of thanking them, Jacobson treated Nin gratuitously, and they had a brief sexual affair in the early 1940s. In 1942, Nin recorded in her diary *Mirages* that "Jacobson discovered a new mixture—the most potent vitamin—which rid me of anemia in three weeks and transformed me physically." It was later determined that some of his "vitamin" shots were actually a mixture of amphetamines, painkillers, steroids, and many other ingredients. He gained a reputation and was visited by celebrities, athletes, and politicians, including John F. Kennedy in later years. He was dubbed "Dr. Feelgood" and "Miracle Max." An FDA investigation would lead to the loss of his license to practice medicine.

Paul Mathieson was a painter and the bisexual lover of Renate Druks, whom he introduced to Anaïs Nin.

Lawrence Maxwell was a bookshop owner who befriended Anaïs Nin in New York in the late 1940s and invited her to make public appearances at his store. He would become an integral part of Nin's "underground force" that kept her husband Hugh Guiler from discovering her relationship with Rupert Pole in California.

Henry Miller (1891-1980), American author of *Tropic of Cancer*, *Black Spring*, *Tropic of Capricorn*, among many other titles, met Anaïs Nin in Louveciennes, France, in 1931. He and Nin shared a passion for literature and for each other—their love affair would last a decade. After both Nin and Miller returned to New York at the onset of war, they began to drift apart and eventually broke from each other in 1942.

Gonzalo Moré (1897-1966) was born in Punto, Peru, of Indian, Scottish, and Spanish blood. He fell in love with the young dancer, Helba Huara, who was married at the time, and fled with her to Paris. He joined the Peruvian Communist Party and associated with the Peruvian poet Cesar Vallejo. He met Anaïs Nin in Paris in 1936 and the two were wildly attracted to each other, carrying on a torrid, emotional love affair for a decade. It soon became apparent, however, that Moré had little practical ambition and was dominated by Huara's increasingly frequent maladies, some of which were imaginary. When war came to Europe, Nin arranged for Moré and Huara to come to New York shortly after her own arrival, where the affair resumed. During the 1940s, Nin and Moré worked together to print her books on an old hand-press and called their enterprise "Gemor Press." When Huara's chronic illnesses and jealousy began to wear on the relationship, Moré became increasingly destructive and violent, which eventually caused Nin to reject him completely.

Joaquín Nin y Castellanos (1879-1949), born in Cuba and of Spanish descent, married Rosa Culmell in Cuba in 1902 and fathered three children: Anaïs (1903), Thorvald (1905), and Joaquín (1908). He rose to prominence in Europe as a composer and pianist, and he had an eye for "*la jolie*," the pretty woman. He fell in love with his underaged student, Maria Luisa Rodriguez, known as "Maruca," and abandoned his family in 1913. He eventually got a divorce and married Maruca. After having been estranged from her father for many years, Anaïs received him at her home in Louveciennes, France, in 1933, and he began to aggressively court her. In the summer of the same year, he and his then thirty-year-old daughter embarked on an incestuous relationship that would last several months. In 1939, he moved in with relatives in Cuba and never saw his daughter again.

Joaquín Nin-Culmell (1908-2004) was the younger of Anaïs Nin's two brothers. Born in Berlin to Joaquín Nin y Castellanos, a renowned pianist and composer, Nin-Culmell studied piano at the Schola Cantorum and the Paris Conservatory with prominent instructors, most notably Manuel de Falla. He gave his first recital in New York in 1936 and later became a member of the music departments at Williams College in Williamsburg, Massachusetts, and, later, the University of California in Berkeley.

William Pinckard (1927-1989) met Anaïs Nin in New York at the age of seventeen and became her lover for more than a year. When he joined the army in 1946, it was his intention to be stationed in Asia, where he had grown up. After his tour, he graduated from the University of California and became interested in Buddhism. He returned to Japan, where he attempted an 88-temple pilgrimage and became ill, spending weeks in a rural clinic. While there, he learned of "go," a game, and became enamored with it, even writing about it. He married a Japanese woman and had two children.

Reginald Pole, born in England, was a heralded Shakespearian actor, director, writer, and playwright, working with John Barrymore and Boris Karloff and garnering rave reviews in the early part of the 20th century. After moving to California, he married Helen Taggart, and the union produced a son, Rupert, in 1919. The couple divorced in 1923, and Pole became artist Beatrice Wood's lover for a time. His behavior became increasingly erratic, and he eventually plunged into severe hypochondria, consuming numerous prescribed drugs and living a vagabond life, going from one dreary hotel room to the next.

Rupert Pole (1919-2006), Anaïs Nin's "west coast husband," was born in Los Angeles to Reginald Pole and Helen Taggart. His mother divorced Reginald and married Lloyd Wright when Rupert was a young boy. In the early 1940s, Rupert began a short and unsuccessful stage career, appearing in a few plays and on the radio. He was drafted into the army in 1943, refused to bear arms, got very ill in boot camp, and was medically discharged. He was briefly married to Janie Lloyd Jones, a cousin of his stepfather. Pole met Anaïs Nin at a party in February 1947 and became her lover. He invited her to drive from New York to California with him, and she accepted.

Lila Rosenblum (1925-2000) was a friend of Anaïs Nin who acted as her personal typist in New York. Her reminiscences of Nin can be found in *Recollections of Anaïs Nin by Her Contemporaries* (1996).

Clement Staff was a New York psychologist who treated Anaïs Nin between 1945 and the early 1950s.

Jean Varda (1893-1971) was a Greek/French friend of Henry Miller and an artist best known for his collages. After discovering Anaïs Nin's work through Miller, he sent her a collage entitled "Women Reconstructing the World" in 1944, sparking a friendship between them that would last for the rest of his life. Varda lived a bohemian lifestyle on an old ferryboat, called the Vallejo, which was moored in Sausalito. It became a gathering place where guests would come for wine, good food, storytelling, and rides on Varda's homemade sailboat.

Gore Vidal (1925-2012), a renowned American novelist, essayist, and playwright, was twenty years old when he met Anaïs Nin. Although homosexual, he developed a close relationship with Nin and proposed that they get married and have outside lovers, a notion Nin considered, but ultimately rejected. As an editor at E. P. Dutton, he was able to convince Dutton to publish some of Nin's fiction, beginning with *Ladders to Fire* in 1947. Vidal dedicated his second novel, *A Yellow Wood*, to Nin.

Helen Wright (née Taggart; 1892-1977) was married to actor Reginald Pole when their son, Rupert, was born. Taggart divorced Pole in 1923 and married architect Lloyd Wright a short time later. With Wright, she bore a son, Eric Lloyd Wright, who became an architect as well.

Lloyd Wright (1890-1978) was an architect and the son of Frank Lloyd Wright and his first wife, Catherine Lee "Kitty" Tobin. He moved from the family home in Oak Park, Illinois, to California in 1911. In 1922 Wright married actress and artist Elaine Hyman (known as Kyra Markham), and they divorced in 1925. Shortly thereafter he married Helen Taggart, and her son Rupert Pole became his stepson. Wright's first important work was the Taggart House, built for Helen's mother. He went on to design and build many structures in the Los Angeles area, and perhaps his most-known work is the Wayfarer's Chapel on the Palos Verdes Peninsula, which is made of steel and glass and surrounded by redwood trees.

INDEX